German Prisoners of
the Great War

Translators

Alison Abbey
Emily Bagshaw
David Booth
Lucy Bradbury
Keith Bradshaw
Anne Buckley
Ryan Bury
Ken Cockburn
Emily Darroch
Sheila Goodhall
David Hall
Keith Hewitt
Nigel Holden
Lauren Jones
Catriona McLachlan

Mhairi Montgomery
Hilary Potter
Alan Roberts
Sally Roberts
Isabella Rosenthal
Sabine Schlüter
Toni-Marie Simcott-Omar
Charlotte Smith
Caroline Summers
Matthew Turner
Alison Tyas
Sue Vickerman
Ada Whitaker
Hannah Williams
Hannah Willmore

German Prisoners of the Great War

Life in a Yorkshire Camp

Edited by Anne Buckley

Translation edited by Anne Buckley,
Caroline Summers, Alison Abbey and Ada Whitaker

Pen & Sword
MILITARY

First published in Great Britain in 2021
and reprinted in 2023 by
Pen & Sword Military
An imprint of Pen & Sword Books Limited
Yorkshire – Philadelphia

ISBN 978 1 52679 868 8

A CIP catalogue record for this book is
available from the British Library

Typeset by Mac Style
Printed in the UK by CPI Group (UK) Ltd, Croydon, CR0 4YY.

Pen & Sword Books Limited incorporates the imprints of After
the Battle, Atlas, Archaeology, Aviation, Discovery, Family History,
Fiction, History, Maritime, Military, Military Classics, Politics,
Select, Transport, True Crime, Air World, Frontline Publishing, Leo
Cooper, Remember When, Seaforth Publishing, The Praetorian Press,
Wharncliffe Local History, Wharncliffe Transport, Wharncliffe True
Crime and White Owl.

For a complete list of Pen & Sword titles please contact

PEN & SWORD BOOKS LIMITED
47 Church Street, Barnsley, South Yorkshire, S70 2AS, England
E-mail: enquiries@pen-and-sword.co.uk
Website: www.pen-and-sword.co.uk
or
PEN AND SWORD BOOKS
1950 Lawrence Rd, Havertown, PA 19083, USA
E-mail: Uspen-and-sword@casematepublishers.com
Website: www.penandswordbooks.com

Contents

Foreword

by Wolf Kahler, grandson of Fritz Sachsse

I first met my grandfather Fritz Sachsse in 1944, towards the end of the Second World War when I was four years old. We had moved to an eastern part of Germany to a farm belonging to friends of his in order to escape the British bombing on Kiel. On my grandfather's visits from his home in Stralsund he was a very caring and gentle man and was there for us. He built a kite for me and showed me how to fly it in the fields around the farm. Of course, the prisoners had flown kites in the camp very effectively. After the war, the second global conflict for him and many others of his generation, Stralsund, now in a divided Germany, became part of East Germany and he couldn't visit us back in Kiel freely. But when he came he always spent time with us children and showed and taught us things like various card games and I learned the Gothic writing from him in my early teens. In his later years he moved to be with his older daughter in Göttingen, West Germany, where he died in 1954. He was old enough by then to be allowed by the East German regime to leave for the West.

When I was contacted by Anne Buckley about the book my grandfather Fritz Sachsse had edited about life in the prisoner-of-war camp in Skipton in Yorkshire during the First World War, I was very pleasantly surprised that she and her colleagues from the German department at the University of Leeds were translating the book into English. The prisoners had smuggled the pages out of the camp on their release. Although I knew that a book with a big red spot on the cover belonged to our family and I had opened it and had read some of it, I was not aware of its significance as a text detailing the experiences of prisoners of war in England and how German and British cooperation was achieved among them. Anne told me that my grandfather, my Opa, had played a major part in encouraging the prisoners to keep and open their diaries to put the book together and he had inspired the men in many other ways and had helped to organise the life in the camp and look to the future, to life after the camp.

I had known through my family that my grandfather had been a prisoner of war in the First World War in the north of England and had escaped from a prisoner-of-war camp in Japan after the Japanese had invaded Tsingtao, where his ship, the *Iltis*, had been scuppered. But when I and my wife, who is from Leeds herself, came to unveil the information board at the actual site of the original prisoner-of-war camp surrounded by many smiling local people I was very moved and felt privileged to have been given this opportunity to be close to where my grandfather and his fellow prisoners and the guards had spent the last years of that war. The prisoners had been fortunate to have been in this particular camp at Skipton.

There is so much in this book, so much detail about the men's daily lives as prisoners of war, about the problems that had to be overcome and the preparations for their eventual return to Germany. It is written with such communal spirit and humour, it is so surprising to see how this all was achieved in captivity.

My grandfather in his foreword said, 'let this book make its way into the outside world'. Exactly a century later I am delighted to see this English translation of his work make its way into the world and I hope it will show the reader that humanity and understanding and suffering and hope as described in this book still play a part in our lives and give us a deeper sense of the impact of war.

Thanks and Acknowledgements

This book represents the culmination of five years of work by a large number of people. Many were directly involved in the production of this book, whilst still more were involved in closely related work which influenced the final product.

Firstly I would like to thank the translators (listed on p. ii) and my co-editors Dr Caroline Summers, Ada Whitaker and Alison Abbey for their enthusiasm and commitment to the project, for their efforts in making sense of words written a century ago, and their painstaking attention to detail in our work to capture these messages in English.

I would also like to express my gratitude to proofreaders Christine King, Heather Hughes, Professor Sally Johnson and Rob Sanders who made many valuable suggestions for improvement to the English text, in addition to spotting our errors.

I am extremely grateful to a number of scholars who are experts on the subject of prisoners of war and internment for the support, encouragement and advice they have provided to me as a newcomer in this field: Professor Panikos Panayi, Professor Matthew Stibbe, Dr Brian Feltman, Dr Oliver Wilkinson, Dr Reinhard Nachtigal, Professor Isabella von Treskow, Dr Berhard Lübbers, Professor Stefan Manz and Professor Tim Grady. I appreciate hugely the detailed advice and valuable feedback offered to me by Professor Tim Grady while I was working on the introduction to this book.

I would also like to thank my colleagues in the German department at the University of Leeds who have supported and encouraged me: Professor Ingo Cornils, Professor Ingrid Sharp, Professor Frank Finlay, Professor Stuart Taberner, Dr Helen Finch, Dr Chris Homewood, Dr Jane Wilkinson, Dr Corinne Painter, Dr Stephan Petzold, Anne Markovic, Judith Eberharter and Wolfgang Keinhorst. Among these I am particularly indebted to the German native speakers for their help with the comprehension of archaic and obscure parts of the German text. A very special mention must go to Dr Caroline Summers who started the project to translate *Kriegsgefangen in Skipton* in 2014 and has been most generous with her advice and support. I am also grateful to Dr Hilary Potter, who assisted with the supervision of the student translators and with public engagement events.

Other colleagues at the University of Leeds have also generously given me their time and assistance: Professor Alison Fell, Dr Jessica Meyer, Dr Claudia Sternberg, Professor Mark Mon-Williams, Dr Tom Jackson, Professor Holger

Afflerbach and Professor Richard Cleminson. Professor Richard Cleminson was another who kindly provided considered advice on the introductory chapter. Thanks are due to Gareth Dant in the Press Office and Dr Alexa Ruppertsberg, Head of Public Engagement with Research, who have supported me in my efforts to tell the story of the Skipton camp to a wider audience. I am also indebted to Alex Santos for his design work.

Additionally, I would like to thank Alice Craft and Joe Everitt, who were student interns on the Q-Step programme in summer 2019, for their enthusiastic hard work in verifying data sourced from the records of the International Red Cross and for producing maps and statistics, some of which are contained in this book.

I am grateful to the Q-Step programme, the Cultural Institute, the School of Languages, Cultures and Societies, and the German department at the University of Leeds for providing the funding for student internships in translation and data analysis. I would also like to thank the First World War Network for providing me with training and mentoring and for provision of a grant for an information board at the site of the camp.

It has been fascinating to exchange findings with those researching other camps in the UK and I would like to thank the following people for their collegiality: Andy Jepson, David Sutherland, Alison Jones, Vicky Crellin, Colin Chapman, Dr Jon Finch, Graham Mark, Jane Middleton-Smith, Dr Mike Noble, Professor John Beckett, and David Stowe.

During the First World War centenary period I worked closely with the *Craven and the First World War* project, based at Craven Museum in Skipton. Within this wider project I learned from and was encouraged by many individual people. A special word of thanks goes to Project Officer Rob Freeman for his endless enthusiasm and creativity. I am extremely grateful to Alan Roberts for his contribution to the research into the camp and the German prisoners. I would like to thank the archaeology team, led by John Mitton and Janis Heward, for their work in finding some of the remaining evidence of the camp. Professor Nigel Holden, whose U3A course about the camp led to people coming forward with additional information, also kindly proofread parts of the text and his enthusiasm, hard work and support have been invaluable. I am also grateful to Steve Howarth, Dr Steve Wilkinson and Ralph Chester for their contribution to the project and to the local people who attended talks, exhibitions and information evenings, and shared their knowledge and stories of the camp. In particular, I would like to thank Monika Butler for providing a correction to the paperback edition. I am indebted to the late Ian Dewhirst, Keighley local historian, for his support of this project and for his permission to use the photographs of the funerals, Plates 14–16. I would also like to thank Clive White, Lesley Tate and Viv Mason of the *Craven Herald* for their support of the Raikeswood Camp project and for publicising our work.

I have been assisted in my research by staff at a number of libraries and archives. I would like to thank staff at Skipton Library, Keighley Local Studies

Library, Bradford Local Studies Library, The National Archives in London, the German Military Archives in Freiburg and the archives of the International Committee of the Red Cross (ICRC) in Geneva. I am especially grateful to Fania Khan Mohammad of the ICRC archives for her assistance in tracing the record cards of the German prisoners. I would also like to thank Ian Walkden and Andy Wade of the *Men of Worth* project and Shirley Penman of Clitheroe Civic Society for their assistance in tracing documents and newspaper articles related to the camp. In addition, I am grateful to Tim Hardy for his work to restore some of the photographs of the camp.

I am very grateful to Corinna Meiss for her work in tracing some of the descendants of the German prisoners. This work enabled me to make contact with the grandsons of Fritz Sachsse, Helmut Kähler and Wolf Kahler, to whom I am extremely grateful for their support and encouragement in bringing the story of their grandfather and his comrades to an English-speaking audience. I would like to thank Wolf for writing the foreword to this book and for coming to Skipton to unveil the information board at the site of the camp. I would also like to thank Ernesto Brucker, son of prisoner Georg Brucker, for his support of this project and for permission to use his father's photograph of a group of officers in the camp on the cover of this book (Georg Brucker is back row, second from left). I am also grateful to Dr Michael Good for sharing his knowledge about prisoner Karl Plagge.

I would like to thank Rupert Harding at Pen & Sword for commissioning this book and for his support and advice during its creation.

I owe a huge debt of gratitude to my parents who supported me financially during the three months of unpaid leave I took from my lecturing job to do the bulk of the editing work. I would also like to thank my sister, Dr Christine Buckley, who proofread the text and took the photograph that is Plate 19 while I was on holiday.

Finally, this book would not have been possible without the substantial contribution of my partner, Triss Kenny, who has spent much of the first two years of his retirement assisting me on this project. He has worked tirelessly to construct a database of prisoner information, sourced from the ICRC records, and which can be seen in an abbreviated form in Appendix 2, in addition to proofreading the entire text and assisting me with the formulation of the wording.

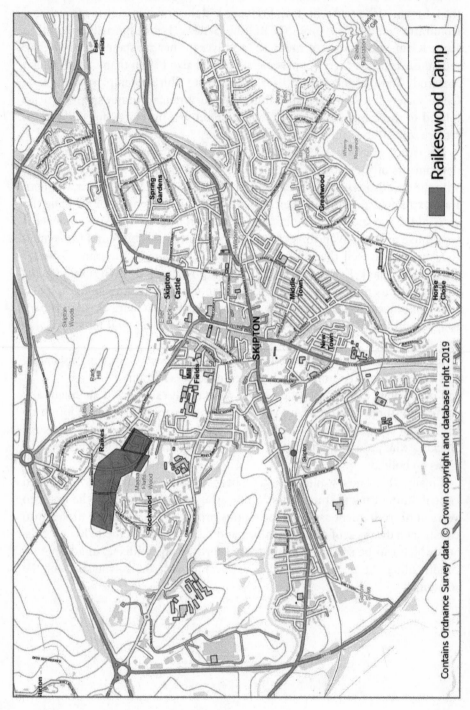

Raikeswood Camp

Contains Ordnance Survey data © Crown copyright and database right 2019

Location of site of Raikeswood Camp, Skipton.

Introduction

Background

On 27 October 1919, almost a year after the Armistice which brought the First World War to a close, a group of 600 German prisoners of war (POWs) boarded a train at Skipton railway station to begin their journey home. After a long and painful wait for repatriation they were finally on their way back to Germany, some of them after more than five years in captivity. A number of the men carried with them written accounts, diaries, sketches and poems about their time behind barbed wire in North Yorkshire. The following year, two of the prisoners, Fritz Sachsse and Willy Cossmann, made use of this material when they published their book: *Kriegsgefangen in Skipton*.

In 2014 the staff at Skipton library mentioned the book's existence to Professor Alison Fell, director of the First World War centenary project, *Legacies of War*, at the University of Leeds. A copy had been kept in an old shoe box in the library, along with some yellowing newspaper clippings about the POW camp, a few photographs and some handwritten translations of parts of the book. A small number of local people had been aware of the book's existence, but how or when a copy of the book made its way to Skipton, nobody seemed to know.

The book contains a valuable insight into life in a First World War POW camp in Britain and the experience of captivity, bearing witness to a rarely explored perspective on the war and its immediate aftermath as seen through the eyes of the German prisoners. Realising its historical significance, Professor Fell brought the book to the attention of staff in the University of Leeds German department, who began a project to produce this English translation. One of the motivations was to involve students studying translation in a collaborative project.

When work started on the translation project, it became clear that very few people were aware that the Skipton camp (known locally as Raikeswood Camp) had even existed. The development of the eastern part of the site into a residential area began in the 1920s and the western part was built over when the Rockwood housing estate was constructed in the 1970s (see map on p. xii). No obvious trace of the camp remains and it has never appeared on maps of the area. Another important factor is that, when it comes to the two world wars, Britain's memory culture is focused on commemorating its own war dead; the fact that over 120,000 Germans were incarcerated in Britain during the First World War[1] has until recently received little attention.

This lack of knowledge, together with an interest in the men behind the stories in the book, provided an incentive for further research into the camp and its prisoners and guards. The camp became an area of focus for the *Craven in the First World War* centenary project,[2] whose work drew heavily on the information in the book and the extended research. One example is the use of plans, sketches and descriptions in the book, cross referenced with local maps, to identify locations for archaeological investigations. In another project activity, local children used stories from the book and information obtained through research to create a cartoon strip story book and an animation film.[3]

The following sections of this introduction draw on both specific and wider research to give the reader contextual and supplementary information to further enrich the vivid portrayal of life in the Skipton camp provided by the German authors. Firstly, an overview of the historiography of POWs is given. It is this scholarship that allows the story of the Skipton camp to be seen in a wider context. Secondly, background information on the camp and the German prisoners is provided, along with detailed biographies of the two main authors, Fritz Sachsse and Willy Cossmann. Archival information and local newspaper reports are then drawn upon to enhance understanding of the camp administration, the escape attempts and the health of the prisoners. Next comes the continuation of the story of the camp and the prisoners, beyond where *Kriegsgefangen in Skipton* takes us, with information on the subsequent use of the huts, details about the post-war lives of some of the prisoners, and the fate of the graves of the prisoners who died. Finally, the production of *Kriegsgefangen in Skipton* in 1920 is considered and the reader is provided with an explanation of the translation process and the decisions that were taken in producing the English text.

Historiography of German Prisoners of War in Britain

During the First World War, nearly 9 million of the 70 million soldiers mobilised globally spent time in enemy captivity.[4] However, until the 1990s, First World War POWs as a whole received comparatively little attention from historians. This has been described by academics as a 'missing paradigm'[5] and a 'forgotten history'.[6]

Some of the earliest research into the POW camps came not from academic historians, but from local historians and philatelists. In this respect, Graham Mark's 2007 study of postal correspondence to and from British POW camps led the field.[7] Mark includes detailed descriptions of fifty-seven major camps in the UK, including Skipton, and in an appendix he lists 693 civilian and military camps and hospitals compiled from records in The National Archives. Of these, eighteen are identified as officers' camps, Skipton included.

Of the First World War prisoners, the German military prisoners who were held in Britain have received the least attention,[8] a group that numbered at least

100,000.[9] An excellent in-depth study of this group is Brian Feltman's *The Stigma of Surrender*, which focuses on how the stigmatising and emasculating effects of captivity and imprisonment affected the prisoners' responses to captivity. The shame and emasculation felt by the Skipton prisoners is clearly articulated in *Kriegsgefangen in Skipton* and their desire to demonstrate continuing loyalty to Germany and the German war effort through their actions while imprisoned supports Feltman's conclusions.

Feltman's work built upon Panikos Panayi's study, published in 2012,[10] which covers the experiences of both military prisoners and civilian internees in Britain, and was the first academic publication in this field. It is a broad study which combines personal narratives with analysis of the wider context, for example, state policy, the development of the camp system and the role of relief agencies who provided charity to the POW camps. Panayi's work enables the Skipton camp to be seen as part of the wider British camp system.

In order to further contextualise the experiences of the German prisoners as described in *Kriegsgefangen in Skipton*, other scholarship that has examined German prisoners in the Second World War and British prisoners in Germany has been useful. For instance, the organisation of cultural, sporting and educational activities by POWs and civilian internees to usefully occupy their time and create a sense of purpose has been discussed by Oliver Wilkinson,[11] Clare Makepeace[12] and Matthew Stibbe.[13]

Of further relevance is Heather Jones' detailed comparative study[14] that covers the treatment of First World War prisoners of war by all belligerents from the moment of surrender. Jones discusses the escalation of violence on all sides 'as countries reciprocated the behaviour of which their enemy stood accused'.[15] An example of such violence described in *Kriegsgefangen in Skipton* is an incident where German captives were shot shortly after surrender.[16] There is also mention of instances when German prisoners were threatened and robbed of personal possessions while behind enemy lines.[17]

Chronology of the Camp

Raikeswood Camp to the north-west of Skipton was built in late 1914 and early 1915 as a military training camp for the Bradford Pals. The 'Pals' battalions were formed after the Secretary of State for War, Lord Kitchener, decided to raise a new army of volunteers and General Henry Rawlinson had the idea of encouraging men to sign up alongside people they knew.[18] The first Bradford Pals battalion, recruited in September 1914, became the 16th battalion of the West Yorkshire Regiment. A second Bradford Pals battalion, which began to recruit in January 1915, became the 18th battalion of the West Yorkshire Regiment.[19]

Initially the Bradford Pals trained at a roller-skating rink on Manningham Lane in Bradford until the purpose-built training camp was constructed at

Skipton.[20] The camp was funded by the Citizen Army League, a group which was formed to 'raise, clothe, equip, feed, house, train and administer the Battalion until the Army Authorities were prepared formally to take it over'.[21] The *Bradford Weekly Telegraph* of 6 Nov 1914 reported on the new camp:

> It would have been difficult to find a more suitable site in the Craven District. It is well elevated, and there is an excellent water supply. The camp will consist of wooden huts, each hut being a barrack room 60ft. by 20ft., and good accommodation for horses etc. Water and gas will be laid on, and the necessary drainage is to receive the most careful consideration. The work of construction will commence at once, and it is expected that 1,200 men will be in residence in about four or five weeks.[22]

The men of the Bradford Pals gave names to the huts in the camp, for example *Buckingham Palace, One Step Nearer* (Plate 1), *Intelligence Department, Dew Drop Inn* and *We Can Whack 'Em*.[23] Some of the names are also listed in *Kriegsgefangen in Skipton*.[24]

Other battalions also trained at Raikeswood Camp, including battalions of the Black Watch, the Durham Light Infantry, the Leeds 'Bantams' (17th Battalion West Yorkshire Regiment), the Labour Corps[25] and the Wool Textile Pioneers (21st Battalion West Yorkshire Regiment).[26]

When the British needed somewhere to accommodate increasing numbers of German prisoners of war, one solution was the military training camps, such as Raikeswood, which had been vacated by British troops. A benefit of such sites was that much of the needed infrastructure was already in place. Raikeswood Camp was to be a camp for German officers, but the first Germans to arrive on 11 January 1918 were non-officers sent to prepare the camp.[27] The local newspaper, the *Craven Herald and Wensleydale Standard*, described their arrival:

> Guarded by a number of sturdy Tommies, with fixed bayonets, the vanquished soldiers of the Kaiser emerged from the somewhat narrow entrance to the station and deposited their bulky luggage on a waggon which afterwards conveyed it to the camp. [...] These particular German prisoners could certainly not be called a smart or a handsome lot. Numbering probably between 50 and 60, and mostly wearing dark grey uniforms with red facings and the familiar round German caps, they looked as if they would have been none the worse for a good wash. Some were smoking large curled pipes, others were laughing and joking, while few of them appeared to be in any way dejected by their misfortune. Standing about the height of an average Englishman they were inclined to be on the lean side; and one could not help comparing their sallow skins and low foreheads with the ruddy complexions and well-fed appearance of our 'Tommies'. Standing somewhat apart from his comrades was a Prussian Guard, said to be 7ft. in height, wearing a brighter looking uniform than the others.[28]

The first group of fifty officer prisoners arrived on 17 January 1918. This group of officers, along with a further two groups of fifty who arrived in the following few days, were transferees from the Colsterdale camp, near Masham,[29] which is where the Leeds Pals had previously trained.

Examination of the records of the International Committee of the Red Cross (ICRC)[30] shows that prisoners continued to arrive at Raikeswood Camp individually or in groups right through until August 1919, some from the Front (usually via a transit camp) and others from military hospitals or as transferees from other camps. The records also document transfers from the camp and thereby illustrate that there was a degree of prisoner turnover. Raikeswood Camp was home to German POWs until the repatriation of the final group of about 600 men in October 1919. The camp was dismantled in mid-1920.

The German Prisoners

Using the records of the ICRC,[31] it has been possible to identify 916 of the Germans who were incarcerated in the camp in Skipton during the almost two years of its existence. It is believed that this represents at least 99 per cent of the total number. As Skipton was an officers' camp, the vast majority of these men were officers, but there were also enlisted men and NCOs who acted as orderlies to the officers. The peak occupancy mentioned by the German authors in *Kriegsgefangen in Skipton* is 560 officers and 120 men.[32] A report relating to a camp inspection visit on 24 February 1919 provides similar figures of 530 officers and 124 orderlies.[33]

The men came from various different branches of the military. While the majority were from the Army there were also some naval personnel including fourteen U-boat officers, of whom seven were commanders.[34] These included Ralph Wenninger, who was one of the most successful U-boat captains of the First World War.[35] There were at least twenty-six airmen, including flying ace Joachim von Bertrab.[36] Of the 916 men, 592 were reservists whose main occupations included doctor, accountant, baker, bank manager, judge, chemist, dentist, butcher, barber, gardener, engineer, plumber, waiter, teacher, tailor, shoemaker, locksmith and student.[37]

The German prisoners came from all over the German Empire as can be seen on the map in Appendix 1.[38] Local identity was clearly important to the men and they formed regional societies in the camp.[39] A further and much more serious consequence of this regional spread arose after the war, when Germany lost 13 per cent of its land and 10 per cent of its population following the Treaty of Versailles.[40] This meant that some of the Skipton prisoners returned home to areas that were no longer part of the German Empire or areas that were transferred to other countries shortly afterwards following plebiscites. These areas included Alsace-Lorraine, which was returned to France, Northern Schleswig, which became Danish, Malmedy, which was given to Belgium, and most of West Prussia, which went to Poland.[41]

The Authors: Fritz Sachsse and Willy Cossmann

Fritz Sachsse and Willy Cossmann are named as the authors of *Kriegsgefangen in Skipton* and, as such, would have undertaken the task of compiling the material produced by over sixty of their comrades, ready for publication. The following sections provide an insight into the lives of these two men.

Fritz Sachsse

Fritz Sachsse was born in Hohenthurm in Saxony-Anhalt in 1875. He entered the Imperial German Navy as a cadet in 1894 and by time of the outbreak of the First World War he had reached the rank of *Korvettenkapitän*.[42] At this time he was stationed in Tsingtao (Qingdao) in the German Leased Territory of Kiautschou Bay in China where he was the commander of the gunboat *Iltis*.[43]

When war broke out, Britain requested support from the Japanese against the German Pacific positions, and on 15 August Japan issued an ultimatum to Germany demanding that it withdraw its fleet and relinquish its military power in China. The refusal to comply by the German Governor of Tsingtao, Captain Alfred von Meyer-Waldeck, resulted in the Japanese mounting a siege on Tsingtao and ultimately defeating the Germans in November 1914.[44] During the siege of Tsingtao Fritz Sachsse ordered the *Iltis* to be scuttled.[45]

The Japanese moved their POWs to Japan by ship and, after landing in Moji, Sachsse was part of a group who were taken to Fukuoka. Sachsse was one of five prisoners who escaped separately in November 1915.[46] He wrote a detailed account of his escape for his local newspaper in Germany, the *Stralsunder Tageblatt*, in thirteen instalments in March 1938.[47]

Using a French calling card provided by the camp interpreter as ID, Sachsse was able to make his way by train through Japan and Korea to the German Consulate in Tientsin (Tianjin), where he spent several weeks. From here he travelled to Shanghai, where he met up with three of the other Fukuoka escapers, the fourth having been recaptured.[48]

Sachsse and Herbert Straehler decided to travel together from Shanghai, aiming to reach Germany via China, Afghanistan, Persia and Turkey. They set off in January 1916 using the passports of two German teachers, which had been obtained for them by the German Consulate. Taking two German-speaking Chinese servants they made their way west, initially using sedan chairs carried by donkeys. They later changed to a donkey-drawn cart and then to horses. After crossing the Gobi Desert they reached Karaschar in mid-April. They then found that their route was blocked because the Chinese government, tipped off by the Russian Embassy in Peking, had ordered local officials to stop any suspected Germans.[49]

Sachsse and Straehler had no choice but to turn round and return to Shanghai, where they arrived on 6 June. They parted company in Shanghai, each looking for a ship to take them to the United States. Sachsse managed to secure employment as a fourth officer on a steamer, *Justin*, which departed on

31 August 1916 and took him to Seattle. From there he took a train to Chicago where he stopped off to visit some relatives. He then travelled to New York where he met up with Straehler again.[50]

After several weeks Sachsse and Straehler managed to stow away on a Norwegian passenger ship, the *Bergensfjord*.[51] However, on 15 November 1916 the ship was searched by the British while off the Orkney Isles, and the pair were discovered hiding in a laundry room under a pile of mattresses. As they presented themselves as civilians, they were taken to the civilian internment camp at Knockaloe in the Isle of Man.[52] In June 1918 they revealed their true identities in the hope of being transferred to Holland as part of an officer exchange agreement.[53] Instead they were sent to become prisoners of war in Skipton, where Sachsse would later become the senior German officer.[54]

Shortly after his repatriation in October 1919 Sachsse was promoted to *Fregattenkapitän* with a further promotion to *Kapitän zur See* in 1920. He retired as a *Konteadmiral* (rear admiral) at the end of 1922.[55]

Willy Cossmann

Willy Cossmann was born in 1883 in Berlin. He studied theology with philosophy, German language and literature, and classical and oriental languages at the Friedrich Wilhelm University (now known as the Humboldt University of Berlin). He undertook postgraduate study in Hebrew and Talmudic literature[56] and in 1914 completed a book about the Old Testament prophets which was published in 1915.[57] When war broke out he was working as a senior teacher at the Kant Gymnasium school in Spandau. He was called up in 1914 and given the rank of *Leutnant*. In 1915 he was awarded the Iron Cross 1st Class and, following recovery from a severe wound, he went on to become a battalion commander in Serbia. He was later awarded the Austrian Knight's Cross.[58]

Cossmann was captured at Cantaing during the Battle of Cambrai on 21 November 1917 and taken to the Colsterdale camp, near Masham in North Yorkshire.[59] He was one of the 150 POWs who were transferred from Colsterdale to Skipton when the camp opened for officers in January 1918. In the camp at Skipton Cossmann led a group of teachers who organised an *Abitur* (A Level equivalent) course for a group of younger officers who had not completed their schooling.[60]

Cossmann returned to his teaching post in April 1920,[61] where he remained until his retirement in 1950. His obituary notes his enthusiasm for his work and the good relationships he enjoyed with his pupils.[62] Alongside his profession Cossmann was also an active and committed Freemason. He joined the Spandau Lodge in 1929, but this and all Masonic Lodges were dissolved by the Nazis in 1935. Cossmann was one of a group who reopened the Spandau Lodge in 1946. In 1957 he became a Grand Master and he was instrumental in the unification of Germany's two Grand Lodges in 1958.[63]

Camp Administration

The treatment of prisoners of war during the First World War was legislated by the Hague Convention of 1907 for all signatory states, which included both Britain and Germany. Amongst other things, the convention stipulated that prisoners should be treated humanely and that they should be interned in a 'town, fortress, camp, or other place'.[64] The same agreement stated that officers were exempted from being utilised for labour.[65] There were also bilateral agreements between Britain and Germany concerning the treatment of POWs.[66] An agreement in July 1918, for example, stipulated the minimum amount of personal space each officer should be afforded (which increased according to seniority), the provision of communal dining, recreation and study spaces, washing and toilet facilities and the right to orderlies.[67]

In Britain the responsibility for dealing with POWs, and thus for meeting the standards of the Hague Convention, lay with the War Office.[68] The Skipton camp came under the jurisdiction of Northern Command in York, headed up by General Officer Commanding-in-Chief John Maxwell at the time of the arrival of the prisoners in Skipton.[69] He was replaced in 1919 by Ivor Maxse.[70] The German prisoners describe visits to the camp by these generals and it is clear that they did not hold either man in high esteem.[71] They even wrote a formal letter of complaint about the perceived lack of respect shown by General Maxse to the German Officer Corps on the occasion of his visit.[72]

The commandant in charge of the Skipton camp was initially Lieutenant Colonel W.C. Hunter, with Lieutenant Colonel Eley as assistant commandant and Captain Parkhurst as adjutant.[73] Parkhurst is sometimes referred to in *Kriegsgefangen in Skipton* by his name and at other times by his nickname, *Icankillyou*, the origin of which is discussed on p. 55. Hunter was replaced by Colonel Ronaldson in September 1918[74] and Parkhurst was promoted to the rank of major and became assistant commandant.[75] The German prisoners describe their respect for Ronaldson and express their gratitude for the way he treated them.[76]

Much of the administration and work in the camp was undertaken by the Germans themselves, including the preparation and cooking of meals. This is described in the sections of *Kriegsgefangen in Skipton* written by Hans Kohlenbusch and Fritz Sachsse.[77] Sachsse had assumed the role of senior German officer and head of camp administration in March 1919,[78] taking over from Major von Bültzingsloewen and Major von Kleist who were both named as senior German officers on the March 1919 camp inspection report.[79] German prisoners had been informed by the German government via the Swiss Legation that military rank hierarchies continued to function in captivity,[80] which was to the benefit of both prisoners and captors. For the prisoners it brought continuity and the retention of their military identities while for the captors, leaving the POWs under the supervision of their own superiors meant less manpower was needed.[81]

In Skipton, the senior German officer and the camp commandant had a daily meeting, during which the German officer would typically negotiate improvements to conditions and the commandant would respond to complaints, convey regulation changes and communicate any disciplinary issues.[82] This kind of meeting would appear to have taken place throughout the POW camp system in both Britain and Germany.[83] It was in the interest of both captive and captor to create an orderly and well-disciplined camp and this cooperation was an interesting contrast to the conflict between their warring countries.[84]

In the case of military officers' camps, such as Skipton, this cooperation was enhanced by a 'common code of military honour and a sense of cultural community'[85] that was shared by officers of different nations, who 'had more in common with each other [...] than they did with their own men'.[86] An example of this is the parole system, effectively a gentlemen's agreement, whereby officers were allowed out of the camp to take a walk if they gave their word of honour that they would not escape.[87]

The treatment of prisoners of war was monitored by a neutral power, who carried out camp inspections. In Britain, this role was performed by the United States until it entered the war in 1917, from which time the Swiss took over the responsibility.[88] The Skipton camp was inspected by the Swiss Legation twice in 1918 and once in 1919.[89] In the February 1918 report the facilities were described as 'fully adequate' but the inspection concludes by stating that: 'The general effect of this camp upon a visitor is not particularly pleasant, but this may be attributed to the fact that the roads and paths in the camp have been somewhat cut up owing to the recent building and re-organisation.' Three months later things had improved and the inspector reported that: 'Skipton camp now has a very different aspect from that presented at the time of my previous visit and compares favourably with the most well-organised of officers' camps.' The final inspection in February 1919 showed further improvement. The Swiss Legation was also a body to which the German prisoners could submit complaints, examples of which are referred to in *Kriegsgefangen in Skipton*.[90]

Escape Attempts

Escape stories have become a popular aspect of POW narratives, despite the fact that only a minority of prisoners escaped and even fewer were successful in making it home.[91] A 1920 War Office report claimed that only seven military prisoners (three officers and four men) and five civilian internees evaded capture following escape from camps in Britain during the First World War, with two of the officers known to have reached Germany.[92]

Kriegsgefangen in Skipton includes a section on escape attempts[93] but only one of these attempts resulted in the escapers spending more than a few minutes on the run. The two men, Hans Wallbaum and Hans Laskus, escaped in July 1918 and made it as far as Chatburn, near Clitheroe, 16 miles west of Skipton, where they entered the Black Bull public house. It did not take long for the landlord to become suspicious and the German prisoners were soon recaptured. The story was reported in detail in the *Clitheroe Advertiser*[94] and the *Clitheroe Times*,[95] and can be seen in Plate 10.

Two other prisoners had 'escaped' with Wallbaum and Laskus but had hidden themselves in the camp where they remained undetected for two to three days. One of them, Hans Kraus,[96] had previously also escaped from the Kegworth officers' camp in September 1917 in a mass escape by twenty-two German officers.[97] Following each of his escapes Kraus was sent to Chelmsford Detention Barracks for several weeks.[98] Presumably this is where he made the sketches of 'English prison cells' that he contributed to the book.[99]

The fact that Wallbaum and Laskus walked in a westerly direction suggests that they may not have been making a serious attempt to get back to Germany and, in *Kriegsgefangen in Skipton*, contributor Wilhelm Kesting mentions other motivations behind the attempts at escape from the Skipton camp.[100] Firstly, planning an escape attempt provided a challenge and a break from the tedium of camp life. Secondly, the prisoners yearned to be back fighting at the Front with their comrades. Finally, an escape attempt meant that the captors required more manpower in the form of more guards and/or police. This would cost the enemy money and detract from their war effort. Indeed, many POWs felt that it was their duty to try and escape[101] to either try to get home and re-join the military war effort or to cause disruption to the enemy. Feltman and Wilkinson[102] discuss similar motivations to those mentioned by Kesting, the former with regard to German prisoners in Britain and the latter with regard to British prisoners in Germany. Both also mention escape as a response to the shame and dishonour of having been captured by the enemy and Feltman claims that it allowed the prisoners to reassert their masculine identities.

Health of the Prisoners

In *Kriegsgefangen in Skipton* there are only a small number of references to the battlefield injuries sustained by the prisoners. However, analysis of the records kept by the ICRC[103] shows that, of the 916 Skipton prisoners identified, 322 (35 per cent) of them had injuries at the time of capture and 18 (2 per cent) of them were sick. Of the 322 prisoners with injuries, 249 (77 per cent) had sustained gunshot wounds – this represents over a quarter (27 per cent) of the prisoners. There were 5 men with amputations (a leg, an arm, a hand and 2 with finger loss) and 20 men had fractures, 12 of the leg or foot, 6 of the arm or wrist and 2 of the jaw.[104] Some men had multiple injuries, one of whom had suffered a compound fracture of the skull in addition to fractures of the tibia and femur.

The influenza pandemic of 1918–20 is estimated to have killed over 50 million people worldwide, taking place in 3 waves beginning in the spring and summer of 1918.[105] The German prisoners report an outbreak in Yorkshire in July and August 1918, which killed a number of the British guards.[106] Some of the prisoners became ill at this time but they all survived. It was a different story when another outbreak hit the camp in early 1919, claiming the lives of forty-seven of the men. This is described in detail in *Kriegsgefangen in Skipton*.[107]

As well as physical health problems there were also issues with mental health. The ICRC records mention only one man suffering from shell shock at the time of capture[108] but many of the prisoners developed psychological issues during captivity. In *Kriegsgefangen in Skipton* the prisoners describe how their mental health was adversely affected by the lack of private space and by living in an all-male environment, in addition to the uncertainty about how long it would be before they would be repatriated. The psychological effects of captivity are well documented. The Swiss physician Dr Adolf Vischer, who visited some of the camps in Britain, published a book in 1918 entitled *Barbed Wire Disease: A Psychological Study of the Prisoner of War*.[109] He believed that 'very few prisoners who have been over six months in the camp are quite free from the disease' and that 'if it has developed to any extent, recovery must entail a long period'.[110] Of the prisoners who spent some of their captivity in Skipton, by the time they were repatriated 391 men had been in captivity for over 2 years, and 25 of these men had been held for over 5 years.[111]

A number of scholars have also explored the emasculating effect of captivity[112] and the effect of this on a prisoner's mental health. There is evidence in the book that the Skipton prisoners experienced these same feelings of emasculation, for example on p. 278 they describe being 'cheated of [...] a man's duty to work for his family'.

In addition, there was some worry about how the men would be received on their return to Germany as a German code of conduct in 1918 stated that, 'For a man to allow himself to be taken prisoner by the enemy without having defended himself to the utmost is a dishonourable act equivalent to treachery'.[113] (This may have motivated some prisoners to attempt escape as a means of redeeming their honour and demonstrating loyalty to Germany.)

The psychological strain on the German prisoners increased after the Armistice. Some of the possible reasons for this have been identified by Brian Feltman.[114] Firstly, the fact that the POWs were unable to demobilise with the rest of the German military personnel left them further isolated from their comrades and from Germany. Secondly, the men often felt inadequate because they were not able to provide for their families, who were frequently left without their main breadwinner. Thirdly, the men were concerned about missing out on employment opportunities. Finally, some of the men believed that the German government was not doing enough to secure their repatriation and they felt abandoned. Feltman argues, however, the German government did as much as was possible but had limited influence as the defeated power.[115] The first three of these issues are mentioned in the letter written by the Skipton prisoners to the Swiss Legation on 27 January 1919 in which they protest against their continued captivity, stating it to be unjust and inhumane.[116]

After the signing of the Treaty of Versailles in June 1919 the situation intensified further, with the uncertainty about the timescale for repatriation causing considerable anxiety. This is described in the final section of *Kriegsgefangen in Skipton*, and in the 17 October issue of the local newspaper the *Craven Herald and Wensleydale Standard* there is a story about one of the prisoners escaping from the camp and making his way to the station saying that he wanted a train for London. The newspaper reports that 'his mental condition was defective'.[117]

Legacy of the Camp

Finally, on 27 October, the men's waiting came to an end and the prisoners were able to leave for home. An article in the *West Yorkshire Pioneer and East Lancashire News* describes the scene in the camp following their departure:

> [T]he walls [of one hut] were hung with maps, notably of sections of South America and of adjacent seas. The maps were not printed, but drawn in chalks and coloured inks, and one gave prominence to the waters around Coronel, and to the Falkland Islands. [... There was] a splintered draught board, broken up savagely, doubtless, at the last minute, as an expedient unfit to see the day of repatriation. For the rest, an assortment of empty tins littered the floor, a pair of mildewed sabots were the sole tenants of a remote corner, while a rude shelf bore a substance which while labelled coffee, had every appearance of tobacco, and emitted an odour which defied investigation. [...]
>
> There were other huts in which the men had seriously tried to live outside their narrow horizon. One man – or more – had taken refuge in mathematics. His examples lay scattered about the floor, disdained in the moment of leaving. Someone else had neglected to take with him an 'exercise book' which bore evidence of a determined struggle to learn the language of his captors, and he was wrestling apparently with the implacable English idiom, when release came to him.[118]

The camp was dismantled in 1920 and the huts and equipment were put up for sale. Advertisements appeared in *The Times*' 'list of forthcoming sales' for several weeks beforehand.[119] On 11 June the *Craven Herald and Wensleydale Standard* included detailed advertisements for the sale of huts and equipment (see Plate 19).[120]

The *Craven Herald and Wensleydale Standard* of 25 June 1920 reports the 'high prices reached' in the sale of the huts and equipment with £7,742 being realised from the huts and an estimated £2,500 from the equipment. An average price of £117 10s. for each of the thirty-nine living and sleeping huts (60ft by 20ft by 10ft) was achieved, 'the largest reached at any sale in the Northern area for that class of hut'. Buyers had travelled from as far afield as Manchester and London but a number of the huts remained in the Skipton area.[121]

The guards' dining room (77ft x 21ft) was reported as having been purchased by a Colonel Maude of Rylstone for £210.[122] This became the village hall for the villages of Rylstone and Cracoe and was named the Rylstone Memorial Hall. It survived until 1998, when it was finally replaced by a stone building.[123] The villages of Tosside[124] and Embsay[125] also utilised huts as their village halls and another became the Arncliffe Gun and Rifle Club hut.[126] Three other huts were used as classrooms at Ermysted's Grammar School.[127] Angus' Garage (now Peter Watson's) on Otley Road, Skipton purchased one of the larger buildings[128] and the roof trusses were still incorporated into the present structure at the time of writing.

Post-war Lives of the Prisoners

Some research has been carried out into the post-war lives of a number of the former Skipton prisoners. This work is in its early stages but has already revealed some interesting biographical information, illustrating a diverse range of careers and interests.

One former U-boat commander, Claus Lafrenz, was elected mayor of the town of Burg on the island of Fehmarn in 1931. In 1933 he refused to fly the swastika flag of the Nazis from Burg Town Hall and, as a result, was removed from office. He was found dead in 1937 in mysterious circumstances, although the death was officially recorded as a suicide. On the eightieth anniversary of Lafrenz's death in 2017 a plaque in his memory was erected on Burg Town Hall with the words 'In memory of the former mayor Claus Lafrenz, who obstructed the National Socialists and was removed from office. In doing so he gave hope to many people'.[129]

Another former U-Boat commander, Ralph Wenninger, resumed his naval career after the war, gaining promotion to *Korvettenkapitän* in 1926 and to *Fregattenkapitän* in 1931. He was further promoted to *Kapitän zur See* in April 1934 and then in October of the same year he transferred to the Luftwaffe. He was appointed to the position of German Air Attaché at the German Embassy in London in April 1936, and remained in post until the outbreak of the Second World War in 1939. He was also Air Attaché in The Hague and Brussels from 1936 to 1940. He died in Merano, northern Italy in March 1945.[130]

Ludwig Hofmeister was a reservist observer with the Royal Bavarian Air Force.[131] Before the war he had been a goalkeeper for the Bayern Munich and Stuttgarter Kickers football teams.[132] He made his first team debut for Bayern Munich in 1903 at the age of 15 and by 1912 he had made 200 appearances for the club.[133] He played one season for Stuttgarter Kickers in 1913/14 and also played two matches for the German national team before the war. Following his repatriation, he returned to Bayern Munich, where he played two further seasons from 1920 to 1922. He died in 1959.[134]

Walther Bremer, a reserve infantry officer, was already an eminent archaeologist by the outbreak of the First World War, having come to particular prominence for his excavation work and publications on the Stone Age village of Eberstadt in the German state of Hessen.[135] He made use of his time in captivity in Skipton to continue his work and to make considerable progress on a book, supported by British archaeologists Sir Arthur Evans and Duncan Mackenzie.[136] It is highly likely that it is Bremer who is referred to as 'a walking brainwave, a future professor of archaeology' in *Kriegsgefangen in Skipton*.[137] Bremer is credited with writing the first section of the book, which describes the camp and its surroundings, and provides historical and geographical information. Following his repatriation he was appointed to a lectureship at the University of Marburg, ultimately becoming Professor Extraordinarius in Prehistoric Archaeology.[138] In 1925 he was appointed Keeper of Irish Antiquities at the National Museum of Ireland in Dublin.[139] However, he died the following year following a recurrence of the malaria that he had contracted while working in Greece before the war.[140] A number of obituaries emphasise the considerable contribution he made during his short time in Dublin and the great loss to his academic field.[141]

Helmuth Schreiner had begun his studies in theology in 1911 and completed his First Theological Examination in 1914.[142] He delivered a number of sermons in the camp and contributed a section to *Kriegsgefangen in Skipton*.[143] In 1921 he achieved his doctorate in the philosophy of religion and was appointed Professor of Practical Theology at the University of Rostock in 1931. He was one of the founder members of the *Jungreformatorische Bewegung*, a group formed in 1933 with the aim of keeping church reforms free from political influence. However, in 1937 he was removed from the group because of his criticism of the racial policies of the National Socialists. He became a minister in Münster in 1938, and in 1946 was appointed Professor of Practical Theology at the University of Münster. He retired in 1957 and was made emeritus. He died in 1962.[144]

Lieutenant Karl Plagge was twenty years old when he arrived in Skipton as a POW in January 1918.[145] Following repatriation, he studied chemical engineering at Darmstadt University of Technology. Plagge joined the National Socialists in 1931, believing that the economic policies of the party would be beneficial to Germany. However, he did not agree with the racial ideology that emerged when Hitler came to power in 1933, and he was dismissed from his position as a scientific lecturer in 1935 for refusing to teach this. At the beginning of the Second World War, Plagge was called up into the Wehrmacht and put in charge of a vehicle workshop in Vilnius. He used his position to save some of the Jewish population from execution by the SS by providing them with employment in skilled positions in his workshop, despite many of them not being suitably qualified. Plagge's story was uncovered in 2000 by Dr Michael Good, the son of one of the women he saved, who had begun to research his family history. Thanks to the efforts of Dr Good and other descendants and survivors, Karl Plagge was named a 'Righteous Among the Nations' in 2005 by the Israeli Holocaust Authority, Yad Vashem.[146] Dr Good has written a book about the story and assisted in the making of a documentary on the subject.[147]

Graves and the Memorial at Morton Cemetery

In *Kriegsgefangen in Skipton* there is a detailed description of the influenza outbreak that hit the camp in early 1919 and claimed the lives of forty-seven of the German prisoners.[148] As can be seen in contemporary photographs of the funerals at Morton Cemetery in the neighbouring town of Keighley (see Plates 14–16), the British authorities treated the German dead with considerable respect. There was clearly some local sympathy for the German influenza victims as the *Keighley News* of 1 March 1919 reports on 'the painful sight of the funeral of five German soldiers' and goes on to say that 'respect was shown to the enemies who have died in our midst by the attendance of a firing party who fired over the open grave'.[149]

After the war, the Yorkshire German community held an annual memorial service at Morton Cemetery and there are reports of individual relatives visiting the graves. For example, the *Kriegsgräberfürsorge* (German War Graves Commission newsletter) in August 1930 includes a report by 'H.R. of Chemnitz' who visited his brother's grave. He explains how, before he departed, he praised the elderly gardener for his care in tending the graves.[150] In July 1937 the *Keighley News* reported on the visit of a German widow who was part of an exchange organised by the women's section of the British Legion.[151] In March 1938 the *Keighley News* reported that a party of fifty Germans had attended the annual memorial service and that the German Vice-Consul in Bradford, Mr John H. Groth, had laid a wreath on the memorial to the British soldiers following the service held at the German graves. The reporter commented that 'Old enmities give way to respect for common heroism as these German visitors never fail to pay their sincere tribute to the memory of Britain's war dead also'. The article continues by describing that 'British and Germans stood side by side on Sunday silently praying that never again shall such a catastrophe as that which brought the two great nations face to face in battle overtake the world'. However, there is a photograph of the Germans raising their hands in the Nazi salute at the close of the ceremony[152] and the Second World War would break out the following year.

In 1936 the Hindenburg airship flew over Yorkshire on its return journey from America to Germany and as it passed over Keighley a package was dropped out. It contained a bunch of carnations, a small silver cross, some stamps, pictures and a letter asking the finder to place the flowers and the cross on the grave of Franz Schulte, one of the prisoners who was buried at Morton Cemetery. The package was from Franz Schulte's brother, Father John Paul

Schulte, who was one of the passengers on the airship – he was known as 'The Flying Priest' as he was the first priest to hold Mass in the air. The parcel was found by two boy scouts, Alfred Butler and Jack Gerrard, who placed the carnations on the German memorial in Morton Cemetery,[153] and the event was filmed by British Movietone News.[154] The story has continued to capture local interest and has reappeared in the Yorkshire press on a regular basis. In 2003, local historian Oliver Denton published a short book about it,[155] and in 2015 a group of Keighley primary school children made a film about the Hindenburg's flight over Yorkshire and the find by the boy scouts.[156] Jack Gerrard's death in 2014 was reported in the *Keighley News* with the headline 'Riddlesden man made famous by crucifix-find dies aged 89'.[157]

The graves and the memorial designed and funded by the German officers remained in Morton Cemetery until the early 1960s when the graves were exhumed and moved to the new Cannock Chase German Military Cemetery, to where all German war graves in Britain from both world wars were relocated (approximately 5,000 in total), excepting those already in military cemeteries in Britain.[158] It is likely that the stone memorial was broken up and put into the vacated graves, as this was the instruction from the German War Graves Commission (*Volksbund Deutsche Kriegsgräberfürsorge*).[159]

The *Keighley News* of 20 August 1960 reported the decision to move the graves with the headline 'Morton to lose graves of prisoners of war'. The article goes on to explain that 'The War Graves Commission states that there is no question of the graves at Morton having been neglected but they are being moved for convenience of maintenance'.[160] The headline seems to indicate a sense of loss to the town and years later the newspaper printed photographs of the 1919 funerals in the 'Down Memory Lane' section.[161] The south-east corner of Morton Cemetery where the graves were located has not been reused.

It was not only in Keighley where local people had taken an interest in the German war graves. In various places in Britain people had been tending the graves and in some cases had contact with the families of the deceased in Germany. In addition, German families would come to Britain to visit the graves in the location where their relative had died. Therefore, in moving the graves a continuing opportunity for interaction and reconciliation between Britain and Germany at a local level has been lost.[162]

The Creation of *Kriegsgefangen in Skipton*

Kriegsgefangen in Skipton contains the work of fifty-four different named individuals. However, the total number of contributors is higher than this: three contributions are attributed to 'X' and one to 'Kober and others', and there are excerpts from the diaries of unnamed men. It is not known whether the individual contributors smuggled their own work out of the camp or whether the editors Fritz Sachsse and Willy Cossmann had already collected all the material together before the men were repatriated in October 1919. Presumably the two editors would have worked further on the text before the book was published in Munich in 1920. Both editors are known to have had a period of leave in early 1920, during which time the work could have been completed. The personnel reports of the school where Willy Cossmann taught (Kant Gymnasium in Spandau, Berlin)[163] state that he was granted 'leave for recovery' until 1 April 1920 following his return to Germany in October 1919. Sachsse had a period of leave from 19 March until 15 July 1920.[164] It is not known whether the original text of the book is still in existence but some of the original illustrations are in the German Military Archives in Freiburg im Breisgau.

In his foreword Fritz Sachsse discusses some of the reasons for producing the book. An analysis of the text suggests that another likely motive is that the Germans wanted to demonstrate their loyalty to Germany and to show that they had used their time in captivity productively in preparation for making the best possible contribution to Germany's future. The shame that German POWs felt at having been captured by the enemy and the concerns they had about how they would be received back in Germany have already been mentioned.

Kriegsgefangen in Skipton was reviewed in the *Times Literary Supplement* on 21 April 1921[165] and is described as 'the first book of its kind that has appeared in Germany'. The reviewer summarises the content of the book and goes on to say that 'We miss the humour and determination to keep the spirits up that are to be found in most of [*sic*] British prisoner-of-war books', completely overlooking the humour that appears throughout the book.

The Production of the Translation

In a fitting parallel to the original, the translation has been a collaborative effort containing the work of around thirty translators. University of Leeds translation students working on internships have gained valuable experience in translating sections of the text under the supervision of staff specialising in translation. Volunteers from the Skipton area have also made a valuable contribution to the process, providing local knowledge that was vital in producing accurate translations of the descriptions of the geographical features and the buildings in the area surrounding the camp. The text was edited during 2018–19 by Anne Buckley, Caroline Summers, Alison Abbey and Ada Whitaker to ensure accuracy and consistency.

We have used endnotes throughout the translation to provide explanation or context to the reader where we feel that more information is needed to fully comprehend the text. However, we have tried to limit the use of these notes and in cases where a term could be easily looked up we have not provided a note. The footnotes within the text are those of the German authors.

Because of the way the material is organised there are occasions where it would useful to be aware of a particular piece of information that appears later in the text. For example, we only discover in the section about the orderlies (p. 259) that forty-nine enlisted men arrived in December 1917[166] to prepare the camp for the arrival of the first officers in January 1918. In the translation, notes have been added to refer the reader to sections further forward in the book where the later information provides valuable context.

Kriegsgefangen in Skipton contains German translations of documents, including newspaper reports, that were originally written in English. We have tried to locate the original documents and, where we have been able to do so, we have used the original English wording. In cases where we have been unable to locate the original document we have translated the German wording back into English. In each case we have used a note to explain how the text was obtained.

There are a small number of minor errors in the German text, for example the incorrect spelling of the place name Arthington as Harthington. We took the decision to correct the majority of these errors so as not to disrupt the reader. We feel that the German authors would have wished for these unintentional minor mistakes to be corrected in a future translation or reproduction of their work, given their meticulous attention to detail. It is a testament to their thoroughness that the number of errors is so small.

The German authors did not distinguish between 'English' and 'British' and although they have used 'British' on a small number of occasions in the book they have used 'English' for the majority of the time. We took the decision to change this to 'British' on the occasions where it was clearly incorrect, for example, 'British government' and 'British War Office' but otherwise we have left it as 'English' as this represents the world view of the German prisoners.

As translators we have tried to capture the different voices of the individual men within the book, from the solemn tones of the portrayal of the influenza outbreak that hit the camp, killing forty-seven of the men, to the rather verbose description of the camp's administration written by Fritz Sachsse himself, to the humorous description of daily life by August Düne.

We have tried our best to translate the jokes in the text but some of these were very difficult to capture in English, particularly those involving a play on words. One example is *Gaulasch* instead of *Gulasch*, *Gaul* being a German word for horse (the goulash was made using horse meat). We have translated it as *goulass* in an attempt to convey the derogatory sense in which the word is used.[167] In the cases where we could not find a way of retaining the joke an explanation has been provided in a note.

One concept that recurs throughout the book is that of *Schiebung*, which we decided to retain in the German as the concept existed in many other camps and the German word is retained in other English scholarship and writing on First World War POW and civilian internment camps.[168] Retaining the term will allow scholars to locate examples more easily. The men in the Stobs camp in Scotland defined *Schiebung* in their camp newspaper, the *Stobsiade*, as 'a curiously elastic term with a whole range of meanings. Usually it refers to the seizing of small advantages, the quest to obtain something before others, discovering a jealous neighbour, announcing malicious tongues to the camp'.[169] Michael Foley describes it as 'an act by which one gained an illegitimate advantage'.[170] In *Kriegsgefangen in Skipton* it is generally used to convey the sense of obtaining goods by some kind of underhand dealing.

Throughout the book the German authors use the term *Prisonör* to refer to themselves, in addition to the German *Gefangener* and *Kriegsgefangener*. This is a phonetic representation in German of the English word prisoner and is similar to the use of *kriegie* by Allied POWs in the Second World War. The term *Prisonör* would appear unusual to the German-speaking reader of the original text and in retaining it in the translation we keep this element of unusualness and simultaneously remind the reader that the authors are German.

Overall, our intention in producing this translation was to capture the thoughts and voices of the German authors, from a text written a century ago, to create an engaging English text for the twenty-first-century reader.

Conclusion

It is thanks to the work and dedication of the prisoners involved in the production of *Kriegsgefangen in Skipton* that the memory of the camp has been preserved. The original book has been referred to in a small number of First World War academic histories but, prior to this translation project, local knowledge of the camp was disappearing. It is hoped that this English translation will help to rewrite the story of the camp back into the history of Skipton and that it will be a valuable resource for a wider readership and researchers who do not speak German. It is an account of local, national and international history that still resonates with us today and that contains a narrative that deepens our understanding of the local impact of a global war.

Kriegsgefangen in Skipton

SKIPTON

IMPRISONED
IN SKIPTON

The story and lives of German
prisoners of war in an English camp

A collaboration by many comrades, compiled by

Sachsse	and	Cossmann
Captain in the Imperial		Former Lieutenant of
German Navy		the Reserve

Originally published in German by Verlag von Ernst Reinhardt,
Munich 1920

Arrival of new prisoners.

In a sea of blows we could not withstand,
Our enemies' fortune in heated war
Forced our weapons from our hands
And exiled us to a distant shore
Far from home.

Sighted by day, in darkness blind
We stare at the valley's floor.
And though we are within mountains confined,
Our thoughts a thousand times and more
Make for home.

We lived in hope, we lived in pride
When Germany smiled in sun;
With sorrow we trembled, in pain we cried
When darkest night sank down
Upon our home.

We captives soon will return from the fight,
From this strange, barren place.
And though unarmed, our armour shines bright
In our hearts, strong as faith;
Love of home.

X.

Contents

A note on the cover illustration:

The English gave any prisoners (initially all NCOs and men, then also officers) who were not in possession of a uniform when they arrived, a colourful assortment of old English peacetime infantry and cavalry uniforms in various shades of black, blue and brown, to use as work clothes. In order to mark the prisoners of war as such, a circular piece of red or blue cloth was sewn on to each item of uniform. The artist felt that it could not be more fitting than to use this dishonourable symbol brandished on the back of every prisoner as the cover illustration.

List of Illustrations

Preface

This book, which depicts the life of the German officers and men who were prisoners of war in the English camp at Skipton in Yorkshire, was written during the time of our imprisonment in the camp itself and, with some difficulty, smuggled back to Germany on our return home. It has several objectives. For those dear comrades who were forced to share many painful days far from home and behind barbed wire, and who now rejoice again in glorious freedom, it should serve as a reminder of that strange time with all its challenges and diverse experiences. It is intended to assist all those who wish for some insight into the life of German prisoners of war. Furthermore, it offers itself as a source for historical research into the war. We also keep in mind the families of our deceased comrades: through this book they may come to know the community in which their loved ones spent their final days.

The book is the result of the collaborative work of many comrades who offered contributions and opened their diaries to us. The German administration of the camp provided reports and documents and went to great pains to prepare the manuscript. The artists in our camp willingly submitted their drawings for us to use, and in so doing significantly increased the value of the book.

As far as the historical accuracy of this book is concerned, it should be noted that the conditions in the Skipton prisoner-of-war camp were quite reasonable, and that no firm conclusions can be drawn from our experiences about conditions in other camps.

And so let this book make its way into the outside world! Let it salute our dear comrades who once spent difficult months and years behind barbed wire, and let it renew old bonds of friendship. Let it tell of our life far from home, and let it bear witness to the unwavering loyalty of our souls, in times of hope and in times of fear, towards our Fatherland and its fate.

Summer 1920
Sachsse
Captain in the Imperial German Navy

Our Camp

The English town of Skipton, in the county of Yorkshire, is pleasantly situated at the bottom of a valley below an impressive Pennine ridge. The town has a population of 13,000 and lies on the 54th parallel north, the same latitude as the Baltic Sea coastline of Mecklenburg-Pomerania. A narrow silver band snakes its way through the valley from the north-west: this is the River Aire. It is here that it gains a major tributary flowing from the south-west as it makes its way from the Pennine moors, which reach almost the same height as the Central Uplands of Germany. About two days' march from here, the waters of the River Aire unite with the other Yorkshire rivers in the Humber. Although Skipton lies a little to the east of the Pennine watershed, from where the waters run westwards into the Irish Sea, it is still somewhat protected from the cold north-easterly wind by the Pennine hills. Nonetheless, one has to get used to the fact that in winter the water freezes in one's wash basin. This exact spot in the middle of the Pennine Chain marks the easiest point of west-east passage through the range of hills, which spans almost two degrees of latitude. It is therefore not surprising that this valley has been settled from as early as the Roman and Anglo-Saxon periods and can look back on a distinguished history. In more recent times it has become particularly important because the canal system, which links Liverpool with both Leeds and the Humber, cuts through the Pennine range here. Skipton's industry (particularly cotton spinning) is not so conspicuous that it detracts from its real character as a true country town where the most important events are the livestock markets. To this day the town remains essentially the same as it was in the early Anglo-Saxon period when it was called Sceptone or Sheep Town. It is the raising of livestock on the extensive moorlands and bleak hillsides that gives the landscape its character, rather than the local industry, whose chimneys rise up every so often in the valley like palm trees in a desert oasis. The district of Craven, with Skipton as its major town, is said to contain some of the most romantic landscapes in Yorkshire, but as closely guarded prisoners of war we were able to feast our eyes on this picturesque natural beauty in only limited measure.

It was to this Skipton, then, that we came as German prisoners of war in January 1918 to take up residence in a British Army camp that had been converted into a POW camp. After we had been led through the town, a formidable gate opened in a fence in front of us. 'This Land is for Sale', declared an adjacent sign. We interpreted this proclamation as a good omen, but after a full year had passed the site of our imprisonment had still not been sold. After we had passed through the gate we caught sight of the camp to our right: ramshackle wooden barracks, surrounded by barbed wire which was as high as it was wide, and gantries that towered above it for the benefit of the guards. We had a premonition of the storms which would whistle through the cracks in the wooden shacks, and of the rain which would drip onto our beds through the roofs, which were constantly in need of repair. We could already hear the nightly calls of the sentries, familiar to us from other prison camps, which would pass monotonously round the camp: 'Number three, all well'. A set of strong double gates, reminiscent of lock gates and covered in steel sheeting, opened and swallowed us up.

After our persons and our meagre belongings, still knotted in red handkerchiefs from Le Havre, had been searched for any forbidden and subversive items, we entered our barracks. We could no longer be disappointed because we were already very familiar with them and their fixtures from other camps. The huts were of a long, draughty construction, open to the rafters, with a door at each end, and six windows along each side. The beds were arranged in pairs on either side of the windows, with their heads against the wall in military fashion, leaving a narrow passageway in the middle of the room, which was suitably cramped thanks to the washstands placed at the ends of the beds (one between two). The middle of this passageway was rather charmingly punctuated by the only thing that breathed any life at all into the barrack block – the iron stove. The windows, as a safety precaution, were placed so high that one could only see out of them from a standing position. The walls were adorned with just one small shelf above each bed and some clothes hooks fitted below this. Below the window between every two beds stood a pine chest of drawers. For later arrivals this exquisite piece of furniture was replaced by a box with iron fittings. Furthermore, instead of iron bedsteads they were given low plank beds and so would cast some envious glances at the 'old hands' with their more comfortable furniture. Finally, each one of the twenty-four officers who had to look upon such a barracks as their home for months and years on end was provided with one further possession: a chair.

We went out to explore the site of our confinement, surrounded by barbed wire and marked out by watch-posts: this was to become our world while we lived in the barracks. But we found nothing there either to gladden our hearts. The weather made sure of that. We were already aware that blue skies were not particularly inclined to smile down on Britannia, but even so, this veil of cloud that generally tended to envelop us seemed overwhelmingly dark and unfriendly. It rained, rained without cease. I once read somewhere that 'the English summer is made up of three fine days and a thunderstorm, and the only apples that ripen in England are baked ones'. And this really was the case, even though Wagner expressed his distrust of such language in the Easter walk scene of *Faust*.[1] Only those who have experienced the winter rain in the mud of the French trenches can begin to imagine the original state of the paths in the camp, some of which, even later on, benefitted little from attempts to improve them.

On the lower slope of the hill, outside the barbed-wire perimeter, were the English barracks. Leaving the camp through the main gate, the huts where the guards lived and their canteen, nine barracks in total, could be seen on the right-hand side at the edge of a small patch of woodland that marked the southernmost boundary of the camp. The administration huts, meanwhile, stood side by side along the road that led up from the town to the main camp gate. Built in parallel to these huts at the north-west[2] corner of the camp stood four barracks: the English officers' accommodation and officers' mess. On the large rectangular patch of grass between these two lines of barracks, stretching along the eastern edge of the camp, we could admire the guard detail at their daily morning drill, enjoying their often vain attempts to handle and load their weapons with German precision. But when spring came, even this morning pleasure was denied us. Just as, throughout England, efforts were being made to turn pasture into arable land to counter the economic crisis, here too the Tommies were obliged to try their hand at growing crops, and the parade ground became a potato field. However, as in most other locations we had the opportunity to see around the Skipton area, the success of this venture failed to live up to expectations, thanks to the unrelenting English rain of 1918. At the south-east corner of the parade ground stood a flagpole flying the Union Jack, a constant and visible reminder of our situation.

Within the camp itself, on the eastern side, a wide path ran along the wire fence: the prisoners' main promenade. In good weather, the 'parades' (that is to say the prisoner roll call) also took place here. On the other side, the promenade was bordered by a very conspicuous building, the long barracks. Its long, uniform façade, with a row of fourteen small windows just below the roof, blocked all other barracks from view. Each of its five doors was reached by a flight of steps, shorter at the north end and increasing in height towards the southern end as the land sloped downwards. At its southern end, the barracks stood so far above the ground that there was room for a basement. This had originally contained store rooms, but had then been converted using bricks and corrugated iron into the camp's only draught-proof construction: a double row of tiny, bare compartments, each with an iron-barred window-hole just below the roof line. They were hardly ever used for their intended purpose as detention cells: following escape attempts and similar punishable actions the German officers were mostly held in a sort of 'gentlemen's detention' in some other room in the camp. As a result, following the Armistice these rooms served the theatre group as a store for their props and scenery. A brief glance through the open door would reveal the camp's artists, with paint-pot and paintbrush, hard at work on a backdrop, or our esteemed stage technicians using hammer and saw to conjure up red upholstered sofas out of nothing.

On the main floor of the long barracks, at each end, were the rooms for enthusiastic intellectual labour, the 'common rooms' or 'quiet rooms', known as A and C, which will feature often in the accounts set down here. A neighbouring room housed the canteen, the only place where the prisonör could buy essential items: trouser braces and brushes, shirts and box-building materials,[3] football boots and tiger nuts for a sweet wander down memory lane – in short, necessary and unnecessary items, all made in England, everything so expensive and yet of poor quality. The remainder of the long barracks, from the canteen to Room A, had originally been a long hall lacking any furniture: the sign above the door revealed that it had been originally intended as a recreation room. Since, however, we Germans do not follow the Muslim tradition of sitting on the floor, and since the coal shortage meant that the stoves were not capable of adequately heating this so-called Room B, it stood empty and deserted for some time, used only for roll call when the weather was poor or after dark; a few stalwarts would often use it for daily exercise, plodding round in a circle, one behind the other. Later, however, once the prisonörs had learned to build walls using wire, sackcloth, old newspapers and porridge paste, this large room offered ample opportunities for activity. Next to Room A, a smaller and a larger teaching room were partitioned off. In another corner of Room B, to meet a general demand, an office was created for the officers of our postal administration and theatre group. Finally, a small room was created next to this for the camp library, the contents of which were not especially rich, but were diverse enough to offer something for everyone, whether he be interested in Schopenhauer or Mrs Courts-Mahler's novels, in tropical agriculture or Hanns Heinz Ewers' horror stories.

The remainder of Room B continued to serve as a wet-weather alternative for the walkers, who could avail themselves of the opportunity to study the latest announcements on the noticeboard managed by the camp administration, which took up most of the wall space. Numerous English camp orders were posted there. Notices from the German carpentry and cobbler's workshop announced the names of those whose turn it was to hand in and collect items. A prisoner could scan the list of walkers and the endless lists of clothing that had been mixed up in the laundry. The camp administration posted its accounts, the Swiss Legation's standardised answers to our complaints, and money lists on which it was possible to sign up for withdrawals from one's personal account on the next payday. We could also read announcements from the education administrators (timetables, announcements of special lectures), from the sports committees and from the music and theatre groups. And between all these hung a motley collection of 'classified advertisements': items lost and found, offers and inquiries, shower lists, important personal news from home and much more.

Directly behind this long building and running parallel to it, though about half its length, stood the Old Mess. Following our arrival in the camp, when we were still few in number, we had at first taken our meals here, which is how the hut got its name. At the north end of the Old Mess, two small rooms had been partitioned off, which were initially occupied by two German majors. Later, these 'apartments' were used as detention rooms for recaptured escapers and similar felons until they had been sentenced by the military court. However, after any illegal wanderlust had died out in late autumn 1918, as our hopes of a return home increased and there was no longer any chance of helping our brothers at the Front, several high-ranking officers took up quarters here. The remaining part of the Old Mess was a large room, the southern end of which contained a small stage with a room partitioned off on either side. In two separate groups, all the camp's occupants could comfortably gather here to enjoy the performances of the orchestra and the theatre group and to listen to the general lectures. The camp's religious services also took place here. The corner rooms housed the German camp administration on the right, and the mess administration on the left. Since the stage quickly proved too small for our musical and theatrical productions, it was doubled in size by the addition of benches at the front, and the rooms at the sides were also extended forwards. Colourful Indian scenery drawn by our camp artists decorated the stage walls, disguising the flimsy construction of wire and old newspapers. In May 1919, most probably as it was no longer seen to be a fitting backdrop for serious artistic offerings, this delightful wall decoration was overpainted with an agate green stone wall.

One of the back corners of the Old Mess had been set up by the mess administration as the 'Bar'. Although this name paints too rosy a picture, in our circumstances we actually found it quite pleasant there. Blue curtains divided the bar space off from the main room, and cheerful pictures livened up the walls. The furniture consisted of small chairs and tables, completed by a counter consisting of a board covered in oilcloth. Here, one of our orderlies acted as 'barmaid', and at set times of the day it was possible to buy apple cider, weak English beer, and, for those who were feeling temporarily well-off, occasionally also a bottle of generally splendid wine for between 7 shillings and sixpence and 12 shillings. Several small groups of companions would often assemble in the bar after lunch in order to pontificate on the latest events over a cup of coffee, but the cosiness of the bar came to an abrupt end when, with the camp now filled to capacity, mealtimes for a number of dining groups were moved back to the Old Mess and the blue curtain had to go. And so the bar became as cold and bleak as the rest of the barracks.

Due to the lie of the land, the stage end of the Old Mess stood on a high framework of stilts. The only thing underneath was a small hidden enclosure made of planks. From time to time of an evening, a mysterious something-or-other could be seen protruding down into this hidden enclosure: a wooden box, secured to the boards above it. Only those in the know were aware of its significance: it concealed the feet of the theatre prompter, who would sit on the floor in front of the low stage and let his legs hang through a hole especially sawn in the floorboards.

In the long barracks and the Old Mess, the intellectual life of the camp's inmates was at its most lively. Here, our minds worked towards the future and found some source of relief. The facilities that provided for the physical wellbeing of the prisoner were close by. Firstly, the kitchen was located diagonally opposite to the Old Mess: it was without a doubt the most eye-catching building in the camp, with its numerous chimneys and the extensions protruding from the two middle entrances. The occasional aroma of bacon or cooked fish that hovered around it was sometimes temptingly inviting and at other times less so. But we could not go in, since the mess administration had declared the 'kitchen area strictly out of bounds'. So a layman could not hope to lift the veil of mystery that surrounded the kitchen. The most we could do was cast a glance into the extensions protruding on either side. The sections at the back served as crockery and drinks stores and were not as familiar to us as those at the front, in which the grocery provisions were managed by a lance corporal who was truly well liked. Here, from time to time, and especially after the signing of the Armistice, there were occasionally items available to buy, and during business hours there were long queues here. But patient waiting did not always bring rewards: rumours such as 'eggs in the store' would suddenly do the rounds, whipping up a storm of excitement and causing one comrade after another to turn away looking disappointed. The smirking faces of the rumour's originators, however, could be seen at the windows of the opposite barracks. Even the nooks and crannies between the kitchen's long building and the grocery store in the annexe were put to culinary use: this was the space for the waste bins, whitewashed in summer, whose contents were removed daily by the English soldiers and used to fatten up their pigs; in another space a wooden frame had been set up, which on certain days of the week held 500 herring with mouths wide open in anticipation of their fate. The three barracks behind the kitchen, along with one to the south of the building, had been set up as messes, in which the prisonörs would assemble in tables of eight 'mess mates' at designated mealtimes. These rooms were later painted and fitted with curtains. The English initially forbade us from entering these rooms outside of mealtimes, but as the camp became full and space more limited, they relaxed this rule. Later still, they served as a space for band rehearsals, teaching, and much more. These mess barracks were part of a large group of huts that made up the main part of the camp and were generally designated as living quarters. They were similar in type to the official British Army huts, and most likely also satisfied English sanitary standards, with constant draughts coming through the floorboards, the walls and the badly fitted windows and doors. Indeed, a through draught seemed to be the most important remedy in the English doctors' repertoire. The draughts even came through the floor, since the slope of the land meant that the barracks were not built into the ground but rather met it at its highest point and, for the most part, were supported by a framework of beams. This also meant that the ground below could also be more easily searched for secret tunnels.

Proof of the unsuitability of these barracks as long-term living accommodation came in an article in the *Bradford Evening News* on 16th September 1919. By that time, our return home was in sight, and so the English camp administration was hoping to sell the barracks to the town of Skipton.

> "The possibility of transforming Raikes Wood Camp into housing in order to relieve the current housing shortage has been a topic of great interest in the town and has been discussed at length by its inhabitants. The local Housing and Town Planning Committee has studied the proposals in detail and has come to the conclusion that the plans are not practicable, due to the amount of work that would be needed to convert and adapt the huts. The Committee, it seems, does not approve the proposals, based on the view that, even in the event of the costs being met, the huts would be inadequate as a temporary solution to the housing shortage."[4]

So even costly improvements could not make these barracks habitable for the English! We, of course, were mere Huns!

A few of these barracks deserve particular mention. First, there were the three huts used by the English administration, which stood next to one another on the wide promenade that extended past the long barracks. The first of these was the office of the commandant and paymaster; the second was the censorship barracks, from which our parcels from home were distributed to us. The last of the three served as the quartermaster's office. Here, it was sometimes possible to buy replacement crockery; it was also from here that the bags of laundry were handed in to be sent to the laundry in the village of Gargrave. The three barracks were surrounded by a special, high barbed-wire fence.

The two barracks in the north-westernmost corner of the camp served as the camp hospital. One of these was divided into several rooms, in which the doctor held his consultations, the dentist saw his patients and the English medical orderlies lived; the other served as a hospital for infectious diseases. The neighbouring barracks housed the German orderlies. Since our enlisted men had, to some extent, also taken on the job of the officers' laundry, in dry weather this whole area was used for hanging washing out to dry, presenting quite an obstacle course for walkers. Also in this corner, by the barbed wire that separated the camp from the sports ground, stood a little cabin with a cement floor and barred windows. It had originally served the needs of the English supply sergeant, then had been used as a provisions store by the mess administration and had finally been turned over to the use of the music director. This 'music store', as it was now delightfully named, housed one of the rented pianos and was used for rehearsals by the orchestra and chamber musicians. All kinds of sounds could be heard coming from this wooden hut all day long.

But the list of the camp's noteworthy architectural structures does not end there. The plan of the camp also shows a number of buildings orientated in a north-south direction and not east-west like the accommodation barracks. First of all there were the semi-open washhouses which had water piped directly into them and primitive toilet blocks which were similarly supplied with water, although we often had to provide some encouragement to get the toilets to flush properly. And, most importantly, there was also the shower block, the destination of each prisoner once a week. Further along there was another hive of industry: the craftsmen's barracks. On its gable end the word 'Sport' was written in large letters. Below this were the noticeboards on which the camp's sports announcements were displayed, especially the daily allocation of practice areas to the various sports teams. Work was carried out in the three craftsmen's workshops from early in the morning until late at night.

Come on. Hans. Wir lassen uns Wasser
— von Deutschland schicken —

Wendel.

'Come on, Hans. Let's have some water sent over from Germany.'

The first housed the German tailors; the second, the cobblers and carpenters; and the third served as a barber's shop. Those in need of some essential sprucing up would begin to gather here, even before their morning coffee, in order to be the first in the queue for a shave. The final room in this barracks was intended by the English to be a drying room, but for a long time it remained unused. It was, however, eventually made available to us, and was then used for all sorts of things. From time to time the music groups practised here, before our stage technician set up his workshop, or the drawing club might meet for a session here, with pencil and paper in hand. Finally the room passed into the permanent possession of the chess club, which fought its silent battles here. The last building that should be mentioned contained the enlisted men's kitchen and dining area; this hut lay between the craftsmen's workshops and the hospital. The dining area was also used for the orderlies' social gatherings and for Roman Catholic worship.

One more structure deserves a mention: a low altar-like construction located to the side of this kitchen. There was always a fire burning inside it, and a grey column of smoke continually rose upwards from it. But the gods of Ancient Greece would have been unlikely to command the Horae to open the heavenly gates to the aromas from this sacrifice. And in fact the smoke from this sacrificial altar did not usually rise freely up into the heavens, but rather crept slowly and

Chess.

laboriously along the ground as though weighed down by some unconsecrated sacrifice. Only those devoid of any imagination could ascribe this to the high atmospheric pressure of the rainy English skies. The adverse wind often drove the smoke back into the camp, and it is probable that no inhabitant of Skipton will ever forget the penetrating stench, from which there was often no escape. It was the incinerator in which all the camp's rubbish was transformed into ash. A second incinerator was positioned in front of the craftsmen's hut.

The south-west corner of the camp, not occupied by barracks, was taken up by the vegetable garden. This was organised by the mess administration, under the direction of gardening experts, and provided the kitchen with a welcome supply of potatoes, peas, cabbages, among other things. Volunteers could find plenty of digging and watering to occupy them here. The garden administration was also active in improving the appearance of the camp. They sowed grass on the area of land north of the large kitchen, planted it with a few bushes and laid two small paths across it. Other gardens came into being thanks to the initiatives of various individual comrades.

Incinerators.

Finally, mention should be made of the remains of a tennis court between the enlisted men's kitchen and the main path. The levelling of the ground for this purpose had begun with lively enthusiasm and in great style; at one point many of the officers took on the task of breaking up the ground or digging, and carried baskets and sacks of soil from one place to another. But when the gas and water supply pipes were unexpectedly uncovered, permission was withdrawn, and afterwards there was nothing but rubble to show for this once grand plan.

The centre of life in the camp was to be found on the main promenade, which ran alongside the long barracks, and on the main pathway through the camp, which led at a right angle from the promenade into the centre of the camp, between the long barracks and the English barracks. The roads and paths in the camp had no names. No notice was paid to a few faded signs with street names, like *Downing Street*, left over from the English occupancy of the camp. The individual huts, too, had been named by their previous occupants: *Clock House*, *The Vicarage*, *In the Jungles*, *Boys of Rest* or, quite ironically, *Buckingham Palace*. The German staff officers' barracks, on the other hand, attempted to present an example of true family life: *Happy Family* was written above the door. These living arrangements never felt so homely for us that we felt the need to give them names, as we had once done in the trenches and dugouts at the Front.

Even when the rain made the rest of the camp paths unpleasant underfoot, the promenade was always still busy with walkers wandering up and down alongside the barbed-wire fence. This track was always the best maintained, as it also had to be used by all the vehicles that came into the camp. A large sign on the wire fence warned: 'Do not cross the barbed wire: danger of death. By order.' Through the barbed wire was a lovely view of Skipton, better still from the small raised platforms at the top of the steps leading up to Rooms A and B. The view to the right was obscured by the small woodland bordering the southern edge of the camp. Further to the left, it was possible to see a good distance down the Aire valley to the south-east. On the tops of the hills which bordered the river valley one could see the remains of a number of old watchtowers which had once dominated the valley. Peeping through the green trees in the foreground on this side of the main valley, however, were the red roofs of an elegant, modern residential area built on the hillside above the little town. Here also was the girls' school that was already known to us before our arrival from a newspaper report. From time to time we would see the pupils playing outdoor games. Over some newer detached houses immediately to the east we could see towards the old part of the town, characterised by the stubby shape of the church tower, typical of English gothic architecture. The church dates back to the late 15th century and is the final resting place of members of the House of Clifford.

This family also owned the old castle behind the church, now obscured by tall trees. The castle was built by Robert Clifford in around 1300. We could make out the two substantial round towers of the main gate next to the church. Above the gate the motto of the Clifford family was written in large capital letters: *DESORMAIS*. Behind this gate stood both the old castle and a new one, the latter now occupied by Lord Hothfield. In the old castle visitors can still see the rooms in which Maria Stuart,[5] was held. We were looking down from the camp upon a real piece of English history. The weak King Edward II frequently spent time here until he was dethroned by his own wife and murdered in 1327. During the course of his battles with Scotland, through which the Scots achieved independence, there was also a Scottish attempt to capture Skipton Castle in 1318. It was unsuccessful. From that time onwards the Cliffords were involved in almost all of the countless civil wars of the English Middle Ages. During the thirty-five years of the Wars of the Roses, Lord Clifford, known as 'The Butcher', fought for the Red Rose of the House of Lancaster. In 1461 he fell, along with 40,000 others, at the Battle of Towton not far from Leeds as they battled against the victorious Yorkists. Clifford troops also played an important part in the defeat of the Scots at the Battle of Flodden in 1513 during the reign of James IV. In the wars of religion that followed this, the walls of Skipton Castle were successfully defended in 1536 against a motley collection of forces opposed to the dissolution of the monasteries. The Cliffords also remained loyal to the crown during the reign of Elizabeth I. And so Maria Stuart was held prisoner here by Elizabeth, and when the Earls of Northumberland and Westmoreland rebelled against the Queen, the Lord of Skipton remained loyal to her. When civil war broke out in 1642, the Cliffords sided with the King. After a long siege their castle was captured in 1645 by the Parliamentarians, and shortly afterwards it was partially destroyed in accordance with Cromwell's orders. A few years later the castle was in fact rebuilt by Anne Clifford, and it is in this form that it has survived to this day.

We must return to our view of the town. We could see little of Skipton itself apart from the castle and the church. Further to the right, towards the

View to Skipton church tower.

residential area, a few imposing chimneys stretched upwards, and in between we were able to see some drab rows of houses, this being the industrial part of the town. We could see nothing of the other fifteen churches and chapels in the town. This large number is indicative of the sectarianism that exists in England. It was only by reading Sutcliffe's[6] novels, which are mainly set in this area, that we were able to picture the animated activity going on, when, for example, on market days the farmers would be selling their wares down on the marketplace in front of the parish church. We did not get to know the people themselves, even when we were allowed to pass through the town's streets on our walks. They generally treated us with indifference, though of course there were also times when young lads in the street would throw stones and other objects at us. But after one incident when a drunken soldier threw an iron bar at one of the German officers (on which occasion, incidentally, the English soldier supposedly assigned to protect us immediately vanished into thin air) all walks that involved going anywhere near the town were once again banned. If we base our opinions of the people of Skipton on their complaints about us marching on our walks and the fact that they refused to accept our sick soldiers into their hospital when the influenza epidemic broke out in the camp, then they will just have to accept it.

On the other side of the valley our view of the town was framed by a long, bare hill which sloped quite steeply upwards. Halfway up was a quarry up to which we sometimes climbed on our walks before the aforementioned ban on walking through town came into force.

An old road led northwards along the hillside here, a post road dating from the time when the valley below was still impassable. Of course it is the same at home in Germany: main roads dating from the Middle Ages frequently run halfway up the hillside along the sides of the valleys. To the north and in front of this hill was a flatter one, the top of which had been completely cut off by quarry works and which was only partly visible from the camp. But the daily noise of explosions resonated in our direction, awakening memories of days past when we were still permitted, full of hope and with weapon at the ready, to do our duty for the Fatherland.

To the north as to the south, the camp's wire enclosure was bordered by a narrow strip of woodland, on the other side of which was a public road. At first, we were not permitted to enter this woodland on our walks because of 'military installations'. Once we had explained to the commandant, however, that we were well aware that tripwires had been set up throughout the woods for our safety, this route was eventually opened up to us. Where the woods came closest to the wire fence, the view into the camp was blocked by a high screen, because one Sunday afternoon the Skipton Salvation Army had come to play for us, and the young ladies of the town were all too keen to use the path as a promenade.

In fine weather, opportunities for physical exercise were offered not only by the paths in the camp but also by the sports ground adjacent to the western edge of the camp, which could be accessed at certain times of day via a narrow passage through the barbed wire that was normally closed off by several gates. Like the camp, the sports ground too was enclosed by barbed wire – though not so thickly – and surrounded by guard-posts. In 1919 these guard-posts were removed and replaced by a book at the entrance to the ground, guarded by an English soldier, in which we would sign a written pledge not to escape. The ground sloped so steeply here that it could hardly have been more unsuitable for sport. Just outside the barbed wire at the opposite end of the field, under a group of trees, stood a small stone hut with a stone tablet inserted in the wall announcing that the area had in fact been intended as a recreation area for the children of Skipton, donated by a Miss Isabel Brown who had died in 1908. The lively sporting activity that took place here when the weather was even the slightest bit bearable will be described elsewhere. At this point allow me to mention only the circle of sunbathing figures gathering around this hive of activity in the centre on sunny days, and those who circled restlessly around the very edge of the wire cage, always walking one behind another, sometimes slowly, sometimes quickly, always going round to the right from the main gate, following the instinctive human tendency to move anti-clockwise. For the sake of politeness the author will say nothing about the vivid variety of outfits that enjoyed an airing in the fresh summer breeze, from the African-inspired lava-lava skirt made from a hand-towel to the long blue German officer's overcoat. He must, however, describe the view that presented itself to the eye from this spot, providing an unparalleled image of a typical English scene: on the one hand the smoking chimneys and wretched, claustrophobic terraced houses of the town's industrial district, and on the other, surrounded by endless meadows on the edge of the park, the manor of the ruling caste.[7] To the west, the view was restricted by a wall and an old hay barn, but to the north-west the eye could see across a little valley with its meadows and verdant hedgerows towards a country house,[8] partly concealed in the shade of its own parkland, and beyond this the skyline formed by the sharp contours of three gritstone hills. Further round to the right, on the hillside as it sloped gently up towards this country house, were the modest buildings of the Craven Heifer inn, named after an imposing, prizewinning cow that, two generations previously, had made the district of Craven famous throughout England. It was depicted in a life-size painting above the door of the inn. The inn stood on the main road leading north from Skipton, well known to all the camp's walkers. Further up the road, not visible from the inn itself, was the 'Green Palace',[9] an ivy-clad mansion with three Italianate towers that was so often the destination of the camp's walkers. To the east of this road began yet another chain of hills, climbing gradually in terraces and stretching out to the east: Embsay Moor. On the lowest of these terraces, closest to the road, if one looked carefully it was possible to see the ruins of Norton Tower, described by Wordsworth in his *White Doe of Rylstone* – a poet who is also known in Germany thanks to his warm posthumous tribute to

Schill[10] – *tempora mutantur!*[11] Not far from the ruined tower, the craggy, almost romantic little valley of Waterfall Gill was also found by a select few of us on one of our walks. It was also possible to follow the southern slope of Embsay Moor some distance eastwards and to look down on the green meadows in which the sheep, like tiny dots, romped around between the stone boundary walls; in the middle distance there were a number of modest farms and farm buildings. The view to the north-east was blocked by the aforementioned foothill, which was almost entirely chiselled away by intensive quarrying – a proper 'little Switzerland', in the words of 'Aunt Frieda', one of our interpreters. From up here we could see very little of the town itself that we could not already see from the camp promenade, only perhaps a little more of the factories and the wretched rows of workers' houses. But looking southwards we could see before us the wide east-west valley through which ran the Leeds-Liverpool canal. In spring and autumn, a good proportion of the valley was often flooded, forming large stretches of surface water. We would often stand and look down into the Aire valley to the south-east, through which one day – who knew when? – a train would surely have to take us back to the coast – to take us home, which in pride or in pain was constantly in our thoughts. But thoughts travel more easily than people. Even while our barometer of hope rose or fell from day to day, the harsh reality of prisoner life, not influenced by these varying moods, continued with the same drab monotony within the small space set out for us by our pen of barbed wire and the bayonets held by those temporarily in power.

The Guards

The life of each individual prisoner was also shaped by the guards, whose faces we saw every day high up on their watchtowers outside the wire fence. So, to finish, a word or two about them. The camp was originally guarded by the RDC (Royal Defence Corps, similar to the German *Landsturm*) from Leeds. These were old fellows, getting ever older as time went on due to the conscription of increasingly older men to meet the needs of the British war effort. Following the Armistice this guard was relieved, thanks to demobilisation, by a combined guard of two King's Own Regiments (the Yorkshire Light Infantry Regiment and the Nottingham and Derby Infantry Regiment) and the Stafford Regiment. They were young men back from the Front, or in some cases former prisoners of war from German camps, who must have had good memories of their imprisonment since they often tried to strike up a conversation with us in German, with varying degrees of fluency. This company was then relieved in part by the Bedford Regiment in early March 1919. These men no longer took any pleasure in military life, particularly the Nottingham and Derby men, who were only committed to serve for up to six months after the end of the war and so on 11th May 1919 expected to be relieved of their duties. Such extensive riots as those reported by the newspapers from other areas of the United Kingdom did not occur in our camp, but it was very common for the guards to throw away their belts and weapons and leave their posts for a time or even for good; there were also stories of larger-scale soldier strikes – stories that seemed plausible given the small number of guards turning up for duty. Once, in mid-June, we learned from the English that thirty-five men had been sentenced to imprisonment for this reason. In May there was yet another change: only remnants of the original four regiments remained, and these were replaced once more by the RDC. These were supported by two replacement transports of Devonshire Men who arrived in early June. Most of the Bedford men were sent to Ireland or Archangelsk. For, while the whole of England was preparing for a celebration of the peace won under the pretext of democracy, British imperialism continued to fight its wars in almost all parts of the world to extend the reach of English dominance and power.

Bremer.

Notes on the sketches of the camp

Area of the camp:	approx. 30,500 m^2
Area of the sports ground:	approx. <u>16,500 m^2</u>
	approx. 47,000 m^2
Built-up area:	approx. 6,280 m^2

Barrack design: timber frames with outer cladding – similar to the German style used for temporary, ancillary buildings, sheds, barracks, etc., particularly with regard to construction, timber joints and design. Excavation of building plots only for solid floors (concrete, in the officers' and enlisted men's kitchens, shower block, wash-house and lavatories). All other barracks built without excavation and supported by specially made substructures due to the sloping land. Building material is pine wood throughout: for the structural posts, floor frames, wall frames, rafters and beams as well as for the cladding and flooring.

Accommodation barracks

Substructure: wall frames rested horizontally on posts sunk into the earth at intervals of 1.5m; similarly the floor frames were laid on sunken posts and strengthened in part by struts at the gable ends.

Gable and side walls: timber frames, with horizontally mounted and overlapping cladding on the exterior down to ground level, and vertically mounted tongue-and-groove cladding on the interior down to floor level.

Floor: untreated surface made of 3.12cm-thick tongue-and-groove timber floorboards, nailed onto joists.

Roof: Low pitched roof (pitch of approx. 20°) – trussed roof – trusses laid onto the frame at intervals of 55cm. Horizontal bracing provided by a plank serving as a ridge beam. Each truss held together by a central cross beam. Struts connect the trusses to the window uprights.

Roof covering: Parallel to the ridge and the eaves, a covering made of tongue-and-groove timber boards nailed onto the rafters. This timber boarding then covered by roofing felt laid parallel to the ridge and the eaves, with nail heads exposed, in the style of a flat felt roof.

Windows and doors: Six square windows (1.18m x 1.18m) down each side of the barracks. Each window divided into six panes by one horizontal and two vertical glazing bars. The top half, hinged at its base, could be opened inwards. Doors: hinged single wing, frame of 4cm thickness strengthened by a 2.5cm-thick horizontal rail across the middle and two diagonal braces. Door cladding consists of vertical tongue-and-groove timber boards.

Heating: A small round stove in the centre of the barracks, sheet iron casing, fire clay lining, cast-iron base and lid. The smoke was removed by a vertical metal pipe that was badly and insufficiently shielded from the roof using asbestos board. With a barracks capacity of approx. 338m³, this heating was entirely inadequate.

Common rooms: Substructure, gable ends, side walls and flooring as in the accommodation barracks. Roof: purlin roof needed due to the larger span. Purlins mounted parallel to the ridge at intervals of 1m supported the casing for the covering material. Rafters needed only for the main trusses, spaced at intervals of 4m. For each of these trusses a tie beam was needed: this was either solid or made up of two parts connected in the centre using a scarf joint. The rafters were supported by two small posts and attached to the tie beam by an iron bar. Additionally, double diagonal timber struts connected the tie beam to the rafters.

Windows and doors: Windows measuring 1.45m x 1.18m, divided into twelve panes by one horizontal and five vertical glazing bars. Doors: double-wing, otherwise the same as those for the accommodation barracks.

Kitchen: Two smaller extensions built onto each of the east and west sides of the kitchen barracks to serve as storage for food and drink or for washing up. Constructed in the same style as the common rooms. Concrete flooring. Water supply. Furnishings: two long tables down the sides of the barracks. In the centre, six large cauldron-like cooking pots, seven cookers each with fire compartment adjacent to oven. Each pot and cooker had its own flue pipe. Three air shafts had been built into the roof to provide ventilation.

The use of poor-quality materials, combined with leaks from the fire compartments and flue pipes, meant that the kitchen was often filled with smoke and soot; at the same time, a significant fire hazard was created by the poor shielding of flue pipes near the beams and roofing.

Bird's eye view of the camp.

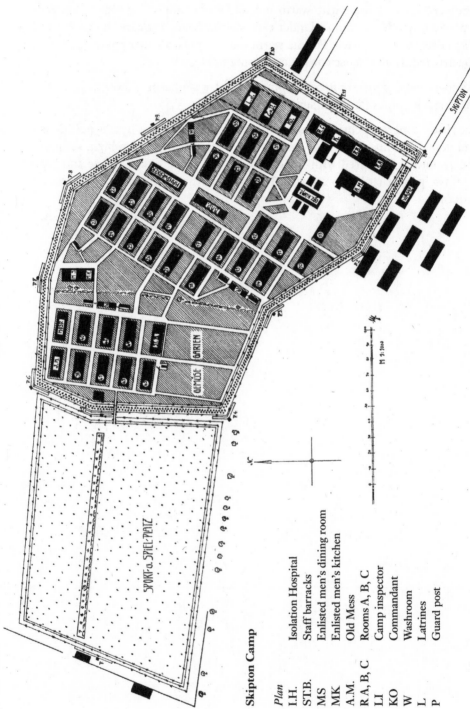

Skipton Camp

Plan
I.H.   Isolation Hospital
STB.   Staff barracks
MS   Enlisted men's dining room
MK   Enlisted men's kitchen
A.M.   Old Mess
R A, B, C   Rooms A, B, C
LI   Camp inspector
KO   Commandant
W   Washroom
L   Latrines
P   Guard post

Shower block: showers with warm and cold water supply. Individual showers separated by side partitions. Under each shower head, a square shower basin, 10cm deep, with drainage. For the warm water supply, a boiler house had been constructed. Boiler house constructed using bricks.

Wash-houses: concrete flooring, long rows of wash basins down the sides of the barracks, pipes for water supply.

Latrines: concrete flooring, lavatories separated into cubicles by side partitions and doors at front. Covered by a flat roof. Wide clay pipes, 1m high, set into the ground and covered with wooden seats; they were linked to one another by waste pipes that led to a sewer. Automatic flushing from suspended water cisterns.

J. Matthies.

The Story of our Camp

(A) From Colsterdale to Skipton

Near the village of Colsterdale, in lonely, practically barren hill country, the brown wooden barracks and high wire fences of a double camp stretch out down a stony hillside. 700 German officers and around 200 German orderlies are housed here in the 'tender' care of the English. With clothing still bearing the traces of battle, around 150 warriors move somewhat timidly amongst this large crowd: that is us, the newer prisonörs, still 'green', caught up in the stroke of luck that gave the English victory in the two battles at Cambrai (November and December 1917). After all the unrest of battle and the less than pleasant journey through France and England, we have now at last reached a German oasis in the foreign wilderness. In the company of comrades and under the energetic direction of the German camp administration, our tormented and exhausted spirits can now find some peace. The much-loved feast of Christmas arrives. In the spacious double hall, decorated by artistic German hands, the Christmas sermon paints a picture of home and a peaceful future before our longing eyes. Christmas dinner treats us to a wonderful roast goose that makes us shudder with delight before applying ourselves in earnest to the gratification of our senses. The holiday rushes by in the glow of the Christmas lights, the sounds of the camp orchestra, the rapidly dwindling supplies of the Christmas stollen and of the gingerbread that reminds us of home. On New Year's Eve, for one last time the old year unites campaigners far from battle and conceals all painful thoughts and memories with its entertaining performances.* We make our New Year wishes in good faith, glad of the comradeship that wove a web of homeliness around many of us during the tranquillity of Christmastime – and so the news that a new prison camp has been set up somewhere in Yorkshire arrives like a thunderbolt. Those in the know even have a name for it: Skipton. 100 members of our large family at Colsterdale (soon the number has risen to 150) are to be carried off there. There are few who would voluntarily leave hospitable Colsterdale for a train-ride into the distant unknown. And so the camp administration is forced to give the order that those officers newest to the camp, i.e. mostly the Cambrai men, must

---

* Former prisonörs, think only of the dance of the fire-worshippers, or of Duvinal's delightful song, *When I was still a Prisonör in Colsterdale*, or of the drumming, the melody and harmony of the violins, the 'twelve chimes' and the heart-felt good wishes for the New Year!

make the hard journey. It is truly painful for us. Anyone with good friends and trusted neighbours in the inner circle of the administration begins, with the innocence of a dove or the shrewdness of a snake, to assert his inestimable value to the educational and artistic life of the camp. The camp administration, with the best intentions, examines each appeal: some men may stay. But for the rest of us, who cannot escape our fate, nothing remains but sweet hope, man's loyal comforter. Soon, favourable rumours about the new camp begin to circulate: for example, that our new Eden in Skipton enjoys a mild climate. How harsh and barbaric our craggy outpost in Colsterdale seems now!* Other stories tell of a little town nestled up close to our new home: oh imprisoned soul, you will see other human beings, children's faces with their peaceful warmth, girls with 'proud, disdainful spirits',[12] the bustle of life – Colsterdale, how grey is your deserted, stony wilderness! Quiet and unseen, a joyful hope is also kindled in the prisonör's stomach. The meals at Colsterdale seem to be on a highly regrettable downward trend. Our evening treats of yellow cheese and white lard – do you remember, poor heart! – are disappearing and the grey spectre of extinction is stretching out its scrawny hands to claim the last strength and mainstay of any prisoner's stomach still clinging to life: our morning porridge – but the epicurean delights of Skipton are a beacon on the horizon of the near future. One more thing gives the prisonör the courage to move camps: the illusion of freedom to be experienced on the journey through the snow-covered Yorkshire landscape, the memory of the towns and villages of home hushed by snow, the brief opportunity to forget the dreadful barbed wire that reminds us of our imprisonment. And so we learn to accept our fate.

The days of our migration came. In the grey dawn of 17th, 19th and 21st January, fifty prisonörs each day tore themselves away from the sweetness of sleep. For the last time, they drank their coffee in those homely surroundings, then delivered themselves into the hands of the interpreters and sergeants who, with notable and affectionate curiosity, searched our paltry belongings and then our persons, in some cases down to the shirt and socks, for any items that could be used during the journey to jeopardise the survival of the United Kingdom and Ireland. And yet with creativity and cunning, it was not infrequently possible to trick those spying eyes and to smuggle through valuable items such as compasses, large scissors etc. Unfortunately, the present writer's finely tuned modesty prevents him from describing in detail the bodily parts that were found to be useful for concealing and carrying these treasures. Soon, the 'double gate'[13] (to be taken literally!) spat the nomads out onto the snow-covered and icy country road. With tender glances at the bundles in our hands, whose limited contents were ennobled by the humble philosopher's adage *omnia mea mecum porto*,[14] and in rows of four flanked by British bayonets, we lined up and set out along the smooth, icy road that took us up and down the hills of the

---

* According to reliable sources, on 9th January one of the English guards – who were mostly older men – even froze to death on duty at his post.

surrounding area, past tidy little village houses and small farms with fortress-like stone walls, past desolate wintry fields bordered by hedgerows and dry stone walls to keep in the sheep and cows that even in these hard months were plodding away their existence in the open air. After two hours' tiring march we descended into Masham, the last stop on the railway line, and were stowed away with our guards in comfortable carriages. The train soon transported us into the sparsely populated flatlands of Yorkshire. We lazed around comfortably on the soft red plush upholstery and made a few faltering attempts at English conversation with our Tommy guards. They were old men, who harboured no hatred of 'Fritz'; without guile, they made no secret of their aversion to the endless war. Harrogate, Weeton, Arthington and Ripon sped past. Albion's sons gazed with curiosity and peaceful astonishment at the 'Huns'. A few ladies and young girls, their hair curling around their necks, made a show of indignantly turning their backs to us – even in the fairer sex, the less favourable view – but we were not disheartened since, for the most part, the front-view of these ladies exhibited neither the austere features of classical beauty nor the sweetness of the ideal German girl. The train finally arrived in Leeds with its thousands of smoking chimneys, where we felt keenly how England's wheezing breath was struggling against Germany's iron grip. We left our carriages here, marvelling at the enormous signs ('Buy War Bonds!'), and climbed aboard the new train. Our guards left us here and a detail sent from Skipton took over the escort duty, much to our appreciation. The English officer was very pleasant: he was a large man who cut an enviably corpulent figure and had a coarse, fleshy face; his imposing chin was visibly at odds with the customary angular junction with the neck, repeatedly thrusting itself forward with a powerful offensive and thus creating the self-satisfied, domineering impression of a superbly trained triple chin. In memory of our gas masks from the field of combat, we later nicknamed him *Triple Action*.[15] He brought comforting news: our new commandant was a kind, gentle sort of man, and the accommodation was of a good standard. Our anticipation increased. The train brought us into a charming valley, where a little river (the Aire) wound playfully around the railway tracks. Travelling via Keighley, at around 3pm we eventually reached our destination: Skipton. And there you were, *Icankillyou!** Dear *Icankillyou*, our self-important camp adjutant! We gazed at you in wonder: your diminutive, graceful figure, those short legs and your comically earnest expression, the darting, piercing little

---

* How few of us know his real name! *Icankillyou*, on the other hand, resounded throughout our imprisonment in Skipton and had great emotive power. The history of the nickname is unclear. Legend has it that the 'little fellow' had been commandant of a camp for German prisoners in France and had threatened rebellious Germans with his startlingly large British pistol, thundering ominously, 'I can kill you'. Another report has it that once, in the heat of a raging battle, he had held the aforementioned murder weapon under the nose of an unarmed German and showed his confidence in his own power by claiming 'I can kill you'. Perhaps new sources will be able to clarify this contentious issue.

eyes and slightly ruddy nose – our knowledge of humankind aroused sneaking suspicions that were sadly to be justified. And how you then sprang into action and in one inimitable, jerking motion your hand sprang up to your cap as you greeted your assigned flock! Yes, we knew even then that *Icankillyou* was a tough fellow and wanted to show the world's most disciplined officer corps that an English captain was their equal. How mysteriously the three black ribbons fluttered at your back!*

Under his direction we proceeded onto the station concourse and organised ourselves into a marching column. In an orderly manner we strode through the streets of Skipton. The whole town had turned out. Dark, animated crowds of locals lined the pavements. They were dignified in their manner towards the 'Huns'. Astonishment and curiosity adorned their simple faces; here and there a finger was raised to point out a 'remarkable' individual amongst us, here and there a witticism was uttered. Proud joy was plain on all their faces: Huns, captured Huns in English hands!

Die Häupter unserer Lieban :
Herr Major „Kill you".

'The Heads of our Loved Ones': Major 'Kill You'.

And we German officers were walking through the midst of them! A variety of emotions surged within us. Our diaries bear witness to this: 'Under those thousands of British eyes I was overcome by a feeling of defencelessness. Under their gaze, everything in me that had been strong and manful now seemed torn to pieces and defiled.' 'I had to lower my eyes in shame. A feeling of regret washed over me, that I had not thought to avoid such an eventuality by instead letting my life be ripped to shreds.' 'I was ashamed for my Fatherland. And I knew that my presence gave these strangers their scornful feeling of superiority at having overcome German strength. That was unbearable.' Many begin to feel defiant. 'I was gripped by a wild feeling of defiance. I had always done my duty, and it was simply the fortunes of war that had delivered me into the hands of the enemy. I felt myself and my nation to be undefeated, and this enabled me to maintain my pride in the face of these crowds.' 'I pulled myself together, conscious of the fact that even this bitter walk was a service to my Fatherland.' Even now, we did not lose our feeling that we had loyally done our duty in battle and were members of a great, proud and undefeated nation. We straightened our backs and regimented our steps. With calm faces and defiant

---

* According to unconfirmed sources: a regimental emblem.

eyes, even with some quips and jokes, we strode through the crowds: we could not let these strangers believe that we Germans felt broken and humiliated.

Marching more quickly, we pushed on past the crowds, past the tidy houses of the town, some adorned with flags, and the shops with their displays of goods long unfamiliar to our eyes that sent alarming reverberations through our prisonörs' stomachs and the more materialistic element of our minds. Gazing out at us with proud yet knowing eyes from the gawping crowds were also numerous wounded British soldiers, dressed in their blue hospital tunics with red ties under loose, white collars. One more thing caught our attention: the channel crossing had revealed to us the English fear of our German U-boats. An incidental remark here and there from English lips had spoken of the highly regrettable food shortages in England, and the replacement of foodstuffs with dummy products in the shop-window displays of Skipton seemed to confirm this; the numerous agricultural machines on the roads suggested an unusual increase in arable farming and therefore also a state of emergency – and yet these English men, women and children betrayed no signs of wasting away, quite the opposite: even in peacetime, nowhere in Germany can one see so many plump representatives of the human race as here in Skipton. In particular, many of us can still picture in our mind's eye the rotund figure of the girl standing outside the Royal Oak, a female giant in miniature.

The street opened up into the market place, behind which we could see grey walls and a venerable old tower; a wide gateway with the inscription *Désormais* allowed a view into the deserted castle courtyard. We turned left into a side-street that sloped downwards, leaving the cramped town centre for the genteel and spacious residential area with its pretty gardens. After only a short distance we are led up another street to the right, a wooden gate opens, we begin to climb upwards; the view that opens up to us stops us in our tracks, pained and surprised. Across a wide snow-covered area, our gaze falls on our new cage. Here, again, we are greeted by double rows of high wire fencing, and behind them – oh poor, deceived prisonörs – the comfortless, much-hated brown, black-roofed wooden barracks climb up the hillside. Closest to us, grinning scornfully at us, was a particularly long and stilt-legged specimen of those delightful dwellings. Farewell, stone buildings, farewell, sweet dreams! 'Now that's a cheat and a stinking disgrace', grumbles an admirer of Reuter, in his thick Berlin accent, summing up all of our feelings in such a profound classical expression. With bowed heads we creep towards the 'Kaffir Kraal',[16] and another double gate opens and swallows us: we are 'home'.

(B) The Early Days

(17th January – 21st March 1918)

The interior of the camp presented a bleak picture. Heavy rain had softened the surfaces of the camp's paths, none of which had been paved. We trudged forwards, ankle-deep in mud. In the large central room of the aforementioned large barracks, *Icankillyou* checked once more that none of his flock had gone missing. Here, already, there was almost a confrontation between us and the little captain. He carried himself like a sovereign duke and expected us to behave like new recruits. While we were happy to extend the necessary formalities of behaviour towards the English officers, we were nonetheless determined to defy any ungentlemanly and humiliating arrogance on the part of the British. *Icankillyou* gave way in the face of our loud and indignant verbal resistance, just as over the course of time he was obliged to abandon many of his harsher demands. And now a scene played out that would so often repeat itself on the arrival of new prisoners. We trooped laboriously over to the mail censorship barracks. Under *Icankillyou*'s supervision, we were searched here again by the English sergeants, in some cases fastidiously down to our shirts. Two English interpreters enabled verbal communication. One of them drew our attention immediately with his schoolboyish behaviour: Mr Snee, who managed to stay on in Skipton until our return home. He had attended a grammar school in Kassel and spoke fluent German, with a vocabulary that even stretched to schoolboy and student jargon. Unsubstantiated rumour had it that in peacetime he had even held a professorship at a South African university. His years in Germany seemed to have endowed him with a certain understanding of German ways. But we gradually recognised that there was no honest disposition behind this 'natural' friendliness and that he was therefore not to be trusted. Later, we were particularly discomfited by his self-important habit of bringing us all manner of wild rumours, probably in an attempt to make himself popular; the rumours would stir up useless excitement in our imprisoned hearts and eventually, inevitably, lead to disappointment. The second, bespectacled interpreter, a Semitic type with a pale, scholarly face, was an openly calculating fellow from the outset and ensured that we felt keenly the shame of our situation. All books and written materials were kept back for inspection. We decisively refused to give our written word of honour that we were not carrying any cash, since the German government does not permit us to make this kind of oath. The Englishman shrugged and released us into freedom – within the wire fence.

Our comrades in the German administration showed us to our places in the barracks.[17] As in Colsterdale, the spectre of miserable living conditions loomed large. We had hoped to find stone buildings in Skipton, small rooms to be shared by a few like-minded souls, but now it seemed that mass quarters with their disturbances and lack of intimacy had become our daily 'home'. We were herded together into barracks of twenty-four men. The wind whistled through the cracks in the raised wooden floorboards and through the draughty timber walls. We were gripped by a profound feeling of spiritual and physical discomfort, and a sense of being far from home. After the kitchen had at least pacified our rebellious stomachs, on this first evening in Skipton, tired out by our journey and by numerous disappointments, we soon crawled into bed.

Miserable, uncomfortable weeks lay ahead of us. The vast rooms stretched out bleakly around us and we did not feel in the least at home. It was hardly possible to spend time in the barracks before 2pm, since the War Office had ordered that they not be heated before this time – coal deliveries were said to be limited. If anyone had the audacity to light the fire early, causing a merry billow of smoke to emerge from the thin chimney, the beady eyes of *Icankillyou* or his underlings would quickly spot the infringement and we would be inundated with warnings and threats. Full of resentment and anger, we would watch the smoke rise early each morning from the English barracks. But even when the happy moment arrived and we were permitted to light the fire in our single stove, there were only a few fortunate beneficiaries: those who inhabited the centre of the barracks. Occupants of the two ends continued to freeze to their hearts' content. Since, as the adage goes, all life is drawn to the sun, it is little wonder that any joy in our existence was centred around this stove. The ranks of the exiled formed a circle, large or small, around this warming, black goblin. All the problems close to our hearts, whether great or small, were discussed here, and so throughout the camp 'stove councils' or circles of 'fire-worshippers' inevitably emerged – they will often feature in this text. This obligatory, inhospitable coldness of the barracks until 2pm was all the more uncomfortable as Skipton's weather failed to fulfil the great hopes raised in us by the mockery of mischief makers. True, here we rarely saw the heavy snowfall of Colsterdale or felt the same ferocious cold, but instead it would often rain for days on end; storms would rattle our wooden shelters and whistle through holes and cracks. The barracks were pervaded by damp air; we shivered constantly. The damp permeated our blankets and the clothes hanging against the walls; timber rotted, and metal developed a coating of rust.

And where would the English, in their humanitarian benevolence, have us seek shelter for our freezing bodies until 2pm? The attempt on the first morning to warm our cold, shivering limbs with an early-morning walk to view our surroundings met with only limited success. It was heavy going through the muddy camp paths, and we paid the price of our foolhardiness with wet feet and extremely dirty boots. Again and again, our German sense of organisation and strong sense of social welfare wondered at the thoughtlessness of the English and their lack of care for our wellbeing. The camp had housed English troops for several years, but little or nothing had been done to improve the paths. Under these conditions, we were initially forced to give up our hope of the many benefits to be derived from camp walks. The English had an answer:

Playing *Doppelkopf*.

we were advised to spend the hours before 2pm in the common rooms, where the use of the stove in the mornings was permitted. Sadly, only one such room was available to serve all of the prisoners: this was not at all sufficient, having no more than a few tables and chairs and only one single, often smoking, stove to call its own.

Our prisonörs' fate felt more bitter than ever in those early days. We were almost all 'new' prisoners (from the Cambrai battles), the majority had still not been able to make contact with home. There were no letters from home to bring reassurance or comfort, no parcels to reveal the caring love of our nearest and dearest. There was no camp library to strengthen, delight and nourish our longing minds. No theatre, no music, no recitals to offer comfort by raising us out of the misery of our individual plight. Desolate and empty, daily life stretched monotonously ahead of us. Desperate times called for desperate measures. That was the heyday of our *Doppelkopf* and *Skat*[18] playing (usually not for money, since we had little or none); each of us contributed to the opinionated, endless speechifying, born of necessity and famous throughout the camp, which was at least one way of killing time with words. Those prepared to take action were still fragmented and each of us individually had to come to terms with the difficult process of settling into our new surroundings. For the individual as much as the collective, it was a time of turmoil and of change. Only gradually did German skill and German energy take up the tasks that lay before our little enclave.

As in all of England's prisoner-of-war camps for Germans, in the Skipton camp the British placed the administration of internal affairs in German hands. It was a convenient arrangement for the British, sparing them much tedious work. For our part, we welcomed it for two reasons. We often noticed that the English lag far behind the Germans in streamlined and transparent organisation. Any improvement to conditions in the camp, no matter how small, required a time-consuming process of obtaining permission from higher authorities in Leeds, York or even London. Bureaucracy seemed to hold even more power here than at home. For example, the barracks' lamps were covered with sheet-metal domes to conceal their light from German aircraft: these covers were removed within two days since they plunged the prisonörs into an almost tomb-like darkness. Following repeated complaints on our part, the order was given to close one door in the mess rooms and set up windbreaks in the accommodation barracks, as a defence against the weather. Naturally, despite our explanations to the contrary, it was the doors on the unaffected side that were closed, and these then also got the windbreaks.

In such conditions, it was a relief simply to be able to arrange our own affairs without interference from this inhibiting incompetence. This work, albeit on a small scale, also allowed us to enjoy a small taste of the German way of life we so dearly longed for.

At the head of our entire German camp community was our senior officer. He was assisted by a managing director of the camp administration itself. A tightly-organised administration supervised all individual areas of business. The two rooms beside the stage in the Old Mess were assigned as administration offices.

The German administration also took on the entire responsibility for the management of our meals. The English simply provided the raw ingredients. According to the Hague Convention, we officers were entitled to the same provisions as officers of the captor state, i.e. England. And our jailers constantly claimed to be upholding this ruling – but we were often more than a little doubtful of their claims, contradicted by the small portions on offer and the loud testimonies of our hungry bellies. Meals were prepared in the officers' kitchen by German orderlies. The kitchen administration faced considerable difficulties as, for example, the number of cooking pots and the coal supply proved to be insufficient.

At mealtimes during the first few weeks we congregated in the Old Mess. The six to eight occupants of each table formed a dining community – to use marine terminology, a group of 'mess mates', each of which had a captain. Each group of three to four tables would be served by a German orderly. In the early days, the food was truly plentiful: two cups of coffee in the morning and a bowl of porridge, our daily ration of bread (which for many younger comrades, admittedly, was far from sufficient); at lunchtime, for instance, soup, a goulash made with tinned meat, omelette or fish with potatoes (sometimes rice). Vegetables were entirely lacking, and the fat content was far too low. Fresh meat was not supplied during these early weeks: its first, isolated appearance on 4th March was a significant event in the camp. During the afternoons we were allowed two cups of coffee or tea. The evening menu consisted of another bowl of porridge and usually also a hot meal: there was a regular rota of peas, beans, lentils, macaroni, herring, rice and tapioca. Stricter rationing from the beginning of March had a devastating effect on our diet. We looked down in horror at our bowls, now only part-filled. Agonising pangs of hunger often plagued us throughout the miserable day. Our mood and our willingness to work, as far as we had any, suffered extraordinarily as a result. When the news of the rationing broke, some 'money men' bought up considerable stocks of valuable foodstuffs from the canteen: porridge, tinned fish, etc. However, the less affluent prisoners (and this was most men) had no choice but to suffer. They were only occasionally able to scrape together enough to allay their hunger with an apple or some nuts. In this exceedingly sad time, the kitchen administration faced a difficult task. It was a stroke of luck that we were able to find a professional amongst our band of comrades who could take over the running of the kitchen. With his wealth of experience, he managed to achieve whatever was possible: despite scarce resources, our food became tastier and more varied. With tenacity and perseverance, Mr James, the canteen manager, was persuaded to cooperate and we embarked on a road towards successful *Schiebung*.[19] In March, in order to enable starving comrades to purchase food more cheaply, the kitchen set up its own store, in which items bought through *Schiebung* were sold at cost price wherever possible. Without this *Schiebung* we would have gone under, especially whilst food parcels from home were not yet reaching us.

In February, the Old Mess was cleared following the order from the War Office that it was to be used as a general recreation room. Mess barracks 10, 11, 12 and later 13 were set up one by one as dining barracks. We were obliged to have the walls painted at our own cost; curtains arrived later to soften the otherwise dismally stark appearance of these rooms.

The difficulties described above indicate the significance of the camp canteen. And it therefore merited making this our very first port of call. It was located in the large barracks and the shop itself was a long room, with several back-rooms for storage and a small yard protected by wire fencing. Many treasures were on display here before our amazed eyes: underwear, boots and all kinds of shoes, toiletries, stationery, sports kit, wicker armchairs, cushions and much more. In the beginning certain foodstuffs could also be had here: tinned sardines, condensed milk, porridge, fruit such as apples, dates, figs and nuts. The sale of alcohol was not permitted. Unfortunately our modest means permitted no luxurious purchases, since of course money parcels from home had not yet started to arrive. We inmates had no access to English money. The English gave us only our so-called camp money, made up of metal coins with the values of 2 shillings and sixpence, 1 shilling, and sixpence.[20] To compensate for the lack of small change, the administration also brought 'paper pennies' into circulation.

Lagergeld.

10s. 2/6s 1s 7/6 s

Camp money.

To our great joy, in the canteen we were able to acquire tobacco, without which our joyless prison existence would have been simply unbearable – and we had not been able to do this at Colsterdale. But after a short time this free market had to be suspended, since mass purchases by some prisonörs had disadvantaged the others; and tobacco rationing had also come into force throughout England. From this point on, each of us received 3 ounces* of the precious plant monthly. All tobacco now went straight to the tobacco administration, which controlled distribution.

Entering the canteen, one would be met with a friendly smile on the round countenance of the man to whom our physical wellbeing was so indebted: Mr James, the canteen manager, who exercised his useful and profitable duties with the help of a few extraordinarily corpulent assistants. All the canteens in the English army and prisoner camps were military outfits run by the Army & Navy Stores (Managing Director: Mr Bourne), and all canteen products had to come from the large warehouses of this military business. Mr James, the manager of the Skipton canteen, knew how to take advantage of his position. His prices were quite high, and it was rumoured that he became very rich. He also knew, however, that the key to his wealth was to be open to a more clandestine approach. And so he would also bring goods from other sources into the camp, or would order more than the quantities specified by the English: in short, he subscribed to *Schiebung*. Our camp administration, carefully but energetically, exploited this tendency of his to the advantage of the prisonörs. Looking back, there is no doubt that our dietary arrangements in the camp would have been dire if Mr James had not been prepared to act outside the letter of the law. The fact that his ledger nonetheless always added up is due to the skill of our finance officers. It was less pleasing for the camp majority to see individual comrades sneaking through the yard door into Mr James' room for confidential transactions. 'Popular opinion' took a decisive stance against this private form

---

* 1 ounce = 23.34g. 1 pound sterling = 20 shillings (sh.). Exchange rate: £1 = approx. 20 Marks 40 Pfennigs. 1 shilling = 12 pence (d.)

of *Schiebung*; the administration gradually put a stop to the underhand dealings of certain individuals, as far as was possible.

The invigorating effect of the German administration was evident even in its earliest days. It energetically went about organising the repair of the camp paths. These were in a very bad state, which was in part due to the unfortunate ground conditions (a layer of peaty soil around 30cm deep, lying on impenetrable clay and only superficially strengthened by weak fascines). The limited material available for the repair work consisted of waste rubble from a nearby quarry and ash from Skipton's factories. In those early weeks, old and young, tall and short, senior and junior officers lugged the stones into place and placed them skilfully along the line marked on the ground. After this, the surface of the path was covered with cinders to level it out and carefully fill the gaps. In this way, a network of narrow paths emerged, firstly between the earliest huts and mess barracks to be occupied. The drainage ditches on either side of the paths were deepened to drain rainwater away as quickly as possible. This babbled merrily down, often building up to real torrents, especially when the thin iron pipes carrying the camp's water supply burst, adding their own roaring deluge to the rainwater. Our honest work, as our director of works complained, remained nothing more than a temporary solution, since the tools at our disposal amounted to one wheelbarrow, a stone hammer, a pickaxe and a few spades. Since the ash was very soft, it was easily trodden down and was soon washed away by the rain. Despite this sorry state of affairs we at least managed to make the paths passable to some extent, meaning that in bad weather in some spots one would only sink down into the mud up to the ankle – whereas when the camp had been opened, one's calves were forced to share this misfortune. Later, the work was continued by between two and six of our men, who were paid 3 pence per hour and enjoyed a supplementary food ration.

One room in the drying barracks soon became host to the barber's shop. Two of our orderlies worked here to help the rest of us maintain a civilised appearance worthy of German officers. In order to manage business, each 'customer' paid a shilling for a subscription card of eight units; the orderlies paid sixpence. A shave cost one unit (i.e. 1½ pence) while a haircut cost two, or five units including a shampoo, and so on.

The barber's shop was soon joined by the cobblers and tailors; the opening of these workshops was vital, since we were for the most part still going about in our clothing from the Front, which had often suffered much wear and tear and was in need of repair. And our boots in particular suffered due to the poor weather and were in constant need of the professional attention provided by our trusty craftsmen orderlies. The dire state of our boots and clothing was all the more pressing since we had not yet received replacements in parcels from home. The necessity of going around daily in this dirty, often badly worn Front uniform also took its toll on our mood. The eventual extent of our craftsmen's work, and the particular problems that these workshops faced, will be described in later reports.

Even the difficult laundry problem was immediately solved. Only the wealthy amongst us enjoyed the luxury of owning a second set of clothing; initially a good many prisoners owned only the clothes on their backs. So it was essential to get things washed quickly. One group of comrades followed English orders and sent their things to be washed in the village of Gargrave. Others, who preferred or needed to take a shorter route to the cleaning of their precious, perhaps only, items, accepted the help of the orderlies, who in turn welcomed the opportunity to earn a little extra. Other industrious comrades of lower rank took the fate of their clothing into their own hands. The observer, smiling in wonder, might be treated to the charmingly unfamiliar scene of sweating figures bent over with their sleeves rolled up in the wash-house.

Our concern also immediately turned to the upholding of moral standards, professional honour and comradely attitudes and behaviour, by retaining the court of honour.

Immediately after the founding of the camp, the then senior German officer issued a special *Provision for the Application of the Supreme Decree of May 1874 and Amendment* and this was regularly communicated and explained to the officers. The senior officer took on the role of a division commander; due to the size of the camp, only one senior officer was entrusted with the duties of commander. At first two, but later five council-of-honour groups were formed, each of which elected its own representatives. As our imprisonment continued, the commander and the councils of honour had increasingly to focus on practical means of guaranteeing the honour of the individual and settling minor disputes in a manner befitting the upholding of a dignified, comradely community. This final arrangement gave rise to the difficulty that referral to Army High Command, as envisaged by the amendment of January 1897, was at first a practical and from late 1918 onwards also a legal impossibility. We attempted to circumnavigate the resulting lacuna in the application of the procedure of the court of honour with a system whereby, in cases in which the council's findings or decision remained unsatisfactory to the affected parties, even after the adjudication of a second council of honour appointed by the commander, the appeal should be put before all those remaining councils of honour not yet involved in the case. Should any party refuse to accept the decision passed by a majority in this collective council of honour, with the approval of the chairman and the commander, the whole council of honour should pronounce the following: firstly, on what points the dissenting party infringed against the shared honour and morality of the officer corps; secondly, that the decision of the collective council of honour resolved the dispute to the satisfaction of the parties involved and the officer corps as a whole for the duration of their stay in the camp, and also that the dissenter, through his refusal to accept the decision, relinquished his right to protection of the concept of honour and of the judicial provisions of the camp officer corps.

The responsibility of the councils of honour to resolve minor matters of honour in the interests of upholding dignified communal living conditions was fulfilled, in so far as in all disputes an appropriate settlement was always found in the first instance. The commander and the councils of honour were guided in this by the shared conviction that the particular conditions of imprisonment also demanded a particular approach to matters of honour. Constant, cramped cohabitation in a single barracks with twenty-four men of varying ages, enforced inactivity, the lack of the most basic necessities of life and physical wellbeing, the constant waiting and mood swings between despair, anxiety and hope, these must have mental and material implications that would never arise in an officer corps at home and can only be fully recognised and appreciated by those who have experienced them for themselves. Taking this into account, certain cases had to be seen as minor and conducive to a complete settlement, which at home would probably have been considered 'of considerable significance'. Taking into account our particular conditions, in all cases a settlement was not only appropriate but also possible.

When, in July 1919, the new constitution of the German Reich dissolved the military courts and with them the councils of honour, we introduced in the camp a special 'arbitration system', which all officers accepted.

Gradually we found our feet in our new surroundings. We saw that our organisation of affairs led to progress and wherever possible attempted to alleviate the wretched life of the prisonörs. Each man built around him his own world of people and objects and learnt to fit in. The dreary barracks became part of life and, in the company of comrades, part of German life. As far as our meagre resources allowed, we created 'comfortable luxury' for ourselves, and where reality truly was too sad to bear, our youthful humour and optimism tried to salvage an illusionary golden world from our unfortunate circumstances. One comrade who, as an 'original prisoner' (in contrast to those who came later), had a wrought iron bedstead and a sturdy cupboard, tells us in his diary of this period, in almost Homeric language, about ...

The Prisoner's Belongings

"Sunday afternoon in captivity. And alone. Where have the rest of them got to? Well, the appearance of some pleasant sunshine, rare in this part of the world, probably enticed them out for a walk. I feel so pathetically miserable. I keep looking at mother's picture and then at Gretchen's sweet face on the other side. How wretched I feel! Come on boy, come on, you were always boasting about your skills in the art of living and now you have been seized by utter misery. Damn it! Why don't I see with the eyes of *Leberecht Hühnchen*?[21] Think about it, young man – don't you have quite a pleasant and comfortable life here? Here in the barracks you have 2.5m x 1.7m that belongs to you alone. This is your kingdom, your home, coveted by nobody else. My kingdom! How could I have failed to see that! But now, now I am taking ownership of it with proprietorial awareness. How the black, cast-iron bed frame extends alluringly across a wide space: you, my bed, are a precious resting place, a downy cushion for my clear conscience with a mattress in two sections, so often allowing my most noble part to sink into the gap between them, with the firm grey-covered pillow on top of a sausage-shaped bolster for my precious head, with four venerable old blankets that I have learnt to roll up lovingly and ingeniously every evening fashioning a sleeping bag to provide my body with warmth and protection and a gentle caress; you are also a splendid chaise longue for a restorative midday snooze, a soft seat for welcome friends who perch on you like sparrows on a telegraph wire. Above you, protruding from the wall are three blackish, gracefully curved hooks for my 'extensive' wardrobe. Further up, a plank protrudes from the woodwork onto which I may place whatever my mood or intellect dictates. On the left, the window opens majestically, its six panes of glass providing the eye with an aesthetically pleasing panorama and revealing the comforting sight of the pitch-painted roof of the neighbouring barracks. I am fully entitled to half of the sturdy, yellowish cabinet: one shelf, one pull-out box and one drawer. Tenderly I look at the greenish, splendidly patterned bedside rug, which caringly protects my bare feet in the evenings when I dare to launch myself from it into my slumber-inducing nest. The blue trunk made in the carpentry workshop lies proudly under the bed; it tore 16 shillings from my bleeding heart but now it smiles out at me reassuringly and waits with me for the journey home. Dear, dear trunk! My little table, fragile but charming you stand on your thin legs; how artistically the craftsman created you to reflect the precarious existence of the prisonör! The mirror at the window shows me the other-worldly features of an incorrigible rogue. Suitably flattered, I turn away. At the end of the bed I am greeted amiably by the dark wooden wash stand with the white earthenware basin, bulbous jug and soap dish embellished with a lid. There is even a water bottle and glass. And peeking out almost shamefully from right underneath the lower shelf is a splendid chamber pot – on many occasions it has saved me from a night walk in storms and bad weather.

With a calm, contented smile I sink down onto the dark chair – even this is my own. I fold my hands together across my wiry body and think while twiddling my thumbs 'how rich you really are!' And how actively I have increased my wealth! Under the window ledge there is a small shelf. Lying here companionably are a brush to smarten me up and a comb to pull through my locks, along with some aromatic bay rum hair tonic and some fragrant hair cream. Two cloths, in a calming blue with white flowers, neatly cover the cabinet and table. A simple rack on top of the cabinet – the carpenter willingly made it for me for 2 shillings – holds just a few splendid books for intellectual stimulation, for study or for pleasure. Two small picture frames carved by myself, working every day for three weeks with an unskilled but faithful hand, coloured black with ink and shoe polish, embrace those I yearn

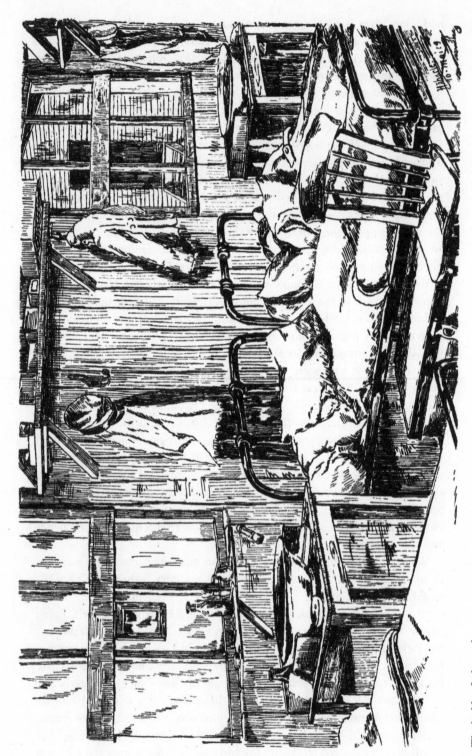

The inside of a barracks.

for: the pictures of my devoted mother and my eternally young love Gretchen with her rosy lips, which I used to kiss so often at home. Away, thoughts, away – you cause the prisonör so much pain! Down from the shelf and over the hooks a green curtain sweeps, and a gossamer-thin, snowy-white net curtain nestles against the window. From under the bed my boot jack grins up at me with a wide-open mouth; in the evenings, he tugs the boots from my tired legs with a firm grip. I open the rectangular drawer: laid out here ready for me are handkerchiefs, woollen and linen shirts, trousers and socks, only a small number but sufficient to enjoy a weekly change. These items were sent caringly by my devoted mother. Still reflecting, I open the small box above it: pan after pan, all my own handiwork, made from tin cans, their contents consumed long ago. Alongside these are forks, knives, spoons and plates. I bought them from Mr James at the same time as I acquired you, the large, blackened cooking pot there under the bed; you have made me so much excellent custard but in exchange I had to part with 9 shillings from my sighing wallet. A small frying pan also became mine – hammered into shape by lacerated fingers with great effort from a rectangular fish can. It has a long wooden handle firmly secured to the tin vessel with thick wire.

This is my world! This is what I call my world!”

X.

The Parcel List and the Post

Parcel list.   Paketliste.

At the end of January and in the first weeks of February, most men received the long-awaited news from home. Who can imagine the quiet bliss, the jubilant elation as we held that first letter or that first parcel in our hands! A thousand questions, a thousand worries had burdened our souls. When did the news reach home that I was missing? How they must have worried! When did the reassuring news from the Red Cross arrive? How are they all back home? Mother and father, wife and children, siblings and friends, they were at the forefront of our thoughts and yet an enormous distance stretched between them and us. Now, however, we held their loving words in our hands; now, thoughts and feelings could flow back and forth. A piece of home had arrived into our desolation; we were no longer so lonely inside. The healing power of home swept over us once more. It was as if an electric current had passed through us when we heard, 'letters are here!' When the sound of our faithful bugler's trumpet announced that the parcel list had been posted, a swirling stream of men poured out of every building and from every pathway.

The Parcel List

What's all the rush; what's going on?
In all the camp a shouting throng!
The canteen's really got milk or eggs
Not just the idiots who pull our legs?
Has Noericke* opened up his shop
To sell us porridge without stop?
No, this excitement, laughing, running
's not about *Schiebung*, not for cunning;
Just now has sounded out the call,
Electrifying one and all
To get a move on.

'Hard Labourers' in rooms C or A,
This worthy group who dream all day
Or think, or copy out whole volumes
Spring from their chairs and rush from warm rooms.
And ramblers seeking quiet places
'Gainst nature's splendours turn their faces,
Abandon any other aim
Than hastening back here to the same
Old well-acquainted noticeboard
To gather there with one accord
By Mess 11.

---

* kitchen officer.

There: pushing, shoving, heaving, bustling,
Too often even selfish hassling.
A cry, 'Nothing again for me!'
But others wreathed in smiles you see.
The rest, whatever is their rank
Stare at that wall and hope to thank
Their lucky stars when on that list
They find their names. They've not been missed!
Yes, yes, a parcel!

                                                            Steinmann.

Our postmasters tell the story:

"There are only three questions that concern a poor POW on a daily basis.
These are: when will we be exchanged, what is there to eat today and how many
letters or parcels will arrive today? Everything else is a matter of indifference
to him and passes over him without notice. Truly, what it means to spend
months, no, years, in enemy territory, forced to remain behind barbed wire,
under lock and key – this is something that can only be appreciated by those
condemned by fate to be there. One becomes indifferent and unreceptive to
everything. But post! It is the bright star in our darkness; it raises the spirits
of even the most tired and demoralised prisonör. The postal service provided
us, the postmasters, with plenty to do on a daily basis, and required good
nerves and patience. One cannot imagine how many thousands of questions
overwhelmed us. It was impossible to be seen out on the camp pathways for
more than five minutes without being asked about postal matters by some
chap or other. And it was almost always the same questions: Have the letters or
parcels arrived? How many letters or parcels are coming today? Have I finally
got a letter or parcel today? What does my parcel look like – small? large?
Could there be sausage in it or maybe just books? There are newspapers in
my parcel – can you manage to bring it out to me without the censors seeing
it? When will they be handed out? Will there be letters this afternoon too?
When did you write the latest mail appeals? Do you know who the sender of
my parcel is? Yes, and other cheeky questions besides. Our policy was to give
everybody a satisfying, friendly response. This was actually rather mean, but
how else were we to satisfy the questions and wishes of each comrade? Once,
we counted all the questions we encountered in a single morning. In the time
between 8.30am and 12 noon my comrade was asked 236 and I was asked
223 such questions, from which one can get an idea of the intense interest
in the post, but also put oneself in the often difficult position of the poor
postmasters who genuinely wanted to keep everybody happy.

    To provide a small insight into the job I must describe our work. The
letters are generally brought into the camp by an English soldier at around
9 o'clock in the morning and then checked by the censors. At 9.45 we collect

the letters and then sort them in our office into pigeonholes according to barracks. Already by this time the door of our office is besieged by impatient men. Some of them, however, having waited in excited anticipation for the distribution, leave again disappointed and empty-handed. At around 11 o'clock the postbags are driven into the camp. Following English orders the parcels are opened and checked by English sergeants, and only then may they be handed out to the comrades. After the names are written down in order with a note detailing the number of parcels, the list is pinned to the noticeboard provided for this purpose. The distribution then usually takes place after lunch at about 2 o'clock, with the officers called in turn. The German orderlies hand out the parcels and the English sergeant opens them and checks their contents. It is amusing, particularly at sports time, to observe the sometimes quite bizarre clothing of those waiting. That chap was clearly in the middle of a game of football and has come along with his coat wrapped around him to collect his parcel. That fellow over there has obviously just been asleep, as he arrives with his hair in disarray, and his sleepy eyes show that they are not yet adjusted to the daylight; he is also only half dressed, and all this just to collect a box from mother! Then suddenly, during the distribution, a comrade comes up to me: 'My parcel today absolutely must not be opened as it contains English money, schnapps and German newspapers.' 'What number are you?' 'Number 53.' 'Hm, thanks, it will be taken care of.' A quick glance and my postal comrade understands. Five minutes later the offending parcel is outside unnoticed despite eight English eyes; in this way four or five such 'dangerous' consignments are smuggled out almost every day. Yes, if only the cunning English knew all this! A comrade is sent a bottle of rum which, if he's unlucky, is confiscated from him as a forbidden item. Dismayed, the owner comes running to us asking us to pinch the bottle back from the English as soon as possible using our innate craftiness. We then head innocently into the censorship room in the afternoon to ask the censor something or other. One of us keeps him talking while the other hunts around for the bottle. Supposedly looking for something, he disappears with the bottle to hand it over to the beaming owner. Could we ever have even imagined doing such a thing in the old days!"

Nickel & von Lilienhoff.

A diary entry tells us:

"The arrival of the letters conjures up moving scenes. We can hardly wait to hold the loving words in our hands. And then each comrade sits on his bed and reads with such reverence. One face looks calmly and contentedly at the contents; sunshine, bright sunshine radiates from the eyes of another. Jubilantly one cries out, waving the piece of paper, 'Just listen, folks, to what my father says!' And everybody listens to what father says. But some sit quietly or hastily put the letter into a pocket and go outside; there must be something difficult to digest.

How the crowds flock around the mail censorship barracks at distribution time! Each man is carefully carrying a small box or bundle under his arm, since we are not allowed to have the packaging from home in case those cunning Germans have magically contrived to secrete anti-British material within it. And now look at these happy men, how they strut back to the barracks with their treasures after the distribution. Like princes they stride along, surrounded by enquiring, curious questions and exclamations: 'Gosh, you're lucky!' 'Boy, oh boy!' And the boy stands with joyful eyes and hands scrabbling furiously trying to unwrap the treasure that has been sent with true love from home into the foreign wilderness: bread and sausage and cheese and cake and butter and cigars and tobacco and uniforms and ... and ...

Packetausgabe.

Parcel distribution.

and ...! Every one of the precious items is revealed, touched, sniffed, inspected. Dear, dear home! You loyal well-wishers across the sea! Lieutenant X complains, however. Mother sent him nuts but the English have not handed them over. Oil, alcohol, medicine or peppermint could not be sent to the prisoners of war.*

Lieutenant Y suddenly lets out a cry of jubilation. He has pulled out a smuggled letter from a seemingly harmless tin can; it brings us important news from home! Cigarette papers also concealed many important little notes from keen English eyes. The English sergeants did not think of this method of infiltration. They only occasionally opened food cans. With larger consignments they only gave out the cans one by one as they feared large stocks could form welcome, easily transportable supplies for escapers. We were also glad to receive the Dutch packages that arrived on behalf of our relatives through the intermediaries of the German and the Dutch Red Cross. At the time they were actually very good. They contained cheese, sausage, ham, butter and tobacco products (priced at 10-20 Deutschmarks)."

We also very much welcomed the arrival of the first consignments of German money, which allowed us to buy items of clothing and underwear. The money reached us by post, via the Red Cross or via the Deutsche Bank. Unfortunately we lost a lot in the exchange – this became even more significant later with

---

* Nuts could be used as containers for small notes, peppermint provided chemicals for invisible ink etc.

the worsening of the political situation. For 100 Deutschmarks the Deutsche Bank paid 70 to 80 shillings (at one point it was over 90), the Post Office 46 to 66 shillings (at one point it was over 90) and the Red Cross about 60 shillings. Towards the end of our time in captivity we received not much more than 20 shillings for 100 Deutschmarks.

We ourselves were only allowed to write letters twice a week, on Mondays and Thursdays, on a rectangular sheet of shiny lined paper, which made the use of invisible ink impossible. The letters were taken to the camp post boxes. The postmasters sorted them alphabetically and handed them over to the English censors. How little one could entrust to that small slip of paper – and yet our hearts were so full of wishes, questions and tales! Our tender sensibilities often felt the oppressive gaze of the alien eyes that perused our correspondence with home. Some prisoners failed to contain their fury: strong words about captivity, the merits of home and the enemy's spite would flow from the pen. Regularly a hot-headed letter would then be returned from the censors back to the commandant and the unlucky man whose heart had overflowed would be given the obligatory reprimand or punished with a mail ban. The lengthy delivery time also depressed us. At that time it took four to six weeks (sometimes three months) for the post to reach its destination. What a long wait for hopes and worries!

Parade.

Communication with home brought sunshine into our daily routine. It was otherwise, particularly in those early stages, quite monotonous:* 8 o'clock coffee; 10 o'clock parade; 1 o'clock lunch; 2 o'clock parade; 4 o'clock coffee; 6.45 parade; 7 o'clock dinner.

At 10 o'clock all prisonörs had to be in their barracks and were counted again there. After the 'Good night, gentlemen!' or the more friendly 'Guten Nacht, meine Herren!'[22] from the mouth of an Englishman the light was turned off; we were then not allowed to leave the dormitories. During the night, patrols scurried or stomped through the barracks making a great deal of noise; they often disturbed our sleep.

Parade

A young comrade paints a picture of these parades for us:

"A quarter to ten in the morning. A gloomy sky hangs over the camp. A cold wind howls around the few leafless bushes and tugs at the barracks. A few hardy prisonörs out for a stroll battle their way along the camp paths. But look! Here he comes, no, thrusts forward what in normally developed people would be called his body, on bulges that would normally count as legs, swinging a clanging bell with considerable force with his bulbous right hand while his fleshy left hand grips a silver-handled riding cane with a gracefulness peculiar to the corpulent. This is the English sergeant major, our Yorkshire boar. Yorkshire's fat swine were famous throughout the world for gratifying the stomach, although the same could not be said of our sergeant major, despite the fact that this portly representative of the regular British Army did share the same physical characteristics that earned this fame with the much loved animals of his local area. For almost a quarter of an hour, watched resentfully by the German officers, he wanders through the prisoners' El Dorado from north to south to the incessant clanging of the bell. Then he steps onto the 5-metre-wide parade ground – a path alongside the long barracks, bitterly reviled by the present authors – huffs and puffs his way up the steps to the commandant's barracks and now stands there proudly waiting, presenting an imposing image with his massive bulk: he calls the checkmated warriors of the Hun empire to parade.

This call triggers feelings of reluctance in almost all of us. It interrupts our valuable reading of the 'objective' English newspapers; we struggle to tear our intoxicated eyes away from the 'perfectly formed' examples of female English beauty depicted in the *Daily Mirror*. Understandable agitation and offence at the thwarting of their hallowed aspirations is also felt by those with a preference for lying-in or having a nap. The last ring of the bell results

---

* One day a barracks outside the camp burnt down and the English officers lost a large number of their possessions. During the blaze we had to line up on the parade ground. After that, the camp fire brigade practised more frequently.

in interrupted dreams, stony glances, and the crushing effect of enforced movement on the diligent students working hard in the quiet rooms. Those with their noses in weighty tomes look up in bewilderment as if to say 'what do I care about what's going on in the world when I'm enjoying my book!' But there is no choice in the matter. Kant will have to continue criticising his pure reason alone; the old clay fragments just excavated with Schliemann and Doerpfeldt are flung aside; the questions of the Shakespearean stage are angrily laid down on a pile of books. From all directions the last trickles flow onto the parade ground: down the steps of the work rooms, out of the accommodation barracks, the barber's shop and the l....* A few always arrive late deliberately** and have to atone for their inadequate practical knowledge of the concept of time, so significant in Kant's theories, by humbly excusing themselves to the commandant, or enduring English cautions of varying severity and the threat of extra parades.

With the barbed-wire fence and the English guards in the background, lined up in two long rows and organised according to barracks, the prisonörs are finally standing ready to respond to the friendly, daily, repetitive inquiry from the British as to our presence. A kaleidoscopic picture emerges. The colours of the uniforms span a wide spectrum of shades. Crude laced shoes and tall boots from the time of the Holy Commissius,[23] delicate yellow slippers and elegant riding boots, patent leather shoes and rubber galoshes, brightly-coloured sports socks, gaiters made of leather or woollen strapping, long trousers, jodhpurs, elegant breeches in a bewildering array of colours, tunics, short uniform jackets, old-fashioned and new-style litewka jackets, here and there clothing on that ambiguous border between military and civilian, stand-up collars, fold-down collars, civilian white collars, ties in a wonderful array of matching and mismatched colours, saucer-like flat caps for the enlisted men, 'proper' officers' headgear in a variety of shapes from the proudly tall to the modestly short and often the quite crumpled, brown woollen turbans for those deprived of their caps, steel helmets for those newly arrived[24] – infantrymen, cavalrymen, grenadiers, airmen, sailors, transportation troops – young men with innocent, youthful faces and then the whole spectrum of maturity up to the silver-grey hair of the grandads, beardless faces, jauntily styled moustaches, bushy beards, goatee beards with the single icicle-like point or in the more extravagant double-pointed style, long flowing manly beards, laughing, chatting, serious lonely faces, stony-faced, turning around, beating time with their feet, frequently taking another forbidden glance at the newspaper or at a letter from a loved one – here you have, dear reader, a visual image of our camp community.

---

*   = latrines.
** A believer in accurate historical transcription has asked us to include the remark made with a knowing nod that these 'few' were always the same ones.

We wait. Above us the fat man also waits. He is holding a watch in his hand as he has been brought up to be conscientious. From the church tower down below, ten chimes strike, but the mass of flesh continues to stand and wait. The loathsome wind is cold and damp as it rages around us. How often have we been made to stand here in all kinds of inclement weather!* The fat man rolls his harmless eyes and shoots chastising looks at the chatting groups and, in a sudden burst of agitation, points to a particularly revolutionary member of our circle. He intends to wait, wait, wait, until … well, a prisonör with an increasing awareness of the unlimited amount of time he has on his hands can wait a little longer. The reserved German mentality also decides not to grant the fat British sergeant the pleasure of the courtesies we usually bestow upon English officers. Finally this realisation dawns on him too. He taps on the door with his outstretched sausage-like index finger and announces sharply 'All right, Sir'.

Die Häupter unserer Lieben:
Serg. Major Green,
der Yorkshire-Eber.

'The Heads of our Loved Ones': Sergeant Major Green, The Yorkshire Boar.

The commandant appears: a man of average height with a bowed head, an untidy gait and shy eyes, holding his stick behind him. The prisonörs raise their hands to their caps and the Englishman acknowledges this: a short, reserved greeting from both sides. This procedure is carried out ceremoniously on the days when *Icankillyou* commands the parade. The precise eighth turns which the little man executes through three points of the compass and the jerky lifting of his jointed limbs always cause us amusement and genuine delight at the small gentleman.

Slowly our captors make their way down the rows. At the fore is the interpreter, who reads out the names of the prisoners with more or less correct pronunciation. Today this herald is a powerful figure of a man, with a truly child-like face. He trots along with small careful steps and we are continually surprised that he does not trip up over his own feet. Shyly and awkwardly the frightened child-like eyes inspect the rows of the dangerous Huns, the former 'baby-killers'.[25] Should his gaze encounter a firm manly stare, his face adopts a startled expression, which almost seems to declare his innocence with regard to our imprisonment and to offer a remorseful apology for his presence. This harmless young man, who would later leave the camp in tears, was given the nickname Pepi or Aunt Frieda. *Icankillyou* eyes the prisonörs sharply. I do not wish to describe him further here as the reader already has sufficient knowledge

---

* Only in the case of extremely bad weather did parades take place in Room B or the Old Mess.

of him. He is also not entirely sober today. Behind the commandant we catch a glimpse of the orderly officer: today it's Uncle Dozy or Opapa. At seventy years of age he is no longer capable of the posture or facial expression appropriate for official duties; he bumbles his way through procedures with listless eyes. The old man, whose gait is more of a stumble than a walk, is followed by his less than beautiful dog, which, in mindlessly trotting along behind him, dutifully replicates the essence of the geriatric old man in its own animal behaviour. Marching along at the rear is our fat man. The deep concentration in his eyes and his murmuring mouth indicate to us that he is a man with an important task to perform. Indeed he has. While the interpreter establishes the valued presence of each particular individual by calling his name, the fat man presides over every individual detail and while he follows ancient Pythagorean principles in recognising number as the essence of all things, he recognises our value only in the entirety of our numeric existence: in other words, he is counting us. Thus the sextet traipses past us. Not infrequently does its progress falter, occasionally a cry to the camp director rings out and our fatherly camp administrator patiently listens to *Icankillyou*'s complaint or warning; this or that German officer is not wearing a cap, has appeared in open-toed sandals or has not shown the appropriate courtesy to the English gentlemen, etc."

Dear reader, we are telling our story here with a sense of humour. And yet, how often during these parades has its bitter seriousness cut into our souls! One only has to read the diaries!

"At one time we faced the khaki-clad figures, like the ones who are inspecting us now, with weapons in manly battle. Now we find ourselves here unarmed while they are still dressed for battle. They command. We listen."

"Allowing ourselves to be counted like cattle by English sergeants, to accept reproaches from English officers – how difficult this is for German pride to accept!"

"If the morning newspapers have reported successes and the island gentlemen then walk among us with pride on their faces, I always feel like going for their throats. But we hide our suffering behind assertive defiance and a provocative indifference. When our men have won a victory, however, I never conceal my pride and my laughing eyes. That is poetic justice."

But back to our parade.

"The English have already reached the end of the German lines. Why can't we fall out? Two hundred German necks stretch forwards, discontented eyes glance to the left. Somebody is pushing back the front line over there, his fat legs pushing forwards, beating an even rhythm with his index finger and agitatedly spitting numbers out of his fleshy lips; the fat man has lost count again. With sympathetic smiles from his waiting victims he once more attempts his difficult duty of counting to 200. This time he's in luck. 'Two hundred, Sir!' The commandant instructs the camp director: 'Dismiss the parade, please!' Him to us: 'The parade is finished, gentlemen!'

Again cool greetings are exchanged and the mass of uniforms disperses throughout the camp."

Brüll.

A few weeks after the opening of the camp our lives had taken shape in a way that made the miserable situation of being in captivity more bearable. Our existence became more varied, and gloomy thoughts were quashed with pleasant distractions.

Just like the English prisoners in Germany, we also had the right to take walks. These took us through Skipton and out into the surrounding area. We hiked up and down on the good country roads or even scrambled up the hill opposite our camp, past the quarry, and looked down onto the town and our temporary home or away towards Keighley on the other side. These hours, at least, provided us with some refreshing vigorous activity, a diverting change of view and the feeling of longed-for freedom. Each prisoner was permitted to take part in one such walk every fourteen days. An English officer escorted us. We were obliged to give our word of honour not to escape and not to do any harm or damage to the British Empire on these walks.

The shower block in the middle of the camp found particular favour with us. According to the regulations we were permitted two showers per week. In the early months this was also what we got: on Wednesdays and Saturdays the prisonörs could be seen in the most fanciful of attire streaming barracks by barracks to the gushing (hot and cold) showers. The shower officer reports:

The Shower Block

"A stove, which required about twelve buckets of coal on a shower day, heated a boiler from which the hot water was piped to two storage tanks that supplied the showers. There were three shower rooms equipped with twenty, ten and ten showers respectively. It took half an hour to fill the storage tanks but the contents only sufficed for about twenty-four showers; this meant that a half-hour break had to be scheduled between shower sessions, which were organised according to barracks. The lack of taps to turn off the hot water supply was keenly felt. They had been promised to us by the English administration but were never fitted, allegedly because the engineer had declared it impossible to install them.

A large number of officers showered daily in cold water, early in the morning, and even in the winter about twenty comrades continued to do so. Due to the lack of gymnastics apparatus in the camp, after showering we did exercises without equipment to strengthen body and mind. The camp hospital contained a gas-heated bathtub for the use of patients."

Wülfing.

Baden.

Going for a shower.

In mid-February the promised books finally arrived from our original camp of Colsterdale and soon our library opened, initially in the Old Mess. It was only small and its few books didn't always do justice to the heights of our German literature. And yet how valuable this intellectual stimulation was to us! We could once again escape from the bleakness of camp life, delving into diverse worlds even if only by means of inner vision and imagination. A new camp species emerged: the book worm.

Newspapers

Soon after the camp opened, English newspapers were made available to us. In the first few weeks they were almost all we had to read. Our first newspaper officer reports:

"The newspapers are here! Word quickly gets around the whole camp. That is the end of the tranquillity, even in the quietest room. Everybody hurries to collect his newspaper. These men enclosed by wire stand side by side in groups and search in the newspaper for new information, good news about the Fatherland and their own destiny, about war and peace. The events provoke lively discussion, often resulting in disputes even at the stove council. Each man believes his strategy and diplomatic approach to be right and tries at the top of his voice to persuade the others that his views alone are valid. The newspapers bring life into the prisoner's lethargic and dreary world. A small boy brings them into the camp. Heavily laden, he tramps up here every morning, noon and evening and hands over his burden, so yearned-for by the prisoners, to the newspaper officer. He in turn has the copies delivered to the readers by the mess orderlies and to the newspaper reading group who, via a skilful translator, read out the day's news to those prisoners with no knowledge of English. We pay monthly for these expensive newspapers – Mr James collects in £40 to £80 a month for them but claims in spite of this not to be making any profit. During the difficult period of reprisals[26] however, when we were not allowed newspapers, a kitchen hand helped us out in our time of need. There was at least one newspaper in the camp, which was read aloud in the mess barracks after the midday meal.

Of the newspapers generously allowed us by the English, the most widely read in the camp is the *Manchester Guardian*. Its liberal point-of-view is shared by the *Daily News*, Lord Burnham's *Daily Telegraph* and the weekly *Common Sense*. Unionist and conservative views are found in the *Yorkshire Post* and in the *Morning Post*, the newspaper favoured by polite society. The newspapers of Lord Northcliffe, the great rabble-rouser, are particularly popular. The

Morning newspaper.

Politicians.

heavily illustrated *Daily Mirror*, the Sunday paper *Weekly Dispatch*, the *Daily Mail* and the *Times* offer splendid examples of loud-mouthed English rabble-rousing. In the last English election, Northcliffe was still an advocate of Lloyd George and loyal to the government, but soon afterwards, for the sake of a bit of variety, he swapped sides and is now against the government. One wonders who might have paid him to do this!

The current government newspaper is the *Daily Chronicle*, and the Sunday *Observer* is also loyal to the government. Minor publications that are nonetheless read in the camp include the *Daily Graphic*, *Yorkshire Evening Post*, *Bradford Evening News*,[27] *Sunday Pictorial* and *News of the World*. The *London News*, *Sphere*, *Bystander*, *Tatler*, *Sketch* and *Country Life* are much-read weekly magazines. As far as special interest magazines are concerned, we receive the *Architectural Review*, *Papermaker*, *Engineering*, *Rowing and Sporting*, *Economist*, *The Churchman* and *The Church Family Newspaper*. All these publications are adept at propaganda in words and pictures. Social-democratic magazines such as the *Labour Leader* and the *Nation* are banned, since the entire British armed forces are also forbidden to read them. Those of us involved in business and commerce have been infuriated by the ban on the *Times Trade Supplement*. From France we receive *Le Matin*, *Le Temps* and the risqué *La Vie Parisienne*; towards the end of our imprisonment there were also Spanish newspapers.

German newspapers are of course banned for the Hun prisoner. After all, from the English newspapers he can learn enough to understand that glorious England is the protector of culture and of the small nations against the Huns, and could only ever be defeated by a world of jealous enemies. Nevertheless a good number of German newspapers are smuggled through in the parcels, and these are then usually read overtly."

Lt. Fricke.

A book purchasing group was also set up by the camp administration and we were allowed to order English and German books from a London bookshop. We were permitted to send one letter per week to London with our orders. In this way many men acquired reading material for their university studies or other professional qualifications.

With the growth of this intellectual activity and the increased requirement for quiet spaces for undisturbed work came a gradual need to create more common spaces. For this reason in February the southern end of the long barracks was also set up as a 'quiet room' (A). Like C it was equipped with a few long tables and chairs. However, the number of places still failed to cater for the number of visitors. In addition, the natural human tendency emerged, on the part of the hard labourers, to claim their own bit of space at the tables in these rooms, as we had no tables at all in the barracks where we slept. The demand for tables was heard repeatedly over these months. Fortunately the camp administration was able to help with this. In February they had opened a carpentry workshop with two competent craftsmen, as carpentry work was also needed generally in the camp and English help could not be counted upon. Hundreds of small tables were built by the carpenters. Even if they were not particularly elegant or incredibly sturdy, in our imagination they were 'writing desks' nonetheless and became beloved work areas.

Our lives were enriched. The productive, purposeful German spirit created areas of activity for itself. The first educational courses commenced. Programmes of study were set up. Spanish and English language courses, business courses, lessons in shorthand and other subjects were organised. On several occasions large groups of comrades gathered in Room C for lectures (offered by our 'Humboldt Academy'). The workshop produced a lectern. On these Tuesday evenings, comrades spoke from a personal perspective of their experiences in foreign lands; insights into the present economic situation were given, important religious developments and modern religious questions were considered. During the dreadful time of the food shortages (in March) one expert calmed our minds in an extremely useful lecture, in which he demonstrated that the food we were receiving provided us with just enough calories. 'Calories' became a catchword in the camp for a long time.

On 27th January, the Kaiser's birthday inspired us to hold our first large communal celebration. We had no idea then that this would be the last time we honoured this day. With enthusiastic devotion and joyous pride we celebrated as German officers and men. The short time since our arrival in the camp and the lack of resources prevented us from having an extravagant celebration but for us the day was still a high point. In the morning the senior German officer gathered all the officers in Room B. This man, who had once been a general staff officer in von Kluck's army, gave a short review of what had been achieved in the war so far and then explained to us the anticipated strategy for future combat. We all had an idea of the likely magnitude of this conflict and proudly hoped for its success. The evening found us at a 'banquet' in the Old Mess. Thanks to the efforts of the kitchen administration our stomachs were also offered something better on this day. Each man was even entitled to six bottles of English beer (obviously quite inferior); a few of the 'better-off' treated themselves to port. A comrade gave the ceremonial address, in which, proceeding from the Kaiser's rejection of Bismarck, he accounted for the merit of the then young ruler's policies on the basis of Germany's mission in the world. Our male-voice choir, which had been formed on our second day in the camp, delighted us with German folk songs. Recitals, both amusing and serious, performances and communal singing kept us together for a long time: after all, the commandant had given us leave until 12 o'clock.

The occupancy of the camp soon increased and considerably exceeded the 150 original prisoners. In February there were further arrivals of larger units from Colsterdale (two groups of 40 men). Formerly wounded comrades, now recovered, arrived from military hospitals (Manchester, Belmont). Others came from Chelmsford, in other words from the prison. They were 'escapers' captured by the English and had been locked up there to atone for their transgressions. Cromwell Gardens Prison sent us airmen and submariners.[28] The British government had imprisoned them as a reprisal for German actions (conviction of Captain Fryatt,[29] and sanctions against English airmen who had dropped propaganda leaflets over the German people). Other new arrivals, who came from the transit camp in Southampton,[30] had been 'picked up' during operations at the Front. In late March an English medical commission arrived to decide upon the exchange of wounded or sick comrades. The queue to be examined was not insignificant but only four chronically sick or badly wounded comrades were sent to the exchange camp in Kegworth. A naval comrade who had been captured by an American warship was transferred to America.[31] Our total number at the end of March was nearly 250.

Initially only the lower quarter of the camp was occupied (barracks 28-33). The area of the camp at the top of the slope was totally deserted. The new arrivals therefore had to move into the less well appointed barracks of the upper camp. The older officers were able to move into the staff officers' barracks in the middle of February. This hut was divided by wooden walls into twelve so-called boxes. Here each comrade had his own stove and his own light. This at least enabled the older officers to have a space to call their own, a privilege missed so very painfully by the others. Loneliness is not the cause of the prisoner's greatest suffering, but rather being forced to live together with so many men in such a confined space.

Our general state of health was good in these initial months. Comrades who fell ill reported sick on a sheet of paper which was posted daily on the noticeboard. They reported to the doctor at 10.30 or requested a visit from him. Medical care was in the hands of an English military doctor, rarely the same one. We took a very dim view of the professional competence of English doctors. Their casual way of conducting examinations, the often completely absurd diagnoses and the lack of medication stripped us of all confidence so that we avoided any extensive medical treatment wherever possible. In addition, the English doctors often displayed such a lack of gentlemanly behaviour that the German camp administration had to repeatedly and insistently complain to the commandant. Seriously ill comrades were taken to one of the two hospital barracks. Those who required major medical intervention were sent to Manchester, which however had such a bad reputation for its food that our comrades would go there only reluctantly.

On 19th March the sports ground was finally opened. It provided more space for the walkers and enabled comrades to participate in sport. Until this time only a very limited amount of sport had taken place. Comrades could occasionally be seen speeding by on training runs through the camp and in the evenings individual comrades could be observed enthusiastically performing exercises, practising stone put or diligently stretching using special apparatus.

But these examples had been few and far between. Now team sport could really begin.

On 20th March the 'bar' opened. It was the place to find either peace and quiet or noisy gatherings. Many walkers would often call in for the occasional small glass of beer or cider. Many an hour was spent here chatting to dear friends and comrades.

This is how we lived our lives in our small world behind the barbed-wire fence. We had settled in, and a sense of calm entered our existence. And yet in those weeks of February and March there was a sense of agitation moving through the camp. A sense of anticipation and speculation gripped us all regarding the question of the great spring offensive.

The Offensive: Feelings in the Camp

A comrade writes about this time:

"Condemned by a cruel fate to the role of extras in the terrible worldwide drama, the exiles attempt to maintain their vigour with hard work and endeavour. Yet no amount of work seems to provide the desired distraction and release. All too often the eyes of those studying wander away from the open page of the book and a restless hand reaches time and again for the newspaper. Automatically the eyes are drawn to the military reports of both allies and enemies in order to study them again in more detail in an attempt to find something between the lines. These reports are the only source of news that the barbed-wire fence does not hold back. Yet, on the fronts, everything still appears to be calm.

What an awful lot has happened since the prisoners were last involved in battle! The Russian bear has been defeated. Peace has been achieved. The English press is making a poor job of covering up the population's unrest about the flood of German troops advancing westwards. Finally the exhausting defensive battle seems to have come to an end – a victim of itself. 'Onward!' will now be the cry heard in the west.

In the accommodation barracks, huddled around the warming stove, the War Council hold meetings that last for hours. All members are motivated by the sacred ideal of German freedom for which they have suffered and fought in happier times. Only the route to the target remains to be planned. The crackpots who hope for salvation from the new German peace proposal are shouted down in no uncertain terms. Others, the political realists, promote the belief that this time our enemies will seek a compromise settlement because those loudmouths will never dare to take on the combined German forces in the west. With a certain, almost superior, smile these speakers refuse to look at the secretly produced maps of the Front, which are now distributed by the supporters of the 'battle to the end'. Yet they remain undeterred as they have by far the largest number of supporters. And if a hypothesis could be proved by the enormous momentum it gives to its creators one would have to blindly follow these stalwarts.

There is a wealth of map information available. What is striking about it is that, on the western battleground, the artists appear to have devoted less attention to Paris, the old target of wars in the west. By far the greatest care and attention has been dedicated to the coast. The Italian Front has also by no means been forgotten. Maybe the first blow of the hammer will fall there, particularly as the system of 'one at a time' continues to be so brilliantly maintained. The boldest even dream of the possibility of a double offensive: they believe Germany consists only of sky and soldiers.

And then the tangible facts are considered. All sections of the Front are examined and particular attention is given to those where recent reconnaissance missions have taken place. Here and there the fleeting hand of the artist adds in a newly mentioned small village or little stream and then the extent of the prisonörs' knowledge is exhausted. The sadness of wisdom

Die Frühjahrsoffensive bei uns.

The Spring Offensive in the camp.

consisting of 'maybe' and 'however'! Anxiety about one's own powerlessness often fills all our hearts. Why keep trying to stay ahead of events? Only one wise course remains for the prisoners and that is 'wait, wait!' What is the purpose of this agitated yearning for happier times? Why not instead enjoy the coming spring which reflects our hopes and expectations onto Yorkshire's hills? For surely the budding spring is the symbol of redemption. Who, though, would have believed, despite all the waiting, that on 21st March the prisoners would be so taken by surprise by the stirring news of the German offensive that we expected to bring our salvation?"

Reichardt.

(C) From the Start of the German Offensive to the Armistice
(21st March to 11th November 1918)
The Offensive

Our hopes are confirmed by the English evening newspapers on 21st March and even more so by the morning newspapers the next day: the Western Front is being pounded by Germany's military fist. Everyone is scrambling to get hold of a newspaper. My comrades sit in the quiet rooms, in the mess or in their barracks, and they read, re-read and read again, not once tearing their eyes away from the pages. Their eyes light up and their cheeks are flushed. Excited groups stand around on the pathways of the camp. Maps with little flags appear everywhere. We want to stand alongside our battling brothers-in-arms, even if only on paper battlefields. The English news is so full of hope for us! The British reports from the Front are quite confused and it seems that chaos reigns behind enemy lines. Seeing this, our eyes shine with pleasure and pride, and fervent wishes arise within us and resonate in our sometimes heartfelt, sometimes cautious words. We feel closer to one another as the sons of such a great, heroic people. Soon the first – admittedly garbled – German reports come in: countless prisoners and captured artillery, enemy towns and villages in German hands. Things are progressing! What objective is our Hindenburg pursuing? When will the final breakthrough be achieved? What great consequences it will have! Even the quietest men in our camp are becoming strategists. During the parades we now stand taller, our eyes burning with the elation of victory, and we confront the troubled gaze of the English. This continues for weeks. The roaring flood of our offensive at Amiens falters. Then it resurges towards Armentières. 'Aha!' the strategists declare, 'war of attrition!' Bailleul, Kemmel, Messines Ridge; the names whirl around. The spoils of war mount to Herculean proportions. During this time, the camp always seems sunny. We note the weather and rejoice in the sunshine. When it rains we are despondent and Mr James declares from his position that rainy days are a gift from God for the British, 'God is an Englishman!'

DIE GROSSE OFFENSIVE. Die Karte in der ALTEN MEßE.

The Great Offensive. The map in the Old Mess.

England's fear stares out at us from the newspapers. A despairing Lloyd George calls on America for help, the new Man-Power Bill extends conscription to all men under the age of 51 who are fit to bear arms, our guards are replaced by old men and the Easter holidays are cancelled in England so that the factories can carry on desperately vital work for the war. Soon we are joined by new comrades, fresh from fighting at the Front. They are surrounded and bombarded with questions. Every detail is seized upon; we press them for definitive assessments of the situation. Wild rumours frequently fly around the camp. Everywhere, small groups hold victory celebrations. More and more hammer blows resound from the mainland: from Montdidier, from the Marne, from Reims. The veterans of 1914 know many of these reclaimed towns and villages and proudly tell the younger men about the deeds of the first years of the war. What losses our enemies must be suffering! In the newspapers, the lists of casualties stretch further and further down the columns. The English pin up lists of the names of thousands of English officers recorded as missing and ask our recently captured comrades for any available information about the fate of these men. We all feel the hot breath of battle and continue the fight in spirit. Paris is shelled from afar; likewise Dunkirk; the enemy makes a desperate attempt to cut off Ostend and Zeebrugge; on Whitsunday, London is shaken by German aerial bombing; the Austrians are also making their contribution and appear to be successful.

What a glorious time! And yet the struggle drags on for months. Our hearts become uneasy. When will the decisive blow fall? Can Germany hold fast through these exhausting times? We can almost hear the gasping breath of our Fatherland, and it sobers us. Then the sun sets. The Austrians are defeated. Squadrons of enemy tanks roll over our lines on the Marne, at Montdidier, on the old battlefields of the Somme, at Lille – we are pushed out of Belgium. We cannot believe it, but we must. We want to hope, and yet we no longer can. All our support has crumbled from under us: Bulgaria, Turkey, and finally Austria. Revolution sweeps the old Germany away, and the Kaiser leaves for the Netherlands. It is impossible to think any more, now that everything has fallen apart for us. On 11th November, the outrageous terms of the Armistice are agreed, extinguishing almost all life within us. Now the only options are defiance or despair.

One comrade who is studying the psychological state of the prisoners describes our mental torment at this time:

"'All life is love', as the philosopher of the Wars of Liberation[32] once proclaimed during a time of action and endurance. A hundred years have passed. Deeds are once again being done; inactivity once again being suffered, nobly and in silence. But how different things are today! Then we rose from ashes to glory and now we fall from victory to defeat! And yet this is precisely the story of our times. A time of doing and being done for, of noble deeds and noble endurance, of give and take, of so many contradictions and yet of one single great life force: love. This must be what Fichte meant when he spoke of love. Hatred too is life, but it is only denial. Only that which I grasp with every fibre of my heart and encompass with all the power of my reasoning and will is the fruit of my life and is true experience. So in every respect our existence is a duality of action and passivity; on the one hand acting upon things, the need to do one's duty, creative energy, on the other a quiet, involuntary endurance in joy and pain. This is the contradictory mystery of life, this is its soul, a rushing river, now breaking the banks with its raging floods, now quietly collecting itself between hills and slopes as a deep-blue lake.

We prisoners know nothing of this now. That river of our being is wearily trickling away, almost as though it will dry up. It too was once something flowing and hurtling, action, responsibility; once it too was a quiet repose in spring sunshine. But then the time came when that which was not only the soldier's weapon but the very symbol of freedom and action was taken away from us – the gateway of life fell shut behind us.

Not so long ago I read a poem about us in a newspaper that had been smuggled from home in a tin. Trembling within its lines was our homeland's love for its sons far away in foreign lands. What a comfort! And yet it captured nothing of the true nature of our suffering. It is not simply the external things, the days of hunger, the pitiful living arrangements, nor even this forced obeisance to our enemies that so often deepens our misery: it is the life of our souls withering away.

Life on the Front already had some of this peculiar bitterness. Family relationships had faded to become shadows of themselves. We missed the influence of a mother, of a wife, that quietly gladdening female presence. That typically German yearning for affection and motherly love, for entering personally into the spirit of give and take, was infinitely limited. Yet above it all stood our cause, so great, so unrelenting in its necessity. But there was more to it than that: it was the object of love, the Fatherland. And on the battlefield, the bountiful relationships of peacetime (freedom, work, family and companionship) were replaced by a higher form of give and take. The forceful momentum of events ensured the fulfilment of the soul through a rich abundance of conflict and calm, of hope and the fulfilment of victory.

And now? Our homeland is far away. The time since we last saw our nearest and dearest grows ever longer. Their image is so faint. Perhaps even fading? Meaningful conversation with genuine questions and answers is almost impossible by post. In most cases it is already too late, even if a response to some urgent request is received after three months of waiting. Some of us want to keep working towards a specific vocational goal and need books – but they don't arrive. Even the newer administrative bodies do not always respond. A businessman hears short reports about his business: it's going downhill. A safe pair of hands, just for one day, and much could be saved. But it's no use! Politics, the arts, science? One used to be part of them and feel the heartbeat of German intellectual life. Now every Saturday one looks through *The Economist* for the column about Germany's economic situation, beginning with many questions and ending with twice as many. Oh, this emptiness! How pitiful, wretched and demeaning it is to have to piece together a picture every morning using these half-truths and truncated English reports. Everyone ends up with a different version. And which is correct? Oh for but a scrap of certainty about the fate of our homeland, a trace of German intellect, how glad we would be! Without it, an ocean of bitterness gathers from small drops and larger streams. Some of us become dulled, some irritable, whether in body or in mind – a constant tinderbox only needing a spark to flare up. Moreover, our acquaintance with one another is of course more a product of chance than a natural development. There is still a long way to go between simply being together and being a community; a comrade who is not able to find a friend remains alone. These are situations that also crop up in the normal circumstances of life. But the particular circumstances imposed by imprisonment and the severity not otherwise experienced make of it a bitter pain in which mind and soul can wither. For we are even deprived of the only thing that might help us in our plight: work.

Being occupied is not work. There is plenty to do here. There are even some malicious busybodies who say that no-one in the camp has any spare time. But what is work without a defined purpose, the daily task without achievement? Work must be freely chosen if it is to give satisfaction. What is more, the particular character of many people with a practical vocational background means that they find it very difficult to switch their energies towards their inner life, not to mention sustaining this over months or years. From the perspective of manual labour with its exhausting exertion it is all too easy to see the channelling of physical energy into quiet contemplation through rose-tinted spectacles. But we long for freedom and responsibility in our work. And that is exactly what we lack.

1918 became the most difficult year for us. Across the Channel the battle to determine victory or defeat, the canons' thunder, the death of our brothers and friends, the flutter of victory banners – and all we can do is read reports. Enemy reports, no less. Do you understand? We miss the German soul in them, and you too! Across the sea an empire is being reduced to rubble. In spite of everything, many of us have loved it with fervent devotion – at the same time as being far away, out of action, imprisoned. Not able to take anything from our native land, nor able to give to it in its time of need, such is the experience of imprisonment, its powerless suffering, its life without love.

On the Saturday before Palm Sunday, a quiet tranquillity lies over the camp. A beautiful spring day is coming to an end. The crimson sun has already gone down behind the craggy peaks to the West. The barracks and the common rooms are bathed in a calm twilight. It is a time to read a good book or write one's Sunday letter. The weekend! No sooner are the first lamps lit when suddenly there is a disturbance outside. Noise, loud shouting, a voice, 'A breach near Quentin!' Everybody jumps up. The quiet room comes to life. We jump up, snatch the evening paper and devour it all at once. One man jumps up onto his chair to see better in the lamplight. How dim this English light is even today! And now he reads aloud, shouts, and cheers; his face radiates a saintly transfiguration. Outside, the to-ing and fro-ing intensifies. Nobody can be alone this evening. Now from the orderlies' barracks the bugler belts out the German charge. In the morning, the facts in detail: 25,000 prisoners taken, 400 guns captured. I hear a quiet voice next to me, 'Oh to be in Germany now, to be able to listen, cry and laugh together with our countrymen and to behold the thousands revitalised despite their hunger.'

This turn of events at the Front was for us, too, a call to new hope. When a great river floods right through the soul it can relieve tensions both great and small, reawaken to new life what is lying dormant, wash away what is decaying. Our spiritual being is a multiplicity of contradictions, held in balance as long as they are equally strong. But if this ends in an unproductive stalemate, then it is a relief for a more powerful force to sweep them up. So it is with joy and also with pain. And how aware of that we became! These contradictions, these frictions disappear or lose their vicious bite. Joy and the coming of spring sow the gentle seeds of hope within us. Only during quiet reflection, when we remember our captive state, are we bitter. Our thirst for life and desire for action are restricted by an iron fist to a certain level of inner passivity. These vital forces are not required to stand the test of being put into practice. And for that reason, growth is sometimes stunted.

Weeks later, when the summer had reached its peak and the green beech leaves of our little copse of trees were turning paler, something quite curious happened. Quietly, very quietly, it came closer, unseen and yet so eerily conspicuous, a painful trembling of the most subtle vibrations of the soul. It passed from one man to the next, infectiously contagious, almost like the twitching of an animal in the throes of death. No one knew where it had originated, but we each had to look it in the face. We knew its name: doubt. 'And what if, after all, it has all been in vain, even the recent Spring Offensive?' Scarcely anyone said this aloud. This was the greatest turning point. But what does that matter! How often had something like this happened! But already the certainty was inevitable that 1918 would not bring us home. That was perhaps the first weakening of the defences built by our optimism. But nevertheless our optimism held. We still had so much to live for! One people – now no longer. The recently imprisoned spoke with such sadness and bitterness about that. But one army, one empire? The tables could still turn!

Doubt became worry, worry became pain. Doubt may also lead the way to emotional collapse. For those whose faith was not grounded in any personal experience of eternal realities, but was merely the offspring of personal and national hopes and desires, the expression 'divine justice' became just ridiculous chatter. Political differences soon reared their heads. The search for someone to blame proved dull and unfruitful. It often tore us apart. And yet we were always reunited by love's shared trepidation at the final outcome. Meanwhile, that which had earlier manifested itself as personal creation, in the solid framework of vocational creativity, and in freely chosen rest and relaxation, must now find its way back inward or burst out in unforgiving exchanges between comrades. A sad, bleak psychological drama, full of strife and without peace. But there is also defiant courage, which looks further ahead than immediate events. A defiant courage that is able to wait.

Then came the day, that Sunday, in a haze of wet, cold fog. Then we learnt the truth. It was the day Luther was born, and Schiller, and Scharnhorst too, the creator of our army. Now a day of death. We could not believe it but we had to: finished.

'Army without Kaiser,
Kaiser without army,
No one any wiser.'

The following morning, the final shot. Silence now reigns – across the Channel too. Our hearts have become so bereft of joy! Outside the gates, the guards have jubilantly hung out the flags.

It took a long time for the numbness to fade. Yet resignation came all too quickly. However, anyone with a deeper understanding of history would no doubt also feel something of the significance and momentousness of these events, particularly those concerning German interior politics. They were of paramount interest to us at the time. We learnt to understand them as the necessary reaction to the mistakes of the past, whilst on the other hand, they were also marked by traces of injustice and error. All of this gave us perspectives on the future, and a consciousness of conciliation as well as of inevitable historical processes led us in time to view the situation more calmly. These things were discussed in small groups. That was not easy: attitudes towards the new state of affairs in the Fatherland were all too varied. Too quickly, convictions expressed became the spark for the deepest agitation. Often, views were clouded by the personal values against which many judged the events, whether the delirium of joy at the glorious revolt of the German people, or the icy 'no' of outright rejection of change. On the whole, however, the pressure of knowing so little for certain was paralysing. Even worse the thought that, even here, possibly at the beginning of a new era of history, we could only observe events from a great distance. The curiously contradictory suffering of imprisonment reached its peak: we were removed from the great distress of the Fatherland, but precisely for that reason torn apart and isolated.

In no year of the war was imprisonment as unbearable as in this critical one; at no other time did the trajectory of our mood and our hopes twist and turn so much, and this was doubly pronounced in the more volatile among us. After all, it is only those with a more finely tuned sensitivity who perceive the complete discord of a life wasting away. In contrast we find the more robust or sturdy, who feel the physical aspect more strongly. Both of these personalities appear in widely diverse forms and varying intensities. Doubtless the vitality and rich variety of our company benefited as a result. Thus there were all manner of discussions. But there was also an unnecessary tendency to criticise, and fertile ground for ugly confrontations. Only when each man must play a part guided by a sense of duty, can justice actually come into existence.

Yet nothing could be further from the truth than the assumption that this now made up the basis of our existence. Other things are also apparent to the calm observer. Some, by their own account, found that it was only here that they came to their senses. Imprisonment is a chance for the mind to catch its breath. The predetermination and control of our lives by higher powers can hardly be felt more strongly than they are here. Being imprisoned means being forced to think. The harshest kind of self-criticism demands a hearing. There is a blessing in imprisonment, just as there is a curse. Suffering brings one closer to reality than happiness ever could."

Schreiner.

When comes the day that we'll be free
And let out of this cage?
Departing British guards we'll see!
Will it still take an age?

Till then the time goes oh so slow
We wait and suffer here.
And all the while we do not know
How fares our land so dear,

The land for which we fought and lost
All else that was of worth.
We fought and did not count the cost
For that best place on earth.

Yet here we are so far away,
But keep it in our hearts;
Awake and dreaming, night and day,
Stay loyal as we ought.

And so we find it makes no sense
To say our past was bad,
That pride and glory have gone hence
Leaving us only sad.

It feels just like a nightmare
But is so cruelly real
And our barbed-wire cage reminds us
Of these wounds that never heal.

Not murderousness nor bloodlust
Not ambition was our cause:
We did our duty as we must
And paid the price with scars.

No, our true place beneath the sun,
That was the very least:
Our rightful place was to be won
'Gainst foes from West and East.

And this we now are to accept
Was just a pack of lies?
The best that in our hearts we kept
Must now learn to despise.

Then well might suffer a poor heart
True German to the core
That finds its loyalty torn apart
But could not love its homeland more.

Greiner.

And so the joy of victory was followed by sorrow. We had no inkling of this in the spring. Towards the end of March and especially in May, beautiful sunny days graced the Aire valley. A blue sky stretched above the hills. The hillsides were turning green, the bushes in the camp and the trees in the small neighbouring wood were sprouting buds. Each morning we were awoken by sweet birdsong. Thrushes, robins, blackbirds and finches were nesting in the copses along the line of the wire fence. In the camp's few ash trees we set up starlings' nesting boxes that were soon inhabited. This springtime celebration did us prisoners so much good! From our hilltop we could see across the sun-lit landscape and down into the bustling life of the little town. We could also see the restrictive wire that kept us caged: against it, our wings beat wearily with our yearning and desire to be out in the bright spring world. More of us than ever wanted to go on the organised walks, to wander through the flowering delights of nature and, at least for a few hours, to treat our souls to the joy of sunlight and universal growth that surrounded us.

A Walk

We stroll through fields and flowering meadows,
Whose colours beyond the fence are threaded.
Jubilant children, a lightly dressed band,
Jump over hillsides, hand in hand.
They ask, their eyes amazed and dumb,
what we sentries find such fun.

Over brooks they leap for dares,
in colourful happiness, life without cares.
Is this for us life's shimmering dance,
As youth and happiness fade and pass?
We impotent damned who must retire,
While life inflames us with desire!

Blechschmidt.

There can be none amongst us whose thoughts do not wander homewards on these summer days. If only we could enjoy this blossoming of life alongside our loved ones! This longing for home often verges on a sickness. Look at them, these poor exiles: how their homeland occupies all their thoughts and wishes! Here for example a father, who for months has been toiling away with busy hands producing strange objects. A miniature side-board is starting to take shape, and his masterful hands conjure up wonderful little boxes from the wood of cigar boxes with *Josef, Else, Hilde* carefully carved into the lids: keepsakes for the children at home. And here, another father stands and stretches out his arms. With shining eyes and laughing lips he tells how he used to swing his children around on those strong arms. Oh, how dearly he would love to spin them through the air once more! And do you see all those men sitting alone, their eyes gazing far into the distance? If you speak to them they do not answer, and their gaze is so weary: homesickness! How their eyes shine with delight when letters and parcels arrive! It takes so long for these sweet messages to arrive (still 4-6 weeks) and our longing makes the wait seem eternal. Often there is no delivery for weeks on end. Then the mood becomes oppressive and unsettled. There is a demand for a sharply worded complaint to the Swiss Legation, though sadly the help they give us is mostly very limited. The older prisoners are intoxicated by the sound of the words 'prisoner exchange'. In July, they anxiously follow the talks in The Hague about a new exchange agreement between Germany and England. Great joy abounds! In twelve months' time we should be transported from England to Holland, and in a further six months finally return to our beloved home. We each begin to estimate the size of our 'little hoard', and to order large wooden trunks (20 shillings) or smaller cases (10 shillings). How all these hopes would be shattered!

Diary Excerpts and Poems

Let our diaries tell of our longing for home:

"And so here I sit, holding their pictures in my hand. I'm getting on in years now, and I feel I could weep. Towards evening, little Franz would always sit on my knee, and Thilde would nestle her little hand in mine, lean her head on my shoulder and give me that impish look of hers. And their mother would stand there proudly and look at me, old fellow that I am. Dear God, sometimes I cannot bear it. If only children's hands would stroke me once more and plead 'Daddy, do this for us ... or that!' But here I hear no such voices, and I bend my head in vain for such caresses."

"I am young and passionate, and long for the tenderness and beauty of life, long for German girls, twenty-two useless years of waiting! Everything in me strives for life and pleasure. After all, this is the age to be storing up life experiences; these are the days when I should be collecting priceless treasures to be enjoyed all my life. And here I am, held captive! And yet I am overcome by desire. It is an urgency, a need unknown to those on the outside, and yet the source of our greatest suffering. That is the greatest act of barbarity against our young lives. And it is the reason for the frequent dreaming and musing, the pain and the loneliness inside so many of us."

"Letter came today: mother is dead! I feared as much. Recently, letters from home sounded so strange. She died without her only son by her side. My lifelong hope was to care for her in her old age. And now she has died so young, and I was far away from her! Where can I run to? People everywhere, no peace or quiet, no space for a child's heart to cry itself out."

"Yesterday was a terrible day. I was ill and lay in the camp hospital. The English medics hardly showed their faces. At midday, a few of my comrades visited me, which was kind of them. But as well as the physical pain I began to suffer inwardly too. How utterly irreplaceable is the peaceful, quiet love of home, that serves lovingly rather than out of duty, laying a blessing and a comforting hand on one's head!"

"When the evening sun sits low over these hills, I always see in my mind's eye the tower of the little church at home in the evening glow. The peal of the bells rings in my ears, calling us to Sunday worship. I see the greenery arched around the back door of the house, see father and mother ... home, sweet home, I will have no rest, no peace until I see you again!"

"I was wild once, and a source of pain for mother and father. I felt no strong ties to home, did not care for family life. I felt too strong an urge to see the world. But it dawned on me in a foxhole outside Lille. A cheery young comrade was lying in his own foxhole and firing loyally at the enemy. Then he was hit in the chest. He sank back and cried out once, and that last cry was 'Mother!' The word expressed despair for his young life and yet also the greatest comfort for a child's heart. Since then I have not been able to shake myself free of it. And now, in captivity, the scales have fallen from my eyes. Here, where I must do without love, I understand how this love has followed me quietly, faithfully and almost unfathomably through all my childish stubbornness and error. Captivity has made me a child of my home once more. I see a new life before me."

"Here in the camp, when my thoughts are drawn to the Fatherland, it is basically always a longing for my own little village with its cornfields and woodlands, with its red-roofed houses and its little church, with all its people, some who caused me pain, others whom I loved. Today more than ever, I feel that all love for the Fatherland grows from an attachment to home. That is why we Germans should foster this attachment to home above everything."

"Did I not love my Fatherland before this? But of course, always! But in its suffering the Fatherland becomes even more beloved. And now, to have to sit by so idly, unable to help, binds us by a thousand chains to our beloved country."

"Blood has a voice. It is like something demonic in me. When I see how I am watched over by enemies, separated from the life of the world, when I read the newspapers that treat us with contempt, when all deny kinship with us, then the voice of my blood speaks to me and fills my heart with unending love for all my fellow Germans."

Homeland

Sitting at my barracks window
Hung each side with sun-filled curtains,
Brightened too with painted frame,
Oftentimes I gaze out yonder,
Dwell with longing and despondence
On the hills of the horizon,
On the little town so near us.

Look upon the red-tiled rooftops
Shining radiant in the sunlight,
See the meadows and the woodlands
By the streamlet
That meanders in the valley
Through the fields, a silver ribbon
Snaking off beyond my vision.

And afar my thoughts do journey,
Sombre, though with hope remaining,
On the clouds of scudding nimbus
Vanishing over the skyline.
Clouds that are with greetings laden,
Greetings, reassuring wishes
To our loves in distant homelands.

Luckey.

Family Home

Here's where I'm from
And to this place
The waking of my soul I trace.
The memory's almost gone.

Come oh so far,
Strangest of ways
A journey of a thousand days
As on another star.

Please tell me when
In reverie
Like the child beneath that same old tree
I can find rest again.

Stoltenberg.

Exile

So harsh, so alien,
the winds that hold reign
over this brown terrain.
Will I ever again
hold your hand in mine?

I'm building a rampart
to safeguard my soul
and its secret spark,
that its lighting of our hearts
may never fail.

Stoltenberg.

Gardening Administration

These enchanting spring days also saw an awakening of agricultural consciousness in many of us in the camp, as we began to look around for suitably promising plots of ground. Our gardening director reports on the organisation of our gardening.

"The camp was in possession of an area of about 4,000m² suitable for gardening use and which, on a gentle south-westerly slope directly beneath the hilltop where the camp was situated (about 400m above sea level), was often battered by the predominantly westerly wind. Since the camp's hilltop forms part of the northerly ridge closing off the Skipton valley basin, the south-west side of which is made up of higher hill ridges, the wind either brought rain showers or was very dry, having already lost its moisture over the adjacent hills.

In general, the climate of the Skipton valley can be described as very damp (mild, overcast winters; predominantly cloudy, damp, cool summers). In 1918 it was only in May that we saw a four-week stretch of sunny days. June followed with numerous showers, alternating with strong, dry winds that caused a severe drop in temperature and on some occasions even hoarfrost on higher ground. July and August were predominantly cloudy and damp, while September brought almost four weeks of rain, which was followed by an equally gloomy and damp October.

While such a climate is favourable for meadows and pastureland, it was of very little help for other types of land use: the 1918 oat harvest, for instance, was completely spoiled by rain. Fruit cultivation was barely possible due to the extraordinarily few hours of sunlight; the exception was a few trellis frames, which actually served mostly as wall decoration. Skipton is said to be one of England's least sunny towns, and in 1918 came nowhere near London's annual average of 1030 hours of sunlight – this is itself lower than the figure for Hamburg, which is Germany's least sunny town and enjoys 1240 hours of sunlight per year.

This climate was reflected in the successes and failures of our crops, often chosen misguidedly due to our initial ignorance of the local conditions and influenced by the glorious spring days in May. The tomatoes failed utterly, although cultivated in shelter from the wind and on the south side of the barracks. Some survived long enough to flower, and a few started to bear fruit but were killed by the frost before they could mature. A similar fate befell the pumpkins, planted in early June in the sunniest spots at the edge of ditches and treated with farmyard manure. After the pumpkins, the next greatest failure were the beans. Shortly after germinating they were afflicted by the drop in temperature in June as well as the strong, dry winds, and recovered poorly from this, though they did survive until the harvest. The white-centred varieties fared the worst, while the runner beans were most resilient and could be trained to grow up a frame made from barbed wire. The broad beans had grown well, and had flowered almost too abundantly, when they too were weakened both by the drop in temperature and by a severe aphid problem, so that they had to be disposed of. Of all the peas, it was the short, early varieties that fared well, while the taller, late varieties mostly put out only smaller pods and little roots. Various types of brassica thrived, and lettuces, as well as beetroot and celery. The most impressive crop was the kale, which provided three harvests of leaves before, at the fourth harvest, the heads fell off completely. Since the land had already borne cabbage in the previous year, there were a great number of brassica pests in the area, mostly cabbage moths and cabbage root fly.

Otherwise, the root vegetables managed only a moderate rate of growth, and the onions (even those grown from bulbs) failed completely. The main culprit was most probably the soil quality. The topsoil consisted of soft, very humus-rich soil to a depth of 15cm, a consequence of the pastureland having already been dug up by the English units occupying the camp two years previously. This layer of humus lay loosely on top of a solid, moist layer of clay and so dried out extraordinarily quickly. It also had a limited capacity to absorb the water from the rainfall that flowed swiftly down between topsoil and subsoil. Each time the ground was dug up, the water supply from beneath it was stemmed, and the soil would then also remain so loose that, after the digging in the early spring, the onions, carrots, lettuces and leeks germinated especially poorly from their seeds. Seeds sown later were therefore only planted once the soil had been compacted solid using a flat hoe. This led to good sprouting. But then it took a peculiarly long time for young seedlings to achieve new growth. In almost all cases, this happened only once a few roots had taken hold in the moist clay subsoil.

Initially our garden work was directed by a few green-fingered comrades. They, along with a larger number of other officers, began to dig over the soil in February. Soon, however, the zeal for this work abated, and ultimately the gardening team was reduced to a small steadfast crew assisting the pioneers alongside the garden orderlies who were assigned to the garden work. In early May, having only recently arrived, the present author, being a specialist, took over the garden leadership, supported in this work by the efforts of several comrades. Unfortunately, the majority of the camp's inmates were quick to offer criticism. July, however, brought more active communal participation, as a long period of drought threatened the development of the plants. During this time, each barracks was assigned a piece of the land for regular watering.

We made intensive use of the land. Between each two cabbages in a row there would be a kohlrabi, a lettuce or a cluster of radishes, while between the rows of cabbages were rows of lettuce. Unfortunately our lettuce grown from seed developed late as a result of the unfavourable soil conditions, and in the three to four weeks after it was planted out, the older cabbage plants gained too great a head-start. On the other hand, the seedlings from Skipton, which we had been able to plant out three weeks earlier, developed good heads. Another plot had alternate rows of celery and leeks, and between them early kohlrabi. Between the runner beans, we managed a full radish harvest. Between the onions grown from seed, which germinated very poorly and grew only pitifully, small-headed lettuces provided another good harvest, as did the radishes between the rows of carrots. Of the herbs, the parsley and chives fared best, while the chervil failed. The spinach flowered too early.

Despite all of these adverse conditions, it was possible to keep the kitchen supplied with all kinds of vegetables. Most of all, the daily nutritional needs of the 550 officers were met many times over by the cabbage crop. Since vegetables from Skipton were in relatively short supply they were also unreasonably overpriced, so considerable sums could be saved by growing our own."

Ebert.

Private Gardening and Allotments

"The gloriously warm May days awoke in us a profound urge to tend allotments in the camp. Spades and rakes, which often required a great deal of effort to obtain, were being used everywhere to cultivate the strips of ground alongside the barracks, whether out of a need to top up our stomachs in this 'time of famine' (as was mostly the case), or to simply take pleasure in the sight of blossoming flowers. Who knows how many radishes and how much garden cress disappeared into our hungry bellies from each vegetable patch? The more provident among us planned ahead, and soon lettuces and cabbages were appearing alongside the barracks. Some comrades transformed into large-scale agriculturists. I remember, for example, the 'potato fields' of one such comrade and the large-scale enterprise of two others. Barrack 28 tended more towards individual plots while Barracks 18 and 27 took a cooperative approach, with some men working the land and the others harvesting the crop. The staff officers' barracks also boasted individual plots of cultivated ground. Cress in the shape of U–boats and anchors grew in front of its windows, indicating the former professions of its occupants. The most intensive and extensive efforts were without a doubt those of one comrade who could be seen 'ploughing away' in every corner of the camp. He even constructed a rehabilitation centre to rescue all the diseased and discarded crops, which he lovingly nurtured with horse droppings.

As always happens in allotments everywhere, all–important resting places also began to appear in the camp for those who wished to spend some time in the fresh air. The more furtive amongst us nestled on the grassy banks beneath the hawthorn hedges to take a midday nap while ostensibly engaged in hard labour. Others pined for the bunkers and trenches they had grown to cherish over the course of the war (especially the lads entrenched inside Barrack 32). There was even a machine gun stand in front of Barrack 27: what

Gartenbau.

Gardening.

it lacked in barbed-wire defences it made up for with its thick concealment of flowers and cabbages. Grottos in front of Barrack 28 revealed the extent of our landscape gardening and a very small amphitheatre had sprung up by Barrack 17, although the never-ending rain at the end of the month meant that our planned bowls nights and instrumental evenings came to nothing. But without a doubt, it was our director of administration who took the lead in the creation of these artistic garden endeavours. Unperturbed by snide comments and complaints, he lugged one piece of turf after another, created lawns under ash trees, built up the grassy banks, laid out ornamental beds and, with the patience of a saint, repeatedly restored the constantly deteriorating paths. 'Make your home beautiful!' seemed to be his motto.

It was a shame that, due to the unfavourable weather, the boundless care and willingness to work which was in evidence everywhere failed to reap its rewards."

Ebert.

The cheerful spring and summer weather tore us out of the constriction and confinement of the winter, and life in the camp began to take on a new form. There were more opportunities for sport. The cold showers were always busy. Bodies clothed only in the shortest of shorts lay around on every patch of grass, stretching themselves out under the brilliance and warmth of the benevolent sun. The commandant granted our request for permission to take walks around the camp until midnight. With this new sense of life, exuberant young spirits were revived and sought to defy the misery of captivity with pranks and high jinks. The water fights in particular were famous. One participant remembers:

"Half-naked like the sons of Neptune, armed with full buckets of water and hand-operated water pumps, the storm-troopers launched their attacks in the late afternoon sun. An army of water carriers followed, skilfully passing the empty buckets down the battle line to exchange them for full ones. A small reserve of stalwart fellows waited under cover, ready for the right moment to attack the enemy's rear guard and steal their water buckets and hand pumps. Our merry antics only came to an end when the English guards intervened, horrified by the waste of water. *Icankillyou* himself appeared on the battlefield, and Aunt Frieda declared that this Hun-like behaviour showed us to be extremely 'unruly'!"

Frank.

To their astonishment, late risers would wake up to find their bedsteads in the middle of the camp pathways, or they were pushed under the running taps in the wash-houses. In the evenings, outlandishly dressed groups paraded through the barracks: grinning men with blackened faces and muscle-flexing athletes frightened the timid, while musicians of dubious ability and saucy girls delighted those with an appreciation for the sensory arts. From some barracks, the 'soft' tones of the gramophone rang out from morning until late in the night. The *Skat* tables stood outdoors, meals were taken in the open air and we moved our evening conversations out of the quiet rooms and into the spaces in front of the barracks. Unlike the lonely silence of the winter evenings, these summer nights saw the camp pathways buzzing with life. One comrade writes:

Evenings in the Camp

"What a delightful experience it is to walk around the camp in the evenings, as seems to be the habit of many prisonörs, and to unintentionally overhear a word here, a sentence there, a momentary insight into people and things. 'Would you believe it, the man is waiting for me to say hello!' Two others approach. One is speaking animatedly, his forearms jerkily swinging forwards. 'Differentiate! x^2 needs to be taken out of the equation.' Clearly two hard labourers. 'Integral.' Swiftly around the corner. Here, tuneful notes ring out from the brightly lit mess. How lively they sound! But now they are stumbling on the triplets from high to low, through F sharp and C sharp, and on the second quaver the bass is always a little out of time. Now a triad erupts in E major, and the triplets begin anew. Poor Beethoven! But here comes

Sunbathing.   Sonnenbad.

a company of orderlies from the dress rehearsal of Strindberg's *Creditors*. Criticism, naturally. 'That wasn't so bad, seeing as there weren't so many of 'em.' Smiling, I duck into a side alley, where a white shape moves towards me! My blood suddenly runs cold, and for a second I believe in ghosts again. But I soon get over my shock: it's a human being, with swimming trunks and a Sandow Apparatus.[33] A fierce cry rings out from a nearby barracks, catching my full attention. I can only make out two words: 'Contra!' 'Re!'[34] I suppose it is Barrack 26. But now a trio comes by, excited and agitated. For the most part they talk over each other, though one is drawing figures in the air with his stick. 'I would have every Bolshevik shot dead!' 'But that remark tells me that you know nothing about politics.' 'Scoundrels ... Berlin ... Ghastly, ghastly!' The last words fade away into the distance as a light-footed pair come along, in stark contrast to the last ones: no stick and no hand gestures but their arms linked. Are they too discussing politics? 'I was seeing Yvonne back in those days.' Ah, France and war memories! But now the 10 o'clock signal rings out, and everyone disappears back into the barracks."

Wendel.

These warm days even breathed new variety into our walks. We chose new routes. The group size was increased (50–80), which meant that every comrade was able to escape the primitive huts several times a week. During the hotter months, the walks began as early as 7 o'clock in the morning. Each individual's physical ability was taken into consideration, as the administration arranged walks for 'fast walkers', 'slow walkers' and 'older gentlemen'. The commandant often allowed the senior officers to undertake longer excursions (6 hours). One of these went via Embsay and over the wide open moors into Wharfedale (32 km).

But what exactly does a day in the life of a prisoner entail? A younger comrade paints us a picture with amusing strokes:

The Prisonör's Daily Routine

"At 8 o'clock in the morning, the trumpet is blown. You see, here in the camp we have a real trumpet, which can actually be blown. But surely we have heard better trumpeting in our time. Slowly, we wake up. The 'quiet time' has ended. One after the other, we slowly crawl out of our beds. My barrack comrade N asks me, as he does every morning, 'What time is it?' 'Half past eight,' I reply. 'What time is it?' he asks again, emphasising the 'What'. 'Half past eight,' I say without any emphasis. 'Half past eight?' he replies. 'Yes, half past eight,' I say calmly. 'Well why didn't you tell me that straight away?' he asks angrily. I don't know what I should say to that. I thought I had told him straight away. I expect the reader would agree. I stay calm and say nothing, as I feel sorry for N (the British have had his watch since the Battle of Cambrai). Now someone sneezes, but not just once, no, at least six times (well, it passes the time). Immediately, he responds for the rest of us, 'Bless you! – Thank you very much – You're welcome' – (to maintain the standard of politeness in the barracks).

Now most of us start to get washed, naturally with a great deal of grunting and groaning (this numbs the biting coldness of the water). I want to empty out my water, so that I can give the next fellow a clean wash bowl. Of course, the bucket is full again. Out goes the dirty water in front of the barracks! The water leaps in a high arc in front of the door. But what is this? To my great astonishment, I suddenly no longer have a wash bowl in my hand. It is lying in front of the door with the water, broken in two. That bit of fun will cost me 4 shillings. I think about my poor wallet. Behind me, the whole barracks roars with laughter. Naturally, it annoys me that everyone is laughing at me and making fun of my mishap. 'Well,' I comfort myself, 'why shouldn't the prisonörs laugh? I mean, they'll laugh at anything.' And I, too, have to laugh.

Most of the prisoners leave to go for coffee; only one stays in bed. He has reported himself sick.

At 9.15 drumming notifies the late risers that coffee time has come to an end. (There is a lot of trumpeting and drumming here!) As the orderlies come to clean up, the atmosphere in the barracks becomes very unwelcoming. Most of us go for a walk in the camp; only a few are left behind in the hut. Someone lights the stove (usually he has to do this two or three times). At 9.45 the trumpet sounds again: time to fetch coal. (I think I may have already mentioned that there is a lot of trumpeting here).

At 10 o'clock, it's time for the walking excursion outside the camp. The walking club has split up into two groups (as is the German way): fast walkers and slow walkers. Neither has a 'chair'man (that would be very unusual), but instead they have a front-'runner'. Variety is important in walks, and so we always take the same route. The whole thing is very well organised. We always end up at the 'Green Palace'.[35]

The stove gradually starts to warm up. It's about damned time; outside it is very cold and windy. That is, of course, the prevailing moderate oceanic climate of England. Some of our barracks' residents have already come inside, as it warmed their hearts to see the chimney start to smoke. Four men are standing close together around the stove; it looks as though they are praying to it. No one says a word.

Here come others, carrying the newspaper with them. The frosty silence at the warm stove is broken. One of the fire worshippers asks slowly, 'So, dear B, is there any news?' 'Wilson has ordered his ship to sail to Brest. The Big Five don't seem to be of the same mind. Wilson is insisting on standing by his fourteen points.' Another of the fire worshippers slowly awakes from his religious devotions. 'Who were you talking about just now, B?' he asks. 'About Wilson,' says B. 'What has he ordered?' the other asks. 'His ship,' B says calmly. 'Where did he order it to go?' 'To Brest,' B says, very calmly. 'Wilson ordered that?' 'Yes, Wilson.' That's what I call question and answer! That is the morning's conversation.

Then the doctor arrives to see the patient and asks him what is wrong. 'Head cold,' answers the patient. 'Have you had a bowel movement?' the doctor asks in fragmented German. 'Yes,' the patient answers in English. The doctor prescribes him a 'number 9' (a laxative). With that, the matter is taken care of.

The stove has started to heat up nicely. Those who are not in the hard labour room sit in front of it and read books from the library. Few words are spoken.

It is around 12 o'clock. The walkers return. 'Is the Green Palace still there?' I ask immediately. 'Yes, it's still there.' I breathe a deep sigh of relief. Imagine if the Green Palace was gone! We wouldn't be able to go walking any more. 'Which of the English was there with you?' 'Knee.' (His name is Snee, but we call him Knee, as it's easier to remember.) 'What is there to eat today?' asks one of the walkers. 'Boiled potatoes with goulass.' (No, that's not a spelling mistake). Goulass bears many similarities to goulash, though this variant is cooked mainly using the rump of an English horse.

Then it's time for parade, followed by lunch. Then back to the barracks. Everyone tries to put his pan of water on the stove, so that he can enjoy hot coffee in two hours' time. The stove isn't heating up properly; of course, someone has been fiddling around in there with the poker again.

At 2.30 parcels are handed out – obviously only if any post has arrived. This is announced by trumpeting. (Have I already mentioned that there's a lot of trumpeting around here?). We spend the rest of our time before dinner playing sport, darning socks, and sewing, baking, reading books or (less often) intellectual work. As it happens, today is Saturday, though it could just as easily be Friday. Well, since it is Saturday today, everyone brushes down his Sunday best. R. polishes his brown shoes with devotion, one might even say love. He says he enjoyed this task even before the war. That's not to say that this man used to be a shoe shiner in peacetime. No, in fact he was an intellectual. In our camp, he runs the entire education system. The powers that be have already appointed him our Minister of Culture. And yet here he is, polishing his brown shoes. How simple, and yet how lovely! As he works, he tells us stories about a pastor who would spray so much spittle when he spoke that those sitting near the pulpit were forced to open their umbrellas. How nice! Next to R., another comrade is standing by the stove, keenly attempting to make a porridge pancake. In spite of his constant swearing, it doesn't appear to be working. As he realises that his efforts are in vain, he throws the mixture into the coal box with a rueful smile, and thinks, 'It's all the same to the pancake whether I starve or not. Why won't it cook?' In silence, I marvel at this contempt for the world.

As he cleans his boots, R. continues talking. The conversation turns to our theatre. Apparently Ibsen's *Ghosts* is to be performed next. R., always a reliable source of information, tells us about the piece. Someone asks him

'Are you familiar with Ibsen?' 'Yes,' R. answers. He reflects for a second, then he corrects himself as that wasn't the right answer. 'No, I've never tried ibsing – how do you do that?' Everyone laughs heartily, so heartily that some are brought to tears. I'm sure plenty of people would say 'even Adam and Eve yawned at that joke'. But we prisonörs, we savages, we're better people. The ancient joke makes us laugh and enjoy ourselves frightfully. We aren't yet so smug that we feel we have to yawn at it. We still have the fresh, happy laughter of young men.

It turns 5.30. Since today is Saturday, as I already said, the barracks may bathe (obviously I mean the inmates of the barracks). The men can find out from the blackboard when it is their barracks' turn. Bathing is the only event which is not announced by trumpet as one might have expected, but rather by the call of the shower officer, 'B-a-a-th time!' In order to make his announcement, the shower officer briefly sticks his head through the door (not literally, otherwise it would make a hole every time). Eagerly, we line up by the stove in our colourful bathing attire, which by no means covers all body parts, and await the signal, which we soon hear in the manner explained above. Everyone tumbles out. It's around this point that one really notices how inadequate the bathing attire is. One tumbler tumbles onto his bare knees. At this point someone shouts 'Blank!' as with a blank cartridge. And with much the same relief as that produced by an enemy blank cartridge, everyone calmly makes his way back to the stove. 'What on earth does that mean?' I'm sure the reader is asking. Well, you see, the world is a terrible place. Someone has played a prank on us again by very convincingly imitating the call of the shower officer. As soon as someone realises this, he calls 'Blank!' Sensibly, lookouts are then stationed by the windows to watch out for more potential fake shower officers (who don't emerge – a good joke only needs to be played once). 'Why not do this sooner?' the reader will ask. I will tell you, quietly and confidentially, 'We need to have our fun, of course. This happens every

Ba — a — a — den

Bath time.

Saturday. Think about it – if there were no fake shower officers, it wouldn't be so much fun! Surely you agree?'

Well, in the meantime the real shower officer has come, we have arrived at the shower block, and everyone pushes his way through the narrow door as quickly as he can, so as to get first pick of the showers. Everyone wants the best shower. You see, there is a big difference between one shower and the next. Some produce only cold water; some none at all. Warm showers are a rarity. Like cows: some produce good milk, others don't. If you prick up your ears as you walk past the shower block at bath time, the yells inside will tell you whether the water is warm or cold. Generally, my barracks gets water that isn't warm (I could also have described it as cold, but I refuse to. I'm not like that). Today it is cold as well, and when we're back in the barracks, one man, still suffering from the cold, calls out from the corner, 'Joking aside (as if we are always joking), I think we should finally complain about these showers.' We all agree with him. So what happens? No one complains and everything stays the same. We can't bring ourselves to break with tradition.

Now it's 6.30. The trumpet signals the evening meal. I don't feel like telling you again that a lot of trumpeting goes on around here. This evening, we get custard. Custard. Just custard. It's good, plentiful, and cheap. 'Make sure you eat it all up!' someone shouts.

As I head back to the barracks after the meal, I see W. sitting completely alone at the stove. 'Now then! Haven't you eaten?' I ask. 'No,' he replies, 'I ate yesterday.' In silence, I admire his stoicism.

The barracks gradually fills up again with its inmates. Everyone gathers around the stove once more. Political speeches and debates can be heard everywhere. Differences of opinion clash violently with one another. The hearty custard has reawakened our fighting spirit. After about an hour, the heat of the discussions begins to die down again. Now we come to the usual topics, in this order:

Ba — a — a — den

1. When will we be exchanged?
2. How I was captured.
3. What will there be to eat tomorrow?

These are discussed in order. Then everyone takes to his bed, satisfied.

I think about what I have to do tomorrow. Oh goodness, tomorrow I need to write another letter.

The English come in and count us.

And now a different sort of trumpeting starts.

Slowly, I doze off ..."

Düne.

Dear reader, I am sure that this picture will have left you shaking your head in disbelief more than once. So that you will have an even clearer idea of life in the camp, a few of my comrades would like to tell you about ...

Cabin Fever

"When I moved into the camp here as a very young prisonör," said one of them, "a comrade shed some light for me on how things are here. After lengthy sage explanations, he eventually furrowed his brow sternly and, looking around cautiously, whispered to me, 'And one more thing – a secret illness is creeping through the camp: fimmulus castrensis communis, or general cabin fever!' Seeing the doubt in my stupidly naive eyes, he said with great determination, while looking at me fiercely, 'Everybody has cabin fever here.' That hit home for me. I looked around cautiously, and also took a look at myself, whom I had considered to be normal up until now. And lo and behold, my clever mentor was right. I saw this fever creeping all around, and one day, it had me in its clutches too. However, that was fine by me. I now no longer stood out; I was one among equals. I can see your astonished face, dear reader. I will take you by the hand as Virgil once did to Dante and guide you to the realm of understanding. Sit down in front of a grey wall – good, just like that! And now please look steadfastly at this grey wall today, tomorrow, the day after tomorrow, and yes, for a month, a year, two years! In silence, you roll your eyes and your hands tremble, you develop a strange look on your face. You see, what you can only sense from this imaginary scene, I am really experiencing. Take a look at my grey wall, at which I stare darkly every day, for months, for years, and with eyes that become more desolately dull by the day. The wall is a mosaic, but its dreary lines are always the same and always bleak and boring. For years on end, the barbed wire has clawed at my eyes. I look out of the window; it is beginning to corrode me. I go for a walk; it blocks my way. I search for a view of the countryside in spring; it closes in my freedom-seeking gaze. Wire, wire everywhere, this spiky, tearing, coiled wire! Do you feel how it is beginning to corrode me, sting me, tear at me, coil around me, tangle me? Keep looking at the grey wall! Year after year the same shrill noise four times a day in my ear, and three times a day the monotone of the camp's trumpet sounds across the barracks. Three times a day I go to the trough. Week after week I ply my stomach with the same creations from our trusty kitchen. Day after day I thrash out the same topics of conversation with the others around the stove. Every day the same brown spectres of the barracks grin at me. Every day, I walk along the same crunchy gravel paths – every day, I remind myself of what I am missing – every day, I consider the same future in my ganglion cells – every day – every day – every day ...! You understand, dear reader! And yet I am a young man, Christ Almighty! I want to live life to the full, learn new things and create new things. And yet my thoughts always run the same course and dwindle away, and when new thoughts emerge, they press against this ridiculous confinement and become so small and bizarre, so unnatural and random. The youthfulness in me wants to spread its wings, but due to this eternal monotony it grows weary and dwindles, or torments itself over little things and reaches for suns which do not shine. The will wants to be productive and yet has no aims, nor tools. It often pursues childish follies and, mistaking them for manful pursuits, it becomes excited unnecessarily and never feels itself to be dignified, stable, worthy. I can see it in your eyes, dear reader, that you understand me. There is so much unease, oddness, ridiculousness, comical earnestness, bizarre behaviour, laughing and crying, earnestness and frivolity, wisdom and stupidity, dignity and comedy, purpose and purposelessness, so many highs and unspeakable lows here, and often all within the same individual, at the same time, in the same place.

So now you understand this atrocious bacillus, this prisoners' poison, this fimmulus castrensis communis! Come, wander a little with me through the camp. Have a good look at this child-like face! A full beard is dangling from his boyish chin. This all began overnight, you know. Mass suggestion is spreading its influence. Alarmingly, full beards, goatees (both single and double-pointed), handlebar moustaches in the style of the Kaiser and mutton chops can now be seen on these otherwise fine, civilised faces. Beard ties and oils are constantly in use. And yet, the determined efforts of many are doomed to failure. Three rows and seven individual hairs really cannot create the exhilarating image of a manly beard. These extraordinary appendages on the chins of some of the men are only a poor substitute. Fimmulus ...

Are you looking in astonishment at that gentleman? The sun is gleaming in brilliant white shiny patches on his head. You will see even more bald heads here. Fully shaved heads appear here in abundance. Look, you are now lying flat-out on the ground! You should have opened your eyes! You need to get used to the camp's half-naked long-distance runners and give way to them courteously. Some of them even ran around like that in the harsh winter and pranced about in the snow. The naked men up there on the roof of the barracks? Oh, I see, yes, that's just for a bet. They volunteered to climb naked up the walls of the barracks and onto the roof in broad daylight, in return for a tin of fruit. That's how it is around here. Are you growing pale? Do you think that this barracks is full of lunatics because you have just heard a fearful scream? You are worrying unnecessarily. Sometimes a man simply has the urge to yell all of a sudden, for no apparent reason. Others sing loudly or softly. No, heaven forbid, no murder or manslaughter is going on over there; it's nothing but a lively water fight. What? Do we have foreign races and religions in this camp? No, we are all Germans and good Christians. What makes you think that? Oh, you can see the Muslim priest over there, attired in a long bathrobe, wooden sandals and a homemade fez, with his face artificially browned, and a long tobacco pipe. That is our K., yes, yes! Quickly, step aside! I can see that you are amazed. Yes, how cheekily the prisoners march past, laughing and singing, with enormous suitcases and laundry bags, caps askew on their heads, brandishing sticks! They are only practising marching back to the homeland. Do we have an orthopaedic institute here? Oh, you mean those half-naked people writhing on the lawn, who are managing to perform the most dreadful contortions? They are our gymnasts. The old men among them are attempting to resuscitate their brittle bones.

You will just have to get used to a lot of things here, dear reader. Do we have civilians in our camp? Heaven forbid, we are all German soldiers. But admittedly, we have stopped conforming to the stricter dress codes. That's why you will see many handsome, imaginative costumes which would make the peacetime soldiers' hair stand on end. Yes, and the sticks too! Many of our prisonörs drag themselves along using these props and many use them to express their desire for peace by swinging them around elegantly.

Dear reader, do accompany me into my barracks! Are you looking in amazement at the living space occupied by N ..., my comrade? Yes, he was overcome by cleaning fever fourteen days ago. He went around his square metres of space like crazy with a broom, brush and cleaning cloth, and denounced as a philistine anyone who did not view tidiness and cleanliness as the primary requirement of civilised behaviour. Well, look at the result after fourteen days! A few books and notebooks are lying on the 75cm long shelf on the wall, dusty and greasy. Lard was on sale recently for sixpence and he had brought some back with him after a meal, and had unfortunately left it on top of the books. Afterwards, he had forgotten to eat the fat and, inexplicably, a cigarette and two butts were later found lying in it. On the shelf there are cardboard boxes of all shapes and colours lying around with wood shavings spilling out of most of them. Presumably they contain food from home. A few tin cans, a plate and a defunct porridge box are crowded around these cardboard boxes in ingenious disorder. Spilt porridge, some custard powder, some loose tobacco, a little piece of shaving soap, a few pennies, and most notably, a considerable number of cigarette butts complete this delightful picture. The latter are of some significance. In emergencies –

in other words, all the time – they are twisted together to make new cigarettes. Our N. also owns a box. Initially, there was enough room in it for his meagre assets, but eventually nothing more would fit in there. And yet, he so wanted to have some order! There was still a lot of space under the bed. Just throw everything as far back as possible so that order can prevail! And so all kinds of things were lurking in the gloom under his bed: slippers, wooden sandals, matchsticks, cigarette butts, old notebooks, newspapers, a long-lost knife, an open cardboard box containing a mildewed shirt, a box with eleven half-mouldy potatoes. I'm sure you understand, dear reader: prisoneritis!

The prisonör moves constantly from one extreme to the other. For the first few days of the week, for example, he meticulously carries out profound intellectual work from eight o'clock in the morning to half past nine at night; he only leaves the quiet room at mealtimes. Then, he will simply do nothing for several days, and instead drifts around, completely inert. Today he wakes up early at 6 o'clock in the morning with heroic determination, and tomorrow he sleeps until lunchtime. For a whole week he abstains from smoking with a manly steadfastness, and then for the following eight days, he will smoke like a chimney. He who refused yesterday to pay sixpence for an egg (yes, if only it cost fourpence!), bought himself a Dunhill pipe today for 32 shillings. Many have spent a year of their imprisonment constantly playing music, others have spent the same amount of time fashioning chess pieces out of cotton reels. Comrades who are businessmen by profession and as such should be busying themselves with business correspondence and double-entry bookkeeping, are spouting Kant, whilst you can see career officers learning double-entry bookkeeping. There are prisonörs whose only occupation consists of making porridge oat pancakes and fried potatoes.

Dear reader, do not start up any conversations with the prisoners! Being healthy and inexperienced, you have no understanding of the obstacles to be negotiated in the ocean of imprisoned souls! You could easily get yourself into difficulties. Look, the scholarly A. is giving an astonishingly detailed talk about Schopenhauer over there at the stove. In the middle of the tightly constructed train of ideas, B. suddenly bursts out with the question, 'A., how old are you actually?' Bafflement, rage, a fierce encounter with hard-hitting masculine words, retorts, they are both in a 'huff'. The prisoners get into a huff very easily. Therefore, you ought to be very careful here, dear reader. But that is the way we are. And besides, there is no need to worry: we always make up again just as easily.

Dear reader, all of this is passing you by, just like an amusing picture, but do you not see the pained, struggling face behind the smiling mask? This epidemic of the prison camp came upon us inexorably and gnawed away at our nerves. We tried to defeat it through loud verbal battles, which seemed to continue indefinitely. We sat at the stove, lost in ourselves, for hours, days, and weeks on end. We sneaked into the work rooms, the home of the great intellects amongst the prisonörs. Forlornly, we sought shelter between the wooden walls, where not a breeze was stirring. Yes, sometimes we would even be sitting there at dawn, wrapped up in our coats and in our thoughts. By night, we became wanderers, lost to the world, escaping the colourful goings-on of barracks life with its noisiness and seeking to cool our hot foreheads and our shattered nerves in the piercing night wind."

Frank, Gleich, Lurmann, Sichler.

The feeling of trepidation about the fate of our homeland, the longing for freedom from our confinement, the distress of our souls in our small, monotonous world. These feelings constitute the painful features of our existence as prisoners. And yet, summer life was unfolding outside in such richness.

The Easter celebrations on 31st March basked in the glow of news of German victory. A mass, the first in the camp, was said in Room A to mark Easter Day. The kitchen had also made a great effort to prepare a feast for our stomachs. A joyful mood flowed through this holiday season despite the cloudy sky and the noisy demonstrations of the Skipton locals, who were perturbed by the successful German offensive. Many smiling faces and others irritated and deceived were conjured up in the camp on 1st April. An extensive parcel list appeared on the blackboard, almost the entire prisonör population came flying out, and almost everybody read his name on the precious list with joyful astonishment. An enormous number of delighted men waited at the mail censorship barracks, until the crushing, wrath-inducing news arrived that a prankster had taken the liberty of playing an April Fool's trick with this list. An hour later, a never-ending crowd of people rushed into the canteen. Apparently, matches were being sold there. However, Mr James had to explain to the turbulent flood of people filling the shop that there was not a single box for sale. On the morning of this unhappy day, numerous men, concentrating deeply, could be seen standing with furrowed brows in front of a large placard by Barrack 12. In an article translated from *The Times*, an expert had provided his strictly scientific explanation of the accomplishments of the howitzer *Big Bertha*. Mathematical formulae were applied to the law of gravity, and an astonishingly brilliant insight into the effect of the earth's rotation and the air currents was given. Such a convincingly dazzling picture of the achievements of German ballistics was set before our eyes that many prisoners were hardly able to prevent their excited stream of thoughts from reaching ever higher throughout the day. Only gradually did the realisation sink in that a skilful practical joker had fooled us.

In April, the young performing artists of the camp gathered the prisonörs together for the first time to perform for them. The hardworking male-voice choir sang us beautiful German folk songs and brought back memories of our beloved country. Also, for the first time, the strains of our orchestra sounded through the Old Mess. Since these April days, the performances of both groups have formed the accompaniment to the camp through joy and sorrow. We thank them for many delightful and uplifting hours. On the morning of 1st May, while all was still quiet, the voices of our talented singers rang out jubilantly across the camp and heralded to friend and foe the joy inspired in the heart of man by the growing pleasures of spring. The Tommies by the wire lowered their menacing guns and were completely astounded by the 'wild Huns'. As if to thank us, they also offered us a musical treat one Sunday. Of course, these warriors, armed to the teeth, did not raise their own harsh voices; instead, delightful girls lined the edge of the woodland and sang all kinds of unfamiliar songs to us, to the sounds of lute music. They were from the Salvation Army, whose ministry in the English enlisted men's barracks on numerous Sundays was always

The relaxed Tommy guard.

heralded by the sound of the trombone. We gained the overall impression that the British are enthusiastic singers. The English guards often relieved their boredom by delighting in the joys of singing, with varying degrees of charm. Apart from that, our German eyes, accustomed to rigorous German standards, could not help but notice the relaxed way in which the Tommy guards carried out their duties.

We were able to celebrate Whitsun on Sunday 19th May in the glory of the bright spring sunshine. In the morning, a large service was held in the Old Mess: it signified new life for every individual and for our nation. The kitchen excelled itself. Our eyes had not seen such epicurean delights for a long time: tomato soup, salmon mayonnaise with biscuits, roast beef with peas and potatoes, custard and coffee, and in the evening, herring salad and cress. On the evening of the second day of Whitsun, the choir guided our thoughts back to our beloved homeland through folk song.

Reprisals

A new regulation with truly tangible consequences descended upon us innocent prisonörs on 28th April. The commandant presented our senior German officer with an order from the War Office. It stated,[36]

"The order has been issued by the War Council to notify you that, as a result of the disgraceful conditions prevailing in the prisoner-of-war camps of the 10th German Army Corps, the German government has been threatened with reprisal actions on German officer prisoners of war in one British military district if assurance does not arrive by 27th April 1918 that these conditions, about which we have the most serious grounds for complaint, have been remedied.

I request that you the take the following measures from 28th April 1918 in all officer prisoner-of-war camps located in your district command, unless otherwise instructed in the meantime. It should then be communicated to the officers that we have been forced to take these steps as reprisals for the disgraceful and inhumane treatment of the British officers inside the territory of the 10th Army Corps, under the command of General von Hähnisch, and that the commandants specially appointed by the aforementioned general to carry out his orders (among whom the two Niemayer brothers have rendered themselves conspicuous) are, for the most part, responsible for the restrictions currently being imposed.

The restrictions coming into force are as follows:

    a) 4 roll calls daily at unspecified times.
    b) No newspapers or magazines are permitted.
    c) No outdoor games are allowed.
    d) All national flags, maps, and pictures of rulers, commanders and famous personalities from Germany and allied countries should be removed and handed over to the commandant.
    e) All musical instruments should be confiscated and handed over to the commandant.
    f) Only one warm shower per week is permitted.

If these restrictions have already come into force, the imprisoned officers must be informed that, from time to time, others will be imposed on them, until assurance has been received that British officers in Germany are not only receiving humane treatment, but are also being treated in a way in which officers should justifiably expect to be treated."

The reprisals came into force accordingly. We were obliged to hand in our portraits of the Kaiser. The maps of battlegrounds, which had been produced with such care and were constantly being updated, vanished. The pianos moved back to Skipton, and the other musical instruments were locked in Barrack 15. We found the banning of newspapers to be truly disconcerting, but by means of some *Schiebung* we were able to get at least one newspaper into the camp and, as a result, the most important news stories could be read out at midday during lunch. The most painful change was the increase in parades. We had to turn out four times a day to be counted: at 10am, 12 noon, 2pm and 6pm. We found the 2 o'clock parade particularly disruptive to worthwhile activities: afternoon naps, working, playing Skat, among other things. But we put on a brave face. Prior to the commencement of the reprisals, the choir sang saucy songs on the square in front of the shower block, and the doomed orchestra played their final melodies boldly and cheerfully for the last time. The reprisals lasted until 15th July, and were lifted following the successful negotiations at The Hague between Germany and England.

Pressure generates counter-pressure. A belligerent atmosphere spread through the camp. During the night of 5th-6th June, some mysterious characters paid a visit to the commandant's office. The perpetrators were said to have pilfered a few dumdum bullets and a railway timetable. On this occasion, it emerged that the commandant had not passed on a number of our complaints to the Swiss Legation, despite his promises. Because the English could not identify the culprits, the commander-in-chief of the northern military district ordered the closure of the canteen for fourteen days on 6th June as a disciplinary measure 'by virtue of the Royal Warrant for the Maintenance of Discipline among Prisoners of War (par. 42, sect. 8)'.[37] In fact, the door of Mr James' premises was slammed shut in our faces on 6th June without prior notice.

The indignation among the prisoners caused quite a stir, especially after the commandant had made an announcement that had offended the whole of the camp. This feeling of agitation was followed by determined action: the officers refused to line up for parade. With all his strength, the Yorkshire Boar rang the bell with his sturdy fists, to no avail. The only response that could be heard from the animated groups down the camp's alleyways was antagonistic laughter. The English appeared to be completely helpless. The commandant negotiated with our senior officer, at whose suggestion he retracted the offensive announcement, and allowed us to collectively purchase the most essential items. He promised to pass on our complaints and demand an immediate visit from the Swiss envoy. When faced with this fearful compliance, the furor teutonicus subsided and we subsequently appeared demurely at parade once again. On 20th June the doors of the canteen were re-opened.

Thus the commandant went through a difficult time with his prisonörs. But his sorrows were to multiply to an unimaginable degree. The beautiful weather beyond the wire, the yearning for comrades still fighting, the anger over the reprisals beckoned daring spirits inexorably towards freedom. And so came the heyday of the ...

Escape Attempts

The rainy day casts a gloomy mood over Room A. With strained expressions, several of the hard labourers, usually so industrious, stand at the windows and gaze with apparent helplessness at the camp gates. There, in a long line, our orderlies are gathering to collect the coal from the store outside the camp, as they do each morning. The rain splatters the face of the English guard as he opens the gate and sullenly watches the orderlies pass. He has no desire to count Germans in and out of the camp in this 'filthy weather'. And so he is oblivious to the fact that one orderly too many has left the confines of the camp. Our men disappear hastily into the coal shed and then, slowly and in pairs, return up the slope to the camp with the filled buckets. While the two Tommies guarding the coal shed stare up at the grey sky from beneath their rain shelter, a figure sneaks behind them and disappears behind the corner of the shed. With feline stealth, the figure scales a fence – we see clearly the red flash of the prisoner's jacket … and is gone. We stand there in anxious expectation. Minutes pass. And then there are loud shrill whistles around the camp, the guards rush to find their weapons, officers gesticulate, and patrols hurry out into the valley. More anxious minutes tick away. And then, coming up the road to the camp from the town, a unit of Tommies, in their midst a civilian in a smart raincoat and floppy brown hat, a colourful tie fluttering cheekily at his throat. Poor comrade, how could you possibly know that a Tommy would be looking out of a barracks window at the right moment to see you jump boldly over the fence and then watch in astonishment as, down in the valley, you shed your prisonör's attire to transform into a civilised member of society! In vain, the sartorial masterpieces created for you from blankets and other innocuous materials by our talented tailors; in vain, your clever and secretive procurement of English money! You

English prison cells.

march past us in good-humoured sorrow. The War Office is quick to send its three-man court martial and the defence lawyer in his white wig, and you are sentenced to three weeks 'in the cooler'. *Icankillyou*, meanwhile, is deeply troubled and cannot stop wondering how the escaper managed to make it to freedom. Over the next few days, he personally supervises the coal collectors.

* * *

It is evening. I stand on the steps of the barracks and look out into the dark valley. I watch in bemusement as one comrade walks ceaselessly to and fro between the quartermaster's barracks and the foot of the steps where I am standing. What's going on? I prick up my ears. Whispering and rattling seems to be coming from the ground. I sneak towards the lonely walker. 'Listen, my friend ...' 'Shh!' he says, laying a finger on his lips. 'Tunnelling.' I am speechless. He leads me over to the quartermaster's barracks and pushes up the lowest planks of the cladding, which are cleverly held in place by wires. The space beneath the barracks yawns darkly back at me. In the corner a 'signal lamp' made from an old tin can throws a muted light onto a few figures crouched in a hole. They remind me of the darkest parts of Abruzzo. Their shirts and trousers are covered with a thick layer of dirt, their shoes in pieces, each one has a red handkerchief around his head. Their breathing is laboured and audible. Now and again, a quiet curse can be heard. 'Blast it, lying around for hours in this watery clay!' 'Hey, the entry shaft is deep enough already, get on with the tunnel! Remember, 50cm deep!' 'This damn stony ground! Another great big rock!' The figures straighten themselves up, remove their shirts and tie them together to lift a giant piece of stone out of the hole.

My guide lets the wooden planks fall quietly back into place. The secret hive of activity vanishes.

'How many are you?'

'Twenty-four,' he whispers. 'All well prepared. March together over the bleak upland moors as far as the east coast. March at night only, to avoid catching the eye of the police or the population. The most senior infantry officer will lead us. Then commandeer fishing boats. There will surely be some lying around, and we have a naval officer to take charge of our journey eastwards. Other escapers using this method have already got as far as two miles off the coast of Heligoland – but were caught at the last moment ...'

'What about provisions?'

'All secured. The kitchen is providing precisely calculated rations of coffee, bread, biscuits, sardines and tinned meat. Navy overcoats and blankets have been made into civilian clothes, bedsheets into rucksacks.'

'And do you have tools?'

'Coal shovels, fire-pokers and a bully beef tin that we have converted into a shovel. We liberated one very useful implement from Mr James: a masonry hammer!'

'Are you being careful?'

'But of course! We have lookouts everywhere. Room A has a view of the gates. The change of guard, their rounds, every arrival of an Englishman in the camp, we note it all down in our record book. Every Tommy, officer or man, has a codename, for example *Fishmonger, Winkelried*,[38] *Caller in Battle*,[39] *The Butcher, Triple Action, Censor Orderly* and so on.'

'Oh', I say, doubtfully.

'Keep a lid on it!' barks my guide.

'But my good man ...!' I protest.

'Shht!' he whispers. 'I was only giving a signal to them in there. There's a sergeant coming you see.'

Aha!

When the tunnel was more than half finished, it was unfortunately discovered. This was largely due to the fact that the hopeful escapers had made such progress without significant disruption and had become complacent. The presence of one English sergeant in the camp had not been promptly reported, and so the workers did not pause as he passed the quartermaster's store. He had heard noises that aroused his suspicions. The next morning, he climbed over the wire fence that ran along the side of the barracks and separated it from the rest of the camp, crawled underneath the store and found everything. One of our hopes had been dashed. The English, who had first had to climb over the wire fence and had got underneath the barracks via an air vent, were feverish with curiosity and eager to find out how the prisoners had got in there. Even Captain Parkhurst, our little camp adjutant, was afflicted by this thirst for knowledge. He used a ladder to climb over the fence but, instead of inspecting underneath the barracks, got himself onto the roof, as though hoping to find the solution to the puzzle up there. But it turned out he was not entirely immune to vertigo, and he seemed unable to move properly on the roof's sloping surface, crouching down low over his knees with his hands flat on the roof behind him. He looked a sorry sight. His pose, similar to that of a monkey, and on top of that his ruddy boozer's face, inspired considerable joy in the numerous German officers who had now quickly assembled around the scene. After ten minutes of withstanding the joyful mockery by his inferiors, he finally retreated, crawling along uncertainly. And, climbing down the ladder, he presented to the highly amused spectators a posterior covered with roofing tar.

*   *   *

The sports ground basks in the glory of the bright summer's day. The English guard, fixed at his post and tasked with watching over one long edge of the field, yawns. In one corner of the field, a lively football match is underway. The English patrol guard, there to retrieve the ball if it lands between the wire fences, watches the agile sportsmen. One solitary man is lying in the grass.

Two officers in overcoats approach him and stretch out alongside him. Another comrade strikes up a conversation with the yawning sentry. The countryside is peaceful. The match picks up pace. The ball flies into the fencing, and the Tommy goes after it. At this moment, the two men in overcoats shake off their cumbersome outfits and sneak along the fence, trailing a long string after them. They throw themselves to the ground, the first wire is cut through, they crawl under the tangle of wires, cut through the outer wire – and already they are jumping behind a stone wall. Slowly, the solitary man pulls the 'wire cutters' back on the long string. The countryside is peaceful, the match continues without another interruption. The patrolling Tommy saunters along the fence. And suddenly his eyes widen – whistles – patrols swarm out of the camp – a farmer, who has seen the fugitives, races through the countryside on his old nag. Ten minutes later, the escapers are brought back into the camp. Bad luck!

* * *

Evening falls at the end of a summer's day. A loud whistle signals that the sports ground is being closed for the night and must now be vacated by all prisonörs. The wide expanse soon stands empty, and the sentries return to the guardhouse. The sergeant surveys the grassy area one last time and locks the gates, satisfied that his duty has been done.

The prisonörs have assembled on the parade ground to be counted. The usual list of names is called followed by the endlessly repeated answer, 'present!' Not one of the flock is missing. Meanwhile, the English, totally absorbed in their task, would have been astonished if only they had looked around. Two figures had broken away from the ranks of the prisonörs already counted, disappeared at lightning speed into the long barracks, cast off their officers' uniforms and re-emerged as two orderlies going calmly about their business.

The horn signals that it is time for dinner. Today there is something remarkable, almost exultant, about the way it blares across to the sports ground, as though it had a joyful message to carry to someone there. The evening passes, and the last prisoner count at 10pm is done inside the accommodation barracks. But as soon as the English had checked the first barracks to see that we were 'tucked up tight', two figures already counted, who had been lying in bed fully clothed, sneaked out of the back of the dormitories, wound their way along the dark paths of the camp to a barracks still to be checked, and lay down there in two empty beds. The English come and count the prisoners. All present and correct!

The sweet peace of the night descends on us. The Skipton church tower chimes eleven. Something is moving on the moonlit sports ground. A head sticks out of the hedge, keen eyes scan around and suddenly, out of the bushes springs first one civilian, then another. 'Nicely done! And our comrades covered for us marvellously! They even straightened the grass we had flattened! Now, quickly, hide the uniforms in the bushes, and let's go!' They easily scale the obstacle, leaving no trace behind them. Soon they are walking through the night, happy and free.

The next morning comes and it is time for the prisoners to be counted. The English soon stop short. One 'Here!' is missing, then a second, a third, a fourth! The sergeants race to the barracks – no trace of the absentees. The guard is alerted, and whole teams of Tommies search through the camp. In vain. Patrols swarm the surrounding area and the telegraph springs into action. It slowly begins to dawn on the English that not all of the missing prisoners have escaped. Patrols stalk continuously through the camp. Individual Tommies crawl under the barracks and cock their ears to the rafters. Meanwhile, filled buckets of water seem to slip accidentally out of our hands and spill onto the listeners. One English officer occupies a toilet cubicle and strains his ears to right and left. Soon, a laughing crowd has assembled outside his listening post. And yet two of the missing prisoners are walking around the camp in broad daylight, only creeping from the administration room into the otherwise completely unscrutinised space under the stage at dangerous moments.

It is a delightful time for the prisonörs. The English become increasingly nervous.

Meanwhile, the two escapers have been walking through the night and on the following day they arrive at a village pub. They introduce themselves as American pilots, and receive a warm welcome and make themselves very popular. Then fate arrives in the form of a policeman. He demands to see identification, and that's when things go wrong. They are led away and the landlady bursts into heartfelt tears. On the third day, the two 'internal escapers' reappear to face *Icankillyou* with smiling faces. The flock is all together again.

* * *

One evening an English sergeant unexpectedly visits the camp hospital to deliver medicine to a sick comrade. We had long since earmarked this barracks as an ideal location for tunnel-building, due to its location close to the wire fence. The sergeant hears a suspicious noise coming from an otherwise little used room. The door is locked, and he approaches quickly with a heavy bunch of keys. But none of them fits. He conscientiously takes a seat beside the door and waits. He has every reason to do so. Inside, the Germans are working feverishly. Months ago, they painstakingly sawed a hole in the floorboards, so carefully that there was no trace of it once the piece of flooring had been replaced. The excavated soil was disposed of down the toilet, and a long hose from the water supply was used to rinse it away. And now the Tommy is sitting outside the door, while inside two men are working flat-out. The work is at a critical stage. They cannot get caught. An impromptu decision and they get to work, labouring through the wet, stony ground under the barracks wall and pushing through to the surface outside. Digging with their hands and with a piece of wood, our two heroes exert unimaginable effort to work their way forward. Their exertions are rewarded. Covered from head to toe in a thick layer of clay, they crawl out of the narrow opening and disappear. The guard has been fooled. *Icankillyou* is inconsolable.

* * *

And so none of our escape attempts met with success. And yet they represent a fairly substantial chapter in the life of any prisoner-of-war camp. Almost anyone who has been a prisonör has toyed with the challenging thought of escaping, spurred on by the pull of home, the dreariness of imprisonment and the longing to be back fighting at the Front. And the adventurous spirit of our youth is deeply ingrained in our blood. And what did we have to lose? A few weeks in a cell and then a change of scenery through transfer to another camp. But it provided a pleasant interruption to the monotony of our existence, and gave us 'glorious' memories. These unsettling escape attempts meant that many English soldiers were engaged in guarding us, and the guards had their work cut out. Motor cars squealed into action. The telegraph line buzzed. And our commandant? He was often left quite pale with anger and indignation. How the scornful grins of the prisonörs must have affronted him! And all because of one runaway, who was now brought back to camp in wonderfully scruffy old clothes, smoking a cigarette, turning his smiling face to all and sundry, 'Come and meet me in Skipton, my fine English fellows!'

Our hopes for success with these escape attempts were, admittedly, extremely slim. Only those who could speak English like their mother tongue, who were acquainted with the customs and traditions of the British, who knew how to find their way across the country and had plenty of English money, could expect their plan to succeed. Great Britain is an enormous cage. It was easy enough to find a way through the barbed wire, to hide out in England, but almost impossible to make it home across the sea. On top of this, those who had successfully made it back to Germany were too willing to share the details of their escapes and alerted the English. And so the escape route never went further than the coast.

As autumn approached, the weather became unfavourable for our endeavours. The Armistice came. The futility of escape was clear. And so in summer 1919 there were no more escape attempts.

Kesting.

On 4th August, the anniversary of the outbreak of war, a quiet act of remembrance took place in the Old Mess. Performances by the choir and orchestra framed a patriotic address that looked back on the years of the war and pointed hopefully towards the future. In mid-August, a Skipton photographer appeared at the camp; at our request, the War Office had permitted him to immortalise our handsome figures on photographic plates for posterity. This small, sprightly man was in great demand. After all, the images were to be tributes to loyal comrades and bring meaningful messages of love from the prisoners to their nearest and dearest. Group portraits and individual shots were taken, outdoors and inside the barracks. Each man gave his person the most dignified and cultivated appearance possible; those who were engaged to be married, especially, developed a surprising knack for enhancing their physical appearance and the triumphant masculinity of the warrior's countenance to best effect. On 3rd November an art exhibition was set up in the larger teaching room. Many of the officers had contributed their own artistic creations. Alongside landscapes, portraits, scenes from camp life and textile work there were chess boards populated by baroque-style figurines, gavels complete with blocks, writing accoutrements, picture frames, brushes, dolls' house furniture and other objects to be admired. The kitchen had also sent masterpieces to gratify the appetite: a hand cart made from porridge biscuits, filled with bottles of 'delicious wine', preserves and fruit, a tasty cake, a very appetising roast duck and other delicacies. These gourmet dishes were raffled off, and the winner of the top prize (the hand cart) was the subject of gnawing envy wherever he went for some time. The enlisted men too had contributed to the exhibition, and had produced some true masterpieces. We were once again impressed by the level of German artistry amongst our enlisted men, when a wealth of artwork from England's enlisted men's prison camps was sent to us and available for purchase. Many of us bought valuable objects from this tasteful collection, for personal use or as a memento. The evening of the 3rd November found us assembled in the Old Mess to celebrate the anniversary of the Reformation. The choir and orchestra performed. The two addresses were on the subject of 'Luther's national significance' and 'Luther and his struggles'.

In these summer months the camp's education system blossomed to an unprecedented richness. The variety of subjects offered and the large number of lessons are testament to the tireless hard work of our prisonörs and their responsible awareness that, in time, we would need to serve our shattered Fatherland with all our intellectual strength. Even in dire straits, the German is the model of the profound, cultured individual. Alongside teaching, lectures were held almost every week in the Old Mess. In September, too, the theatre society was formed, which every Sunday and on some weekdays would provide intellectual stimulus, joy and often uplifting artistic delight with a never-ending succession of lively musical evenings, cabaret acts and other artistically skilled performances.

Food Supplies

Food in the summer months did not rise above the level of the March rations: it was scant, very scant, especially in April and May. The thought of swede still makes us shudder slightly. The feeling of hunger could never be completely quelled, and inhibited all our physical and intellectual labour. For this reason, many gave up their intellectual and physical endeavours altogether and lay in listless resignation on their beds for hours on end. The provisions available from the canteen also became more and more limited. Quaker Oats were not often to be had. And what should our stomachs, longing for proper nutrition, do with mixed pickles, oranges, nuts! As ever, there was very little fat to be had. We could only buy very small quantities of margarine, lard, tinned goods and sardines. Some hungry souls received assistance from home, but many did not enjoy this support. On the few occasions that the kitchen store did manage to obtain larger quantities of stock thanks to *Schiebung*, there was a race to buy items and a never-ending queue of men stretching out of the kitchen building.

The reader, and particularly his lady wife, might be interested in a weekly menu card from around this time (taken from a diary, with remarks by the consumer):

Sunday: soup; pot roast (very tough), three boiled potatoes and gravy; carrots; orange dessert (good). (Today I was full.) – Supper: macaroni with fishcakes (tiny), cup of tea (ghastly).

Monday: soup, turnip. – Supper: peas.

Tuesday: potato soup (with peel), cabbage (kitchen list says 'with meat'; I couldn't find any. Tastes terrible.) – Supper: dish of gruel, orange custard (hungry 2 hours later).

Wednesday: soup, 1½ dessertspoons of goulash, three boiled potatoes. – Supper: pickled lentils (good).

Thursday: soup; peas with carrots (good); meat loaf with gravy. – Supper: half a herring and three boiled potatoes.

Friday: pea soup; pickled potatoes, orange pudding. – Supper: swede, fishcakes.

Saturday: gruel, fried fish with sauce, three boiled potatoes. – Supper: rice and gravy (soon hungry again).

In the latter months of this period, food supplies improved. More goods obtained by *Schiebung* began to appear in the kitchen store. Frozen rabbits provided our Sunday roast. On several occasions we would be greeted by the sight of an appetising brown cake covered in chocolate icing on our Sunday table. For special occasions (for groups of regimental comrades, *Landsmannschaften* groups, etc.) the kitchen was able to deliver meals of more substance and better quality.

Our organisation into groups of mess mates had proved very beneficial. Close bonds often formed within the small groups, not only as a result of shared enjoyment of material things. This dining fellowship encouraged a sense of social justice. Each man was only permitted to take his allotted amount from the bowl. And now, dear reader, think of the poor prisonör's starving belly! You can surely understand how greedy and calculating a gaze he would cast on the kitchen's offerings, how he would long to take his portion in full, what great spiritual generosity it cost him to show humility here. Some mess mates elected particularly trustworthy members as food distributors, and some of these entrusted individuals acquired great fame for their unshakeable sense of justice.

It was also in the smaller social circle provided by the mess mates that birthdays were normally celebrated. Oh, those birthdays! The lucky individual who was usually sleeping his way into a new year of his life would be awakened by the particularly discordant sound of a horn, blown from time to time by our old camp cobbler, with more goodwill than skill. He always blamed the instrument and its faulty valve seals. No sooner had the sounds of *Nun danket alle Gott* [*Now Thank We All Our God*] or the *Dies ist der Tag des Herrn* [*This Is The Day Of The Lord*][40] wailed to a close, than the whole barracks would take part in the celebratory ritual. This was a most enjoyable activity, but the accompanying congratulations had to be accepted as an unavoidable stroke of fate by either surrendering or bellowing. You see, some barracks had developed a tradition of using the lucky fellow's backside to count out the years lived. Presumably the older gentlemen must have found this procedure particularly painful. Compensation for this torture was of course the tender attention of the mess mates, who would normally decorate the table with flowers and excel themselves by providing something special, at the very least a cake.

Newcomers

Towards the end of this period, our number had grown extraordinarily. During our offensive and also during the course of the counter-offensive, great numbers of German officers had fallen into enemy hands. Since there was still ample room in our camp, the new comrades were brought to us in larger and smaller groups. By November our number had reached 560 officers, and the camp was almost full. These new prisoners mostly came straight from the Front, others from hospitals. Their clothes and faces still bore the signs of battle with torn uniforms, wool turbans instead of caps, without gaiters or any kind of proper footwear, sometimes in English coats and trousers with the familiar red or blue spot on the back or thigh, their few belongings wrapped in a red handkerchief. All this presented an often shameful picture in comparison to us long-term prisoners, who stood almost like 'gents' before them. We were deeply shaken as we saw comrades arriving from the hospitals. Missing an arm or a leg, or perhaps with only one eye, dragging themselves on crutches; this is how they often arrived amongst us. Alongside our pity for these valiant comrades we often felt anger towards the English, who did not always treat these unfortunate souls with an appropriate level of care. The first few days were difficult for these new arrivals in the camp. The pale, haggard faces of many still mirrored the suffering of recent weeks – and not only physical suffering, but ongoing mental torment too. The nerve-wracking tension of battle, their capture and their treatment behind enemy lines had all sapped their mental strength. In some places behind English lines, the Tommies' endless desire for souvenirs resulted in theft and plunder: prisoners were threatened and forced to hand over money and especially watches. Some comrades had had even worse experiences. One man reported that he and a number of other German officers, not long after their capture, had been ordered to kneel down in a line, and that the English had then proceeded to shoot the defenceless men one by one. He had fled, and was captured a second time by less bestial representatives of the British Army.[41] At night, we would often hear our new comrades leading their units and companies in their dreams; some had to be vigorously awoken to put a stop to their tortured moaning. We tried to make these difficult first days in the camp as easy as possible for them. We founded a loan fund[42] from which they could borrow up to 20 shillings. The kitchen and the store willingly allowed them to buy special rations on credit. Prisonörs who had been in the camp longer helped them with their purchases and supported them where possible by giving money, underclothing and items of uniform.

Amongst those who arrived in the summer were some who could look back on a most unusual personal story of the war. Corvette Captain Sachsse and Lieutenant Straehler, the latter from the IV marine division, the former the commander of the *Iltis*, had been imprisoned by the Japanese when Tsingtao was taken in November 1914. In November 1915 they escaped from the prisoner-of-war camp at Fukuoka and managed to reach Shanghai by travelling through Korea. Their attempt to forge a route through neutral Asia and reach home via Afghanistan, Persia and Turkey, was thwarted when they were forced to turn around in Karshan (Chinese Turkestan) by Russian and English protests at their progress westwards. Heading eastwards instead, they reached New York. In November 1916 they were discovered as stowaways on a Norwegian steamer and, having presented themselves as civilians, they were imprisoned on the Isle of Man.[43] When the exchange of officers through

Kapitän Sachsse.

Holland began, they set aside their civilian disguises and, as a result, they were transferred to our camp.

Captain von Ledebur had a painful history. He had arrived in East Africa in 1901 and had been a company commander and district governor there. A year before the outbreak of war, he had moved north and was living near Mount Meru. In September 1916, fighting the English, he was severely wounded and the German medics had no choice but to amputate his leg. Soon afterwards, the hospital fell into English hands. As soon as he could be moved, he was transported to a hospital in Egypt and then to Malta. The German government demanded his repatriation, but it was not until June 1918 that he was transferred from Malta to an English hospital and then to us in Skipton. Lieutenant Commander Wenninger came to us from prison. As a U-boat commander he had sunk 150,000 tonnes of English shipping.

Administration

The camp administration was now working relentlessly in an attempt to meet the growing demands at this time. The individual services in the camp improved and simplified their procedures. To nurture the unified spirit of the officer corps and in particular to make our relationship with the administration more fruitful, August saw the appointment of an officer at the head of each barracks. These men met often, eventually every Saturday, to consult with the officers of the camp administration and with the senior German officer, to communicate the wishes and opinions of their men and, conversely, to take back to their respective group of men suggestions and decisions from the camp administration and to ensure their implementation. The increase in our monthly remuneration from the German government (1 shilling a day for high-ranking officers, ½ shilling for lieutenants), which we received via the Swiss Legation as back-pay for the period from January to August 1918 and from then on every month, gave us great pleasure.

In September and October there was also a change in the English administration of the camp. Eley, the English assistant commandant, had already left us. The unapproachable attitude of this lanky, spindly, spirited representative of English masculinity had made such an impression on us that amongst ourselves we had called him 'Der Graf', or 'The Count'. One prisonör unfortunate enough to be 'caught' using this expression at the evening parade was sentenced, despite his protestations, to several months in the cells, since the English interpreter had mistaken 'Graf' for 'giraffe' and insisted on his interpretation. The commandant left us in September. His replacement was a Scottish colonel, Ronaldson, who had most probably been removed from field duties due to his injuries: he walked with a stick. Colonel Ronaldson was the opposite of his predecessor: an upstanding, jovial soldier who had a natural flair for the military and approached us in an open, humane way. He almost always accepted our requests. Amongst other things, the regulations for the walks were revised and more free time was granted for special evening festivities. *Icankillyou* was awarded the rank of major and became assistant commandant. The role of adjutant was filled by Nicoll, a young captain of whom we had a less than favourable opinion. Aunt Frieda, to his childish glee, was awarded a second (lieutenant's) star.

The health of the comrades during this period was generally good. In July and August, however, a serious influenza epidemic broke out in Yorkshire, from which we did not escape unscathed. A number of officers lay for weeks in the hospital. Various preventative measures were implemented: the barracks' floors were washed repeatedly with Lysol solution, scheduled ventilation of the living spaces was organised, walks were strongly advised and more opportunities were provided. So the disease passed over us without lasting damage, while several of the English guards did not survive. In July, a team of doctors visited us again to decide on the possible exchange of the sick and the wounded amongst us, and sick officers from other camps also came to Skipton. Following this medical inspection, in October four comrades received permission for repatriation.

We were also able to set up arrangements for our dental care.

Die Häupter unserer
Lieben:

Lt. Col. Eley.

'The Heads of our Loved Ones':
Lt. Col. Eley.

"At first it was very difficult to access a dentist, since they all refused to treat German prisoners. Thanks to the mediation of the English commandant, the best dentist in Skipton agreed to attend the camp once a week, on a Sunday morning, and otherwise only for emergency cases; later, he came twice a week. Dental treatment took place in the hospital barracks. The only available drill was an old, rusty piece of apparatus. The English commandant sought assistance from military dentists in York but to no avail. Prices were 10 shillings to 12 shillings and sixpence for a filling, and 5 shillings to have a tooth extracted."

von Recum.

Those with eye problems were permitted several visits to Leeds, escorted by English guards, for eye examinations and the purchase of spectacles.

(D) From the Armistice to the Signing of the Peace Treaty

(11th November 1918 to 28th June 1919)

Armistice

On the morning of 11th November, the day of the Armistice, as the noisy jubilation of the English guards rang over the barbed wire from outside the gates of the camp and colourful bunting fluttered in the wind all over the English barracks, pain and grief arose in our German souls with an intensity almost beyond our grasp. Serious, strong men could be seen weeping like children. Many who, just days before, had so eloquently debated whether Germany might still have a chance of victory, became grim and taciturn; others erupted in passionate outbursts of vitriol or lament. From that day forward, a shadow descended upon our lives in captivity, remaining and then intensifying under the agonising pressure of the events that followed. For two days, the walks did not take place. We neither wanted nor were able to expose ourselves to the triumphant and sneering looks of the English. Most of us could no longer find any enjoyment in the camp's amusing artistic offerings. The musical evenings ceased. The enormity of the burden that weighed on our minds only became truly clear when the initial shock had sunk in. Our every thought strained to comprehend and interpret the new circumstances. In our hurt we clutched at any vestige of hope. Each man sought the company of his comrades, looking for consolation and support from the strong; the passionate struggled against the weary, the optimists against the pessimists. But everywhere, through the agitation of these times, our fervent, deeply wounded love of the Fatherland resounded. This restless searching of our thoughts, this hatred and love, this hopelessness followed by renewed unshakable faith has a harrowing effect on anyone reading the prisoners' diaries. One man concentrates his attention on family and home. He sees in his mind's eye all the dishonour that has been cast onto our great Fatherland heaped onto his father and mother, onto his wife and child and onto the lovely, once blessed life of his home town or village. Another sees Germany's history, and now he clenches his fists and watches as, at the end of our victorious ascent as a people, the end approaches, reducing to nothing our centuries-long struggle for our precious cultural existence. Many contemplate the hardships of war, the death of comrades, our own willingness to sacrifice ourselves during those years of war and our awareness of the divine justice of our struggle, and then like a death cry the realisation, 'in vain'. Fathers and grandfathers talk of the 1870s and appear to weep for the ruins of their work. Hot shame burns through these wild, crushing words, spoken with manly rage and deep hatred: crippling weakness and blind faith often blended together in the same sentence. We agonise about the future of the German people. We question our own futures in these uncertain times. We grapple fiercely with the turmoil of German domestic politics, some asserting their opinions with unrestrained emotion, others looking objectively and rigorously to comprehend the truth and find meaning in it. The reasons for Germany's collapse preoccupy us all. The question of blame drives opposing minds to heated arguments. We sit for hours poring over the English newspapers, trying to read between the lines. However, the English perspective and the cold will to destroy staring up at us from these pages never cease to upset us. Only a few of the more objective English publications are available to us. Some back issues of German newspapers from London are permitted (*Frankfurter Zeitung*, *Berliner Tageblatt*). Later the War Office renews the ban on German newspapers, but the censors are lenient and allow most of the mailings through. However, even our home newspapers offer us no consolation. They only confirm that Germany collapsed both internally and externally. Experts in economic and financial matters give lectures to large audiences and, despite the lack of certainty, search for at least some guidelines for our future. Others would have us reflect on ourselves and the indestructible strength of the German people. At our Sunday worship the preachers seek to shed religious light on the situation to enable us to come to terms with it through the power of our inner lives.

Difficult Times

Outside storms – inside cares.
Yearning with each new dawn.
The path is happed in loneliness.
Only the will to shape the future
Remains, and feeds my strength.

Every day, at all hours,
I let the latest complaint
sink in my silent breast.
Only the will's brightness
Bears me, as I bear it.

You, my heart, and you two hands,
From the ruins of great fires
build my new world.
Much sank. The will holds.
Help me, that I might fulfil it!

Stoltenberg.

O, to be a Titan!

To fight with a Titan's fire and fury
For Germany, slash the tightening noose!
Smash these shackling chains
And forge an everlasting peace.

Then, on feathered wings of eagle and swan,
With voices raised in jubilant song,
Unto the front of storm-tossed skies
Heading for Germany, proudly rise!

And descend, of a sudden, to one small dwelling,
Wherein abides a wife, all swollen-eyed!
Dear God, I think she'll no more cry,
though eyes may blink as our tears come welling.

Stoltenberg.

We had hoped that the Armistice would grant us our freedom. As Germany was now defenceless, there was, militarily, no reason to detain us any longer. But the negotiations in Spa dashed our hopes. Not even a single concession was made in the camp. Bitterness grew amongst us. It was decided, at a gathering of the barrack captains, to lodge a protest with the British War Office via the Swiss Legation against our wrongful continued captivity and to inform the German government of our action. A commission produced the document, which was sent to the Swiss Legation on 27th January.[44] It read:

"In accordance with legal and humanitarian regulations, the German prisoners of war expect their release. The psychological effects of imprisonment are well known already. In the last few years, it has been a constant, imperative demand of humanity to shorten the period of suffering of prisoners of war, and this has been the objective of a series of treaties. During this time of war, we prisoners were sustained by the belief that, in spite of our suffering, we were complying with military necessity, and were fulfilling our duty in whatever way we could by contributing to a victorious outcome to the war. This legal and psychological incentive is now lost. The limitation of freedom in times of war, according to modern sensibilities and laws, should only go as far as is necessary for the fulfilment of military goals. These include the settlement of peace and the implementation of the conditions of peace. However, both of these goals are now, militarily, fully assured. The express objective of the Armistice was to render the resumption of hostilities on the part of Germany impossible, and to subject the country to every one of the non-negotiable conditions set by the Allies. Furthermore, the conditions for a peace settlement, which are usually the content of preliminary peace talks, have already been agreed in President Wilson's Fourteen Points, which constitute the content of the Armistice and have been officially accepted by Germany. After the implementation of the conditions of the Armistice, the state of war has indeed ceased, the basis of the preliminary peace has now been agreed and only requires formal settlement; the establishment, the recognition and the possible enforced implementation of further individual conditions are guaranteed by the military provisions of the Armistice. There is no longer any military necessity for the continued detention of the prisoners of war; there is no longer any legal basis for the existence of 'prisoners of war'. Restrictions of freedom for reasons other than military necessity, however, would have the character of a penal sentence or even slavery, both of which are contrary to progressive, modern sensibilities and which for decades, even centuries, have been excluded from the legal systems of modern states. The conditions of the Armistice do not state, and for humanitarian reasons it is not to be expected, that there should be any changes to the legal rights of prisoners of war. Therefore, if Article 10 of the Armistice states that the repatriation of German prisoners of war should be agreed as part of the preliminary peace agreement, then the implementation of the Armistice and the meeting of the Peace Conference indicate that the time has indeed come to make these arrangements. This moment cannot be postponed indefinitely, arbitrarily or through formalities. Rather, the general principles of law and an interpretation of the wording of the Armistice agreement give us the indisputable right to demand our release.

However, there has in fact been no mention of a formal settlement of the preliminary peace agreement or the question of our release. We therefore remain preoccupied by the dreadful thought that, for no purpose and despite the lack of any real or legal necessity, we are being robbed of our freedom. The effects of this are magnified to an overwhelming extent by the particular circumstances of this war and the present situation in Germany. Each of us has been subjected to imprisonment, not just for months, but for years. On the Front and in captivity, the greatest psychological and physical demands have been placed on each of us for years, and we have been almost entirely alienated from our homeland, our families, and our social and professional circles. Upon cessation of the active state of war, all comrades have returned to their loved ones; even the English prisoners of war returned home in time for Christmas. In addition, radical changes are gaining ground in the social and economic life of Germany which demand the full intellectual and active cooperation of every individual. Another few months, and the possibility of securing a livelihood and adjusting to the new circumstances will be permanently lost to many. Under these circumstances our longing for our homeland becomes so overwhelming that our mental and physical resilience, already shaken, erodes completely; we are beset by psychological and financial harm, which cannot be put right later in life. In fact, the thought of continuing to have our freedom withheld for the foreseeable future without reason and through no fault of our own, and of our isolation from the life of our fellow Germans, torments our souls and causes more pain than the most degrading punishment. It is an irrefutable humanitarian imperative to bring this torment to an end by releasing us, and to make it easier for us to endure until then by announcing the date of our release.

The nature of our accommodation and rations further intensifies both our mental and our physical torment. We live in camps, cut off from all communication with the outside world. Even the officers, from the youngest lieutenant to the captains over 40 years of age, are mostly housed 24 to a wooden hut. For the storage of our belongings, there is usually only one crate each available; each hut is heated by a single stove. There is no possibility, not even for one single hour of the day, of pursuing one's own thoughts away from others, either alone or with one or two comrades. Each room dedicated to intellectual work must accommodate 50, 100 or more officers in an insufficiently heated space, relying on only three lamps. For the purposes of personal hygiene, warm showers are available, but only once per week and in a cold room shared by 24 officers. The allocated rations do not allow us to assemble and prepare even one meal a day in the English middle class style. We receive no German newspapers, nor any new German books. Two short letters per week constitute our entire connection with our homeland but the censors, the delivery time (which can be months), and the restrictions on legal transactions make any real conversation or the realisation of professional or commercial interests impossible. Many of our comrades have found out only months after the event that their closest relatives had been suffering from severe illnesses or had died. On a short visit to these camps, conditions may seem bearable. A third party, however, cannot possibly imagine how this herding together and the suffocation of intellectual exchange affect our souls. It is clear that, until recently, these conditions were in part determined by the state of war and the lack of food. In both respects, however, a fundamental change has occurred, the effects of which have caused these conditions to become unbearable. Even the recent concessions (in particular, better heating and lighting, improvements to our rations, and an overall improvement in communications with home), only implemented after repeated requests, cannot change the fact that our accommodation is worse than that of the reserves immediately behind the front line, and worse than that of the lower classes here and at home. We are housed in wooden huts in a crowded camp, and we are robbed of our physical and mental freedom. In the absence of justification for these conditions, they must be regarded as not only unjust and unbearable but also degrading to every sentient human being, particularly to every soldier who was merely doing his duty and had risked his life to do so. Human decency demands that these undignified and dishonourable conditions should be brought to an end through our release.

It is not only we, the prisoners of war, who are suffering as a result of our continued captivity, but also millions of innocent women and children, fathers and mothers who, for years, have been longing for their spouses, their fathers and their sons, and whose need for their providers and their advisors becomes more desperate every day. And so the result of our continued imprisonment is ultimately that it is not mainly Germany's military might nor the German soldiers themselves who are affected but rather millions of innocents. These innocent people have been promised the blessings of peace, and long for them from deep within their hearts. It is these millions, too, who are pleading for our release at the earliest possible opportunity. However, above all, we make this plea in accordance with our conviction that our demand is simply for the justice that every valiant soldier deserves. Only by agreeing to this can the humanitarian imperative and the principles of justice and righteousness be realised that ought to be the objective of this war and peace."

The entirely dismissive response received on 19th March 1919 came as no great disappointment to us. It proved to us once again how powerless we were and how unenthusiastically our concerns were represented by the neutral embassy. Our indignation with the English and their allies grew all the more, as it was precisely at this time that there was talk in the English newspapers and in Paris of our 'atrocities' during the war and our inhumane treatment of prisoners. This was an insult to our sense of honour. We had all stood on the field of battle and were aware that we had fought the war as a cultured nation. The terrible weapons of annihilation had also been used by our enemies in the same way. Some of our comrades could testify, from their own experience of serving in German camps, that enemy prisoners in Germany had not been treated inhumanely; this was confirmed to us by some Tommies who had recently been released from German prisoner-of-war camps. On the other hand, while behind the Front, we had often experienced treatment from the English that does them no credit. We considered it our duty, therefore, to compile a list of these unfortunate experiences and bring them to the attention of the Swiss Legation. Out of the 500 prisoners in the camp, only 104 contacted the commission appointed for this purpose, less than the total of those affected. The following 'souvenirs' have been stolen from them by the Tommies: 83 watches, 22 chains, 18 rings, 24 cases, 1 medallion, 31 wallets, 25 purses, 2 pairs of binoculars, 1 shaving kit, 1 cigarette lighter, 5 fountain pens, 2 cameras, 1 bracelet, 1 map pouch, 1 shirt, 1 pair of breeches, 3 coats, 1 pair of boots, 1 pair of scissors, 3 pairs of gloves, 1 fur coat, 1 fur waistcoat, 2 pairs of fur boots, 1 cap, 5 sets of underwear and in 26 cases various other items of clothing, numerous medals and epaulettes and 5,210 Deutschmarks in cash. The total value of the stolen items added up to 17,000 Deutschmarks. The Swiss Legation handed this list over to the War Office, which cleverly got itself off the hook. The envoy wrote to us, 'I am writing to inform you that our Legation has received the message from the War Office that it cannot pursue these demands without more precise elucidations which would make it possible to identify the relevant hospitals and first-aid stations.' Who among us was capable of naming the English units that had taken him prisoner and the field hospitals behind the Front to which he had been temporarily admitted!

The Kaiser's Birthday 1919

At this time of intense distress, the day approached that previously had been celebrated with grateful pride and joyful hope: the Kaiser's birthday. Nearly all of us felt connected in loyalty and reverence towards that lonely man in Amerongen, because brute force cannot loosen the ties which had been entered into in freely chosen devotion. But he was no longer our supreme leader, our homeland no longer an Empire. And should we be celebrating, while he sorrowed alone? We resolved therefore to abstain from a large celebration involving all comrades. On the morning of 27th January, all the officers and men in the camp gathered in the Old Mess. The senior German officer made the following speech:

"Comrades,

A new age has descended violently upon our Fatherland. Much that was sacred, and that we treasured, to which we were devoted with heart and soul, has been trodden into the dust; much of it has already been completely lost. The 27th January, too, has ceased to be a national holiday; no longer can we observe the birthday of our Kaiser in the traditional manner.

But for us, it will always remain a cherished day of remembrance. As a display of our shared sentiments, we therefore gather here today to proclaim publicly that our regard for the Kaiser continues unchanged and will remain, and that our devotion to him and love for him will be maintained with German constancy, even though legal obligations no longer exist. Today we do not wish to debate how it could have happened that the Empire lost its Kaiser, and we our supreme commander; we do not wish to make our hearts heavy today with thoughts of the terrible outcome of the war, brought about by events at home.

But it is never too soon to raise our voices in defence of our Kaiser against the brazen attacks of our triumphant, gloating enemies. We owe it to the Kaiser and to our own honour to meet these attacks with outrage and contempt; it is our sacred duty to uphold the pure and unblemished name and character of our Kaiser before the whole world.

We know the Kaiser, we know that all his deeds have arisen from the purest and noblest of intentions; and those who now insult and vilify him, they too once recognised the integrity of his character and admired his virtues, as a man and as a ruler. The rector of Oxford University could not have better expressed the views of the enlightened and educated world about the Kaiser than with the words he spoke when awarding him his doctorate by diploma: 'To an enthusiastic lover of the sciences and patron of the arts – one, moreover, who, by the high ideals that he has pursued and the noble personal example that he has set in [his] reign [...], has appreciably raised the standard of duty and patriotism both amid his own people and among the nations of Europe.'[45]

Yes, duty and patriotism, these are the virtues that the Kaiser, leading by his own glowing example, has planted deep within the souls of his people, and particularly into us, his Officer Corps. With us, comrades, lies the responsibility of ensuring that this seed sown by the Kaiser is not lost in the hearts of our people.

There is no better way of proving our loyalty and gratitude to the Kaiser than by striving to be distinguished amongst our own people through our loyalty, selflessness and love of the Fatherland.

By adapting to the new circumstances at home – as far as our conscience allows – we will continue, each in his own role, to work towards that high aim for which our Kaiser worked, fought and now must suffer: the free development, the prosperity and the happiness of the German Fatherland.

And throughout our labours towards the unity of the German Empire, throughout our work for a free, strong Germany, throughout the defence of our reputation and our national honour against foreign insolence, the proud words of the Kaiser shall serve as our guiding light, our incentive and as council to our conscience: remember that you are a German!

Today the Kaiser must spend his 60th birthday alone, abandoned and far from home. May the country that has received him remain strong in providing hospitality, may the attacks of his enemies be foiled, may the German people soon remember the gratitude they owe the Kaiser, and may they grant him the protection, the tranquility and the peace of our home soil!

In short, we concentrate our wishes into one plea and prayer: God save our Kaiser!"

On the evening of the 27th, small groups of like-minded comrades gathered for quiet celebrations.

Wilson's Fourteen Points and Versailles

In the subsequent months, with heavy hearts, we followed the negotiations in Versailles and the turbulent developments at home. With anger, we heard of the Spartacist battles and the strikes that completely destroyed our economy. We sent both comforting and angry letters to our families, and letters from home with important messages or significant German newspaper reports were posted on the noticeboard. We speculated and argued about the new constitution, about the position of the political parties, the relationship between church and state and about school reform, among other things. The infrequent news from Versailles had us reeling between hope and despair. We clung to Wilson's Fourteen points and did not want to believe that this 'saviour of the world' was a liar or a spineless idealist. But increasingly we came to recognise that our hopes were misguided. The occasional less biased voices in the English newspapers gave unheeded warnings. The English strike movements, upon which those at home were placing so much hope, were really only aiming at domestic political objectives. Victorious peoples do not start revolutions. And how could these movements have been any help to us whatsoever, at this late stage! What use to us now was the slackening of the British Army's discipline, which even we could see from behind the barbed wire: soldiers on duty threw away their weapons and equipment and left, and whole troops of guards went into the town without leave and were later arrested. We saw the pure hatred of the old tiger Clemenceau in his work of destruction. The fact that the English had no interest in our hardship, and wanted only to completely destroy their once-feared opponents, was clear from the words of the English orderly officers with whom we talked on our walks. The limited education of the English, their poor understanding of what it is to be truly human, their isolating pride in their own world view, and their belief in the almost divine right of the British clearly came to light in these representatives of England. We also saw that they were completely under the influence of their own press, which in this free country is subjected to the power of the government to a far greater extent than at home. And the things the press dared to present to the people! Infantile stories, which would have been rejected in no uncertain terms by any moderately educated German. Indeed, one of these noble institutions suggested that 10,000 prisoners should be shot every week, should Germany fail to sign the peace treaty.

Under these circumstances, we were already in no doubt as to the nature of the conditions of the Allies' peace treaty. But when we were faced with the articles in their bare-faced viciousness and brutal destructiveness, we felt as though we had been struck down. Grief, shame, outrage, even hatred possessed us during those days. Even in the camp, we observed the week of mourning organised at home. The administration had the conditions translated into German and provided each barracks with a copy of the document, which according to the will of its creators was intended to introduce a new era of justice and of a new internationalism. In order to expose to everyone the Allies' broken promises, the disastrous consequences for Germany's future and the insult to our German conscience, lectures were held as a kind of demonstration against this most monstrous of treaties, and were attended by many officers and men. The wrath they expressed branded itself on our minds forever: 'We will not forget what you have done' but we do believe in that which is nevertheless true: 'A civilisation that has come crashing down is worth nothing if it does not reflect upon itself and confidently invest everything in its belief in its ancestors and in its future in the world.' It seemed impossible to most of us that Germany could possibly accept this peace treaty. We now forgot our miserable fate; we no longer thought about returning home. The Fatherland was not to take us into consideration: we did not want to become part of the price paid for this disgraceful peace. But the brutal events overrode our ineffectual purposes as prisoners and brought us peace on 28th June. What joyful images we had once had of this day! Now we were experiencing it in sorrow and cheerlessness, and even the certainty that we would soon return home inspired no feelings of joy. Outside, the celebrations of the English guards, the bunting on the towers in the town; in here, broken men!

It was only natural, given the circumstances, that the misery of imprisonment weighed on our souls more heavily than usual. Never did we feel more strongly the violence of the victors, our deprivation, our powerlessness, all the fragmentation of our lives, than in these winter months. Hardship brings people together. So we sought, in a tight community, to overcome our cruel fate and our mutual tribulations together. The winter had drawn in behind the barbed-wire fence; the greater freedom of the summertime had passed by. On the hills and in the valley, a heavy fog descended again. Gales shook the barracks; rain drummed down onto the roofs. The snow arrived late. Now, once again, we were crowded into the close domesticity of the barracks. Winter activity in the barrack communities thrived once again. In many respects, it developed much more pleasantly than in the previous year. The barracks were heated again from 1st October. The supply of coal was more plentiful, though still far from sufficient. Most importantly, however, the new commandant did not renew the loathsome regulation that heating would only be allowed from 2 o'clock in the afternoon. So the beloved stove emitted its warmth in the mornings too, and enticed the prisonörs out of the gloom and the rain of the English winter days, and away from the mud of the camp's paths, into its hospitable vicinity. Now the rooms offered us a more appealing prospect. Most of the prisonörs had hidden the harsh lines of the windows behind curtains, and for protection against the cold and wind had stuffed all the holes and joints in the walls with paper or had even covered them over with wallpaper. The longing of individuals to possess their own homes, places into whose silence and seclusion they could escape, soon gave the interior of the barracks an entirely new appearance. Our comrades built boxes, that is to say they built walls around two or three beds and created the illusion of a room. This activity had already begun in the summer when we created partitions with cloth. However, the actual building phase only began in early winter; we were now working with more experience and with better materials. One comrade describes ...

The Creation, Existence and Sad End of the Box

"Deeply rooted in the character of the German is a longing to have his own roof over his head, for a hearth with its foundations in his own land. So we should not be surprised if two comrades in neighbouring beds in the barracks develop a heartfelt desire to emulate their ancestors or to follow the modern trend by building themselves a house.

The idea was born and became a desire, a decision was made and it grew into action. And how it grew! However, like all innovations, this house-building plan, which went against the traditions, customs and habits of the barracks, came up against both overt and covert opponents from the very beginning. The would-be builders were unwise enough to reveal their ambitious goals to the profane ears of their comrades during a stove council; within just three weeks, this resulted in constant, mischievous questioning on the progress of the work, even about the topping-out ceremony, though it was quite clear just from a glance that the work was still very much 'in statu nascendi'. But it progressed, because these energetic entrepreneurs had taken the decision to subscribe to *The Times* starting from the first of the following month. They decided on *The Times* not because it provided the most captivating divorce dramas and blood-thirstiest defamations against the 'bloody Huns', but for purely architectural reasons. The walls of the villa, including the fireproof partition walls and the roof covering, were to be constructed of paper, considered to be the most modern building material of present times besides reinforced concrete, and one issue of *The Times* was well-known to provide more than enough for a generous covering layer.

The following month was therefore spent diligently collecting material by means of the subscription. Meanwhile, the future financing of the construction was thought out and it was decided that the accumulation of capital from the next payday would be used to negotiate with Mr James for the necessary steel reinforcements. Laymen without the faintest idea of the difficulties involved in preparing such an enterprise seemingly felt some undignified competitive envy (unsurprisingly these were mostly the owners of so-called 'cloth boxes', who attempted to substitute the solid walls essential for a true homestead by hanging up tawdry blue or green fabric), which led them to try and dampen the enterprising spirit of the young builders by offering entirely unprofessional advice under the guise of support, or even by openly offering odds that repatriation or other similarly unlikely events would occur before the topping-out ceremony, and other such undermining tactics. In spite of this, on payday, industrious activity began on the planned building site in the corner. With scant regard for 'damage of royal property', holes were drilled in the floorboards, and the thick wire, which had been successfully purchased from Mr James, was fed through and fixed firmly in place, and then attached in a similar manner to the barracks ceiling, thus creating the corner and door pillars. On the very same day, the transverse and T-beams were installed in the form of thin wire and as evening fell, thanks to the unwavering energy of the builders, the building was structurally complete.

Porridge was to be used as the binding agent or mortar. Porridge can stick, glue or cement anything. Porridge transforms the most implausible of raw materials into ideal structural components, turns little pieces of

Finance.

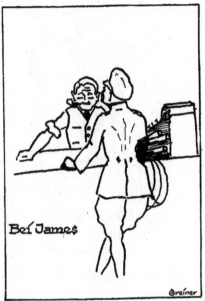

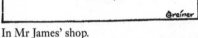

In Mr James' shop.

Laying the foundations.

horse meat into beef goulash with a tasty sauce, makes the most beautiful and palatable chocolate dishes from just a small amount of cocoa powder with added water; without any additional ingredients, depending on how it is prepared, it takes the form of coffee macaroons, gruel, Viennese pastries or crispy brown roasts. Porridge is a general-purpose material, similar to the equally well-known custard powder. Porridge was also to help in this venture, providing the multiple layers of newspaper pages with the necessary energy and willpower to remain upright. Over the next few days, in a show of unparalleled self-sacrifice, the builders each took their own allotted morning rations from the porridge pan and, wasting away, pooled their spoils together in the white pots under their beds. Partly because the Christmas period was approaching, but also partly because the barracks' inhabitants assumed a threatening attitude due to the aromatic fragrance of these mortar pots, the comrades decided the collected stock of porridge was sufficient, and one morning began to spread the mixture neatly onto the opened newspaper pages with the aid of a shaving brush and a hairbrush, before hanging them over the wires of the building frame. And so, soon enough, a structure appeared in the barracks which, showing only heads and feet from the outside, was reminiscent of the public conveniences in the cities of France and Belgium, the only difference being that the outside world was presented, not with an austere, black-tarred blank space, but rather with one which was lavishly illustrated with the most beautiful images from the *London News*, *Graphic*, *Sphere* and other magazines, so that it immediately became a showpiece of the barracks.

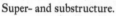

Super- and substructure.   Porridge.

After this quite extraordinary achievement, however, a truthful chronicler is obliged to report that the work did in fact come to a halt, and the derision and scorn in the barracks reached their peak. The Christmas period was approaching, and it gradually became clear to the builders that the current conditions were truly intolerable. After serious discussion, at the start of the week before Christmas they returned to work to complete the construction. In a powerful surge of energetic activity, they filled in gaping holes, hung the ceiling constructed from triple layers of wrapping paper, and then began the interior decoration. Thanks to a loan successfully obtained from the barracks kitty, three rolls of wallpaper were purchased from Mr James: a black lattice pattern delightfully decorated with colourful sprigs of flowers, reminiscent partly of the harsh reality of barbed wire, partly of the poetry of a young girl's bedroom. At the sight of this, the barracks' residents were moved to spontaneously celebrate the exquisite taste of the home owners. It was with a combination of love and a double helping of gruel that this elegant example of wallpaper art was applied to the walls. A renowned artist, who had close links to the theatre group and its supply of paint pots, was able to bring the colourful symphonies of the walls into harmony with the lily-white ceiling by means of a frieze, beautifully drawn in whitewash, whose brilliant white was playfully trying to escape into the deep black of the border.

Fast drying soon curbed any aspirations of the black border to run down like stalactites over the delicate patterns of the wallpaper, ensuring that the impression of polished, peaceful elegance retained complete serenity. The architects heightened this impression through tasteful interior design and

Trial sleep.

The completed villa.

artistic wall decoration. Without further ado, the customary layout of the beds perpendicular to the barracks' walls was dispensed with, and one of these was pushed lengthways against the wall as a divan. The ugly cabinet, which took up so much space, was relegated to the hallway, and its place under the window was taken by the pretty table, made of wooden planks and covered with green canvas. The entrance to this 2½ x 3½ metre delight of a room was screened off by a royal blue blanket hung as a curtain, with a bachelor corner created to the left of the door with the aid of a few issues of *Vie Parisienne*, while the back wall, decorated with prints of rather more serious content, led to a more academic corner where a bookcase held dictionaries and textbooks of all living languages of the European continent alongside publications of a legal and commercial nature. The obligatory green curtains still hung next to the window, which continued to provide Biedermeier-style hanging space as a substitute for the lack of wardrobes.

The other end wall stood out, thanks to its blaze of colours and a painting of a lady in 'bleu' with slender legs and an equally slender umbrella. None of the little touches which give a real home the magic of intimate homeliness were forgotten. A retired potato basket, prettily whitewashed, successfully assumed the duties of a wastepaper basket, sardine tins made themselves useful as ashtrays, the woollen hat from Le Havre served as a laundry bag, the Dunhill collection, the pride of its owners, was resplendent on the wall in a pipe rack made from cigar-box wood, while a further container afforded smokers the necessary tapers: in short, the joyful homeowners were ready to present the fruits of their successful labours to the public, when the falling darkness revealed a serious omission. The room was completely dark; when the curtain draped across the doorway was closed, it did not allow through even a single beam of light from the barracks lamp. What was to be done? Time was short for the builders; there was only one day until Christmas Eve. Anxiously, trusting that necessity would indeed be the mother of invention, they retired to their beds and woke up inspired the next morning. One knowing look was all it took, and by the time of the midday meal they had 'found' a rubber tube in a suitable location, along with a device which seemed to have been created for use as a gas burner. Using cobbler's wax, soap and great skill, they were able to connect these items to the barracks gas pipe, and on Christmas Eve our cosy homestead was no longer lacking that most important of things, a source of light from the ceiling. At that point, no one knew of the dark forces that, according to the English doctor, were being cultivated and had even been incorporated within the fabric of the paper house, and there began a period of complete domesticity and carefree living, probably due mainly to the following discovery. Straight after the official Christmas celebration, the residents returning from the mess at a respectably early hour made the discovery over a bottle of wine that, notwithstanding the snowstorm raging outside and the fact that the stove had gone out, the house itself was warm. Eureka! The problem of modern warm air heating was solved without the need for action on their part. The open gas flame automatically took care of heating the air and the whitewashed paper ceiling prevented it from escaping. What is more, it did not provide only a single level of heat, but rather it was possible to experience and make use of a graduated range of microclimates. In England's normal rainy weather, the usual temperate zone was found at around 'chair height', one's head was quite a few latitudes closer to the equator, while one's feet seemed to make acquaintance with one of the polar regions, and during severe frosts it was not uncommon to find the residents and their visitors standing on tables and chairs while conversing or reading a good book in order to take advantage of the tropical climate near the ceiling, which, to the uninitiated, may at first have seemed somewhat peculiar. But during the normal English rainy weather, as has been mentioned, the quiet and tranquil life of the prisoner continued between the four walls, independently of the heat and light sources in the rest of the barracks. This *buen retiro* became the preferred location for coffee groups and birthday parties. The rest of the barracks' occupants made a pleasant habit of whiling away the time after the evening parade with a friendly tête-à-tête at the draped window, and the popularity of the homeowners grew enormously, particularly in very cold weather. And so things continued smoothly for two months.

In the meantime, however – according to the English doctor – the dark presence had gorged itself and developed in the humid climate of the ceiling. In similar individual abodes which had sprung up everywhere in the camp barracks, similarly sinister forces had taken root, fostered by the absence of light and air – according to the English doctor – and in mid-February they became aware of their own power: influenza bacteria attacked their unsuspecting victims and accompanied them out into the hospitals – according to the English doctor.

Meanwhile, war was declared on the abandoned homesteads. By order of the English doctor, they were torn down and razed to the barracks floor.

The same fate befell our homeowners. Gone was the lily-white ceiling, the end wall was dismantled, the royal blue blanket returned to protecting a shivering body, and a single tall column remained to bear witness to past glory: the bachelor corner, under the neutral guise of a draught-screen, escaped the doctor's wrath."

Schulte, H.

While snow or rain was falling outside, and so often the harsh English winter storms rattled against the walls, our band of exiled comrades now inhabited these box colonies. Fate had brought us together here from all regions of Germany and from all professions. Men of all ages, of the most diverse fundamental attitudes and differing life experiences, had to learn to live together here.

As in the previous year, our dear stove drew heat-loving creatures around itself. There was a flourishing of the oft-mentioned ...

Stove Council

"It has been some time since the mess orderly used the ashtray to signal the official ending of the evening meal*, but still I sit here and, after the usual evening serving of porridge (2 shillings and 2 pence per month), force down my third mouthful of 'tender young peas'. I'm sure the reader's mouth is watering, since the mere thought of tender young peas naturally seduces the soul with the dreamlike image of a magnificent schnitzel with delicious slices of lemon and capers. The harsh reality of life as a prisoner is far removed from this comforting fantasy. Firstly, as my eyes search the plate they see not tender young peas, but old ones, at least three years old; secondly, are they actually peas? Full of sorrow, I search the porridge for the bacon that was advertised on the menu; I find that it is doing an incredibly good job of hiding from me.

The task, more a chore than a pleasure, is finally done. I take to my heels and rush through the rain (does it ever stop raining in Skipton!) back to my barracks. I open the door. My eye is well-trained to spot certain things and it catches two comrades who are just taking their 'home-cooking' from the stove with an almost motherly, loving look in their eyes. I sense the delightful

---

* In some messes, an orderly waved an ashtray to signal that the mess captain had risen from the table.

aromas of the roasting tin wafting beneath my nose. Dark forces rise within me, hideous envy tears at my very soul.

The two gas lamps, which are supposed to provide light to twenty-four men, burn dimly. The wind whistles through the cracks in the floor. An uncomfortable dampness pervades the oppressive gloom. But there it stands, the beloved stove, our best friend. Broad and stocky, it stands in the centre of the barracks emanating waves of warmth. Dangling sweetly above it from the rafters, a pea-meal sausage, a pair of boots, a box on a string containing something mysterious, three pairs of socks and a suitcase: all this simply for the sake of order, as only order-loving types hang up their things to dry. And almost everything is damp here: Sunday trousers, the porridge reserves, bed sheets and towels, shoes and curtains, book spines and hairbrushes.

Now I move like greased lightning to get a chair and secure the best possible position. Every man is thinking the same thing though, and soon enough there are five, then seven, and finally fourteen men sitting around the stove: one is straddling his chair and another is sitting sideways, one is

Der Ofenrat.

The stove council.

squatting and another has his legs outstretched. Twenty-eight eyes bore into the stove, intently enough to frighten the poor thing.

The barrack captain, also known as the 'sheikh' or the 'hut director', arrives back from his evening stroll in a dignified manner. His glance darts over the circle of dozing men, then he lets loose the poisoned arrow. With a sneaky wink, he speaks to someone: 'I'm sticking to it. The farmers have failed. When one man goes hungry and another feasts, where will it all end!' he says, before falling silent. That wakes them up at the stove. 'What!', yells a farmer. 'Do you think we're stupid enough to starve on purpose? Would you have done anything different?' Through a mountain of foam comes the outraged voice of a man shaving at the wash basin: 'Of course, if every man thinks of himself first ...' At this point, a great wave of voices arises from around the stove, engulfing his invaluable final verdict. One man thumps the nearest table and shouts, 'The old government is to blame ...' The learned businessman with his folding table moves closer, rummaging in his papers and interjects, 'The statistics prove it. I know the precise figures ...' But his words too are swallowed up by the torrent of noise. 'So what should Ludendorff do?' 'Don't even mention Foch; my little boy could do a better job!' 'Tell me, how many children do you have again?' The voice of a democrat thunders, 'Ebert, he's the man'. 'Gentlemen,' yells one educated in the ways of parliament, 'no more than five to speak at once.' 'Nonsense,' cries the sheikh, 'that is an unreasonable demand. If each man speaks that bit louder than the rest, he will be heard.'

A few of the men smile at this. But it is good advice. The war of words gets louder. 'How can you accuse me of being unreasonable?' 'In '15, when we were at the Ravka ...' 'Our combat pack was useless too ...' 'If Mr James hadn't ...' 'Hegel, if you take his philosophy of history ...' 'Boy oh boy, the evenings in Cambrai, do you remember ...' 'I will not tolerate ...' 'This bloody coffee ...'

The lanky barrack philosopher sits calmly; he is true to the words which were once composed as a eulogy for him:

> The Sage stays out of their debate,
> Maintains his philosophic calm.
> Determined not to join the scrum,
> He listens by the stove, stays quiet,
> Adjusts his specs, utters a hum,
> Reflects then wisely holds his tongue!

Finally the babble of voices quietens. Two comrades put their heads together and, in hushed tones, discuss the nature of the soul according to Rehmke and Wundt. They are unable to agree on the subject. Two fathers are talking about their children; a wartime student is vividly describing his university. Then the discussions slowly subside. A gloomy silence once again hangs over the drowsy men. One can almost hear the ebb and flow of the silence. 'Doesn't anybody have a 'latrine' for us?'* the barrack sheikh finally asks, attempting to raise the intellectual level once more. "Latrines!' If only there were any 'latrines' worth talking about!', remarks an authority figure from the other side of the stove. I decide to sacrifice myself and restore some much-needed intellect to this situation. 'Did you read that Lloyd George ...' 'Good grief, how many times are you going to tell us that? Firstly, we've all read about it and secondly you've already told us about it twice.' Dejected, I fall silent and, with silent anger, see the malicious glee in the eyes of the others.

Once again, the dull, dark cloud of apathy threatens to envelop us when, with a thud of boots, in comes a young comrade, his face glowing with joy. Fifteen heads spin round, everyone shouts, 'Latrine?' 'Yes, absolutely, it's all true ...!' He throws his hat and stick onto the bed. 'Well, out with it then!' 'Come on, come on ...' Curiosity is at its peak, there is anticipation on every face. The man in possession of the rumour takes a chair, pushes his way into the circle around the stove, looks inquisitively around the group to ensure everybody is curious, and then gives his knee a satisfied rub. 'So, you do know that the English commandant has returned from leave, don't you?' 'Yes, and ...?' 'So, I have it on good authority ...' 'Well it must be rubbish then.' 'Well if you'll let me speak ...' Fifteen voices cry out, 'Carry on, carry on!'

'So, on good authority, that the commandant – because the Tommy who told me, he wouldn't lie to me ...' 'Come on man, what about the commandant?' 'Yes, so the commandant is supposed to have got secretly engaged to a twenty-two-year-old girl while on leave ...' Finally, the secret is out.

There is a lively murmur of voices, applause and objections. 'If that's all you have!' says Karl from Kempten. 'Come on now, if I may be permitted to say so, such an engagement is quite something!' 'What do you actually do, when you want to get engaged?' asks little Ludwig. Karl, the font of all knowledge, now begins a long speech on the subject of how it is done, mentioning the frock coat, tie and collar before ending with some general sex education. The lawyers among us are talking about the legal aspects of engagement in general, the recently-married sheikh and I discuss the expense of furniture these days, two twenty-year-olds consider the influence of weddings upon general popular customs and traditions. Our dentist is holding forth about milk teeth in infants, the farmer is telling a Berliner astonishing things about the mating seasons of cattle, horses, pigs, sheep and other domestic animals, whilst the merchants share their experiences of bridal veils, bed linen and dress fabrics.

And so, the gathering is engulfed in a wave of storytelling, differing opinions and spiteful leg-pulling. For an hour, 'engagement' is the only subject on anybody's mind; the issue is discussed to exhaustion and theorised

---

* Latrine = camp speak for an uncontrolled rumour.

in the context of everyone's occupation and disposition, from the economic, financial, medical, sexual and ethical viewpoints. Incidentally – just between us – of course, the commandant had not become engaged!

But the flow of conversation is interrupted by the shrill sound of the Yorkshire Boar's bell. The pretentious windbags slowly get up. Quickly we brush our teeth and gargle, soon the tips of noses are the only things to be seen poking from under the dark brown blankets. The Tommies come and count us. Then everything is silent, as our thoughts and dreams turn softly towards home."

Kober and others.

Warm–hearted, comforting and carefree life did flourish from time to time in these social circles. After all, we were amongst comrades sharing the same fate, the same hopes and the same concerns. This often got a man through the most difficult of times. And you helped too, dear pipe, with your soothing, billowing clouds, and you, cigarette, dressed in white, with your delicate bluish smoke, and you, expensive rare brown cigar!

A Chapter on Smoking

"There is such a person as a phrenologist. He attempts to judge a person's character by the shape of his skull. There is such a person as a graphologist. He does the same with a person's handwriting. I used to regard such people with a certain scepticism. This has changed since I myself became a nicotinologist. Allow me to explain that this is someone who draws conclusions about a smoker based on what he considers smokeable.

How did I happen to become a nicotinologist? It was easy. I was pushed into it from the first day of my imprisonment. One had no choice, seeing and smelling the smoke all around, and even hearing it (yes, hearing it! Have you never heard the sweet sound of a pipe, like the bubbling of boiling paste?). In the early days, I was overwhelmed by the abundance of sensations on offer. Later, when I was more in the swing of camp life and these sensations became more familiar to me, I tried to restore some kind of order to the chaos, so as to make things clearer. The result follows. I would like to begin by saying that my research was conducted during the time from August 1918 until ..., well, until the exchange that is expected daily; and took place in the prison camps in France, mostly in Le Havre, and in England, in Southampton and Skipton to be precise.

Let me start with a most succinct typology*:

---

* By way of explanation, I am no philologist but many moons ago I studied something similar: veterinary medicine. During the war I became an officer and, in the Skipton camp, a theatre set artist.

I.   Substance: 1. Tobacco 2. Tobacco substitute
II. Form: 1. Cigarette 2. Cigar 3. Pipe tobacco 4. Chewing tobacco 5. Snuff
III. Requisites: 1. Pipes 2. Pipe tools 3. Pipe cleaners 4. Lighters.
IV. Smoker: 1. Who? 2. Nicotinology.

First, then, the substance. Varieties of tobacco are ten a penny; they are legion. Assuming that the reader has sufficient knowledge of tobacco, its origin, its history, etc., I think I can more or less skip this point; the more interesting topic is tobacco substitute.

It is said that there are still people who believe that one cannot smoke everything. Oh, ye of little faith! When I was still at school and used to gorge myself on Karl May's books, I had considerable difficulty in believing his astounding story of desert dwellers using camel dung as a substitute for fuel, and in times of need – and to get to the salient point – even as a tobacco substitute.

This may not be news for smokers who have lived through the last few years of war. How often it seemed that one could still hear the oak wood rustling in one's pipe! Still, I learned a few new things in the prison camps, especially in the early days in France. It was in Le Havre that I was surprised at the sight of a German soldier who seemed to be looking for something by the fence. Now and then he would pick a camomile flower. When I could no longer resist asking what he was doing, he answered in an unmistakable Berlin accent, 'Well, I'll dry it and then I'll smoke it, lieutenant. Guaranteed to work!' It made me think of the times when, as boys, we would stuff our peace pipes with strawberry and chestnut leaves. It would make us feel so wonderfully sick. In Skipton in 1918, we faced the severest tobacco rationing; those were dark days for smokers. One day, a first lieutenant from my table turned up with a pipe stuffed to the brim, much to the envy of the other comrades. Everybody watched as he lit it, but the first cloud of smoke he blew across the table was – well, I'll keep quiet about that – I have to, considering his high rank. He later told me in confidence that he had found a pack of tea, no, sorry, tea substitute, of course – in his first parcel from home. But he reasoned there was no big difference between tea substitute and tobacco substitute. I can vouch for the accuracy of these accounts, and I could even call witnesses to the fact that it didn't stop at camomile flowers and tea. A great many things, from horsehair to – well, to the most unthinkable, went up in smoke before my very eyes, ears and nose in those days of need.

Substance is important, but form is everything. You will agree with this assertion if I mention the example of painting. Paint and paper or canvas are the substance for the artist, and this means a lot, but the painting itself is the form, in other words, everything. Smoking is similar: tobacco, or a substitute, is the substance; the form is … well, the following lines will elaborate.

1. **The cigarette**. Its growing popularity aside, I will mention just a few of the brands which made their mark in Skipton: Three Castles, Three Nuns (some called it 'Three Huns'), Woodbine (probably due to what it was made of), Redbreast (explanation: it made you feel chirpy), among others.
2. **The cigar**. It gives an impression of affluence and is different from the cigarette, in that it is not wrapped in paper, and similar, in that nobody knows what either of them contains.
3. **Pipe Tobacco**. All I will say is this: there are different kinds. The tins can be used as containers for lard, salt, soap and ink and as ashtrays, drinking cups and even top hats for New Year performances; and, last but not least, providing one remembers to turn off the gas tap first, it is possible to use them as oil lamps, if one has any oil.
4. **Chewing tobacco**. It can also be smoked, in which case it is called 'twist'. In combination with other substances it causes nausea, on its own it is deadly. There is some in the canteen, but it isn't that at all, it's chewing gum. It looks like chocolate, and the optimists among us chew it for refreshment on walks or during exercise.
5. **Snuff**. This is something for the older gentleman or for those prisonörs who have tried forms 1 to 4 and are looking for 'something different'. Pepper or toothpowder is a suitable replacement, as long as it smells of peppermint. So that it is clear: substance is important, form is everything. Have you got that, dear reader? It isn't easy.

Substance and form determine the appearance of an object. With tobacco, as with everything else, they only are minor matters compared to the pleasure we derive from it. That is essentially what matters most to human beings. In order to achieve this pleasure though, a lot of equipment and many utensils are needed. Nicotinologists call them requisites, and it is these that I will now address. Pipes take their nigh-on historic first place, but cigar and cigarette holders must be presented alongside them. Here follows a list of the different types.

I. Cigarette holders.
1. In its simplest form, a small tube made of cardboard, quills, elder twigs or wood. Made by the user and cheap; the material can be found in any prison camp.
2. Purchased varieties (does this not highlight brilliantly the contrast of 'simple' vs. 'bought'?). Those who have ever bought anything from Mr James will know what I am talking about. ('I am in the picture,' as my friend Karl says.)

II. Cigar holders. As described under point I, only a little larger.

III. Pipes. I will need to dwell on this subject for a little longer. Dear reader, can you even imagine the magic of the words Dunhill or calabash? I think not.

In which case: there is a pipe manufacturer in England called Dunhill. His pipe bowls are carved from boxwood and they have a white dot on the stem so that the smoker knows which way is up. This is nothing special, you say? Well, of course not, but there are very nice price lists illustrating them. Nothing to write home about either? There's a small aluminium tube in the stem. Still unimpressed? There are people, however, who buy these pipes at abnormally high prices, even though a warranty is no longer provided. You say, dear reader, that a fool and his money are soon parted. You are a hopeless case, you misanthrope! But the calabash! I cry. That shuts you up, ha! However, it is not only called a calabash but has a number of other beautiful names like, for example, Bolshevist's trunk, trunk as in elephant. I pity you, dear reader, when I see you aghast. Somewhere in the dominions of the United Kingdom there grows a kind of squash that becomes as hard as wood and is in the shape of a cow-horn. Cut it off horizontally at its wide and its narrow ends, add a stem to the narrow end and fit into the wide one an insert that is shaped like – for lack of a better expression – a ventilation outlet or perhaps a spectacle frame; and there you have it: a calabash pipe. If you have to pay an extortionate price for one of these pipes, if the insert soon breaks in two and you cannot get hold of a replacement and if you cannot manufacture your own insert from plaster (the mould can be carved out of a $1m^3$ block of wood with a pocket-knife, the opening can be produced by pressing a radish into the moist plaster) – if you can imagine all of this, then you are 'in the picture' about the calabash. Calabash and Dunhill are the most important varieties of pipe for the prisonör. However, there are many other kinds as well. Suffice it to mention medium length, long and very long pipes, cranesbill pipes, health pipes, meerschaum pipes, clay pipes and water pipes; the latter consisting of a mixed pickles jar as the water container, and accommodating two smokers in a recumbent position. (My friend Karl insists that bagpipes have no place on this list and belong in Scotland). There are more varieties of pipe but I must get on.

IV. Pipe Tool. If there is none to hand, use a walking cane, if there is one to hand. I can see the light of comprehension shining in your eyes, dear reader. We call it a pipe poker, a name inspired by the larger tool used for poking around in the stove. It usually consists of three parts: spoon, tamper and spike. Pencils, fountain pens, keys, canes, nails, hammers, bolts, pocket-knives and nail scissors all make suitable substitutes.

V. Kliner, in English 'cleaner'. The simplest type: chicken quills, 1 penny each. The complicated type: small brushes with a wire handle; they are complicated because they tend to break off inside the pipe and make it unusable.

VI. Lighting Paraphernalia. Matches, very popular. In earlier times these were the sort that could only be lit on the brown striking surface, but that was solved long ago. The ones we use today can be lit by striking them against the seat of one's trousers. These matches used to be hard to come by, so hard, in fact, that when a match was about to be lit, the entire hut was summoned to take part in the ritual.

Dear reader, I conclude my observations with a conclusion and the conclusions that can be drawn from it, by which I mean the conclusions concerning the smoker himself. First, in response to the initial question of 'who?', I think I can safely say: all prisonörs. There are a few non-smokers among us, but they too have a connection with the 'smokeable', even if it is merely a feeling of repulsion and contempt.

The most effective way of presenting the conclusions of my nicotinological research is tabulation (a table is always the easiest and most incomprehensible method). Allow me to present it:

The prisonör

who smokes	is
cigarettes	mostly youngish; elegant; if he smokes a lot, not thrifty; a gourmet; passionate; often conceited.
cigars	a little older; respectable; appreciates dignified things; reticent; thoughtful; often a bon vivant.
Twist	if he can stomach it, of a very robust nature.
Dunhill	gullible; with a soft spot for beauty and elegance; extravagant; very particular about clothes and footwear.
Calabash	imaginative, but without a real feeling for beauty; pugnacious; good-hearted but still a revolutionary ('Bolshevist's trunk').
snuff	beyond the pale; taken by long-term prisoners.
substitutes, as listed earlier	not spoilt.
long pipe	a very respectable and amenable citizen.
medium-length pipe	a respectable and amenable citizen.
water pipe	a person of oriental imagination with an appreciation of art, especially drama.
clay or cranesbill pipe	susceptible to the outlandish; in short: simple and without taste.
chewing tobacco	see snuff; also gullible.

Should you, dear reader, have found in the above a grain of truth, I would be delighted, and even more so if you were inspired to do some research yourself. Finally, allow me to add one more thing: even the worst tobacco or substitute becomes bearable when seasoned with a bit of humour – this will turn it into Virginia and Gold-Flake. My heart goes out to any poor prisonör who has lost this essentially German quality. A little dream of home, a joke, a folk song and a pipe of tobacco can always make one forget the bleak hours of imprisonment."

Eberhard Greiner.

The small community in the barracks had also implemented its own rules. We tried, for example, to find regulations for opening doors and windows and to put them into practice. Conflicting proposals and the determination with which they were represented would often lead to serious conflicts. In order to put a stop to the vociferous and incessant prattling of some men after the evening roll call, the time from 11.30 pm to 8 am was declared a 'quiet time'. The same applied to the time after lunch when, for the benefit of those who were in need of a nap or wanted to read in peace and quiet and particularly for those who wanted to work, there was to be silence in the barracks. The following report illustrates the strict observance of this rule:

Quiet Time

Time:	noon, after lunch (porridge soup, turnips).
	The gramophone is playing the Tipperary March.
Place:	an oblong building, called a barracks, with 12 'boxes'. From the central aisle, nobody can be seen, but voices can be heard:
From box 1:	'For heaven's sake! Can't you just keep quiet? It's always the same!'
From box 2:	(in a Bavarian accent) 'I want some peace and quiet!'
From box 3:	'We decided yesterday that this is quiet time!'
From box 4:	'What? Quiet time? In the evening and in the morning when we want to sleep, there are a lot of people who don't observe quiet time, either!'

(The gramophone continues to play, now *La Paloma* for a change. Grunting from the few gentlemen who would like to sleep.)

From box 5:	'Vamba, form of vambum.' 'Fabum, fabam!' 'No – that's wrong.' 'Present tense: Vabaum.' 'That's right!'
From box 6:	'Do you have to read aloud? You're disturbing me.'
From box 7:	'Your chattering after 10pm often disturbs me too – isn't that right, H ...?'
From box 8:	'Don't drag me into this!'
From box 9:	'What a terrific lunch. I'm full to bursting now!' 'Fritz, you idiot, what have you done now?' 'Janek, you little swine, come here a minute!'
From box 10:	'My turn to deal.' '18, 20, 24, 36 ...' 'Your turn!' 'Clubs are trumps!'
From box 11:	'Erm, erm, that's impressive!'

From box 12: 'Put on a Richard Wagner record for a change!'
From box 1:   'There's custard in the canteen!'
From box 4:   (half asleep) 'What is there in the latrines?'
From box 6:   'tan $((A - B)/2)$ / tan $((A + B)/2)$ = $(a - b)/(a + b)$'
From box 4:   'What's the German for *exchange*?'
Voices from all boxes: 'You don't know that? Unbelievable! It's *Austausch*!'
Enter our Bavarian foreign correspondent through the barracks door:
'Have you heard the latest 'latrine'? The camp will be closed by 15th March; I
have it straight from the commandant!' 'Don't talk such rubbish.' 'Ok then!'
A trumpet signal.
Coffee time. Farewell, quiet time!

Luckey.

This peaceful life, eventful on its own small scale, drove many sorrows away.
This was enhanced by the ever-growing enthusiasm for intellectual pursuits
that would flourish especially on winter days that kept us indoors. Allow me
to present here an overall picture of our educational activities.

Quiet Rooms

From the early days of our camp life in Skipton, one of the most pressing
matters was the question of where we might work without being disturbed.
The English camp administration at first allocated room C as a working space.
Since this did not meet our requirements, the commandant eventually gave in

Hard labour.

to our demands and assigned a bigger room (A) as our public working space, a room that had previously been unused and locked up. Until the end of our imprisonment, we had to make do with just these two rooms A and C, where we could work with relatively little disturbance.

In the Skipton camp we kept ourselves busy with lively intellectual activity. A large number of younger comrades, who had been torn from their schools, universities and apprenticeships by war and immersed in the field of battle, used their enforced leisure time to continue their studies and to fill the gaps that the war had left in their knowledge. Most of the older comrades, too, who had been leading a civilian life before the war, filled the long period of time during which they were condemned to inactivity with intellectual self-improvement. As a result, the shared chairs and tables in the quiet areas could no longer satisfy demand. One after another small tables appeared, and the carpenter's workshop had its work cut out to meet the many requests for small desks. Later, in an attempt to render the rooms more homely, the walls were papered up to half the window height, the ceiling painted white, the doors equipped with draught excluders and the windows fitted with curtains. The cost was covered by the officers' voluntary donations. During the winter months, life centred round the few iron stoves that barely warmed the rooms; during the summer months, activities were evenly distributed between the two rooms, and it was only in the evenings that those sitting in the far corners would move closer to the few gas lamps that illuminated our place of intellectual activity.

Bibeljé.

Courtesy of a comrade, a letter home describing the quiet rooms paints a picture of our individual intellectual life as 'hard labourers'.

Skipton, 18th November 1918

My dear German girl!

You say you are being brave back home? Yes, that's how I always imagine you. You have faith in us that we are enduring our fate bravely, that, even as prisoners, we are thinking of home and faithfully serving our Fatherland. My dear fair-haired girl, I would so much like to take you in my arms and kiss your brave mouth. As a reward for your faith, let me tell you today about our conscientious work in the camp.

Up these steps, quickly! But wait, I must pull a magic cloak over your wild hair first. For what would happen if you were visible to everyone in the quiet room! There would be a revolution, compared to which the one in Germany would be child's play. And to be frank, I would also be a little jealous. Into my corner, quickly! Here is a chair, give me your little hand, and now have a look around! Are you surprised? Yes, we ourselves hung the flowered wallpaper on the once dreary walls, with touching diligence and porridge paste. And the white net curtains that soften the rigid lines of the windows, in the style of a doll's house – it cost us a lot of time and money to find a simple artistic way of hanging them. Do you like my desk with the heavy pile of books? Just have a look what's here behind the tomes: your dear picture. Could you feel your ears burning now and then? Whenever I have a headache, I look at you and talk to you. The comrade to my right, the one with the big moustache, is doing the same thing right now. He is a mathematician; just look at his high forehead. He has just been sitting there working hard on a profound analysis of curves. Now he sits up and leans back, his face radiant as his thoughts incline towards Halberstadt, to the other focal point of his life's ellipse. You're laughing? Oh, him over there! He is a fine fellow, a bank clerk who in his quest for general knowledge is reading Kant. But he is struggling. Can you see the worried look on his face? Now he is banging his fist on the book. I bet there is something he hasn't understood. But look, now the light is dawning on his face! He is lovingly stroking the book and his knee; he's got it now. The intriguing face next to him, with a pipe cleverly hanging from the right corner of his mouth? He is a walking brainwave, a future professor of archaeology. His hand, which you can see working so busily, is writing some very learned essays on the Stone and Bronze Ages, which seem to us just mythical. You like the look of the elderly gentleman in the easy chair over there, sitting tall with a comically regal expression on his face, gazing over people's heads: that's our old Schr...., our philologian who has diligently studied English life in countless tomes. Look at the ethereal young man right in front of us who is opening a mysterious little box with an affectionate look and is taking out neatly ordered sheets of paper covered in writing. This is the cradle of his muse's progeny, because his poetic soul allows him to escape the narrow confines of captivity by creating a liberating world of his own, like so many others here. Look at the musing eyes there in a trusting man's face. Kant and Ibsen are lying on his table. This thinker is reflecting on duty and the individual will to live, and he has promised us to give a few talks about it soon. You are serious again now, observing the earnest man over there. Yes, look at him with nothing but respect! Someone like him will bring us all together, hopefully very soon. He is a theologian, quite a cheerful character, but at the moment he has to ponder the problem of free will. His neighbour over there, sunk down in his wicker chair, is quietly reading a book on his lap. He is destined for the Church. He has just put a thick book on canon law aside and is now immersing himself in one of Wilhelm Raabe's novels. He once told me he wanted to enrich his inner life within these narrow confines by engaging in some wider reading. The elegant young man in the wicker chair to my right, who is rolling a cigarette with elegant carelessness, is reading Wedekind; he is enthusiastic about modern literature. My neighbour to the left, with the friendly face, is working incessantly and hardly ever looks at us. He is a hard-working farmer and has been working for a year with countless books around him in order to base his future life's work on real science. He can write an awful lot about animal feed, stabling, agricultural chemistry and agricultural policy, and he can talk about them at even greater length. Here is a young man bent eagerly over Spinoza, and next to him lie Leonardo and Max Klinger. He is ardently following in the steps of the old seeker of truth and his soul clings to the eternal beauty of our old masters. Just a second, my little bunny! There is a gentleman who wants to speak to me. 'Really, your doctoral thesis will be finished soon? I see, about the relationship between Nietzsche and Schopenhauer! Yes, of course you can have Nietzsche's biography! There you go – you're welcome!' Over there, a comrade is putting a huge notebook onto his bookshelf; he has finished yet another volume of his prison diary. It contains many beautiful and refined thoughts; my little sweetheart, perhaps we can read them in print after the war, because he wants them to be published.

Damn it! That unpleasant whispering in the corner over there! Shh! Shh! Of course, it's them again. The tall one and the short one over there are lawyers; they are pointing agitatedly at a book and talking at each other insistently. What legal problem might be waiting for their solution? Shh! The classical scholar with the little pointed beard is looking up in irritation from Birt's book on Romans of distinction, and the German philologian bent deeply over his books by the stove is banging his hand on his Nibelungen text and mumbling, 'How impertinent!' Finally, a comrade with a pale overworked face, whose study of Wilhelm Ostermann's *Interest* requires particular concentration, takes the matter into his own hands. His forceful 'Silence!' echoes across the room. The law, in the form of its two representatives, is silenced. The artist in the corner on the left is adding a few more flecks of sunlight to his native landscape where his thoughts are frolicking away in their happy memories. The tall, hard-working man by the wall – a student of the *Abitur* class[46] – is learning a Goethe poem by heart for his fearsome German teacher, and he mumbles with a wistful face, '*Liebe, Liebe, lass mich los!*' The second neighbour to his left is running his fingers through his hair. This aspiring teacher is staring wild-eyed at a gentleman bent over *Consciousness* by Johannes Rehmke, who is his teacher, his master of pedagogy and the cruel obstetrician of his first psychological studies. To hell with assimilation, association and apperception! You're laughing again, my little flower! Oh, and just look what a face the blonde boy over there is pulling as he designs a bridge using every mathematical and technological trick in the book. 'Achoo!' – 'Bless you!' says the old man in the easy chair in a friendly tone. Everybody lifts their noses from their books. A smile spreads through this temple of learning. Soon silence settles again all around. The stocky man with the fatherly face over there is practising his shorthand by transcribing Otto Ernst's *Appelschnut*. His neighbour on the right is drafting a business letter to Gomez Salvador, Barcelona, in the most authentic Spanish. The man to his left is corresponding with E.G. Wrigley & Co. Ltd. in Birmingham and revelling in his most beautiful English. The man sitting opposite him is bravely poring over a huge tome, Rothschild's Commercial

Handbook for Merchants[47] and, in desperation, repeatedly consults a very busy but amiable gentleman, who each time abruptly breaks off future trade relations between Germany and Argentina. My little one, you're trying to understand the fragmented words coming from behind two doors in the wall. 'Gentlemen, it's not *mai soui* but *mais oui*! French liaison... .' '*Ljubisch li tü sladkija wina*?' You're looking at me questioningly? Well, there are French and Russian lessons next door. But what's going on now? Don't get up, my little love! There is no fire. It's the arrival of our newspaper orderly. Everybody is fighting for a copy of the paper. See? Now they're all back in their seats again. The books will be forgotten for a good while. Our thoughts now go out into the world, mainly towards home, trying to find out anything that can be read between the lines of the English reports.

Are you happy too, my brave little pumpkin? The prisoners here have been held behind barbed wire for many, many months, but they have not forgotten that waiting for them at home are a profession, a Fatherland and fellow countrymen anticipating its rise from the ashes, and that even here in these narrow confines they must serve future goals by working diligently and broadening their minds. You look at me with glistening eyes. Yes, may the day come soon when we are both at home, you and I, my courageous wife and an industrious husband! Believe in this, as I do,

Yours, Georg. X.

Educational Courses

From early on, many officers expressed the desire for organised classes in order to benefit from the richer or more varied specialist knowledge of individual comrades, both for personal interest and for use in the future. Officers soon came forward who felt ready to quench the thirst for knowledge of their fellow imprisoned comrades, and so the first courses came into being.

From most modest beginnings, our education system developed to an extraordinarily high level. The first timetable contained 9 hours per week; the final version contained around 180. The lack of suitable classrooms presented a huge obstacle to the rapid and unhindered development of the education system. Initially, Room A was allocated to us by the camp administration for educational use only in the afternoons. The teachers and students would sit at the table in the middle of the room whilst those comrades who were not participating in the lesson worked at the surrounding tables. We are all aware of how disruptive it is to have other people present in the room who are not participating in the lesson, no matter how quietly they are working. It is equally obvious that spending hours on end listening to lectures from various teachers on a variety of subjects which are not at all related to one's own work is not conducive to successful intellectual work.

After many attempts we eventually received permission to partition off, at our own expense of course, part of the large room next to room A that was used for roll call. We did not allow this difficulty to deter us. A wall made from canvas was constructed and covered with several layers of newspaper, with porridge from the kitchen serving as cement. The resulting room was further divided by a second wall, constructed in the same fashion to form a small room that would serve as a classroom for lessons with a small number of students. The walls of both rooms were either wallpapered or painted. The large blackboard was installed in the large room and the smaller blackboard, built in the camp carpentry workshop, was placed in the smaller room. After several weeks of frenetic activity (captains and lieutenants in their shirtsleeves carried out this unaccustomed work) both rooms were as good as ready to be moved into. Classes could then recommence to their full extent. There were some minor disadvantages that we had to accept. The paper walls were, of course, by no means soundproof. If two comrades with powerful lungs happened to be teaching in the two rooms at the same time, they would cause considerable disruption to each other's lectures; whoever had the loudest voice had the advantage. It was, in addition, not possible to heat the smaller room. Any heat came through a hole in the wall, behind which stood a stove in the larger room. This heating vent was opened during breaks; when teaching was in progress it obviously had to be kept closed for acoustic reasons. In spite of these problems we were nevertheless happy to have found a permanent base at last.

The best way to get a sense of the gradual growth of the education system in the Skipton camp is to take a look at the extensive timetables on the noticeboard, although this did not include the classes for the *Abitur* courses or later, teacher training courses.

The following overview shows the courses available during the existence of our officers' prison camp:

Open Courses in Skipton Camp

I.   **Languages**: 2 beginners Latin courses; 3 beginners Greek courses; 3 beginners English courses; 1 advanced English grammar course; 2 English conversation courses (beginners and advanced); 1 French conversation course; 2 Spanish courses (beginners and advanced); 3 Russian courses (2 beginners, 1 advanced); 1 beginners Dutch course; 1 beginners Portuguese course; 1 Gothic course; 1 Hebrew course

II.   **Mathematics and Sciences**: botany; microscopy course; metallurgy; differential and integral calculus; chemistry

III.   **History and Art History**: art history; German culture and society

IV.   **Business and Commerce**: professional business training; accountancy; business and commerce

V.   **Forestry**: forestry course

VI.   **Stenography**: 2 beginners stenography courses; 1 advanced stenography course

Bibeljé.

Associations of Subject Specialists

Alongside these courses, meetings of subject specialists took place almost every evening of the week.

From the very first days of our imprisonment at the Skipton camp, the …

Teachers' Association

came into being, about which its last chairman writes:

"Years of life on the battlefields lay behind us. While our thoughts were still predominantly preoccupied with our more fortunate comrades on the various front lines, we also soon gave thought to the future. Our strong will to live made us turn our attention to our future working lives, about which we had once been so enthusiastic. As we looked into the armoury of our minds, we were shocked at the gaps and voids we found there.

This revelation led to the establishment of the Teachers' Association in the Skipton Camp on 1st February 1918. The number of participants was small; the shortage of books* and the inhospitable rooms were far from ideal. But this merely strengthened the desire for intellectual work. The fact that colleagues from so many different regions of our vast Fatherland found themselves together in our circle also proved advantageous.

The aims of our work were defined following a lecture on the development of the German Teachers' Association. While it was clear to us from the outset that lectures could in no way be a replacement for study, they could nonetheless act as a stimulus. Each subject area came into its own as time went on. Numerous themes from general as well as educational psychology, general educational theory and didactics, in addition to the specialised methodology of the individual subjects, were introduced and discussed, all with reference to the great educational theorists and taking into account all the aims of modern education. It was extraordinarily invigorating and inspiring that psychology became the point of direction and orientation throughout the curriculum, and that the experiences of the majority of the German teaching body, who had fought in the war, should be important in shaping the curriculum and the future development of the German school system. We did not lose sight of this aim even after the collapse of Bismarck's great creation.

The eighteen-month existence of our Teachers' Association did not always run as smoothly as it may appear. Old shadows stretched even into this backwater and new threats appeared, rooted partly in the depths of the individual soul and partly in past experiences, but allowed to develop fully here. The prisoner experiences dramatic mood swings between apathy and enthusiasm, which constitute a severe hindrance to any steady progress. There were often noticeable signs of this amongst our circle too. Nevertheless

---

* Even the organised support work of our loved ones at home did nothing to alleviate this.

it was possible through a fortunate combination of freedom and constraint, to guide our little boat through storms and towering waves and around cliffs and whirlpools. Although thoughts of returning home were a constant distraction, colleagues and classmates worked hard until the very end. We have not been amassing quantities of useless specialist knowledge, but have instead armed ourselves to help with the rebuilding of a united people with strong hands and stout hearts by immersing ourselves in the preparation necessary for German secondary school teaching, engaging in didactic and educational methodology, based on psychological theory."

Schmidt.

The numerous businessmen of the camp also felt an increasing need to form a closer bond for mutual encouragement and purposeful clarification of the confused status of their profession under the new conditions brought about by the war. This led to the formation of The Businessmen's Association, the chairman of which now reports on the ...

Occupation of an Imprisoned Businessman

The involuntary idleness of imprisonment obliged us businessmen, like others, to use the opportunity to extend our knowledge and to equip ourselves for peace. Time is money. Our younger comrades were particularly concerned about how best to use their time. Many of them had perhaps only just finished their apprenticeships before following the flag, others had interrupted their apprenticeships and some had not yet even begun, so we found many would-be businessmen among us. They must have felt the need, much more than the older comrades, to pursue studies which could be of use to them in their future careers. This, however, was easier said than done, as the most precious skill which defines the very essence of a businessman cannot simply be acquired by theoretical study. By this I mean business proficiency and competence, which are the fruits of years of experience and business activity.

What could we do then? It was only natural that, as businessmen, we began with the study of foreign languages, in particular English. We had plenty of opportunities thanks to the numerous English courses on offer. The second most popular language was Spanish, whose worth was becoming ever more apparent to businessmen, since South America is indeed the only large area which will be open to us in the future. In the spring of 1918, we were fortunate that a Russian course was set up and was attended by many businessmen due to our close business relations with Russia before the war, and also due to their even greater post-war significance for us. A Portuguese study group materialised in December 1918 and, when Spanish classes had been running for more than nine months, a study group devoted to Spanish business correspondence was also established.

Alongside these courses, assiduous individual study of the aforementioned languages must not go unmentioned. This was especially true of those who already possessed a good knowledge of the language and simply wanted to study it further. It was a shame that the request for a native English speaker to come into the camp and teach was declined by the commandant. So we were reliant upon the newspapers and books. Small groups of three or four comrades had been formed here and there, with the aim of practising the spoken language and business correspondence. There seems to have been relatively little interest in French, with only a few study groups. Perhaps French was being written off.

Knowledge of foreign languages alone, however, does not make a businessman, and so the desire for further training inevitably became more and more apparent. Double-entry book keeping was taught by experienced colleagues in courses and also in small private groups, so that probably every businessman here has worked on it in depth. A significant amount of time was also dedicated to the study of the monetary system, the banking system, the stock exchange and economics.

Numerous textbooks provided the opportunity to engage with these subjects. Economics in particular seemed to attract increasing interest in light of current developments. It is also worth mentioning at this point that, although the business textbooks were the personal property of some of the comrades, they were always shared willingly. In fact, many of the books were probably in a perpetual state of circulation.

One comrade, commendably, undertook the difficult task of teaching commercial practice and in the summer of 1918 delivered a course on the operation of a Hamburg import and export business, including accountancy and business correspondence. In December of the same year, he also gave a series of lectures on the topic of money and currency problems and focused especially on the question of whether and how the gold standard could be abolished; a lively debate then followed.

In the summer of 1918, some businessmen began to feel the need to learn the fundamentals of commercial law and at the request of a few of the men, an older comrade (a district court judge) declared himself willing to lecture on commercial law on Friday evenings.

This is by no means the full extent of the business studies teaching. From the beginning of 1919, a course in international trade took place, which proved to be both informative and inspiring, thanks to the rich experience of the tutor. In March and April of 1919 a comrade gave a short course on trade with India and East Asia, followed by a course on English business correspondence. In May there was a similar short course on the trade of coffee and colonial goods, and another on insurance.

The desire to continue these business evenings was eventually voiced by some of the younger officers, with the aim of making the experiences of the older comrades accessible to a wider circle through the exchange of ideas. This led to the formation of the Businessmen's Association, which met weekly. They sought to achieve their aims by organising lectures and responding to subject-related inquiries. The lectures were usually on the subject of the particular area in which the lecturer had worked. These topics included: paper manufacture and the paper trade, semi-precious stones, Zanzibar, bankruptcy law, iron and coal. More general topics were also covered during these evening meetings, for example the question of emigration and evaluation of balance sheets. A lively debate would always follow the lectures. The head of the Businessmen's Association attempted to alleviate the shortage of books in the camp by compiling a list of textbooks owned by various comrades, resulting in an inventory of all the books. We also created a list of all the businessmen in the camp with details about their previous employment, their areas of business specialisms, etc. The intention was that, in this way, the businessmen would get to know each other even better than before and form closer bonds. The list also provided each member with the opportunity to re-establish contact with the others at a later date.

Alongside the daily newspapers, we were always eager to receive magazines whose main focus was trade and commerce. Thus many copies of the well-known *Economist* came into the camp and were eagerly studied. Those who read it regularly will certainly have gained good insight into the economic life of England and acquired a fair amount of general business knowledge. The *Trade Supplement* of *The Times*, which is a good source of news from all corners of the world, unfortunately only found its way into the camp a few times. All our appeals to the commandant and our efforts to acquire it regularly were in vain; the English would not allow it to be brought into the camp. This is telling. However, the opportunity to obtain books from London was exploited extensively and some prisoners will have considerably enlarged their personal library thanks to English textbooks.

As businessmen it is of course our duty to pay close attention to the events of the outside world. The war was after all partly an economic war. Even if not economic in its origins, it certainly became increasingly so as it continued. This is evidenced by the 'black lists' which were not abolished until the beginning of May 1919, and also by the many attacks on German private property in foreign countries, as well as by the expulsion of Germans from China, at the instigation of the English of course. The efforts of the English and the French to shut down our trade and industry also testify to this. I am thinking here, for example, of the paint industry or of the influential Englishman Dr Bunsen's trip to South America, where he was lobbying on behalf of the British Board of Trade.

The new budget gave the British colonies a preferential rate of duty on sugar, tea, coffee and other products. With this move Britain went down the road of protectionism. But might it not become a doubled edged sword? Be that as it may, it was of great importance for us as businessmen to follow this development. Britain was the traditional land of free trade; it was what had made Britain great. How would Britain's allies react to such preferential treatment of British colonies? As you can see, the events continually provided us businessmen with new questions.

Over time we witnessed how America, and similarly Japan, increased their share in world trade. The big European nations are increasingly falling behind these two powers. The trends in international shipping were an obvious sign of this. The submarine war had cost England around 7¾ million tonnes of shipping capacity. America, on the other hand, whose fleet had previously been insignificant, was making more and more progress. We were greatly alarmed to discover that we were obliged to hand over our superb modern merchant ships and we clung increasingly to the hope that we would at least get some of them back. We felt very strongly that our merchant fleet represented something special and we were proud of it. As Georg Friedrich List said, 'Those who have no access to the sea, are excluded from all the good things and honours of the earth; they are the step-children of our dear Lord.'[48]

What is there left to do? We must take back what has been taken from us, recapture what we have lost!

Boecker.

Our farmers and gardening enthusiasts attended lectures on agriculture, animal husbandry, fruit farming and horticulture several times a week. Engineers and technicians were taught in specialist lectures on mechanical engineering, metallurgy and its application in workshops, autogenous welding, and foundry processes. In an art history colloquium, discussions took place on the most diverse aspects of classical, medieval and modern art. A small group of comrades regularly occupied themselves with questions of prehistoric archaeology. Once a week, the lawyers discussed practical legal issues under the guidance of an experienced senior comrade, but it is not possible to list all the subjects that were studied in the camp. And all this in the most unfavourable conditions imaginable! What difficulties we had in obtaining the core literature for each field of academic study! Three months would often go by before the books ordered from Germany arrived, and those ordered in London were mostly not available. And yet, for a large number of the prisoners, the time spent in the camp was not completely useless. This was in particular the case for the younger prisoners who have been able to sit the final school exams (the *Abitur*) here in the camp, entitling them to a place at university.

The *Abitur* Course

"In May, several officers approached some older comrades who had been secondary school teachers in civilian life to ask for help in achieving their goal of passing the school-leaving examination (*Abitur*), which would guarantee them a place at a German university. The war had deprived them of their final years of schooling, making it impossible for them to sit this examination. They wanted to study properly, just as in school, with the help and under the supervision of older comrades so they would be able to complete their school education by sitting the examination as soon as possible when they returned home to Germany. Their wish was granted. It was not difficult to find teaching staff, since a sufficient number of secondary school teachers and graduate trainee teachers were available to enable every subject to be taught by a specialist.

And so it came about that, deep in enemy territory, a German secondary school was established with ten teachers and, initially, eleven students. It was in actual fact an amalgam of the three variants of the Prussian secondary school: the *Gymnasium*, the *Realgymnasium* and the *Oberrealschule*. On 3rd June, formal lessons commenced. With fresh and joyful intentions and glowing with noble motivation, teachers and students alike went about their shared work. The curriculum was exactly the same as that of Prussian secondary schools. In frequent meetings, members of the teaching staff would exchange views on the students' knowledge or lack thereof, their ability and motivation, and the question of how long it might take individuals to achieve their goal. Great obstacles to this educational work persisted for a time. Like migratory birds, the group had to move from one classroom to another and lessons sometimes had to be postponed for a few days or even several weeks. After much effort, we were eventually granted permission to partition off part of Room B at our own expense to form a small room that was to be our base. We were, in addition, able to use Teaching Barrack 45 for some lessons and, after it was allocated to us in October, the larger Room B, which we had in the meantime also prepared for use. On 27th October, after weeks of disruption, we were finally able to resume teaching.

But we still had further difficulties to overcome. Acquiring the necessary textbooks took an inordinately long time: at least three months, often longer. For a long time we had to make do with a single copy, and circulating it from one comrade to the next was often an unsatisfactory experience. The chemistry teacher appealed to the commandant, with the full support of the senior German officer, for permission to acquire the most essential chemical apparatus and enough chemicals for a few simple experiments. However while we were requesting exactly the same as what English officers imprisoned in Germany were allowed, our application was refused out of hand by the War Office. So the chemistry and physics lessons had to be limited to descriptions of experiments, when actual demonstrations not only would have enlivened the lessons significantly, but would more importantly have often facilitated the students' understanding. But these difficulties did not deter us, for we followed our chosen path purposefully and confidently, and this eventually led to complete success.

In order to obtain recognition for our work with our younger comrades from the relevant authorities at home, we sent the following request to the Prussian Ministry of Education and Cultural Affairs in August 1918.

'Skipton, date: ...
Officers Prisoner-of-War Camp

The following report and attached request is submitted by the undersigned to the Royal Prussian Ministry of Education and Cultural Affairs.

In the Skipton prisoner-of-war camp are a number of officers who have been called to war from the final years of their German education. Their service on the battlefield has made the continuation of their studies impossible, meaning that their advancement after the war will be hampered considerably. For this reason, a number of other officers, mostly qualified secondary school teachers and graduate trainee secondary school teachers, have taken the decision, in the interests of their younger comrades, to set up a preparatory course for the *Abitur* examination. There are eleven students. The lessons are planned using the same textbooks that are in use in German secondary schools. In addition, the design and delivery of the syllabus follow the official regulations stipulated by the German education authorities.

The undersigned hereby inquire most respectfully to the Royal Ministry of Education and Cultural Affairs as to the possibility of official recognition for this course, for example in the sense that regular attendance of the course is to be considered equivalent to completion of the final year of secondary school. A concession of this nature would be advantageous to our active cadet officers for the acquisition of their commission and also for students intending to continue their schooling in Germany after the war.

If this were acceptable, on completion of our course we would supply our students with a certificate of attendance, a report on their attainment and their written assignments as marked by the teaching staff.

Should official recognition not be possible, the undersigned would be grateful if the Royal Ministry of Education and Cultural Affairs would acknowledge our work and declare its approval.'

To this request were attached a detailed syllabus and timetable, in addition to a list of the course teachers and students. At the same time, the teaching staff decided to increase the number of lessons per week and to make regular attendance at lessons obligatory. At this time the number of men in the camp was continuing to increase, and consequently the number of our students also increased to sixteen.

On 4th December 1918 the written response from the Ministry arrived via the Swiss Legation in London. The answer we received exceeded our expectations. The Prussian Ministry of Education and Cultural Affairs had recognised our *Abitur* course and even granted the teaching staff permission to organise a 'provisional' school leaving examination here in Skipton. The staff decided immediately to organise an examination, following the official rules for implementation to the letter. News of this spread quickly throughout the camp. This had a two-fold effect on our students: on the one hand they were delighted to be able to be assessed by a commission of comrades with whom they felt a communal spirit through months of working together. On the other hand the spectre of the examination was now suddenly looming perilously and tangibly near.

Even though everybody had worked with such diligence since the start of the course that increased effort could hardly be considered possible, on receipt of this decision from the Ministry the industriousness of the students reached an almost pathological intensity. From 6 o'clock in the morning (and getting up at such an early hour in the cold, dark, wooden barracks certainly required considerable willpower) until late in the evening when the bell signalled time for the evening roll call, these young comrades worked undaunted, with enthusiasm and indefatigable diligence, barely taking time off for meals. The teaching staff increased the number of lessons to 47 per week.

Meanwhile the disastrous Armistice agreement was concluded, hope of an early release from captivity shone like a ray of hope before us, and yet above all we wanted to formally complete the examinations before our repatriation. So the teaching staff scheduled the written examinations for the period of 13th–20th January and the oral examinations for 28th, 29th and 30th January, recorded as were all our procedures in the documentation required by the *Regulations for Secondary School Examinations*. The teaching staff set the required standards in accordance with *Regulations for Examinations of Participants in the War* sent by the Ministry. According to these regulations it was then possible for all sixteen students who had regularly attended lessons to be entered for the examination. On 13th January, intellectually well-prepared, our students embarked upon the written examination.

Questions for the final written examination

German: To what extent does the figure of Götz portray the personal development of Goethe and also the general question of the meaning of human life?

Greek: Translation from Greek to German: Thucydides VII, Chapter 83.

Latin: Translation from Latin to German:

Gymnasium students: Cicero, pro Roscio, 37, 105-107.

Realgymnasium students: Livius, ab urbe condita, XXIV, 43, 44 (Coleridge, Macmillan, London edition).

French: Translation from German to French.

English: Translation from German to English.

Mathematics:
Gymnasium students:
1. In a triangle $a=80.349$cm, $c=85.627$cm, $m_b=75.243$cm. Calculate the missing information.
2. A civil servant with a starting salary of 2400 Marks, which was increased annually by 100 Marks, earned a total of 90,000 Marks during his entire service. How long was he in office?

3. A offered 600,000 Marks cash for a property; B, 696,000 Marks payable after 3 years without interest; C, 729,000 Marks payable after 4 years without interest. Who offered the most if 5% compound interest is calculated, and how much more than the others did he offer?

4. A rectangular flowerbed 3m x 4m is surrounded by a uniformly wide strip of lawn whose surface area is ten times that of the flowerbed. How wide is the strip?

Realgymnasium and Oberrealschule students:

1. What is the shortest distance in kilometres between Hamburg (latitude $\phi 1$ = 53° 33' 6", longitude $\lambda 1$ = 9° 58' 30") and New York (latitude $\phi 2$ = 40° 43' 48", longitude $\lambda 2$ = 71° 29' 12")?

2. Point P_1 (?, 6) lies in the 2nd quadrant of the ellipse with semi-axes a=5, b=10. Point P_2 (4, ?) lies in the 1st quadrant on the parabola with the parameter 1. Point P_3 (?, 3) lies in the 1st quadrant on the hyperbola with the semi-axes a – 4, b – 4.
   a) What are the co-ordinates of the points P_1, P_2, P_3?
   b) What are the equations of the perpendicular bisectors of the triangle P_1, P_2, P_3?
   c) At which point do the perpendicular bisectors intersect?
   d) What is the equation of the circle circumscribed around triangle P_1, P_2, P_3?

3. A square piece of card has sides of length a. From the four corners equally-sized squares are to be cut out. The resulting rectangles of the piece of card are folded upwards to create a box. How long must the sides of the cut-out squares be to maximise the capacity of the box?

Physics: What is movement and how does the physicist describe the different forms of movement (with the exception of rotation)? Consider in particular the vertical, horizontal and diagonal projections.

Chemistry: The production of hydrochloric acid and its transformation into chlorinated lime by the Weldon process.

1. How does hydrochloric acid occur in nature, and why is common salt the most important compound of hydrochloric acid?

2. How is hydrochloric acid prepared from common salt? The set-up of a factory with muffle furnace and condensation plant should be explained by means of a sketch.

3. How is chlorine made from hydrochloric acid according to Weldon, and how is the chlorine transformed into chlorinated lime?

The results of the written examinations entitled all candidates to be entered for the oral examinations. On 28th January, teachers and students gathered in Room B for this purpose. The camp was represented by the senior German officer, who had expressed his full approval of the *Abitur* course on more than one occasion and had encouraged our endeavours with appreciation. Our course leader informed the students that, in accordance with the constitution, the teaching staff did not have the authority to exempt students from the oral examination, but had they had this authority, they would have exempted six comrades on the basis of their excellent performance throughout the year and their written assessments. He then continued by saying that this was likely to be the only example of German prisoners of war, in the middle of enemy territory and constrained by their adverse circumstances, taking their examination and thereby acquiring the rights to which this examination entitled them.

The oral examinations were carried out strictly in accordance with the *Regulations for Secondary School Examinations*. They took three days and lasted from 8.30 in the morning until either 5 or 7 o'clock in the evening. These were long, hard days full of effort and exertion. But the work and the strain of the preceding weeks and months were wonderfully rewarded: every comrade who had taken the examination passed. A provisional certificate provided details of a student's performance which, along with the minutes of the teaching staff meetings and the students' written assignments, was to be submitted to the Honourable Minister on our return home, for verification and confirmation. In a short ceremony attended by the senior German officer, the course leader handed out these provisional certificates to the successful candidates and gave an address which he based on the words of Nietzsche: 'Of what account is my happiness? I strive for my work.'

But those who rest, rust. So after a longish break we resumed our work together, though in a different way from before the examinations. Teaching was now conducted in a more academic manner. There were inspiring and informative lectures on all academic subjects, delivered by teachers and students. Teachers also made an effort not only to help their students maintain their level of knowledge but, wherever possible, to deepen and advance their understanding. The course continued right up until our release.

We were also able to assist another group of comrades to prepare for their future careers, thanks to the concession of the Ministry. Having been recognised by the Ministry as an examining body, we further utilised this authorisation to examine those officers desiring certification of their competence in Latin, Greek and Hebrew.

In another case, the teaching staff was regrettably unable to help. Eight comrades from the officers' prisoner-of-war camp in Holyport had completed an *Abitur* course and, after written communication with Skipton, they had contacted the War Office requesting a transfer to Skipton, because the teaching staff of our course was at that time the only examining body in a British prisoner-of-war camp that was recognised by the Ministry. The War Office declined the request outright, probably because of the terrible influenza epidemic rife in our camp in Skipton at that time. So, unfortunately, we were unable to help our eight young comrades from Holyport to achieve their goal.

Alongside our *Abitur* course we also ran a modest teacher training course enabling younger comrades who had not yet been employed as teachers to gain practical and theoretical experience of their future career through lectures, tutoring, assessed teaching practice, etc. under the direction of officers who were already fully qualified and experienced teachers."

Bibeljé.

Teacher Training Course

A teacher training course was set up in the camp from 25th October, to continue the education of those younger officers who had entered military service before taking their final qualifying examinations. This advanced training course, comprising 34 hours of classes every week, covered every subject on the school curriculum and also teaching methods. Teaching practice was somewhat makeshift, with students giving lessons to their comrades. Initially, the teaching staff consisted of three secondary and seven primary school teachers.

In January 1919, the course teachers sought recognition for their work from the Prussian Ministry of Education and Cultural Affairs. They received this, in the form of the following ministerial decree, dated 21.03.19, Berlin:

"I was very pleased to hear of the professional training which has been running in the officers' prisoner-of-war camp at Skipton since mid-October 1918, for the benefit of eight imprisoned Prussian student teachers. I recommend that the course be aligned as far as possible with those of Prussia's teacher training institutions, and am prepared, under the prevailing circumstances, to credit a period of regular and successful participation in the course as equivalent to time spent on a course completed at a Prussian teacher training institution. Course leaders must therefore provide participants with certificates stating the duration and frequency of their participation as well as their competence and the subject matter covered. This certificate, along with a short *curriculum vitae* and a police check certificate, is to be submitted as soon as possible after repatriation, with reference to this decree, to the Regional School Council responsible for the teaching course that they previously attended. The Regional School Council will then make the necessary arrangements as soon as possible for the training to be continued or the first teaching examination to be completed."

The course was not immune to change, some of which was particularly painful. Not only did the influenza outbreak of spring 1919 force a prolonged interruption of our work, but it also took from us two dear colleagues.

The members of the course will be forever grateful for their loyal work.

The last five remaining student comrades, with a teaching staff of eleven involved in their training, worked tirelessly right up to the end of our imprisonment.

Reuter.

Lectures

While discussing pedagogical activity in the camp, it is also worth mentioning the lectures delivered by individual comrades. In these, they shared the wealth of their experience and knowledge with their fellow sufferers. Over the course of the camp's existence, the following open lectures were held in the Old Mess, which was often full to capacity.

1. Modern Greeks
2. Persia (3 Lectures)
3. Chile through a Merchant's Eyes
4. Argentina
5. Religion and Modern Man
6. Religion and War in Ancient Semitic Thought
7. Mining and Smelting Iron
8. The Economy and Politics (2 Lectures)
9. Nutritional Science and Camp Provisions
10. Bismarck, the Statesman (2 Lectures)
11. China (3 Lectures)
12. Problems with Currency: 4 Lectures
13. An Economic Perspective on Trade
14. Germany's Post-war Financial Position
15. Ibsen's *Rosmersholm* (4 Lectures)
16. English Secondary Education
17. Ibsen's *Ghosts*
18. The Peace Treaty, Law and Justice
19. The Peace Treaty and German Industry
20. The Peace Treaty and German International Relations
21. The Peace Treaty and the German Army
22. The Peace Treaty and the German Conscience
23. Ireland

Bibeljé.

The Camp Library

Our two camps of origin, Colsterdale North and Colsterdale South, whose inmates as veteran prisonörs were well aware of how a good book can while away many a dull hour in captivity, willingly donated books from their rich libraries as we were bundling up our worldly goods to establish a new empire in Skipton. This meant that we had around 350 books at our disposal from the outset, and many a prisoner who had escaped our sad reality for moments, even hours, by reading a good book remembers with gratitude the considerable efforts of the two library officers who, even in the first week following our transfer to Skipton, organised a book lending system to shorten the grey hours of waiting that their comrades had to endure. From these modest beginnings, the camp library expanded its collection to 1,284 books through new acquisitions, donations, books sent from home, etc.

The two or three officers who managed the library were also responsible for repairing particularly well-thumbed books and for rebinding torn and dirty ones. Each borrower paid 3 pence. This money went towards repair materials, glue, paper and cardboard. According to the rules each comrade was allowed to take out one book per day. There was no limit on the loan period for academic books. Order slips had to be submitted by 11.30 in the morning. Two catalogues were displayed in the Old Mess, and later in the entrance to the library. Books were distributed daily, after lunch, in exchange for the return of the old books. Non-academic books could be kept for three days. If anyone kept a book for an unreasonable amount of time, he would, one day, suddenly find his name on a list on the noticeboard. Loaned books were registered by means of a two-card system. Excluding academic books, around 100 to 150 books were requested every day. Demand for the library was at its highest after the influenza outbreak, when Rooms A and C had still not been reopened for study. We sent 150 books to distract and entertain our comrades in Keighley War Hospital.

Regular audits took place, for which purpose all books had to be returned so that updates could be made to the catalogue.

At the end of the camp's occupancy, all the books (with the exception of those lent to the library by individual officers) were shared out among the comrades, or collected by Dr Markel, the head of the Prisoners of War Relief Agency in London, and put to an agreed use.

Book Inventory

Book Origins:	Non-academic books:	Paperbacks published by Reclam:	Astronomy books:	Academic books:	Foreign language books:	Total:
Brought from Colsterdale	310	26	9	-	6	350
Made available by the Society for the Delivery of Charitable Gifts to Imprisoned Academics, Berlin	46	1	2	106	5	160
Donated by the Swedish Red Cross	7	-	-	4	1	12
Purchased in London using the camp account	100	-	-	-	31	131
Donated or loaned by individual men in the camp	352	120	12	66	81	631
Total:	815	146	23	176	124	1,284

The Camp Newspaper

At the turn of the year 1918/19 the first camp newspaper appeared. As well as contributions in verse and in prose, some more serious than others, concerning the times in which we lived and our daily camp life, it also contained a large number of illustrations of our barracks community and its surroundings. Because the whole print run was snapped up immediately, clearly demonstrating demand, the enterprising director of entertainment decided to publish a monthly camp newspaper with the help of several comrades, in order to record in words and pictures impressions from the Front and from the experience of imprisonment, significant events in the war and in the camp, and characterisations of the English officers and sergeants who were our guards. These newspapers, printed in the camp itself with the aid of a duplicating machine, acquired an extensive readership, and many comrades took them home later as paper mementos of many a dull and dark hour, but also many a cheerful one, showing the unbroken German courage and cheerful labour of their fellow sufferers, created in bleak circumstances in a foreign land.

Bibeljé.

Alongside these academic efforts, artistic endeavours also flourished in the camp.

The Male-Voice Choir

On the very first day after the arrival of the Skipton Camp's original 150 prisoners, a meeting was held between 25 comrades who felt strongly the importance of upholding the German tradition of the male-voice choir, even in exile. They founded a choral society in the hope that the sound of German song might lighten their own burden of imprisonment and conjure up a vision of home for their comrades for a few hours in the midst of their miserable existence. And they succeeded. How often we listened, full of profound emotion and full once again of unbowed pride, to the sound of German song, sung by German men! How often the sound of popular German song evoked a tangible image of our homeland, the land which bore and raised us, and to which we owe allegiance from the bottom of our hearts.

The choral society made its first public appearance as early as 27th January 1918, for the Kaiser's birthday celebrations. The singers gave faithful and harmonious renditions of *Kennst du das Land der Eichenwälder* [*Do you know the land of the oak forests?*] and *Durch tiefe Nacht ein Brausen zieht* [*The wind is roaring in the night*, also called *Deutschland*], and earned the gratitude of all the comrades who had gathered in the Old Mess to listen. Over the course of the following months we were frequently able to enjoy the sounds of home as we were treated to a whole series of evening concerts organised by the choral society. On several occasions they even joined forces with the orchestra to shorten their comrades' long, cruel wait for repatriation. German song accompanied us through all of the happy and sad moments of camp life. On 1st May we were woken early in the morning by a song which we used to sing so often ourselves to greet the merry month of May: *Der Mai ist gekommen, die Bäume schlagen aus*

[*May has arrived, the trees are budding*], and dawn was greeted with *Die Sonn' erwacht! Mit ihrer Pracht erfüllt sie die Berge, das Tal* [*The sun is awakening, it fills the mountains and the valleys with its splendour*]. When the English tried to oppress us and drive us to despair by imposing reprisals, they were met with magnificent male voices full of unshakeable strength, belting out their song into the bright morning: *Was glänzt dort vom Walde im Sonnenschein? ... Das ist Lützows wilde, verwegene Jagd* [*What glistens there in the forest sunshine? ... That is Lützow's wild daredevil hunt*]. On Whit Monday 1918, a number of popular songs, performed with warmth and depth of feeling, carried us away to our homeland for a few hours. *Totensonntag*, the annual Lutheran memorial service for the dead, was enhanced by the choral society's rendition of Hegar's *Totenvolk* [*The Dead*] chorus. When we gathered together in the Old Mess for a quiet dignified celebration to remember the forty-seven comrades who had been taken from us by influenza, the choral society performed the old hymn *Wenn ich einmal soll scheiden, so scheide nicht von mir* [*Be near me, Lord, when dying, O part thou not from me*], providing a solemn accompaniment to the words of the senior German officer in memory of our deceased comrades.

This small group of enthusiastic singers celebrated their first anniversary on 31st January accompanied by the thanks and accolades of their comrades. We shared with these trusty musicians the feeling and conviction expressed by one of our number to the celebrating choir.

> You enfold us in bonds of friendship,
> Touch our hearts with a gentle hand,
> You carry us away with glimpses of home,
> From this unwelcoming enemy land,
> We'll treasure and cherish you, songs of home,
> Whatever our unfolding fate may demand!

Rarely did our beloved tunes sound as fresh or as festive as they did that evening. We all shared in the rejoicing, and were all delighted by the ebony baton, embellished with silver, that the grateful choir presented to the deserving choirmaster to commemorate the time he had spent leading a German choral society in enemy territory.

Bibeljé.

The male-voice choir found its counterpart in our excellent orchestra. The orchestra's energetic conductor, a sensitive interpreter of musical works, took over from the extremely dedicated founder of the music society, and will now tell us about ...

The Camp Orchestra

"If the attentive reader of the pieces collected in this book has gained an awareness of the crushing mental depression which is the inevitable fate of a prisoner of war, then he will also have come to understand the fervent longing, born of this, to plant a seed of the atmosphere of home amidst the bleak monotony of life behind a barbed-wire fence, a reflection of German scholarship, German art and German humour. If at times the chains of a prisoner's everyday life threatened to suffocate the blaze of enthusiasm that had been stirred up in combat and labouring for the greatness of our Fatherland, within our hearts it still trembled, yearned, and hoped not to be silenced in tight-lipped resignation. A strong vibrant yearning for home is surely what showed our little band the way when they, hesitantly at first, took up violins and cellos to conjure up the sunshine and peace of home through the sounds of familiar harmonies and tunes. It was with true

ORCHESTER

Orchestra.

joy, if also with plenty of critical scrutiny, that this nascent ensemble was greeted when it came into the lives of prisoners so hungry for simple cheer.

Could there have been technical and material constraints insurmountable by the first rush of joyful enthusiasm? I do not believe so. Instruments and suitable sheet music were helpfully made available to the German POWs by K.E. Markel of London. They very soon found their way to us and, with great eagerness, the difficult yet indispensable preparation and individual practice began. There was no shelter, no building that would not have been a welcome venue for our musicians and their daily practice! Unoccupied barracks, the mess halls, and yes, even the cool damp shower blocks were filled with the music of indefatigable diligence. Admittedly this was not always to the delight of their unwilling audience, forced to suffer painful if unintentional discordance. Only when the baton of the orchestra's founder forcefully unified all of the individual contributions and the first modest concert gathered together the camp's many music-lovers in the Old Mess – only then did this group of musicians start to feel, from the warmth of the approval they received, that from now on even their 'tuning troubles' would be met with goodwill. And this is what happened.

There remained the challenge of matching the selection of works to the technical abilities of what was, after all, a severely limited number of musicians. The orchestra consisted of eight violins, two violas, one cello, one double bass, one flute and one piano. Using suitably adapted arrangements, they managed to play renditions of fantasias on operas, short solos, and light music. Aspirations to higher accomplishment were brought to an end by the reprisals to which the English most unfortunately subjected the camp, condemning every joyful note to silence.

July, August and September 1918 saw the return of a number of unambitious but entertaining concerts, and saw the players' technical abilities develop steadily. Their efforts to hold everyday camp life at bay for a few hours with familiar melodies were rewarded with great success.

When the little storehouse on the playing field was made available for full orchestral rehearsals, practice became more tightly organised. Skills were trained systematically and the words of the great Hans von Bülow, 'in the beginning was rhythm', were brought to life. So it was no surprise that even the more difficult tasks no longer seemed insurmountable. Ambition did the rest.

Our awareness of increased skill in general and of successful performance in particular led to a desire for a wider audience, and our director of entertainment, who promoted the interests of both the theatrical and the musical societies, had by the end created a vibrant colourful portrayal of the fine arts within the camp. Skipton Camp had acquired its own modest little temple of the muses. It goes without saying that the Old Mess often seemed to struggle to contain the number of appreciative listeners.

The long, dull winter posed diverse challenges.

Although a profound appreciation of music inclined some of our receptive listeners, and especially the musicians themselves, towards works of our classical German masters (as far as performing them was within their capabilities), there were still a number of obstacles to this ambitious goal. For the most part the orchestra was restricted to the music provided for the camps by K.E. Markel through a system of mutual exchange and this, it has to be said, remained an idiosyncratic mixture. What is more, sheet music of good quality German works did not seem to be stocked by English music publishers. An obvious solution, therefore, was to try to satisfy the demands of the musically less discriminating in the camp and to make some room for the more frivolous muse alongside more serious, significant pieces. This meant that New Year's Eve of 1918/19, for instance, saw a considerable crowd gathered together in the Old Mess, all determined to see in the New Year with a smile, listening to the sentimental melodies of Johann Strauss' waltzes, or brisk marches and dance tunes.

Increasingly, the orchestra had the pleasure of helping to enhance special occasions in the camp. The powerfully simple Christmas service banished our loneliness in this foreign land through the sounds of German Christmas carols, and in many a service the powerful harmonies of familiar chorales flowed forth from the instruments.

It would have been natural to combine the efforts of the actors and the musicians, perhaps to bring to life a little traditional German *Singspiel*. However, the lack of suitable voices (female, in particular) put paid to this notion. As a result, the orchestra was only able to support the theatre by providing accompaniment at a few gala performances.

Although the camp had no 'knights of the swan', no representatives of the highly popular *Heldentenor* [heroic tenor], a few comrades were able to make use of their pleasant, well-trained voices in concert performances. One lent his sonorous bass to a number of operatic arias, with great effect, while another became a sensitive interpreter of German *Lieder*.

The practice that we undertook with such earnestness and enthusiasm, together with many full rehearsals, laid the groundwork for a number of new concerts. The gala performance on the occasion of the camp orchestra's first anniversary (27th April 1919) will have demonstrated to all of those involved that honest hard work paves the way to worthwhile goals. Alongside the overture and the *Athenian March* from Massenet's *Phèdre*, we performed three movements of Tchaikovsky's *Symphony in B Minor* (*Pathétique*). The orchestra consisted of eight first violins, six second violins, three violas, three cellos, one double bass, one flute, two pianos and one harmonium. That evening, the senior German officer joyfully expressed the camp's gratitude towards the choir and its laurel-crowned conductor:

'The full houses to which our camp ensemble has always performed; the recognition that their achievements have always earned; most of all, the thunderous applause that has just filled the room with such force that these ramshackle beams are still shaking – all of these things leave me in no doubt of your support in dedicating a few words to our ensemble on your behalf.

Gentlemen! From modest beginnings, through tireless effort, you have overcome all obstacles to ascend to your current heights. You may yourselves have derived great joy and satisfaction from the exercise of your talents, but the greater part of your work has been a sacrifice for the common good. I am myself no judge of your achievements, but – believe me, gentlemen – the knowledgeable among us praise you beyond all measure.

I have to admit that I have nothing against a nice big kettledrum and a bit of decent *Schrammelmusik*, but your achievement lies precisely in the fact that, from the outset, you have never resorted to that kind of music, and instead have always striven to play the best and highest forms of music. Unfortunately, today I am unable to wish you every success for the future, as one would with any other young ensemble that had just completed a happy and successful first year. On the contrary, I hope that you, Sir, may lay down your baton very soon, and that you, gentlemen, may very soon pack up your instruments and go your separate ways.

But rest assured that our camp orchestra will always have pride of place among the few happy memories of Skipton that we will cherish.'"

Appendix

By 1st August 1919, twenty concerts had taken place (forty-two, including repeat performances). The following works were performed:

Overtures:
Iphigénie en Aulide, Gluck
Egmont, Beethoven
The Marriage of Figaro, Mozart
Der Freischütz [*The Marksman*], Weber
Euryanthe, Weber
Athalie, Mendelssohn
Festouverture, Nicolai
Phèdre, Massenet
The Thieving Magpie, Rossini
Fra Diavolo, Auber
Dichter und Bauer [*Poet and Peasant*], Suppé

Symphonies (including excerpts from symphonies):
Symphony No. 41 (Jupiter), Mozart
Symphony No. 8 (The Unfinished Symphony), Schubert
Andante con moto from Symphony No. 5, Beethoven
Symphony No. 6 in B minor (Pathéthique), first, second and fourth movements, Tchaikovsky
Kol Nidrei, Max Bruch

Assorted Works:
Gavotte, Bach
Lento from the Double Concerto, Handel
Turkish March (Marcia alla Turca), Beethoven
Marche Militaire, Schubert
Canzonetta from *Don Juan*, Mozart
Wedding March, Mendelssohn
Einzug der Gäste [*Arrival of the Guests*] from *Tannhäuser*, Richard Wagner
Andante from String Quartet No. 1 Op. 11, Tchaikovsky
Marche Hongroise, Berlioz
Hungarian Dances Nos. 5 and 6, Brahms
Phantasie auf ungarische Volksweisen [*Fantasia on Hungarian Folk Themes*], Liszt
Two Norwegian Dances, Grieg
Ballet Russe, themes 1, 2, 4 and 5, Luigini
Träume [*Dreams*], Richard Wagner
Melody in F, Rubinstein
Two dances from *Nell Gwyn*, Edward German
Athenian March (Phèdre), Massenet

Plate 1. Bradford Pals at Raikeswood Camp, Skipton in front of *One Step Nearer* hut. (*Reproduced by kind permission of the Ellwood family, V. Rowley, and North Yorkshire County Council, Skipton Library*)

Plate 2. View from the camp over the parade ground, looking towards Raikes Avenue. Photograph taken by camp guard Lieutenant Frederick Fitzgerald Barry (Royal Defence Corps). (*Photograph courtesy of Peter Barry and Charles M. Whittaker*)

Plate 3. Fritz Sachsse in 1920. (*Reichsmarine (Marineschule Mürwik)* – *Archiv des Wehrgeschichtlichen Ausbildungszentrums der Marineschule Mürwik*)

Serial Number.	Surname.	Christian Names.	Age or Date of Birth.	Rank.	Military Particulars, Home Address, etc., and Birthplace.	Place of Internment.	Place and Date of Capture, Wounds, etc., etc.
180594	Petermann	Willi (Karl August)	27 ans	Osamt.	See S.N. 23326 C; List 179. Stadtisch Mördkappe Winterfelde. Stettin	Cai.34528 (10/1)	Kp.S. (S.M.S. Königsberg.)
180595	Hieronymus	(Hermann)	25 ans	N.Z aya	See S.N. 29289. C; List 183. Reformierter Schulgasz 3. Leer (Ost?)	Cai.34458 (9/1)	S.M.S. Königsberg.
181299	Butz	Paul (Otto)	30	Poff.	-Marine Engineer-. R. Eric Butz: Stahnsdorf, Teltow (B). Schönebeck a/d. Elbe (B).	Oat.8593 (8/6) Bro.18648 (15/7)	See also S.N. 89673 List 122 (Civilians).
181300	Sachsse	Fritz (Walther)	10/6/75	Kervk.	(Seeoffixier). Frau Maria Sachsse: Kiel, Beselerallee 56 (H). Hohenthurm, Halle a/Saale, Sa. (B).	Skp.581 (18/6)	The internment of this P/W was previously notified under S.N. 79041 in List 115 (Civilians) under the assumed name of Edelen, Hans. He has now furnished his correct name & personal particulars.
181301	Nielandt	Arthur (Karl John)	27/3/86	M.	T.D.2,Kp.5; R.(Seeman). Herr Nielandt: Hamburg, Niebuhrstr.4/II (H a B).	Hfth.20443 (16/6)	See also S.N. 4682 C; List 21.

LIST No.204 OF GERMAN PRISONERS OF WAR - EUROPE - NAVAL FORCES - MAIN LIST   21272   Form I.B. 20

Plate 4. Record from the International Committee of the Red Cross showing Fritz Sachsse's transfer to Skipton on 18 June 1918, following his revelation of his true identity. (*ICRC archives [ACICR C G1]*)

Plate 5. Crew of German submarine *U-58* surrendering to USS *Fanning*, 17 November 1917. One of the officers, Friedrich Müller, was imprisoned in Skipton from 7 March 1918 until his transfer to the United States on 9 April 1918. (*NH54063, Naval History and Heritage Command, Washington, DC*)

Plate 6. Officers and crew of the German submarine *U-58* entering the Fort McPherson Camp, Georgia, United States in April 1918. Friedrich Müller, who had been imprisoned in Skipton (see Translation Note 31), is one of the men in the front row. (*U.S. National Archives, Local Identifier:165-WW-A161(4)*)

LIST No.187 OF GERMAN PRISONERS OF WAR

EUROPE

NAVAL FORCES

APPENDIX II

17840

Form I.B. 90

Serial Number (1)	Surname (2)	Christian Names (3)	Age or Date of Birth (4)	Rank (5)	Military Particulars, Home Address, etc., and Birthplace (6)	Place of Internment (7)	Place and Date of Capture, Wounds, etc. (8)
					The Pa/W named below were handed over to the Authorities of the United States of America for transfer to the United States of America, as they had been captured by the Naval Forces of the United States of America. The date entered in the Eighth Column is the date on which the Pa/W embarked with a view to their transfer.		
153513	Röpke	Heinrich			List 171	Stbs.12549	9/4.
153514	Stoffels	Hans			List 171	Stbs.12547	9/4.
153515	Rippe	Hermann			List 171	Stbs.12548	9/4.
153516	Grunert	Ernst			List 171	Stbs.12556	9/4.
153517	Steinau	Josef			List 171	Wg.2399	9/4.
153518	Kretzschmar	Kurt			List 171	Wg.2419	9/4.
153519	Rauscher	Ernst			List 171	Wg.2420	9/4.
153520	Bornheim	Viktor			List 171	Stbs.12550	9/4.
153521	Haupt	Artur			List 171	Stbs.12552	9/4.
153522	Sammüller	Michael Franz			List 171	Stbs.12554	9/4.
153523	Birk	Eduard			List 171	Stbs.12555	9/4.
153524	Meyer	Philipp			List 171	Wg.2422	9/4.
153525	Schneider	Kurt Alfred			List 171	Wg.2392	9/4.
153526	Wissemann	Heinrich			List 171	Stbs.12553	9/4.
153527	Trumpold	Paul			List 171	Wg.2402	9/4.
153530	Amberger	Gustav Andreas			List 171	Keg.865	9/4.
153531	von Ritgen	Johannes Ernst Otto			List 171	Keg.866	9/4.
153532	Müller	Friedrich Wilhelm Heinrich			List 171	Skp.372	9/4.
153533	Schroeter	Robert Paul			List 171	Keg.867	9/4.
153534	Selberg	Willy			List 171	Wg.3421	9/4.

Plate 7. Record from the International Committee of the Red Cross showing the transfer of Friedrich Müller from Skipton to the United States of America in April 1918. (*ICRC archives [ACICR C G1]*)

Kopie aus dem Bundesarchiv

Plate 8. Programme for a concert held in the camp on 9, 10 and 11 February 1919. (*Bundesarchiv-Militärarchiv, Freiburg im Breisgau, MSG200/1971*)

Plate 9. Programme for theatre production of *The Doctor's Dilemma* by George Bernard Shaw, held in the camp on 23 and 24 March 1919. (*Bundesarchiv-Militärarchiv, Freiburg im Breisgau, MSG200/1971*)

Clitheroe Times.

FRIDAY, JULY 5, 1918.

* * * * * *

The Germans invaded Chatburn last Sunday. There were only two of them and they entered the village by stealth but left ignominiously in charge of a constable and in the full glare of publicity. In fact, the village was in a veritable ferment for a short time. Rumour had it that the men had escaped from a camp at Skipton, and for once in a while the roumour was founded on fact. The names of the men were Hans Wallbaum (24) and Hans Laskus (22), and with two others they decamped on Saturday evening. Their escape, however, was not discovered until late the following morning and a description of them was immediately circulated. Reaching the village, they entered the Black Bull Hotel and sought to impress the landlord by saying that they belonged to the Royal Flying Corps and had come to inspect the district, for what purpose they did not explain. Their purpose was to engage lodgings and they were ultimately accommodated—but not with the comforts they had anticipated. Information of their arrival was conveyed to P.C. Hawkwood who hurried, post haste, to the hotel and without any beating about the bush accused them of being Huns. Realising that the game was up, Laskus, who could speak English almost without a trace of accent, admitted the truth of the accusation and said, " We escaped from Skipton. Quick work getting a message. We are officers in the German army and will pay cab fare." The constable allowed them to do so, and they were conveyed to Clitheroe Police Station and placed under lock and key in one of the cells. To make assurance doubly sure, they were guarded throughout the night by members of the special police. Each man had a parcel of bread and meat and both had a plentiful supply of cigarettes. In money, however, they had only threepence between them. On Monday morning an armed guard in charge of an officer arrived to escort them back to captivity. They left shortly after noon, a large crowd gathering outside the station. It is to the credit of Clitheroe people, however, that there was no demonstration, but it was noticed that the men travelled " third class." P.C. Hawkwood's astuteness in effecting their arrest was publicly recognised at the County Sessions on Monday morning when Ald. J. T. Whipp, chairman of the bench, said they desired to compliment him on his clever work and expressed the hope that the officer's conduct would be brought to the notice of the Chief Constable for the county. Supt. Palmer promised to carry out the wishes of the magistrates. The other two defaulters were captured on Monday. The capture has soon brought its reward, the announcement being made yesterday that P.C. Hawkwood has been promoted to the merit class.

* * * * * *

Plate 10. The recapture of escapees Hans Laskus and Hans Wallbaum in July 1918. (*Johnston Press plc*)

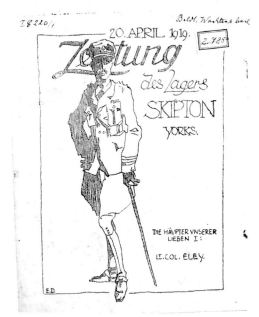

Plate 11. Front cover of Skipton Camp newspaper, 20 April 1919. (*Bundesarchiv-Militärarchiv, Freiburg im Breisgau, MSG200/1560*)

Plate 12. Sketch drawn by a Skipton prisoner of war showing a volleyball game in the camp. (*Bundesarchiv-Militärarchiv, Freiburg im Breisgau, MSG200/2188*)

Plate 13. POW footballers in the Skipton camp. (*Bundesarchiv–Militärarchiv, Freiburg im Breisgau, MSG200/2730*)

Plate 14. Funeral at Morton Cemetery, Keighley, of Skipton prisoners who died in the 1919 Spanish flu outbreak in the camp. (*Photograph courtesy of Ian Dewhirst*)

Plate 15. Funeral at Morton Cemetery, Keighley, of Skipton prisoners who died in the 1919 Spanish flu outbreak in the camp. (*Photograph courtesy of Ian Dewhirst*)

Plate 16. Funeral at Morton Cemetery, Keighley, of Skipton prisoners who died in the 1919 Spanish flu outbreak in the camp. (*Photograph courtesy of Ian Dewhirst*)

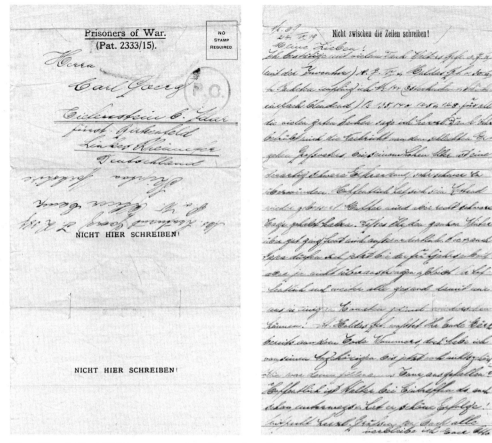

Plate 17 and Plate 18. Letter written by prisoner Otto Goerg to his relative (likely to be his brother) Carl Goerg on 24 April 1919. Translation of the letter:

With thanks I confirm receipt of letters from Walter (07.03 with the inventory and 07.04) and Halda (30.03). I have received packages numbers 144 (splendid Easter cake and ham), 135, 140, 145 and 148. Thank you very much for the wonderful things. I am very saddened to hear that Grandfather has not been well. At his advanced age such a serious illness will be difficult to overcome. I hope his condition has improved. They will have been very difficult days for Mother. I am extremely happy to hear that she has been well throughout the winter. She and Dad mustn't overdo it now in the spring work and hopefully you will stay healthy so that we can see each other again in a few months in a good state of health. According to Halda's letter you both already knew about [someone's name]'s death but I have not heard anything yet from his relatives. How did the [name of a family or place] dance go? Hopefully by the time this letter reaches you, Walter will be well on his way and will be successful!

Very best wishes to you all. I remain yours, Otto.

(Letter reproduced courtesy of Ben McKenzie)

G. R.

MINISTRY OF MUNITIONS.

By Direction of the Disposal Board
(Furniture Section).

CAMP EQUIPMENT AND ENGINEERS' STORES.

For Sale by Auction at
RAIKESWOOD AND PRISONERS OF WAR
CAMP, SKIPTON, YORKSHIRE,
On Tuesday and Wednesday, 15th and 16th
June, at Eleven a.m. Daily.
comprising :—

2000 BLANKETS,

182 Wood and Spring Single Camp Bedsteads,
231 Malta Pattern Bed Cots,
310 Stick Back and various Chairs,
220 Tables, 36 Table Tops, 69 Wood and Iron
Trestles, 180 Forms.
56 Iron Coal Boxes,
878 Coat Hangers,
20 "Simplex" Fire Extinguishers, 9 Dry
Earth Buckets,
58 Bacon Tins, 39 Tea Pails, 4 Mincing
Machines,
51 Metal Meat Dishes, 250 Small Enamel
Basins, 51 Carving Knives and Forks,
3 Sets of Scales and Weights, 28 Hand Fire
Pumps.
171 Brush Handles, Platform Scale, Butcher's
Scale, 5 Butchers' Blocks, 63 Enamel
Plates and Mugs, 21 Enamel Wash
Basins,
271 Brush Trays, 45 Ash Bins and Urine Tubs,
59 G.I. Coal Tubs, 173 Table Cloths,
472 Towels, 542 Palliasse Cases, 617 Pillow
Slips,
262 Fire Buckets, &c., &c.

The Engineer's Stores include :—
Electric Switches, Wires and Batteries, 38
Three-Burner Lamps, 500 Coat Hooks,
50 Inverted Gas Brackets, 3 Rolls of
Felt.
39 New Lamp Globes, 48 Small Lamp
Glasses,
100 Tin Gas Shades, 2 Sun Boilers complete
with Pipes, 4ft. Fire Range, 30 New
Fire Bars, Tub of Pitch,
30 Bath Sprays and Piping, 30 New Posts, 1
Flag Pole, Coil of Barbed Wire, &c.,
&c.

The Furniture, &c., may be inspected on
Saturday, 12th June, between 9 a.m. and 3 p.m.,
and on Monday, 14th June, between 9 a.m. and
5 p.m., by Catalogue, or by Authority from the
Auctioneer—

MR. T. H. TAYLOR,

Caroline Square, Skipton (Tel. 226).
Full particulars in Catalogues to be obtained
free from the Controller, Surplus Government
Property Disposal Board, 18 Queen Anne's
Gate, London, S.W.1, or the Area Office,
Hotel-de-Ville, Leeds ; or the Auctioneer.
Note.—For particulars of other Government
Property for sale see "SURPLUS." price 3d.,
at all bookstalls or by quarterly subscription of
2s. post free in the United Kingdom, payable in
advance to the Director of Publicity, Ministry
of Munitions, Whitehall Place, London, S.W.1.

G. R.

MINISTRY OF MUNITIONS.

By Direction of the Disposal Board (Huts
and Building Materials Section).

SALE OF HUTS

At RAIKESWOOD AND PRISONERS OF
WAR CAMP, SKIPTON, YORKSHIRE.

On Friday, June 18th, at Eleven a.m.
comprising :—

39 MEN'S HUTS, 60ft. by 20ft. by 10ft.

1 R.E. Workshop and Guard Bath House,
92ft. by 13ft. by 9ft. 6in.
2 Drying Rooms, 21ft. by 29ft. 6in. by 12ft.
6in., and 21ft by 21ft. by 9ft.
1 Orderly Room and Verandah, 112ft. by 29ft
by 11ft.
1 Recreation, Reading Room and Canteen,
200ft. by 29ft. by 13ft.
1 Y.M.C.A. Dining Hut and Theatre, 93ft.
by 21ft. by 13ft.
1 Guards' Dining Room, 70ft. by 21ft. by 11ft.
1 Guards' Cookhouse and Stores, 31ft 6in.
by 21ft. by 11ft.
1 Barrack Warden's Stores, 62ft. by 21ft. by
11ft.
1 Officers' Cookhouse, 60ft. by 28ft. by 12ft.
1 Servants' Cookhouse and Dining Hall, 71ft.
by 25ft. by 10ft. 6in.
1 Cart House, 82ft. by 21ft. by 12ft. 6in.
1 Stable, 34ft. 6in. by 21ft. by 10ft. 6in.
1 Coal Yard, 64ft. by 51ft. by 7ft. 6in.
2 Bath Houses, 34ft. by 15ft. by 9ft. 6in.
16 Latrines and Ablution Sheds.
1 Meter House, 16ft. by 11ft. by 6ft.
13 Sentry Boxes, 3ft. by 3ft. by 7ft. and
Gantries 60ft. by 4ft.
1 Canteen Stores, 41ft. 6in. by 20ft. by 10ft.
1 Canteen Coalhouse, Stores and W.C., 29ft.
by 5ft 9in. by 9ft.
2 Store Rooms, 21ft. by 11ft. by 10ft.
1 Work Shop, 78ft. by 20ft. by 9ft.
1 Brick Built Boilerhouse, 7ft. 6in. by 15ft. by
13ft.
3 Wooden Horse Troughs, 12ft. by 2ft. 9in.
each.
1 Ideal Sectional Boiler with 3 tanks.
10 72-inch Double Oven Cooking Ranges.
13 Portable Farm Boilers.
3 Brick Incinerators.
850 Posts, 10ft. 6in. long.
3000 Posts 4ft long.
400 Posts, 5ft. long.
2000 Yards of Barbed Wire Entanglements.
N.B.—All the Huts and Buildings are in excellent condition.

The Huts may be inspected on Saturday, 12th
June, from 9 a.m. to 3 p.m., and on Monday,
14th June, from 9 a.m. to 5 p.m., by Catalogue
from the Auctioneer.

T. H. TAYLOR,

Caroline Square, Skipton (Tel. 226).
Full particulars in Catalogues to be obtained
free from the Area Disposal Officer, Hotel-de-
Ville, Leeds ; or the Auctioneer.
Note.—For particulars of other Government
Property for Sale see "SURPLUS," price 3d.
at all bookstalls, or by quarterly subscription of
2s. post free in the United Kingdom, payable in
advance to the Director of Publicity, Ministry
of Munitions, Whitehall Place, London, S.W.1.

Plate 19. Notice of auctions to sell the huts and equipment from the camp, *Craven Herald*, 11 June 1920.
(*Reproduced courtesy of the* Craven Herald)

Plate 20. Prisoner Friedrich Siems directed the Skipton camp theatre and wrote the section on the theatre on pp. 183–7. After the war Siems became a successful actor and theatre director in Germany. He was artistic director of the theatre of Cologne from 1948 until his death in 1963 at the age of 67.

Friedrich Siems
als Don Karlos

Plate 21. Prisoner Dr Friedrich Eppensteiner at Albert, France, on 26 June 1918, two months prior to his capture at the Battle of Chuignes. Eppensteiner wrote the section on sport on pp. 235–45. Following repatriation, he taught history, German and foreign languages at a secondary school in Tübingen from 1925 until his retirement in 1946. Following his retirement, he became the chairman of the sports club in Tübingen and in 1964 he published a book (*Der Sport*) on the history and theory of sport.

Plate 22. One of the huts from the camp became Rylstone Memorial Hall in the village of Cracoe, 6 miles north of Skipton. It was replaced by the current Cracoe Village Hall in 1996. (*Photograph courtesy of Ralph Chester*)

Plate 23. One of the huts from the camp became Tosside Village Institute. (*Photograph courtesy of Tosside Community Link and Slaidburn Archive*)

Plates 24 and 25. Archaeology on the site of the camp, 2018. (*Photographs: Rob Freeman*)

Plate 26. Ink pots found on the site of the camp in the 1960s. (*Photograph: Rob Freeman*)

Plate 27. German shell fuse found on the site of the camp in 2018. (*Photograph: Rob Freeman*)

Plate 28. German uniform belt hook found on the site of the camp in 2016. (*Photograph: Rob Freeman*)

Plate 29. German trench whistle found on the site of the camp in 2016. (*Photograph: Rob Freeman*)

Plate 30 and Plate 31. German 1 Pfennig coin found on the site of the camp in 2016. (*Photographs: Rob Freeman*)

Plate 32. Editor Anne Buckley with actor Wolf Kahler, grandson of Fritz Sachsse, at the opening ceremony of an information board to mark the site of the camp in July 2019. (*Simon Stevenson*)

Nutcracker Suite, Part 1, Tchaikovsky
Menuett, Boccherini

Solos:
Air for Solo Violin and Orchestra, Bach
Romance for Violin and Orchestra, Svendson
Prelude and Adagio from the Violin Concerto in G minor, Max Bruch
Lied an den Abendstern [Song to the Evening Star], Wagner
Karl V in Wittenberg [Charles V in Wittenberg], Löwe
Cavatina from *La Juive [The Jewess]*, Halévy
The Mayor's Aria from *Zar und Zimmerman [Tsar and Carpenter]*, Lortzing

Dances and Marches:
Künstlerleben [Artist's Life] Waltz, Johann Strauss
The Blue Danube, Johann Strauss
Waltz from *Der Rosenkavalier [The Knight of the Rose]*, Richard Strauss
Barcarolle from *The Tales of Hoffmann*, Offenbach
Estudiantina [Band of Students] Waltz, Waldteufel
Les Patineurs [Ice Skaters] Waltz, Waldteufel
La Paloma, Yradier
Promesse Tzigane, Speranza-Camusat
The Conductor's Song from *Dancing Hussars*, Szirmai
Schleiertanz [Veiled Dance], Funck
Nights of Hadness, Andiette
Regimentskinder March [Children of the Regiment], Fučik
Vater Rhein [Father Rhine] Ceremonial March from *Fräulein Loreley*, Lincke
Kaiserjäger March, Eilenberg
Auszug der Garde March *[The Guards Go Forth]*, Eilenberg

Chamber Music (performed in addition to the main concert programme):
Trio, Op. 68, Haydn
Trio for Cello, Piano and Violin, Handel
Piano Trio No. 2 in C minor, Mendelssohn
Trio in D major, Mozart
Arias, Lotti
Gebet [Prayer], Hiller
Arias, Tartini
Cello Solos from Träume [Dreams], Wagner
Alt-Wiener Tanzweisen [Old Viennese Dances], Kreisler.

Hähner.

Chamber Music

As well as the grand orchestral performances, we had the more intimate activity of chamber music. Soon after the formation of the orchestra, several comrades gathered together in small groups to play chamber music. Once a second piano had been acquired and sheet music had arrived from Germany and London, this more intimate musical activity also began to blossom. These musical gems could often be heard at the main orchestra's concerts when some of the ensemble's members performed solos.

By popular demand, orchestral and chamber music were separated by the foundation of the chamber music society in January 1919. Its members, forty to fifty comrades, agreed to pay sixpence a month. The proceeds from this went towards hiring a third piano, which was placed in the Old Mess. Here, every Thursday afternoon and on Friday evenings during the summer, an 'unambitious' concert was held, implying that the players asked their audience to look kindly on any deficiencies of technique. It was, of course, free for all paid-up members. The piano was moved to the corner of the room opposite the stage, and musicians and audience gathered around it informally.

As well as violin, cello and piano solos (Svendson's *Romance*, Gounod's *Serenade Berceuse*, Kreisler's *Old Viennese Dances*, G. Jensen's *Suite for Violin*), there were also performances of duets by Bach, Handel, and Corelli; violin sonatas by Beethoven, Grieg and Brahms; trios by Handel, Haydn, Mozart, Gade, Mendelssohn, Schumann, Brahms and Volkmann; and piano and string quartets by Haydn, Mozart and Beethoven. Our vocal artists sang *Lieder* by Schubert, Chopin, Loewe, Lortzing, and others. At the request of the audience, the conductor once delivered a commentary on Tchaikovsky's *Symphonie Pathétique*.

These informal gatherings were always uplifting and meditative for all of those involved.

Sichler.

The Gramophone

An account of the camp's musical pleasures would be incomplete without mentioning the instrument whose music was soon to be heard coming from one barracks or another with varying degrees of tunefulness, alternating wildly between military marches and arias from *Cavalleria Rusticana*, repeatedly assuring us, while we were at the barber's, that love is a gypsy invention,[49] or reminding any officers who happened to be passing the kitchen that it was 'a long way to Tipperary'. At ordinary barracks parties and formal gatherings alike, and generously placed at our disposal by its magnanimous owner, it was the gramophone that seasoned the simple meal, the serious or the light-hearted speech. In the kitchen, the kitchen orderlies would be so enraptured by it that they would forget about the cooking, or over-salt the food, or let the porridge burn. In the end, however, the hard rubber records were so worn that even we deprived prisonörs chose to forego the pleasure of listening to the gramophone, or rather its creaking and squeaking; and so it was consigned to oblivion. However, it was revived in the form of one of its components, when the expectant sports-day crowd was informed of results through the horn, which worked perfectly as a megaphone.

Bibeljé.

The flourishing artistic life of the camp was also enhanced by the enthusiastic and successful contribution of the theatrical society.

Our Camp Theatre

"The bleaker the weather in Skipton became, the more we desired sunshine and light; the closer we came to tears, the more eager our desire for joy and laughter. The restless human spirit lights lamps like welcome oases in an endless desert, to brighten even the drabbest and blackest greyness. The monotony of camp days led to a demand for variety, for distraction, for intellectual and visual stimulation. And this gave rise to the creativity and initiative to establish a number of continually developing ventures for engaging with scholarship and art, not least of which was our theatre.

In September our new director of entertainment accomplished his first and most significant feat: the creation of this camp theatre. He gathered together a number of comrades who were willing to be actively involved as performers or technical assistants. The number of members soon increased and by October a permanent organisation was established, separated into performance and technical departments. The inner circle within the theatre committee consisted of the scriptwriter, the director, the treasurer, the head of the technical department and three actors selected from among the members. The committee's remit was firstly to choose which plays would be performed, secondly to decide on the director, who then had a free hand in the casting, and thirdly to monitor new purchases. The monthly general meetings were not just to discuss business; they also offered cheerful and often frivolous entertainment such as poetry and light verse, and popular songs, in a relaxed environment with coffee and cake, cocoa and cider.

It is not only warfare that involves money, money and more money, but the establishment and maintenance of a theatre is also impossible without this widely sought-after commodity. The Skipton camp community recognised this, and so provided the theatre group with about £50 from canteen funds. This was all spent on building the stage, creating suitably elegant surroundings and purchasing the first basic props and costumes. After that the theatre was completely reliant on income from performances. The entry fee for the first night was only 3 pence; due to exaggerated modesty, combined with a substantial underestimation of both the ongoing running

The Skipton theatre and concert hall.

costs and the financial resources of the camp inmates, it was assumed at the time that no more could be charged. As a result of increased awareness of these factors, the entry fee for theatre productions was later fixed at sixpence. The principle of giving the shows an appropriate and attractive setting, so as not only to delight the audience with the performance but also to increase the actors' enthusiasm, compelled the theatre group to set an entry fee of 1 shilling for the Christmas performance, on account of the extra effort and devotion invested in rehearsing and in decor and costumes. From then on the price was nearly always kept at this level.

The stage, which was built from benches in front of the raised platform of the Old Mess, was 6m wide and 7m deep. A green cloth curtain separated its shimmering world of illusion from the outside world. Paintings designed and created by camp artists decorated the proscenium arch. The triangular space below the roof was filled by a portrait that depicted a bronze-green Buddha, in front of whom numerous Chinese were kneeling in fervent prayer, foreheads on the floor, showing their posteriors to the audience, whilst on both sides of the curtains half-naked devadasis swayed their slender, dark limbs in strangely contorted foreign dances. For acoustic reasons, the Buddha, along with his Chinese army, had to evacuate his tympanum for all musical events. In other words, the painted canvas was rolled up, while the Indian dancers hid modestly behind the curtains during Sunday prayers.

The small offices and the library at either side of the stage served the actors as make-up and dressing rooms. It was unbearably overcrowded there on the days of a performance, particularly for plays with a long list of characters. But good humour and love for the cause made the most makeshift situation bearable. A large number of bright gas lamps beamed a dazzling light over the stage. The lamp nearest the stage was transformed by a reflector into a kind of spotlight, in front of which different coloured pieces of glass could be positioned using a mechanism backstage, thus immersing the stage in red, yellow or blue light. Other devices backstage enabled either the auditorium or the stage to be plunged into darkness or re-illuminated by means of a simple unseen flick of the wrist.

When it came to the creation of the lighting system, the head of the technical department proved to be an unsurpassable champion in overcoming difficulties and inventing new possibilities. But the fabrication of new props and costumes also gave him and his assistants ample opportunities for this. Every single item used on stage was produced under his direction in the theatre workshops, with a workforce of mere unskilled officers. For this purpose the detention cells (which were seldom put to their intended use) were available for use by the theatre. These empty rooms were now also used by the actors for role study, and the hard labourers sitting together in what was vulgarly called the stink room may well have often been inspired to exceptional intellectual activity by the muffled symphony of hammering, sawing and Schiller's lustrous lines.

Jute and wooden slats were the main raw materials from which a constantly evolving backdrop was created. Initially there was a dark, hall-like room, whose leather wallpaper above heavy oak panelling had a simple and elegant effect; and through rearranging the doorways by changing the curtains and drapes, it was possible to keep changing its appearance. There was also a bright, friendly salon, made homely by rich pictorial decoration. This replaced the living room decorated in shades of violet, which was the most frequently-used piece of scenery in the initial performances. Finally, there was a sun-drenched beech forest, which opened up onto a peaceful clearing, and a colourful flower garden, which was bordered on the left by the façade of a summerhouse. There were also a number of further scenes, which were however, for economic reasons, painted over immediately after the production for which they were required so that they could be used again. Several comrades worked tirelessly as scene painters.

Some, but not all, of the costumes also originated in the camp. Most of them were purchased either through the canteen manager or directly from London from the company C.H. Fox, who also provided the wigs and makeup. It proved very useful that our comrades from the Navy kindly put their uniforms at our disposal for plays that required formal costumes. The uniform buttons and badges were covered with dark fabric to make them into immaculate civilian clothes. Over time, the theatre acquired a collection of costumes that included almost all types of formal suits and a number of pieces of fine women's clothing with all the accessories. These were carefully stored in sturdy crates on the other side of the barbed wire under the watchful eye of the English, and were only brought into the camp for the performances.

The highest demand for props and costumes was for the Christmas performance of *Turandot*. One of the camp artists designed the costumes according to the director's instructions, the head of the technical department cut them from colourful, cleverly dyed fabrics, and then a number of group members sat for weeks sewing, stitching and adding trimmings. Twenty complete costumes had to be finished within three weeks, and while one room served as a tailor's workshop, in another fantastical headdresses, wide oriental swords, pointed and twisted daggers and other weapons and equipment were created by the skilled hands of the comrades in the technical department.

The motivation behind the programme selection by the theatre management should be apparent from the attached list of plays. At the beginning there was not a great deal of choice. We were forced to make do with whatever plays were available in the camp. We even had to include musical evenings and cabaret evenings. Steps were immediately taken to acquire literature, with only very limited success. Only K. E. Markel and the German Student Services sent relatively useful things, albeit late. Our requests to other camp theatres did not prove fruitful. But the powerful force of chance nevertheless ensured that the theatre management was able to organise a programme based on firm criteria, even if complete fulfilment of those wishes could not be achieved with the limited resources available and the very particular prison camp atmosphere. From the outset, the theatre management was aware that performances should first and foremost provide amusement and liberating laughter. Nevertheless, we attempted to put on comedies of literary value and interest as well as cheap farce. Finally, for the sake of genuine intellectual stimulation, it was also the aim of the theatre management to make room for modern drama with its profound awareness of social problems. Therefore a 'studio theatre' was established, which evoked keen interest and lively approval in March with Strindberg's *Creditors* and, after a preliminary and explanatory lecture, with Ibsen's *Ghosts* in May. The richness and variety of our repertoire is demonstrated by the programme below. This is how the Skipton theatre, with considerable effort, sought for many months to serve fellow imprisoned comrades. When, one day, we are free to return to our life's purpose, using our strength in the service of the Fatherland, then may the thought of the theatre be one of the shining lights among the many sad recollections, displacing the grey memories of the camp with a conciliatory glow."

Siems.

Our Theatre Programme

Schiller: Turandot
Shakespeare: Much Ado About Nothing; The Merchant of Venice
Ibsen: Ghosts
Strindberg: Creditors
Shaw: The Doctor's Dilemma; Major Barbara
Wilde: The Importance of Being Earnest
Hartleben: A Word of Honour
Schönthan: Der Raub der Sabinerinnen [Romulus and the Sabines]
Freytag: The Journalists
Schnitzler: Anatol: 1. The Question to Fate 2. Episode 3. Farewell Supper
Kotzebue: The Absent-minded Ones
Benedix: The Rusticated Students
Bonn: Sherlock Holmes
Philippi: Die Wunderquelle [The Healing Waters]
Thoma: First Class
Stahl: Tilli; Mädchenaugen [Maiden Eyes]
Malkowski: Zu Befehl, Herr Rittmeister [At Your Orders, Captain]
Wolters: Leander im Frack [Leander in Tails]
Wilhelmi: Einer muss heiraten [One Must Marry]
Kastner: Der Hotelregisseur
Kaibel: System
Belly: Monsieur Herkules
Keller: Ein Kater [Mirror the Cat]

Also recitals, musical evenings, cabarets

All this mental stimulation frequently turned our thoughts and feelings away from the greyness and suffering of our captivity and our people's distress. For whole hours and days, sometimes even forever, it lifted us to heights where we forgot the little things and felt at one with every one of our different comrades. Thus we all became closer. The bond that was established between the comrades was indeed a blessing of captivity. We lived side by side every day; we experienced each other's peculiarities and learnt to accept them. Through others our own individuality became clear, through others we learnt the rights and wrongs of our values, through others our own duties became clear to us. The understanding of the inner life of others brought enrichment to many of us. Confrontation with unfamiliar ideas was often accompanied by intense clashes. In some of our fellow men we found opposing, incompatible minds, whereas in others we found like-minded spirits or we gratefully discovered considerable and invaluable qualities. With some men we agreed on political, academic, artistic and developmental aims, and in others we found loyal companions. In this way, camp life gave rise to many valuable and close friendships, which will maintain their personal and functional value beyond the short period of time spent in Skipton.

Lutheran Worship

Thoughts of distant loved ones, exposure to the events of the World War, our individual fate and that of our country, our future and the endless desolation here often weighed heavily on our souls, so the question of religion occupied us more intensely than usual. One wanted to exchange lethargic idleness for constructive action, nebulous oppressive thoughts for certainties, faltering restlessness for firm desire and faith. One wanted solace for one's own suffering and for that of others. Initially it was the torment of the individual soul, which, left in isolation while the fate of the world was being decided in blood and suffering elsewhere, felt the desire for something strong that could lift up the spirit in this time of human impotence. The best that was in us struggled in the silence in which all true piety grows, but ultimately the soul which possesses only itself and does not live in communion with others breaks down in this solitude. It searches for that power which is also the strength and inner meaning of every other living thing, and so strives towards God the father of us all. It

Worship.

steps out of its narrow circle and seeks to join the other souls who are looking towards the same heights for solace and strength. It aspires to cast itself into the powerful current of eternal life alongside fellow countrymen, and to let itself be carried along. So, early on in our camp, the desire for religious worship arose, the desire to learn through communal reflection and quiet meditation before God to love and to follow the paths which had been found and trodden before us by loyal comrades in the same plight and with the same earnest desire.

Holy Week 1918 brought us the first religious service in Room A. On Whitsunday we gathered in the Old Mess. On the stage, in front of the green curtain, was the altar covered in a white cloth with a black cross. On top of it was a lectern draped in black cloth; to the right and left of this, candles glowed on simple wooden candlesticks. From this time on, all services took place here. Every two or three weeks, 150 to 200 officers gathered for communal worship on Sunday mornings. The hymns we sang together were accompanied by piano, and later by harmonium. A church choir was soon established, which assumed the duty of planning the music for the services. The esteemed choir master reports:

"Some officers from the choral society immediately offered to serve this good cause. Initially only a double quartet, the church choir then gained a few more members, so that soon each part was sung by three or four comrades. There were never more than sixteen voices, but this was quite sufficient for our purposes.

At first we were greatly hampered by a lack of sheet music, as no one in the camp had motets or choral arrangements suitable for church. To begin with, parts of the liturgy or a chorale were sung in the style familiar to the conductor from the Prussian State Church. Later, hymns and motets were also sung. Rehearsals were held once a week, for an hour. The participation and enthusiasm of the singers was quite gratifying. During services we generally sang at the beginning and immediately after the sermon; it was usually a piece from the liturgy or the great doxology at the beginning, and one or two verses from a chorale after the sermon."

Three camp theologians took turns to give the sermons. Taking the enormity and hardships of the time as their starting point, they tried, amid the unsettling turmoil of the world events, to guide individuals to the unshakeable certainty of religious life, to contemplate and affirm the heroic suffering of the German people from a religious perspective, thus preparing a pathway of faith towards a new age.

Services for the enlisted men took place on Sunday afternoons in their dining hall and later in the music store, and major festivals were celebrated in the Old Mess. There were not usually many attendees, generally no more than ten, but this did not discourage the camp preachers. For them it was simply a pleasure to keep seeing the same dear faces.

During the course of our captivity, twenty-five services were held for officers and twenty for enlisted men. They so often lifted us out of the misery and bleakness of our life in captivity to a higher plane and, in giving us solace and strength, brought us closer to God. May their blessing continue to lead us towards God's presence after our captivity and impel us to constructive, manful deeds.

Höhn, K.

Catholic Worship

At the request of our Catholic comrades, the English camp administration enabled Catholic services to take place in the camp from the middle of February 1918. Father P. Bethell from Skipton kindly agreed to conduct the services.

Since the priest was fully occupied on Sundays with his church duties in Skipton, the weekly camp service was arranged for Fridays at 8 o'clock in the morning. The service consisted only of Holy Mass with a reading from the appropriate Gospel, since the English clergyman's inadequate mastery of the German language prevented him from giving sermons. There was the opportunity to take Holy Communion every Friday. When the priest fell seriously ill, services unfortunately had to be cancelled for several weeks throughout Advent and Lent.

It proved difficult to find a room. In the first months, empty accommodation barracks were still available to us, but after the camp became fully occupied we were left with no other option than to hold services in the enlisted men's dining hall, the interior of which was hardly fitting for this holy purpose. During the winter months, lack of heating meant we were restricted to the music room next to the sports ground. The decision to allow us, firstly at Easter and at Whitsun 1919, and then regularly from the middle of June 1919, to hold our services every second Friday in the Catholic Church of St Stephen's in Skipton, was welcomed by all.

As our services had to be held in the most unassuming of surroundings, we attempted to make them more dignified by setting up a small church choir, which successfully performed choral masses and German hymns on holy days. During normal services it later became more common for the whole congregation to sing.

While lacking some of the aesthetic features that we had grown fond of in services and church attendance at home – here too captivity enforces sacrifice – the core of Catholic worship, the Holy Mass, bestows God's mercy and divine blessing even within the prison camp just as it does elsewhere.

Arnold.

Diaries give us an insight into our grappling with religion in our camp. These most intimate and tenuous voices of inner life, with all their contradictions, may give us a picture of the religious beliefs of the prisoners.

The Prisoners' Religious Beliefs

"Oh how the men here in the camp, with nothing else to do, get carried away with grand theoretical ideas! I have never been a philosopher or a theologian, nor would I ever want to be. What do I know of the meaning of life? Is it not all just words? Who can ever make sense of this World War? I am less ambitious. When the storms roar above and tear down walls and houses, I cower down in my little hole in the ground and wait for it all to blow over. Then I crawl out again and look at the tree stumps and the rubble and quietly go on my way."

"Oh, how I laugh at these idealists and religious enthusiasts! It seems to me to be one of the advantages of being a prisoner that every day I can observe and listen to men turning into little fantasists. I see how their God comes into being. When the news of victories came, their German souls were proud and filled with joy – so they created a righteous, strong God. And when defeat and revolution descended, their wings drooped – so their God became unfathomable and harsh. So out of their own wretched condition they create for themselves their highest entity. God, in man's image. Our camp preachers are the same: they make divinity out of their own ideas and naïvely create a fanciful mythological world from an illusion. I laugh at these naïve fools – and while laughing I stick to the facts. I am my own God and can easily construct my earthly life from facts."

"Between the war and captivity, I have lost God. I saw brave and loyal comrades fall while cowardly shirkers triumphantly returned home with their wretched lives. In the machine-gun fire and the hell of shelling I saw no reason, only blind chance. In the terror of heavy fire I listened, trembling, for a comforting voice. But in the screaming of my agonised, bleeding men, in the horror of elemental human violence, in the hammering to pieces of nerves and mental strength I have always sensed the grim senseless pressure that bears down on our human lives. What place is there here for God, and all the solace that is said to bathe us and him with golden light! And now, with our empire collapsed and our loyal devotion sunk so pointlessly into the dust, with the virtue that we held sacred and certain in our hearts scorned and mocked by the world, where now is the justice of world events, and where is the higher spiritual power that champions our truth against all the lies! The war and its peace shatter all faith!"

"Time and again I have wondered how all the harrowing events of war passed some people by without a trace. Many, particularly younger, barely awakened minds have let everything drift by with eyes and hearts closed. They have learnt nothing from the most significant event in the history of the world. For others the impact was only short lived. There they go again, gliding happily and thoughtlessly along the smooth superficial path of life, as though life has no depths. I often ask myself whether religion is not simply a gift and a talent."

"In war and in captivity I have found that no one loses faith and no one finds it. He who loses it never had it in the first place, and he who finds it had it all along flourishing silently within him."

"For me in captivity, it was my feelings about home that reawakened my religious faith. I suffered so unspeakably from separation from my nearest and dearest and felt that only their love for me had made my existence worthwhile. It seemed to me then that the fulfilment of everything important in life stems from love, and that showed me the way to God."

"I have so often poured scorn on religious tradition. But the war and captivity, with their hardships, have taught me to value it again. What gave father and mother and all my ancestors strength, will also be for me, the son and grandson, my staff and support. Often when, in the hardship of the last year, I found no resources within me, I felt the hand of faith reaching out from my forefathers."

"Often, captivity has led me to loneliness or even a sense of abandonment. At such times I became aware that one cannot live so completely alone. Then God came to me."

"The lack of true meaningful activity here in the camp has, it seems to me, also greatly constricted religious life. Our thoughts are weary and the bleakness of each day means that nothing happens. That is why God is so seldom here and his presence barely discernible. I see yet again that God only reveals himself where morality is put into practice. Those who are free to work constructively can see and experience God, and they are never without God."

"In the midst of our great collapse I am not able to think great thoughts as I would only be grasping at straws. But from the ruins I hear a quiet voice constantly urging me onwards: be humble and work as though the fate of your people rests on your purity and your actions!"

"M. is a peculiar fellow. Yesterday he received a letter informing him of his mother's death. I said to him, 'You see, God is dead. The homeland has perished, and now so too has your mother! Life itself is meaningless and cruel!' Then he stood up and said, 'God is dead? Then I will live him back to life.'"

"Without a doubt, the death of young comrades always cut me to the quick but never led me to doubt my faith. Everyone dies once he has fulfilled his task in life, and the decision as to when he departs from this world rests in the hand of God."

"It was here in captivity that the reason for religion first dawned on me. When the Fatherland was destroyed from within and without, I was in agonising despair. But a religious service here in the camp restored light and strength. I saw the old Israelite prophets appear before me; they, too, were in torment and the suffering in their homeland had destroyed almost everything for them, but their faith was indestructible. Now I know that religion in such times as we are now experiencing is a jubilant comfort. I no longer question anything; I do not question the destruction of worldly goods, or the weakness of others – I believe, and I stand firm. Even if everyone else sinks down, if everyone tells me that the world of possessions and love is a mirage, I do not let all this pessimism grind me down. Am I, the believer, not proof that God's world is still active in our lives! I can withstand the pointlessness of life. Through me it is revealed that religion is power and light. I am building a new and yet age-old, eternal life!"

"It is incomprehensible that what is most precious to us has been taken away. I see how so many here in this camp do not possess the religious strength necessary to comprehend this. The blame for this seems to me to lie in part with our religious teaching. God has been presented to us far too much as a loving, benevolent father, and this has failed to provide us with sufficient strength and insight to cope with the worst eventuality. We were not taught enough about the harshness and bitterness inherent in all true religion. The fact that religion also thrusts a sword into the soul and into history is something we should have learnt better and experienced more."

"It is with deep concern that I have felt here in the camp how strongly our modern religion has been smothered by aestheticism. Sermons are often only valued for their formal and rhetorical qualities; no notice is taken of the content. Religion appears only as an artistically harmonious interpretation of the universe and as a finely-tuned receptive conduit of the individual's own soul. However, the fact that religion requires willingness of the soul, acceptance of all life's contradictions, devotion to an ultimate deity, and readiness to undertake difficult tasks in the service of what is real – all of this is missing from the understanding of so many men. Everything to do with religion is so sickly sweet, so delicate and hence of such little substance and so pathetically ineffective. This development in turn must be dragging down the directness and vigour of the German people's spirit. It is a danger against which we must fight."

"Our religious life seems to me to be too strongly bound by dogma. In school and at church we learnt about Christianity as though it were a matter of eternally fixed and never-changing truths. This appears to me to be a basic mistake. God is the eternally new and he enters our souls every day in different forms. God is only immanent. God is an eternal secret revealed to us daily, surprising and delighting us anew. Because He is this enduring life, every religious person must be prepared to see Him anew at all times and to strongly affirm His daily revelations. If they had done so, many here in the camp would have understood God better during these times and would not have allowed themselves to be continually tossed hither and thither by the tides of a wearying and strife-torn life."

"The dreadful events hit me hard. The impotence of our humanity and the guilt that we have all brought upon ourselves have deeply humbled me. Since

I cannot live without strength and yet I do not find this strength anchored in my own being, my yearning for God and my determination that he must exist have grown in me out of this spiritual desolation. I must bind myself to a higher entity in order to live. So, here, I have learned that power can arise from a broken life."

"Religion is the courage to seek the eternal."

"War and life in captivity have forced me to face some difficult questions. I see the whole of humanity in conflict and an immeasurable extent of suffering resulting from it. Since my intellect is focused on understanding and my religious feeling is that God is to be found in all things, I cannot believe that anything can happen without God's help. But then the present forces the most difficult realisation into my life: that God, as well as being the source of all happiness, must also be the creator of all terrible suffering. I feel that as a religious person I must accept this realisation, but it is agony. I can only accept it if I see this terrible side of godly life as a blessing for myself and our people. For this reason it seems to me to be an essential task, especially for the perplexed and confused German people, to consider their terrible fate as a blessed stage in our development."

"World events, with all their contradictions, can only be adequately understood from the viewpoint of pantheism. One should put aside all dogmatic theological rigidity and learn to feel the whole world as a manifestation of an inexhaustible life force. All our little struggles are indeed only part of the great workings of the all-encompassing, immanent divinity. These passionate struggles, this surge of opposing forces to form ever new entities in the great flow of life amount to the coming into being of the Holy Spirit. We ourselves are the elements of this great struggle and from us the divine world is built. For this reason a holy light shines around us, and relentless adversity – including that of the present – will become our happiness because it is essential for the coming into being of God."

"It is said that humanity has only one God, not a specific one for each people and that there is therefore no German God either. Doubtless this is right, because God is the basis of all life and mankind. But here in contemplative captivity, considering the isolation of our people, I have come to the realisation that there is a German faith and therefore also in a sense a German God. God manifests himself through the particular nature of man. The German people have preserved their nature and history, and God has revealed himself to us in a particular way. It is precisely the extraordinary fate which our people must now face and to which no other nation has ever been so subjected that will create a piety which is particular to us Germans. So of course we would refer to a German God."

"We have learnt here to see the events surrounding us from a higher vantage point. Death has lost its sting for us; we no longer fear it. We have learnt to understand the common man now; we have learnt his language, his thoughts and feelings and we bow down before the quiet greatness of his heroism. Many grand things in the world have lost their allure for us. We have looked into our hearts and where we expected strength and altruism, we found hollowness and selfishness. We have learnt how to differentiate between truth and lies. We now know what true friendship and what true love are. We also know one more thing – and we will not forget it – that a being rules over us, before whom we are nothing but dust, but who still looks upon us through a father's eyes and allows us to find him when we look for him. We have sensed God's presence too often in our darkest hours not to have gained an unwavering conviction that God walks beside us through life when we ask him to."

"The present, which binds our individual fate so powerfully to the public and private experiences of the German people, also leads me beyond the lonely personal encounter with God to the belief in the God of history. He who gives value to my own life also confirms the meaning of all existence. It is he who also leads people and nations along dark mysterious paths, paths that lead to a destination."

"During my imprisonment, nothing has given me so much strength and courage as the certainty that even here it is not blind chance that prevails, but that the 'Father in Heaven' speaks to me through the suffering and the waiting, and expects so much of me. There were times when I found everything so strange, so devoid of love, both the people around me and most of all what was happening. Whenever people's ideas made me so uneasy and the Fatherland seemed to me to be so downtrodden, as though by the evil power of an enemy who knew about everything but love, then the figure of the Saviour would stand before me and I would see his eyes full of eternal love and at that moment knew, 'You are not alone'. God was then so near to me and shone a light onto many obscure mysteries. Our Father lives! After all! And so I will believe, work and wait."

"Never before in my life have I become more conscious of the tremendously liberating power of the Lutheran hymn *Eine feste Burg ist unser Gott* [*A Mighty Fortress Is Our God*] than in November 1918 here in the camp. The unshakeable belief that ultimately love and truth must indeed triumph over hate and lies kept me happy and hopeful even in the hardest of times."

"Oh how the people here shock me sometimes! So much about them is petty and philistine and there are only few among them who are capable of very strong faith, as strong as that of a child. Even when one wants to take heart from the best of them, when one gets closer, one sees only their own misery. But they do at least make travelling companions with whom one can share the journey. With them one feels then that no other human being is capable of giving us the last and highest thing, and that brings one closer to God. That is another blessing of imprisonment."

"I thank this imprisonment for turning my life around. I have gone blithely through life without giving much thought to myself or the world. I avoided anything serious and only sought out companions to laugh and joke with. Here, however, imprisonment left me no great choice and I had to measure my trivial life against serious comrades. That was when I began to feel ashamed. I learnt from one or two of them how terribly petty and shallow my existence was. I saw in a few of them a pure strength of will, an unshakeable religious faith, a relentless search for everything that was precious and good. There, in the presence of these men of strong faith, I felt a sense of my childish restlessness and the trivial content of my life. I cannot continue in my old life any more, and I must begin afresh. I often feel a quiet gratitude that God brought me here."

"The cheery high spirits, for which many envied me, were lost in captivity, my peace of mind replaced by moodiness and temper. I felt the burning shame of being a useless parasite here, whilst loyal brothers-in-arms were allowed to die with the word 'home' on their twitching lips because they carried loving thoughts of home with them until their final hour. But I was fortunate in that, like the trees, I could find the waters and wells to revive my will to live. 'I know the thoughts that I think towards you, thoughts of peace and not of evil',[50] as the one whom I may call Father once said to wretched prisoners through his servant. Are the terrible afflictions not also God's judgement? Is it not folly to believe that a few leading statesmen have led the world into so much blood and misery! It was distrust, envy and national pride that divided the nations of this earth and it has become clear to me, sadly rather late, that thoughts of envy, selfishness and resentment towards our neighbours played a part in generating this terrible tension, which had to erupt into violent war at some point. And that I become complicit in the next war if I continue to harbour such thoughts. For this reason, if I try during this time of imprisonment, through unrelenting self-discipline and work, to set aside all that is not good; to work on self-improvement, so that after the war I can quietly work to serve my people; to dispense as much love and kindness as possible and to enlighten all those who do not know what wonders love can do, then I will praise this bleak time in captivity as a gift of mercy given to me by him who has 'thoughts of peace and not of evil.' "

In addition to the comfort provided by the activities in the camp and by one's own thoughts, the walks also offered a pleasant distraction. From the autumn of 1918 one of our staff officers put a great deal of effort into planning these very proficiently, having procured a large map of Skipton's surroundings, and he often approached the English with this own suggestions. The commandant accommodated our wishes. We walked daily for up to 2½ hours and got to know some of the surrounding villages: Carleton, Cononley, Draughton, Rylstone, Gargrave, Broughton (with the beautifully situated Broughton Hall) and Halton East among others. On some days we ventured up onto the nearby ridge of hills through woodland, moorland and gorges. We saw the ruins of Norton Tower and the place where a tower belonging to the Cliffords had once stood.

The gritstone hills.

We could rarely enjoy the view because the area was almost always shrouded in mist and fog.

These walks were of great benefit for the physical and psychological wellbeing of all comrades, some of whom never missed a walk. For a few hours it gave us a sense of freedom. The varied beauty of this charming region delighted our eyes; the refreshing movement improved our posture. The frequent change of route meant we could get to know the countryside, the people, and foreign customs and make comparisons with the Fatherland.

A keen walker paints a picture of our ...

Walks

"When a layman (that is, someone who has not had the privilege of spending part of his life behind barbed wire) hears the word 'walk' he thinks of a leisurely stroll around his little home town, usually with his girl, of wandering down to the nearest hostelry, or even a carefree ramble through fields and woodland. In very much the same way, with only minor differences, the prisonör also takes his walk.

Our own lovely walk along the promenade here in the camp is similar to the one at home. It stretches from the gate as far as the entrance to the sports ground, sometimes not so far if the last section of the path has become impassable due to the pleasantly damp and dust-free English climate. Despite the highly commendable work of our pathways committee, it is not always possible for them to maintain the whole stretch of the promenade in an accessible condition. We stroll alone, or in twos or threes; a threesome is rare and difficult due to the narrowness of the shadowy[51] paths. The word 'shadowy' simply slipped from my pen. However, there is little possibility of shadowing anybody here. The elder tree behind which one could conceal oneself to engage in such an activity is indeed next to the path; in fact there are two or three. However, the most important thing is missing: the courting couple and the rival whom one secretly wishes to shadow. We stroll along the winding path inside the camp at an early or late hour, even at a very late hour after our English hosts very obligingly permitted us to walk 'freely' around the camp even after 10 o'clock at night. Just as we would on a stroll around our own small town, here too we sometimes glance at the window displays even though there is nothing to see other than a toothbrush, a shaving brush, or a small bottle of something harmless. The adorable sales girl is missing too. We only see a face at the window when someone is putting an intense effort into making his hair and visage conform to culturally acceptable standards (as the mirror required for this purpose is usually hanging in the middle of the window). Or a face may be seen in the windows of the barracks down in the lower compound, where mostly older, dignified prisonörs live, looking out with keen interest to see if the porridge is being brought to the messes or if the parcel lists are on their way, or whether the store is looking busy, indicating that some special *Schiebung* has worked out well.

Our walking pace is slow and dignified. In the beginning there were some inexperienced novices who rushed around frantically as if searching for a way out. These men were taken care of and advised as to the dangers of going too close to the wire fence, and particularly on the path that sloped steeply downhill towards the main gate they were held back lest there was any danger of them getting too close to it. There were some foolish characters who were unable to appreciate their stay in the camp and who wanted to leave it without permission, so it was quite rightly forbidden to approach within five paces of the main gate.

And so that sums up walking within the camp. Now let us speak of our excursions out into 'freedom'. Our ever congenial hosts really do go to a lot of trouble to keep us safe. It would be no easy thing for a band of villains from outside to attack us. On the rare occasions the gate is opened for us, it is done so with a display of military power, the like of which I have otherwise only seen to honour the highest dignitaries and of course we duly value this honour. In the early days the commandant appeared in person. The adjutant is nearly always present. Then there is the interpreter, the officer who will lead the walk, usually also the one on guard duty, a sergeant major and a few other guards. One of our comrades reads out the names of those whose turn it is to go out on the walk. Then everyone hands his signed form to the sergeant major. For the edification of posterity its content is as follows:

> 'Temporary parole by an Officer Prisoner of War
> I hereby promise and undertake that, during the period I am permitted to leave this place of internment for the purpose of taking exercise, I will make no attempt to escape, will make no preparation for a future attempt to escape, and will commit no act prejudicial to the British Empire or her Allies.'[52]

The gate is a double one. But, while in Schiller's well-known lions' den in *The Glove* two gates fly open to let two leopards leap out at once, here just one comrade at a time walks slowly out through two consecutive single gates, saluting to the right between the two gates and then again beyond the second gate. He is then a free man, or at least almost as free as those two leopards who exchanged the freedom of the cage for the freedom of the arena. If it should happen that a comrade inadvertently overlooks the English officer between the narrow gates and does not salute him, he has to go back and make up for this oversight. To part without a salute and a friendly look from his host, even for a matter of hours, is something that strict English etiquette cannot allow the prisonör. The first walk outside the camp was particularly impressive in military terms because the accompanying officer had retrieved a huge sword from the armoury of his forefathers in order to defend us to the death. The sword's basket hilt was so large that it could not be worn at the side. It was therefore fastened to the hero's left breast. Nevertheless, the tip almost reached the ground while the hilt protruded over his shoulder – a truly prodigious, awe-inspiring and terrifying murder weapon. Unfortunately, the bearer was a dignified elderly man, somewhat bowed down by the maturity of his years or perhaps even by the weight of his weapon. Regrettably, this man's real name escapes me. Amongst ourselves he was generally known by the name *Winkelried*.[53] He brought the sword with him only once, probably because it became clear that the area surrounding Skipton was, after all, not as dangerous as had at first been assumed.

Once we are all assembled outside the gate, they count us again as a safety measure and then we set off. We are always preceded by an English officer, who has kindly been given to us as a guide through this entirely unfamiliar landscape. That is, however, not enough. At the rear follows another English soldier, who, to our astonishment, is armed with just a bayonet. After all, we are used to seeing the other Tommies ordered to protect us always carrying a rifle and mounted bayonet. I can only hope that he at least has a hidden revolver with him as well. Under this military escort, we then slowly leave the camp's immediate surroundings. Of course, the rate of motion varies greatly between forty or more comrades of various ages, various temperaments and various ranks. The consequence of this is that the line soon becomes noticeably strung out. Naturally, this then puts us at risk. Just imagine a sudden attack from the side and think about the inadequate cover! That could be disastrous. The warrior at the rear is therefore wisely ordered, as a precaution, to give a shrill whistle whenever the distance between himself and the guide seems to him to be too great. He does so reliably and frequently. The walkers at the front stop until the line is once more of the right length, or rather the right shortness, then they set off again. This extremely amusing game is repeated very frequently to begin with, until we have mastered the correct average pace and, above all, until we have given our kind hosts the idea of establishing two walking groups – the so-called fast walkers and the normal walkers. Naturally, I do not wish to imply that the fast walkers themselves were abnormal; it was only their pace that was not always normal. Besides, nothing seems abnormal to us prisonörs anymore. In our home country we are used to walking along the side of the road on a raised pavement, while here we have been shown the benefits of walking on the road itself. The pavement is surfaced with hard flagstones or made from coarse gravel that wears down the soles of our shoes unpleasantly. The road, however, stretches before us with a perfectly smooth, soft, springy surface. In England even the rural roads are surfaced with tar. Walking on the road has yet another advantage, however. After all, we would really like to get to know the inhabitants of this damp island, and particularly its daughters. If while walking on the pavement in a dense crowd one encounters such a charming creature, one only catches sight of her at the last moment. Before one has properly taken in the sweet sight, she has already vanished as if by magic. How different it is walking on the road! Even from a distance, one gets a first glimpse of the enchanting vision. 'Ah, there is something female approaching!' Excited curious anticipation: young or old, pretty or plain? She is getting closer, she really is getting closer and closer! One takes a closer look, and then another look, but then one looks quickly away to the other side, at the pretty cows and sheep that populate the meadows in such large numbers. Oh, we had such incredibly high expectations and the disappointment is often so bitter – true, it was a daughter of Eve who passed by, but whether the blessed Adam would have taken the apple from her hand, I doubt very much. Flat-chested, bespectacled, with the stern features of a nun – to an Eve such as this, Adam would surely have said 'Oh, no thank you, I've already eaten.' In truth, what we saw of the daughters of Albion here gave our eyes little pleasure and our hearts little joy, with very few exceptions.

To begin with, the town itself was strictly out of bounds. It was only after months had gone by that the English dared lead us, rarely at first and then more frequently, through the streets. But then, all of a sudden, we had to avoid the town again. We had been repeatedly attacked in the very centre of the town with stones, pieces of ice and even with an iron bar. Each time, however, the brave English officers successfully warded off these attacks. It has nevertheless been alleged that the Tommy at the rear sought protection in our ranks during the iron-bar attack. But that could well be slander.

At home it is common to take a walk to the nearest hostelry. We do the same here. Admittedly, I am only familiar with one of these convenient inns in the immediate vicinity of Skipton: The Craven Heifer. This whole region is named after Lord Craven and the heifer was a particularly powerfully built young cow from the local area that then also won first prize at a show in London. After all, London is world famous for the large cows within its city walls. So it was pleasing to hear that our Skipton did better than London. Above the entrance to the inn there is a magnificent painting that has unfortunately now suffered from the inclement climate but still decorates the outside of the establishment, a poor likeness of that magnificent animal. We stand at the door of the inn considering whether or not we should fortify ourselves a little within, when we unfortunately remember the cursed slip of paper on which we promised not to jeopardise the English state in any way. How could we then drink up their 'hope ale' and whisky! We are also well aware that we are very well fed by our kitchen 'at home', so we might as well save our money. We therefore turn around and, after an absence of 1½ hours, reach the gate of our fortified camp once again. How we long to get inside! Each man pushes to be the first. But before we enter, our military guard of honour must all gather together and the gate, so under threat, must be duly manned. Then the interpreter reads aloud the list of names and hands each man his declaration, gracious salutes are exchanged and finally we are once again happily at home behind the barbed wire."

Schrader.

The longer walks of the more senior officers were also continued. They were led by Lieutenant Robert or Assistant Commandant Major Parkhurst.

Christmas Celebrations

The winter days passed full of such troubles and their consolations. Our Sunday of commemoration of the dead, *Totensonntag*, celebrated as always in November, affected us more profoundly than ever. That day's sermon impressed upon us that the only true and manful way to honour the dead is by faithfully and bravely continuing to live according to their most noble aims. In the evening, the orchestra's solemn tones filled the Old Mess and the male-voice choir sang Hegar's *Totenvolk* for us. Then came Advent. Separated though we were by a foreign land and a foreign sea from our loved ones, the festive season cast its spell even upon us poor exiles. Back in the summer

Merry Christmas.

months, the camp administration had organised a competition to design artistic Christmas cards. The War Office had authorised each of us to send ten of these cards (with an image of the Skipton camp in the snow) home to loved ones. We ordered Christmas trees and decorations: the green firs soon arrived. Our minds conjured up images of German forests and of hearth and home in Christmas candlelight. Triumphantly, representatives from each barracks brought in the trees and, wherever possible, hid them from the inquiring eyes of the others to increase the surprise. Christmas was fast approaching. The camp administration and the kitchen, the artistic societies and individual members of the community all became caught up in a feverish flurry of mostly secretive activity. Christmas parcels and letters from home had already started to arrive; with joyful hearts we felt the arms of our loved ones reaching out to us. We looked anxiously out at the gloomy, damp weather, scanning the sky in hope of Christmas snow. It came. Over Christmas, a white blanket covered the camp and the surrounding hills and valleys with a festive glow. The messes were transformed into green bowers by masses of foliage. On the evening of 23rd December the orchestra's Christmas concert created a festive atmosphere in the camp.

Programme
Part 1

1. Festival overture *A Mighty Fortress*: Otto Nicolai
2. a) *Aria* (cello): Lotti
   b) *Prayer* (bass solo accompanied by harmonium): F. Hiller
3. Christmas carols
4. *Evening prayer and pantomime (apparition of the angel)* from Act II of *Hänsel and Gretel*: E. Humperdinck

Part 2

5. *Hungarian Dance*
6. *Hungarian Dance No. 6*
7. *Hungarian Dance No. 5*
8. *Fantasia on Hungarian Folk Melodies*

 J. Brahms

The religious celebrations took place in the late afternoon of 24th December. Two religious services for the officers were held, with the service for the enlisted men scheduled between them. In the Old Mess, which had been decorated with greenery, the bright glow of two Christmas trees shone from the altar table. The *Christkindleins Wiegenlied* [*Christ Child's Lullaby*], sung by our male-voice choir, sounded tender and heartfelt in the dimly lit room and our dear old Christmas carols rejoiced in the accompaniment of our orchestra. The sermon spoke to us of Christmas as the celebration of love – of the strong love that, after all the terrible misery and hatred of war, seeks to once again find faith in itself, in others and in the eternal Father. Very gently, this love seeks to build a pure new world from the destruction. It seemed as if father and mother, wife and child, friend and companion back home, were standing before us as we celebrated, and with them we pledged ourselves to the new future. Then at 8 o'clock we sat down to our Christmas meal in the messes, which looked so welcoming decked with all their greenery. The kitchen had done their best. Just imagine it: wine soup, lobster mayonnaise, roast pork with red cabbage, mashed potato, fruit, butter and cheese, coffee! Piled up in front of each person, a Christmas stollen and two bags containing biscuits, oranges and nuts greeted our smiling eyes. At 9.15, a raffle for all kinds of mouth-watering artistic creations from the kitchen took place in Room B. There were cakes, custards and potato fritters, to mention but a few. With a bright smile or a comically disappointed expression, the emissaries returned to their mess mates, some carrying more than others. At 9.30, there was a loud knocking on the mess doors. In a long snow-covered coat with a flowing white beard and gasping under the weight of an enormous sack, the German Father Christmas stomped towards his big Skipton lads. He brought us warm wishes, but also gave us the traditional telling off. Finally though, overcome with great compassion for us, he retrieved well-wrapped little parcels from the large sack usually carried by his companion Knecht Ruprecht. He read a humorous or serious little verse to each prisonör, waiting in feverish anticipation, and then pressed a secret something into his hand. Everyone, even the laziest man, the man who always played tricks and the man suspected of *Schiebung*, received a gift: cigarette and cigar holders, wallets, pocket knives and letter openers, for example. These objects had all been made by German enlisted men in prisoner-of-war camps and were received with great joy in Skipton. With a hoarse but sincere farewell, good old Father Christmas then disappeared, followed by the grateful gaze of his boys. We remained sitting in the light of our Christmas trees, chatting happily to one another. The orderlies served us punch and wine. Nimble hands brought the violins to life, the songs of our choir filled the air and other comrades delighted us with recitals. The celebrations continued in this way long into the night – after all, curfew wasn't until 1 o'clock.

The first day of Christmas dawned with the most glorious sunshine. In shimmering white, the hills glistened all around us. A joyful Christmas spirit enveloped the camp. The camp paths were filled with cheery people out for a stroll. The roll calls were cancelled. In the afternoon, the enlisted men celebrated Christmas in the Old Mess. Then, in the evening, there were separate Christmas celebrations in the individual barrack communities. One comrade tells us about his ...

Barrack Celebrations

"Christmas! Who, at the sound of this word, does not recall the most blessed memories! Who does not remember the magic this celebration brought with it in childhood days? Christmas 1917: victorious against a world of enemies, we thought we saw the guiding light of peace glowing in the lights of the Christmas tree. Christmas 1918: far from home, in enemy territory, robbed of our freedom, powerless in the hands of the enemy! Captive!

The dark grey sky stretches across the land; the future lies dark before us – the prisoners' Christmas! We see the festive time approaching with heavy hearts. Some had silently hoped to be able to celebrate Christmas at home with their nearest and dearest. Yet, now we are still completely and utterly in the hands of the enemy. But 500 German men, united in their dismal fate, know how to celebrate Christmas, even in enemy territory: the Germans' Christmas, Christmas in Skipton!

If the general preparations were fraught with difficulty – after all, everybody ought to receive something special at Christmas – the celebrations in smaller barracks communities required even more thought. I invite you, dear reader, to follow me into my barracks, to experience Advent and Christmas in spirit with me there.

It is evening. We are in bed. The barracks is in darkness. Suddenly, a voice: 'Hey lads, do we want to celebrate Christmas?' Everyone: 'Yes.' 'And we want to celebrate all together, right lads.' Now a buzz of voices is heard, from which nothing in particular can be distinguished. You begin to worry, dear reader. You think that now nothing will come of the communal celebration. Just wait! You do not know enough about the unity of the barracks yet. Because only half an hour later, after each man has vented his opinion and expressed his wish about how he would like to spend the festive period, a decision is made: 'Right then we will celebrate together.' After a bit of discussion back and forth, the Christmas committee is elected and the barracks can sleep peacefully: we will celebrate together!

Over the next few days, you will see something unusual about barracks life. You will notice how people are muttering over here and whispering secretly over there. The Christmas committee is at work! As a precaution, the curtain of the box in which the discussions are taking place is drawn closed to safeguard them against curious eavesdroppers. You watch sympathetically as one poor prisoner sits at the stove, looking melancholy and contemplating his unhappy fate. There is no need to worry about him. He doesn't need your sympathy. The Christ Child is speaking to him and whispering something softly in his ear, hence the contemplation.

Advent moves towards Christmas. The barracks has experienced many noisy periods, but they are nothing compared with the time leading up to Christmas. There is knocking and hammering all day long. You escape with your book to the quiet room, but on the way you do not forget to take a quick look into the box from which the knocking is coming. The Christ Child looks up from his work, startled, and thunders 'Out!' at you in a voice that you would never have expected from him. And all this whispering! Distrustfully, you glance at the prisoner by the stove, who has so much to discuss with the Christ Child.

Advent suddenly comes to an end. One morning you wake up and Christmas has arrived. Dear reader, you would like to join us in spirit for Christmas in our barracks. Have patience. We will wait until after the camp's communal festivities and begin celebrating on 25th December.

But now the day has dawned. Next to the stove, the Christ Child has put up the Christmas tree. See how he has cleverly used the coal scuttle as a base! Today, the dirty black is covered by vibrant colours. All around the tree, tables have been set up. Instead of festive white tablecloths they are covered with dark bed sheets. Dear reader, do not shy away if you do not find here the Champagne and punch that you are perhaps used to drinking at a celebration of this kind. Cider can be just as pleasant. Only occasionally do you see bottles of other wine, and it is no better than cider, though it can compete with the finest German wines in price. Come, sit with us around the Christmas tree!

A trio of voices fills the room with the carol *O du fröhliche, o du selige, gnadenbringende Weihnachtszeit* [*Oh, how joyfully, oh, how merrily Christmas comes with its grace divine*]. Some of the prisoners had got together in the utmost secrecy to rehearse the wonderful old Christmas carols. *Freue dich, freue dich o Christenheit* [*Hail, ye Christians, hail the joyous Christmas time!*] rings out just like at home. The song fades away. One man gets to his feet and leads us in thinking of our loved ones at home, makes us forget our plight and glimpse a brighter future. Homecoming!

And the singing begins again: *Stille Nacht, heilige Nacht* [*Silent night, holy night*]. Hark, do you not hear heavy steps approaching along the camp's snow-covered paths? Father Christmas is coming. Loudly, he raps on the door and, without waiting to be invited in, he stomps into the barracks. He is wrapped in a white fur coat and has a long beard – just like at home. And all the things he is carrying! With a groan, he sets down the heavy sack and lets off steam with the following words:

> 'Gosh, lads, I wandered far and near,
> Till finally I've found you here.
> In years gone by it was a dawdle,
> When simply to the front I travelled.
> This time your nearest-and-dearest explained,
> That you were cooped up over in England.
> So right away I bought a ticket
> And sailed across on the old steam-packet.
> I couldn't describe the journey as good,
> For my German wasn't understood

> And of speaking English I'm no great fan,
> For Nicolas is a German man.
> But, lads, at last, after much travail,
> Enquiring and searching everywhere,
> It finally dawned on my old brain,
> That maybe to Skipton I should aim.
> I'm sure you'll all ask straight away,
> 'What have you brought in your sack today?'
> Let me say first before everything
> That all good wishes from home I bring.
> For those whose conduct's been becoming,
> Gifts from the sack will be forthcoming.
> With every present which here I offer,
> There also comes a well-meant moral.
> To all I wish improved conditions
> And may these presents suit your notions.'

And now he shakes out his gifts. All kinds of things emerge! A child's rattle, a hobbyhorse, a doll, an abacus, a violin, cigarettes, a nightcap, playing cards and so on. And everyone gets their own little verse too. For example, he gives a farmer a large potato with the words:

> If you would work a fine estate
> And wish someday to govern it
> Then you must always make the effort
> To prize and nurture such potatoes.
> Keep growing the biggest over the years
> And the Farmers' Council will be all ears.

Our camp gardener receives natural fertiliser. His verse is as follows:

> Hey, Anon, surely you can't think
> Your reputation will not sink
> When last year's cabbage fails to grow?
> It's rubbish soil! We told you so.
> 'Cos for a cabbage to mature
> It needs a plot with good manure.
> Yes, horse manure revives the soil,
> All else, you see, is useless toil.

See, Father Christmas doesn't even forget the sick! For one man who was suffering from insomnia he has brought medicine:

> Anon knows always every night
> Each thing that happens before light.
> When others are all deep in slumber

He's still a wide-awake old grumbler
Because he's almost always frozen.
He knows the times that Tommy's chosen
To do his rounds, and where it's draughty
And where a window's open. Ghastly!
He knows the names of all who snore,
Familiar with snores galore.
And only when the dawn awakes
Can Anon sleep. So long it takes!
This medicine will let you rest,
With more than forty winks be blessed.
And if you take it you'll soon see
How calm and peaceful night can be.

And there is another man who has often disturbed us with his knocking and hammering. He is given a hammer with the warning:

Who is it hammers from sunrise
Till late at night? It's no surprise!
He thinks the barracks has to be
A workshop for his carpentry.
Ah yes Anon we're sick and tired,
If we'd a choice we'd have you fired.
It's true that everything you do
Shows an ambition grand and true
For carpentry; but give it a rest,
Delay your efforts, don't be a pest.
Better if your banging abated
Until we're all repatriated.

The sword lying there on the table is for one of our active soldiers. Father Christmas asks this of him:

A message from our new Republic:
They know that you are tired and sick
Of serving in the army now
A government you disavow.
The sword of honour's what they offer
And hope that you will turn from scoffer
To loyal servant of your land
To serve it with both heart and hand.

This Father Christmas seems to be a real warmonger. If my eyes do not deceive me, he has even brought a canon with him. Yes, I was right, it is a present for our artilleryman from Baden:

> Anon from Baden hits the roof
> If anyone is so uncouth
> to doubt the worth of lovely Baden
> At this his angry heart will harden.
> The homeland of this little man:
> Baden, a joy since time began!
> But stuck in Skipton you observe
> The foe's in Baden. What a nerve!
> The homeland's waiting, hoping too
> For you to free your home anew.
> Your government wants to let you know
> That, yes, your progress will be slow
> And endless practice you will need
> On this to finally succeed.
> But certain victory will be won
> And you'll free Baden with this gun.

So there is a present for everyone, and each man gets a little verse too. But wait! Here he has an Englishman carved from wood, surely intended for a man who has complained in private about the Tommies. Again we listen to what Father Christmas has to say:

> Good Heavens, our Anon does go wild
> Especially seeing the reviled
> English need to be confronted
> And a complaint is what is wanted
> From our commandant. Not from him.
> Chances he'll say a word are slim!
> But it won't do to simply hate
> You need to learn how to berate
> And more: to take your anger out
> On those who caused it. You can shout
> At this wood figure who will never
> Argue, he'll just agree forever.

At last Father Christmas has handed out all the gifts. He looks around once more, just to make sure, and demands this of us before he goes:

> Now lads, each one of you has got
> A message that I hope you'll not
> Forget and that you'll think it through
> And do what it suggests you do.
> I hope that you will take to heart
> What in these words I would impart.
> T'would mean for our community
> A great increase in harmony.

Yes, dear reader, now you look at me with a triumphant smile because you think that, like you, Father Christmas doubts the unity of barracks. I must admit that there is a modicum of truth in this. But you would not know it this evening. Because no sooner has Father Christmas left than merriment bursts forth, of a kind seldom seen among prisoners. Everything seems to be harmonious. Here humorous speeches are being made, there old German folk songs are being sung and it seems that everything, just everything around us is forgotten. Only too soon we are brought back to reality by the camp bell calling for quiet. And in sleep too we think we hear Christmas bells jingling and in our dreams we are standing around the Christmas tree with our loved ones.

Freue dich, freue dich, o Christenheit [*Hail, ye Christians, hail the joyous Christmas time!*]. The prisoners' Christmas. Christmas in Skipton."

Köstlin.

On the second day of Christmas, the theatre management, in keeping with the Christmas mood, carried us off into the world of fairy tales with a performance of Schiller's *Turandot*. On the evening of 31st December we gathered in the messes again to celebrate the end of the old year around the Christmas tree, which was lit up once more. The first camp newspaper was distributed. Copious amounts of punch and wine gave the prisoners a feeling of freedom and banished their worries for several hours. A festive, even exuberant, atmosphere took hold. Groups in fancy dress roamed about. A married couple presented their offspring – an alarmingly tall giant and an absurdly small dwarf – to the *Abitur* course. Our conjurer astonished us with his little tricks. Travelling minstrels, wild vagabonds, negroes and other characters (including Admiral von Tirpitz!) wandered to and fro. Songs and poems inspired by the camp were performed.

New Year's Song

There was ein deutsche Offizier,
Halt! Who comes there?
Und is now taken prisoner,
All correct, Sir!
The watsch and money
All souvenir
for focking Tommy
Von German officer.
And when stands up the deutsche twit
I can kill you!
Pistole at head from English grip
I can kill you!

In Skipton grosse barbed-wire fence
Halt! Who comes there?
Number of English guards immens
All correct, Sir!
O goldnes liberty –
All souvenir
You are so very far von here,
Von German officer.
In camp goes little Man herum
I can kill you!
Von whisky red the nose und rum –
I can kill you!

Ze little Mann: his Adjutant,
Halt! Who comes there?
He, Aunty Frieda is genannt
All correct, Sir!
Three times a Tage –
All souvenir
He makes Parade
Von German officer.
And that the officers stand still
I can kill you!
Ze little Mann makes sure he will –
I can kill you!

Ein third Person kommt too herein
Halt! Who comes there?
He ist so fat as Yorkshire swine
All correct, Sir!
Mit Fingers counting
All souvenir
The right amount
Von German officer.
For prisoner, wenn Post kommt an –
I can kill you!
He's waiting there too this fat Mann –
I can kill you!

In store of Mr James there is –
Halt! Who comes there?
To make a little business,
All correct, Sir!
All made in England

All souvenir
For plenty money
For German officer
And hidden from the Kommandant
I can kill you!
Schiebt Mr James for Lieutenant
I can kill you!

The prisoner in little hut,
Halt! Who comes there?
Lives very nice, is all caput,
All correct, Sir!
When he is sleeping
All souvenir
Comes water dropping
To German officer.
Each evening Kommandant says then
I can kill you!
Good night! zu all ze gentlemen
I can kill you!

Und kommt der Tag for going home
Halt! Who comes there?
Und all ze deutsche prisoners gone
All correct, Sir!
The camp in Skipton
All souvenir
In deutsche homeland
For German officer
There he is no more prisoner
No I can kill you!
There is the peace und no more war
No I can kill you!

Greiner.

At 12 o' clock the mess captains greeted the New Year and offered their good wishes to the comrades. This was followed by a lively round of well wishing. The excitement and festive atmosphere then lasted for hours, and for many the celebrations only ended with the first light of dawn. Some men, however, had spent the evening deep in thought by the barracks stove; thinking of home and trying to plan for the future was, to them, the best way to bring in the New Year. On 1st January the religious service provided a serious introduction to the New Year, with the sermon pointing us towards the religious tasks and aims of this new period of history.

When the celebrations came to an end, the weeks fell back into their old rhythm. In January, the Bavarians held a Bavarian festival and organised an evening of entertainment open to all, with speeches in dialect, *Schuhplattler* folk dancing and a performance of Thoma's peasant comedy, *Erster Klasse* [*First Class*]. On 27th January small groups gathered for quiet commemoration. *Landsmannschaften* of the men from Oldenburg, Schleswig-Holstein and other areas organised special evenings to remember their home regions.

We had no idea then that we, though often suffering so bitterly both as prisoners and from our agonising concern for the Fatherland, had not yet faced the worst, and that fate would soon plunge the Skipton prisoners into days of unspeakable sorrow. Already, death was waiting outside the camp gate and in the second half of February joined us inside the camp itself. This was the arrival of the great ...

Influenza Epidemic

Influenza had long been raging in the surrounding English towns. We read about its devastating effects in the press and knew that many of our comrades in another German officers' prison camp (Kegworth) had fallen victim to it the year before. We were certainly fearful that this scourge could affect us too. We were well aware that, if it were to cross the barbed wire, influenza would find an ideal breeding ground here in the camp, due to the dire sanitary conditions. We had been herded in, 24 to a hut (the men as many as 34 to a hut). Cold and draughts came up through the gaps between the floorboards, which were raised above the ground. Rain came in through the roofs of most huts. In spite of many complaints these grievances had not been addressed. In the winter months the huts could only be aired briefly and inadequately by opening the top half of the windows. A single stove, often small, barely warmed the long room at all. Officers had to stay in the poorly aired study rooms, with 130-140 in A and 80 in C, from morning until evening all winter long. The cold, damp weather and muddy camp pathways made it impossible to spend much time outdoors. So the imprisoned comrades had to stay indoors constantly, in inadequately heated, draughty, overcrowded, uncomfortable rooms.

The dangers arising from our accommodation were compounded by the poor food. The food allotted by the October rationing was nowhere near sufficient to give the body the strength needed to ward off illness. For our meat ration we received only horsemeat and Chinese bacon. Both were eaten only reluctantly by most officers. What the English themselves thought about this bacon can be seen from a comment in the *Yorkshire Evening Post*: 'No Chinese bacon has been issued for English consumption.' For us Huns, however, this 'valuable' foodstuff was deemed perfectly acceptable in spite of our complaints. Fresh fish was supplied only once a week. The rest of the fish ration consisted of salt herring, which was only edible after soaking in water for days on end. The tiny sugar ration was not enough to sweeten our food properly. Almost the only thing we had to put on our bread was black treacle, which was not popular due to its unpleasant after-taste. Only rarely was it possible, by illicit means, to procure a type of honey. The only vegetables were turnip and common-or-garden carrots, which were old and sometimes rotten. Due to the shortage of cooking fat it was not even possible to prepare them in a tasty or nourishing way. We only received 4 ounces of fat per week, and no cheese at all. The cooking fat that we were given now and then consisted mainly of tallow and water. Peas, lentils and beans were mostly good, but again there was no fat to prepare them properly. Rice could only be boiled in water. There was a severe shortage of seasoning, particularly salt. And so it was that our comrades were not at all well nourished when the influenza broke out. Pulses, porridge and insubstantial sloppy food had been the staple diet for most of the prisoners for over a year, certainly for those who received few if any parcels from home.

The camp sanitation was totally inadequate to combat the outbreak and spread of an epidemic effectively. The camp hospital consisted of two wooden huts that displayed all the same shortcomings as the living quarters. Medical care was provided by an English military doctor, Major Powder,[54] whom we trusted neither as a man nor as a doctor. He was assigned three English hospital assistants and one German medical orderly.

On 12th February, five orderlies fell ill with influenza. The sick were treated in their barracks at first. Only when their condition became more serious were they taken to the camp hospital. The illness soon spread further among the orderlies, and on 15th February it spread to the officers. It would develop as follows: after an incubation period of two to three days, during which time the symptoms were tiredness and a lack of appetite, a fever would suddenly break out, forcing the patient to take to his bed. The fever would be accompanied by fits of shivering, high temperature and a headache. The patient would suffer from constipation and lack of appetite, he would feel weak and appear listless. Additional symptoms were coughing, nosebleeds, backache and aching limbs, and occasionally an ear infection. The fever would peak on the fourth or fifth day, when the crisis point was reached. In most cases the temperature would gradually fall from this point and the patient would begin to recover. However, lung damage and heart problems were often lasting consequences. Unfortunately, complications arose in many cases due to tissue and nerve damage. In such cases the fever did not abate and pneumonia and heart problems ensued. It was very noticeable that almost all who fell sick, and especially the most seriously affected, were no older than thirty.

The camp took on a sombre air. All loud activity ceased. Classes and lectures were suspended. No singing, no music sounded through the Old Mess; no creative works were performed. The usual noisy comings and goings of the mess rooms ceased. The few who were still healthy now ate in the Old Mess at a few sparsely occupied tables and went about the camp with tired faces, strained by anxiety about their own fate. Stretcher bearers became a familiar sight; we asked reluctantly but with heartfelt concern which comrade lay under the blanket. Vehicles rattled their way through the camp gates, stretchers were loaded in. With fear and hope in our hearts, our eyes followed the departing vehicles. Indoors, in the sickbays, bed by bed, our comrades lay in feverish delirium: strong men, old soldiers prepared to bear anything, even death; now frightened men with shattered nerves, preoccupied by thoughts of death. One asked for a rosary, another, a teacher, taught his pupils in the night hours, yet another leapt out of bed in his fever thinking his mother was waiting for him outside. One, the last of four fallen brothers, made his will. Others, in their confused minds, were standing in battle, leading their men with loud commands or quietly spoken orders. Some lay under the covers, pale and apathetic; some readied themselves quietly for the final journey. What would we have done without you, our healthy comrades, in those hardest hours, united in providing selfless aid day and night! You sat by our bedsides to comfort us, you straightened the sheets and positioned the pillows with your faithful albeit unskilled hands, you quenched our feverish thirst, you wrote our letters home, you willingly took upon yourselves even the most difficult and unpleasant sickroom duties. And you did all this quietly and gladly. In the darkness of night you sat like faithful guardians, wrapped in your greatcoats, among your many patients, and when someone called out, you were always on hand, helping with loving care. If it were not for you, how many more would be lying there in that Keighley cemetery! And also you faithful few orderlies who weren't yourselves laid low, during those difficult days, you dealt with medical care and transportation and a host of other tasks, all this tireless effort to help others performed out of love for your fellow man.

The English authorities did nothing to prevent the illness spreading. All they did was prescribe constant fresh air, and the commandant allowed all the officers the opportunity to go walking in both the morning and the afternoon.

The English camp doctor could no longer fulfil what was required of him. As no medical preparations had been made, he faced insurmountable difficulties. The camp hospital was soon overcrowded, so the sick had to remain lying in their barracks alongside the healthy. This was probably the main reason why the disease continued to spread. As the English authorities did nothing to establish proper sickbay organisation, ten barracks formerly used as dining and living quarters were converted into makeshift sickrooms at the instigation of the German camp administration. On 18th February, the English military doctor Captain Melbourne[55] arrived here from Ripon with eleven English and four German medical orderlies. In the absence of any organisation even these reinforcements were not enough. Some of the junior staff were really quite negligent in their duties. Each individual patient was seen by the doctor only once a day, unless an extra visit was requested. Temperatures were measured only once a day; for this purpose, the thermometer was stuck into the patient's mouth. It was observed that the same thermometer was used for several patients without first being cleaned. On several occasions the medical assistants also mixed up the medical notes of individual patients so that incorrect information was recorded. There was little examination of heart and lungs: the entire treatment was limited to taking temperature, stimulating bowel movements and distributing cough medicine. The shortage of bedpans was a great deprivation: the sick were obliged to find their way to the primitive outdoor latrines even in cold, rainy and windy weather. It was clear that some of the sick suffered a worsening of their condition as a result of this. Bed linen was only changed at our insistence.

At first no special diet was provided for the sick; both sick and healthy were fed horsemeat and beans. Only after energetic representations by the mess management was there any improvement in provisions. The commandant took it upon himself to allow the canteen to order in fresh meat (500 English pounds weight for 550 officers), eggs, milk and canned fruit, in addition to which we received an extra 4 ounces of bread a day and a cup of tea with rum at dinner time.

In spite of the overcrowding of the camp hospital with seriously ill patients and the large number of seriously ill patients left lying in their barracks, the English camp administration only undertook the necessary steps for the seriously ill to be moved to hospital after we demanded it. The town of Skipton refused to place their 'military hospital' at our disposal, giving the feeble excuse that it was actually the workhouse and it would not be permissible to deny access to its rightful occupants. Eventually the War Office gave permission to accommodate the sick at Morton Banks Military Hospital near Keighley, provided that beds were vacant there. At first, permission for this had to be sought from the War Office for each individual patient: each application had to find its way through four or five departments before a reply arrived. The sick were taken to hospital in motor ambulances, and transfers were often subject to long delays due to the unavailability of the transport. It was not until they were able to make a whole building at the hospital available especially to accommodate the German patients that all the seriously ill were taken to Keighley.

Morton Banks Hospital, owned by the town of Keighley, had been designated a war hospital since the Somme offensive. The first patients from our camp were admitted on 20th February. Eventually two buildings were allocated to the German patients. Sadly, access to proper hospital treatment came too late for many of the sick, in addition to which they were all transferred from the camp without medical records of any kind, so that the doctor had no indication of the previous course of the illness. Most of the patients themselves were in no condition to supply any details. The doctor made his rounds three or four times a day. Three nurses and two medical orderlies were on duty in each of the three wards during the day, and two nurses and two orderlies at night. One great difficulty in the care and treatment of the sick was the impossibility of communication between patients and carers. At the request of the senior

German officer, one of our comrades was therefore sent to the hospital as an interpreter. He reported on his experiences and observations:

"I was present for all of the doctor's rounds. In my estimation, the medical treatment was quite excellent.

The food ration for the critically ill consisted of fresh milk with whisky or brandy (a ward with 33 patients received 45 litres of fresh milk per day). Patients in recovery received bread, butter and tea in the morning, fish, potatoes and rice pudding at midday, bread, butter, jam and tea in the afternoon and cocoa or beef tea in the evening. Patients whose fever had subsided received bread, bacon or ham, and tea in the morning. The cost of board was 3 shillings per person, per day.

Due to overcrowding, the hospital could spare no further buildings and, as the rooms already allocated to us were not sufficient, quite a number of our patients had to be accommodated on the very draughty verandas. Due to this lack of space, some of the sick were even sent back to camp, still in a very weak condition. Whereas the nurses did their best out of kindness and tireless conscientious care, some of the medical orderlies showed their aversion to us Germans by their insolent behaviour. These people were relieved of their duties as soon as a complaint was made. On giving their word of honour, recovering officers were allowed to go walking in a particular section of the hospital gardens. A Protestant and a Catholic priest frequently visited the sick."

On the occasion of a visit to the cemetery in which our dead were buried, we took the opportunity to express in person the camp's gratitude to the head of the hospital for the excellent care and treatment received by our sick. It must be mentioned, however, that the senior consultant was called to account by the hospital management board for this friendly treatment of the German officers. He is said to have given the honourable gentlemen the only proper answer, that as a doctor he recognised neither Germans nor English, only patients.

Of the 546 officers and 137 enlisted men interned in the Skipton Camp, 324 officers and 47 men became ill. Of these, 74 officers and 17 men were taken to the hospital. 32 officers and 10 men died there, and 5 officers died in the camp.

During the epidemic a representative of the Swiss Legation had visited the camp, and when he returned on 5th July he told us that the Swiss Legation had forwarded a report on the influenza epidemic to the German government on the basis of information given to them by the British government. We expressed our amazement that we had not previously been consulted about this, as we would certainly have had some grievances to air. When we named some of them, he told us that conditions were much worse in the camps in France.

We laid our dear departed comrades to rest in the cemetery in Keighley. In order to pay them our last respects, a detail of 10-14 officers and men was driven from our camp to Keighley on the day of each burial.

We marched from the hospital to the cemetery, some distance away, in solemn funeral processions. The English guard of honour, led by an officer, proceeded at a slow march ahead of the hearse bearing two coffins; we German comrades followed behind.

The coffins were lowered into the grave with great ceremony by the English troops; in silence we raised our hands to our caps in a farewell salute.

The English military chaplain spoke words from the Scriptures and said prayers full of comfort and faith, and concluded with a benediction for those whose bodies we were laying to rest in foreign soil.

The most senior of the German officers present then gave a short farewell address. On one occasion, one of the comrades who also conducted services in the camp spoke briefly on the words of Jesus, 'Because I live ye shall live also' (John 14:19).

Then, following military custom, a three-gun salute was fired and an English bugler sounded the wonderful *Last Post* over the open graves.

We stood to attention in silent solemnity. But then after this last farewell came the sacred vow:

We live to honour our dead

Above the trees
God's heavenly harp
Resounds on the breeze.
Yet we stand quiet with bared heads
Among and between
The many graves of the dead
For, of their number, one is yours.

On high, above the trees
The wind sings its hymn
To the heavenly harp,
And peace grows around us
And all the misery you suffered
Simply sublimely ceases to be.

But we want only stillness and silence
Standing respectful in the shade,
As your glory shines
Now and for ever
In the face of God's own splendour.

On high, above the trees
The blessed harp-winds chorus.
Yet we stand quiet with bared heads
Among and between
The many graves of the dead
Of their number, one is yours.

Stoltenberg.

Lt. d. R. Berleung, 8. J.-R. 4, Kaiserslautern

Lt. d. R. Böhme, R.-J.-R. 263, Schkölen i. Th.

Lt. d. R. Bostelmann, J.-R. 466, Verden a. d. Aller

Lt. d. L. Brandt, J.-R. 84, Lehe a. d. Weser

Lt. d. R. Burgmann, J.-R. 470, Salneck (Baden)

Lt. d. R. Danz, J.-R. 77, Celle (Hannover)

Mar.-Ing. Dietrich, U.-Flott. Fland., Potsdam

Oblt. d. R. Encke, R.-J.-R. 90, Hamm (Westf.)

Lt. d. R. Fiedler, R.-J.-R. 233, Kassel

Lt. d. R. Förster, R.-J.-R. 133, Dahlen (Sachsen)

Lt. d. R. Harter, E.-J.-R. 28, Pforzheim

Lt. d. R. Heydenreich, F.-A.-R. 90, Ilfeld (Harz)

Lt. d. R. Joost, Pi.-Btl. 23, Sensburg (Ostpr.)

Lt. d. R. Kamutzky, J.-R. 152, Pr. Stargard

Lt. d. R. Kisker, J.-R. 84, Charlottenburg

Lt. d. R. Klein, F.-A.-R. 27, Siegen

Lt. d. R. Knocke, J.-R. 395, Lüneburg

Lt. d. R. Kötter, J.-R. 456, Weitmar b. Bochum

Kplt. Krech, 5. U.-Flottille, Berlin-Zehlendorf

Lt. d. R. Lanz, R.-J.-R. 31, Traben-Trarbach

Lt. Laue, J.-R. 84, Wiesbaden

Lt. d. R. Linse, J.-R. 414, Heidenheim a. d. Brenz

Oblt. z. S. v. d. Lühe, U.-Flott. Fland., Schwerin i. Meckl.

Lt. d. R. Mory, J.-R. 84, Gettorf b. Kiel

Lt. d. R. Müller, J.-R. 94, Wittingen (Hann.)

Unsern Toten

In memory of our dead.

Lt. d. R. Priebe, J.-R. 140, Bärenwalde (Westpr.)

Lt. d. R. Rausche, J.-R. 360, Weimar

Lt. d. R. Rother, R.-Jäg.-Btl. 2, Chemnitz

Lt. d. R. Schenke, J.-R. 371, Rudolstadt

Lt. Schlösser, J.-R. 160, Bonn a. Rhein

Oblt. z. S. Schmitz, U.-Flott. Fland., Berlin

Lt. d. R. Schröter, L.-J.-R. 386, Berlin

Lt. d. R. Schüler, J.-R. 50, Lissa i. Posen

Lt. d. R. Schulte, Fl.-Kampfgeschw. 3, Dortmund

Lt. d. R. Strang, 2. See-Fl.-Abt., Kleve, Rhld.

Lt. d. R. Weiser, J.-R. 466, Mittelpöllnitz i. Th.

Lt. d. R. Wommer, L.-J.-R. 387, Eitzweiler (Birkenfeld)

Musk. Bach, R.-J.-R. 111, Heddesheim b. Mannheim

Musk. Behrendt, J.-R. 72, Lübbenau (Brandenburg)

Gren. Borgwardt, Gren.-R. 9, Schwanenbeck (Pommern)

Musk. Brosi, R.-J.-R. 122, Hohenhaslach (Württemberg)

Soldat Dettmann, J.-R. 183, Leipzig

Musk. Hoyer, J.-R. 26, Sucholoua (Ober-Schlesien)

Wehrm. Müller, R.-J.-R. 22, Dortmund

Ers.-Res. Nagel, R.-J.-R. 55, Holsen (Westf.)

Ldstm. Schatz, J.-R. 126, Rorschach (Schweiz)

Gefr. Schwab, B. J.-R. 17, Kirchzell (Unterfr.)

zum Gedächtnis

On 16th March we assembled in the Old Mess for a quiet memorial service. After listening to the sober sound of the Kol Nidrei (orchestra) and the cantata *Wenn ich einmal soll scheiden* [*When I must once and for all depart*] (male-voice choir), the senior German officer gave a speech of remembrance:

"Dear Comrades! The past weeks lie behind us like a terrible dream, in which the pernicious disease, the murderous curse of the Great War, which has spread across the whole world, has claimed many victims from us. We are still living under the shadow of those awful days. We must still force ourselves to acknowledge that all those dear men who loyally shared with us all the little joys and great sorrows of incarceration, who, with all their merits and minor faults, had become dear to us and valued as old dependable comrades-in-arms or as friends newly made through cheerful play and serious work, will never return to us.

Death has torn many comrades away from us over recent years, but death and dying had lost their terror for us in the war. Sadness and pain for our fallen heroes was eased by the knowledge that they were not unprepared for death, that they had laid down their lives willingly in the honest, open, honourable fight for a sacred cause.

Here at the grave of our dear departed we search in vain for similar grounds for consolation, but the pain they suffered and had to endure is too great; fate has too cruelly destroyed their last hopes.

With their masculine pride deeply wounded and their soldierly ambition thwarted by imprisonment, and condemned after years of pride in victory and serene confidence in future victory to become impotent spectators in their Fatherland's time of need, they were forced to endure for long months and years the humiliation of captivity, with its privations and its agonising fluctuations between hope and bitter disappointment.

They had been forced to hear how that which they had achieved and that which they had been fighting to achieve was hopelessly lost, that their proud regiments, their storm-weathered ships, their daring air squadrons had been forced to surrender to the enemy without a fight, that their dear Fatherland had become a defenceless spoil of war.

And the only hope that sustained them in the face of this disaster, the hope that at least now they would soon be returned to their loved ones, even this was denied them. And yet they did not let this defeat them, but bravely held on; worked hard to further their education; passed on their extensive knowledge to others; delighted us with their art; helped us through many dull hours of captivity with their youthful exuberance – until illness defeated them.

But here, on their sick beds, what happened to most of them was that their inner suffering came to the surface despite their apparent calm, how they had been consumed by concern for their loved ones, by their yearning for home. The last thoughts of those already in the throes of death were of the journey home. Deeply moved, we heard one of the sick, in delirium, stammering the words, 'Don't take me, I must go home now, my mother has already prepared everything for my return.'

And at this time we, too, are thinking in heartfelt sympathy of the loved ones of our departed comrades. We can imagine their pain that, after years of fear and hope, their husband, son, brother has been snatched away from them at the very moment when, by all that is humanly right and just, he should have long since been recovering in their arms from the suffering and deprivation of the last few years.

We can find no words of comfort either for them or for ourselves, but as Christians we humbly bow our heads in the face of that which God has ordained.

And now farewell, you faithful comrades, whose final resting place must be in foreign soil. We cannot yet tear our thoughts away from your final suffering. Your dear faces still appear garlanded with flowers before our eyes, and we can still think of you only in sadness. But when we have fought our way through the dark present into a brighter future, when happier times have dawned for the Fatherland for which you too stood in heroic battle, and when we can look back on these days of captivity as merely a test of fate that we passed with flying colours, then shall the familiar old tune ring out clearly and jubilantly from our lips to honour and remember you:

I once had a comrade

You will find no better"[56]

For us it was a sacred duty to erect a memorial for our dead at their place of rest in a foreign land. We chose the designs created by two comrades and we employed an English contractor to carry out the work.

The Memorial

"The unusual way in which our comrades were buried, similar to family burials with five coffins in each grave, and the fact that the graves were only 90cm apart led us to consider treating the whole site as one large family plot by creating a single unified monument using peaceful and yet animated forms and without prioritising any individual grave. There are to be no individual memorial plaques. All the names are to be brought together in letters embossed on the large copper roll of honour, dedicated by the officers and men of the Skipton Camp to the memory of their comrades. This plaque is to be located in a curved alcove in the rear wall, which dominates the whole monument. Boundary walls will preserve the unity of the plot, whilst at the same time setting it apart from the rest of the cemetery. Nevertheless, the structure will integrate well into the whole cemetery and the surrounding area because the walls at the front and sides are to be only about 50cm high, with only the rear wall emphasising the boundary more clearly at a height of about 1.5m, and the alcove containing the memorial plaque rising above it as the central point. Even the building materials and style of the walls will blend with the surroundings. Light sandstone, like that which is quarried locally and was used in the construction of the chapel and cemetery wall, will be used in such a way that the corner pillars are hewn smooth, as will be the coping stones of the alcove. The walls in between will consist of undressed stones laid on top of each other and only the alcove will contain stones dressed like shell limestone. In places where the walls have been built of undressed stone, gaps are to be left free of mortar and filled with soil, where it will be possible to plant hardy perennial flowering plants, whose delightful blossoms will soften the appearance of the border. Campanula bells will tinkle here, and the scent of thyme will fill the air. Daisies will lift their crowned heads, alpines will tumble down the sides, and broad-leaved saxifrage will form soft cushions on the higher parts of the rear wall, whilst fragrant honeysuckle and wild clematis with its white flowers and bunches of silvery seed heads will hang down over the coping stones of the high rear wall. In order to add even more definition to the boundary from the rear and to provide a more effective backdrop to the main wall, a sturdy laburnum tree will grow behind the wall to either side of the alcove. Their garlands of golden tassels, amongst the dark foliage, will augment the floral display, which should last throughout the summer even within the enclosed plot. Like living green flames, slim upright young junipers will keep watch on either side of the alcove without concealing the boundary walls, each assisted in its guard duty by a bold stand of upright irises whose blue flowers will stand out from the light-coloured stone like small flames. A bright carpet of gypsophilia will spread out across the lawn from beneath the dark junipers. Rhododendron bushes will gradually lead the gaze up to the alcove, and between and in front of them, harbingers of spring and summer perennials will peep out: primulas and aquilegia, bellflowers standing tall, cinquefoils and broad-leaved hostas in front, whilst in the midst of them a bold cluster of white irises in front of each of the dark junipers will support their blue sisters by the alcove as torch-bearers. And strong stands of blue delphinium and purple phlox will raise their heads between the rhododendrons, and Michaelmas daisies will offer the last floral farewell to the departed souls before winter comes. Some of their flowering stems will lean gently over the low stone walls. Finally, delicate, delightful sprays of heuchera, dotted here and there, will spring from the inner corners of the low walls, anemones will raise their cup-like heads and the bright pyrethrums, that colourful relation of the marguerite, will open their radiant petals.

And so the burial plot will become a monument that will require little maintenance and will become more beautiful year after year as its wealth of plants and shrubs mature, a peaceful flower-filled resting place for our comrades united in death."

Ebert.

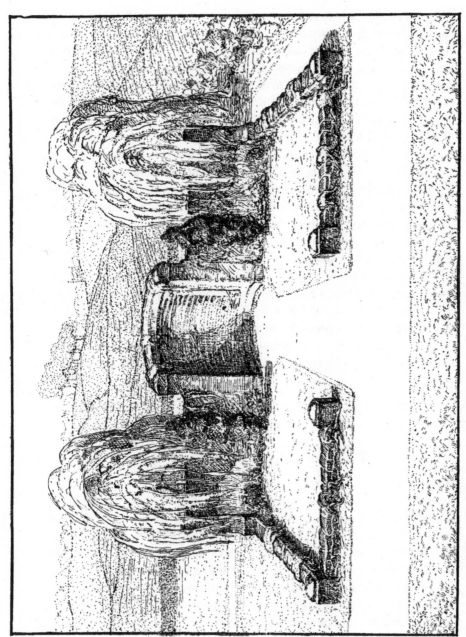

German memorial in an English cemetery.

Another comrade describes the impressive architectural character of our memorial:

"The burial plot is enclosed by a grey-green sandstone wall. The rear wall (about 1.75m high) is raised in the central section and curved to form a kind of alcove. The plaque with the inscription is set there. Whereas the left and right sides are enclosed by continuous low walls (approximately 40cm high), the wall at the front has an opening to indicate the entrance. The end and corner stones of the smaller sections of wall are carefully dressed; the imposing profile of the top of the main wall lends it a particular character. Ornamental detail has been intentionally avoided; the lettering on the plaque in the curved alcove, on the other hand, could well be described as ornamental.

The effect of the architectural construction is considerably enhanced by the garden design. In a few years' time a romantic spell will have been cast over this quiet plot and then nature will have endowed the monument with an ornamentation that could never be achieved by an artist's hand; then flowers will spring from the stonework, and evergreens and climbing plants will embrace it like soft tender arms: a vision of life at this place of death.

The memorial will be effective through its sublime simplicity and wholly classical serenity. There is nothing over-ornate or contrived about it; it reflects the sanctity of the place and is in keeping with the framework of the whole scene in which it is set, precisely those concepts required of modern cemetery design. In fulfilling these requirements, the monument speaks in a deeply serious, ceremonious language, a language that is full of comfort and faith."

Andrich.

The following articles about our monument appeared in the *Keighley News*, the main newspaper for Keighley and the surrounding area, on 17th May 1919:

1. "The German Corner in the Morton Cemetery

However inhuman the Germans may be as a nation in their attitude to and treatment of persons of other nationalities, they are evidently, both individually and collectively, most thoughtful and reverential where their own dead are concerned. That, at any rate, is the impression conveyed by the project of their surviving comrades for marking the last resting place of the officers [and men][57] from the Skipton camp who died in the recent influenza epidemic and were interred in the new cemetery at Morton. These comrades are sticking at no expense or trouble in setting up a memorial which will stand forth in the years to come as a testimony to their regard and affection for those who have thus passed away. They are proposing to lay out the corner of the cemetery reserved for these German burials. The forty-seven influenza victims have been laid to rest in ten graves, arranged in two rows of five each, making a compact group in the right-hand bottom corner of the burial section nearest the entrance to the cemetery. The cemetery paths run along two sides of this piece of ground, and what the members of the camp who have taken in hand the arrangements for perpetuating the memory of their dead associates have now done is to purchase the adjoining grave spaces on the other two sides, the whole space thus secured measuring in all some seven yards by eight. One of the prisoners at Skipton, who is understood to be a skilled architect, has drawn up a plan for enclosing this space by a low wall of local stone, and into this wall is to be set a bronze tablet worked with repoussé decorations and bearing the names of the men resting below."

2.   "An Artistic Memorial Scheme

Another comrade of the buried men, who is skilled in gardening matters, has combined with the architect-designer in drawing up a scheme for the general beautification of the enclosed space. According to the present plans, those portions of the enclosing wall not covered by the memorial tablet are to be laid out as a wall garden, the interstices between the stones being left free of mortar to the depth of some inches for the reception of wall and rock plants of a suitable kind. The actual grave spaces themselves will be levelled and laid out as a small lawn, while the surrounding portion of the ground is to be planted with shrubs and small trees. When these have obtained full growth they will constitute a very attractive setting to the lawn centre. The whole scheme seems to have been most carefully and tastefully planned out on distinctly artistic lines, without any tendency towards excessive display. It is about as unlike the monumental monstrosities which one usually associates with Teutonic ideas of commemorative art as could well be imagined, and in course of time this little corner should become one of the beauty spots of the cemetery, harmonising in most welcome fashion with the general scheme of sylvan and horticultural adornment planned out by the cemetery authority. The whole scheme is estimated to cost some £250, and the money is to be provided, we gather, by a self-imposed levy on the officer prisoners at the Skipton camp. One can only hope that the people of the Keighley district will see to it that the memory of the British and Colonial soldiers buried in the same cemetery is perpetuated in as artistic and reposeful a manner. Now that the war is over it is surely time that some steps were taken to this end."

> As tempests blow among the ears of wheat
> And set the crops a-sway in hosts of gold,
> So all of us, beleaguered by our fate
> And in your tempest tossed, do yet stand bold.
> Our deepest inner thoughts are gently lulled
> When your inspiring breath reaches our heart.
>
> He who knows your presence in his breast
> Knows too, no-one from you can ever flee.
> Whether enraptured by your love, or lost,

Out of the depths of your primordial sea
Will each of us, in heart and mind and being,
Be swept unto your shore at last.

God who is in us, may we hold fast
To you, as you hold fast to us eternally.
Your arms are opened wide to both the lost
And saved who dwell in our fraternity.
This day and for eternity
We will be yours – as you belong to us.

Stoltenberg.

Food Supplies

A heavy burden of responsibility rested on the shoulders of our kitchen administration during this period of illness. Indeed, their task was always an onerous one as they were entrusted with providing sustenance for 550 men. It was not easy to satisfy every request. Strict rationing by the English restricted the possibility of preparing ample, palatable and varied meals, often perceptibly so. This rationing changed frequently over the course of our imprisonment.

Summary of our provisions and their alterations since establishment of the camp.

Weekly rations per prisoner

(n.r. = not rationed)	January 1918	4th March 1918	18th October 1918	6th February 1919	12th May 1919
Meat	6 oz. for 5 days	20 oz. (fresh and tinned)	20 oz. (horsemeat only)	14 oz. (only fresh)	18 oz. (fresh and tinned)
Bacon	Not allowed	Not allowed	8 oz. (Chinese)	14 oz. (American)	14 oz. (English)
Fish (fresh) Fish (tinned)	24 oz. n.r.	} 20 oz.	} 20 oz.	20oz 3 tins	20oz 3 tins
Sugar	8 oz.	7 oz.	7 oz.	7 oz.	12 oz.
Bread	34 oz.	56 oz.	56 oz.	56 oz.	72 oz.
Flour	n.r.	8 oz.	8 oz.	8 oz.	n.r.
Coffee or Tea	7 oz.	3 ½ oz.	3 ½ oz.	3 ½ oz.	7 oz.
Cocoa	n.r.	2 oz.	2 oz.	2 oz.	2 oz.
Potatoes	n.r.	140 oz.	140 oz.	140 oz.	108 oz.
Vegetables (including fresh fruit)	n.r.	30 oz.	38 oz.	42 oz. (oranges allowed)	60 oz.
Pulses	n.r.	16 oz.	16 oz.	16 oz.	20 oz.
Rice, Sago	n.r.	8 oz.	8 oz.	8 oz.	20 oz.

(n.r. = not rationed)	January 1918	4th March 1918	18th October 1918	6th February 1919	12th May 1919
Oatmeal, rolled oats, barley flour	n.r.	10 oz.	10 oz.	10 oz.	10 oz.
Jam	Not allowed	Not allowed	Not allowed	4 oz. (lemon)	8 oz.
Fat	7 oz.	4 oz.	4 oz.	4 oz.	8 oz.
Cheese	8 oz.	3 ½ oz.	3 ½ oz.	3 ½ oz.	Not available
Salt	n.r.	3 ⅓ oz.	3 ½ oz.	3 ½ oz.	4 oz.
Pepper & other seasoning	n.r.	½ oz.	½ oz.	½ oz.	1 ½ oz.
Fresh milk	1 pint per 3 officers per day	7 oz.	7 oz.	7 oz.	n.r.

There was no notable improvement in our provisions following the signing of the Armistice. Until January and February we only received horsemeat. The administration repeatedly petitioned the War Office in an effort to have restrictions lifted on fresh meat but to no avail. To supplement our meagre rations a considerable amount of *Schiebung* was required. The administration proved to be particularly skilled at this and, as a result, were able to procure goods via *Schiebung* to the value of £1,034 in December, £380 in January, £1,046 in the February-March period and £1,100 in April. But behind the scenes there were many challenges to be overcome. The commandant had got wind of one or two instances of *Schiebung* and was keeping a close eye on the kitchen and canteen operations. The *Schiebung* nevertheless continued efficiently, albeit with a little more caution. The total expenditure on food came to £1,940 in April and £1,786 in May. The canteen faced its greatest challenge during the influenza epidemic. The need to disband the mess mates system, the distribution of food to the many sick rooms, the lack of healthy orderlies – new measures had to be introduced on a daily basis to overcome all of these difficulties. The sick needed to be provided with lighter, more easily digestible meals. Fortunately the commandant was prepared to take personal responsibility for authorising a considerable improvement in our provisions at this time. The bread ration was increased and fresh meat, fat, fruit and milk were delivered to the camp in larger quantities. Provisions continued to be supplied at more or less this increased level. The improved food situation in England was also felt within the camp, especially from spring onwards. Eggs, butter, bacon, sausage, jam and so on were available to purchase from the store. Prices did not fall however, on the contrary in fact, the cost of daily meals rose from 2 shillings to 2 shillings and 3 pence. Before Christmas the old German government had sent us smoked *Mettwurst* sausage (1½lb per person) via the Danish Red Cross, and in May the new government sent us tinned meat.

Our kitchen did not just serve up meals to satisfy our stomachs but mixed a quantity of mischievous humour in with the menu. On more than one occasion, the daily menu on the blackboard announced enticing, eye-opening items (such as Bolshevik soup) that made the prisonörs' eyes widen. One comrade reports here on the hope and disappointment he experienced over the ...

Chicken Surprise

"Chicken surprise this evening! These words are chalked in large letters for all to read on the blackboard hanging from the kitchen door. The prisonör's eyes widen, his apprehensive heart opens wide, his easily excited imagination leads him on to anticipate the epicurean delights for which the chicken has sacrificed itself. He is intoxicated by the very thought of the delicate juicy flesh of a roasted chicken leg, and the justifiably much-loved health-giving properties of chicken soup steam temptingly at the edges of his memories of chicken. All of this flashes through his mind in an instant. In the very next moment he knows with fatal certainty – chicken? Here? – Impossible! In a trice his castles in the air come crashing down. And yet he still has some hope and comfort. Once real chicken is out of the question he titillates his taste buds with the thought of something exceptional, something extra special, a delicacy beyond the everyday fare. So the prisoner starts work and, in his subconscious, it hammers away, it keeps bursting forth, filling him with a secret joy and a sense of expectation: Chicken surprise! Chicken surprise! That is, at least, until he receives clarification from an authentic source, which sobers him as if he had been doused with a jet of icy water. Chicken surprise is in fact a euphemistic description for a concoction of beans and beets, a dish to stultify the taste buds, animal fodder. It is a dish closely related to Irish stew, and the German one-pot dishes *Pickelsteiner* and *Leipziger Allerlei*, and classified in the category of necessary evils. And yet even this much-reviled dish gains a certain consecration. It is rehabilitated, as it were, by calling it 'chicken surprise', surrounding it with an ennobling halo that lodges itself like a limpet in the prisonör's mind as he makes his way to the dining hall that evening, so that it swirls around him like incense as he shovels his share of the bean and beet concoction from the bowl down his gullet. And it did taste good, that chicken surprise! Whimsically, from now on he will see his whole wretched existence as a chicken surprise! And even if the road he travels in life is bumpy and dirty, impossible and impassable, it will be transfigured by this illusion, the magic of chicken surprise will bring him safely through."

Metzroth.

The lack of sufficient food in the messes often forced us into self-reliance, enabling ...

Cooking in the Barracks

to prosper, as two of our comrades explain.

"As the main meals in the messes were not able to sate the prisonörs' intensely ravenous hunger, an extensive, peculiar sort of culinary art very quickly began to develop in the barracks. Historical research into the early days of the camp showed the supplementary food created by totally inexperienced cooks, and the kitchenware required for eating and cooking it, in a very poor light. The basic ingredient of all our cooking and baking goods was always porridge (pronunciation: por, redj), i.e. oatmeal or Quaker Oats. In the direst of times, all our dietary hopes were pinned with the most immense fondness on these yellow cardboard boxes of squashed grain. Even in better times, we also found manifold uses for it. The importance of porridge as a staple food is reflected in the various expressions used in the camp, such as 'porridge head', 'porridge belly'; we even spoke about 'the porridge of life'.

The kitchens served this noble dish as a soup every morning and evening.
'A meal of porridge is the way
we start and finish every day' ...

Porridge.

1 Raw form
2 Before coffee
3 In between times
4 For lunch
5 In the afternoon
6 Before dinner
7 Before bed
8 Eating it dry

... was an adage that found its place in the camp vernacular. There were not many who, in the most difficult gastronomic emergencies, did not turn to it with an all-consuming love. At the peak of the barracks cooking phenomenon, porridge was the shibboleth of all self-sufficient men. In the early, uncultured days of our captivity we were content to boil the mixture up into a type of gruel in water with a pinch of salt. In order to give this 'soup', so innocuous to mind and body, a bit of a stronger flavour, the more fortunate of the prisonörs added cocoa or sweeteners – if they had been lucky enough to get hold of these glorious delicacies at the camp store. Gourmands whose tastes inclined towards piquancy even drizzled delicious condensed tinned milk into it. It is said that, for some, the little pan, filled to the brim, was never off the stove.

The inevitable progression of the desire to tickle our taste buds resulted in new culinary endeavours and brought with it useful results – we progressed to baking. We would rub the dried oats between our palms, turning them into flour, then we would mix this with water to form a stiff dough. The mixture would then be spread over hot stove plates and soon our longing eyes would be greeted with the sight of golden-brown crunchy biscuits. This led to the creation of the so-called 'Bolshevist cakes', which enjoyed great popularity.

They were a good bread substitute. If, in a rash moment of wanton extravagance, fat, sugar and chopped nuts were added into the mixture, a culinary marvel would be created, the taste of which would have made even Lucullus – about whom we knew more then we could stomach – smack his lips. Other pioneers made successful inroads into producing homemade fritters. To make these, one would mash the moistened oats with a fork until they softened and then bake them in something fatty. The pan was often greased only with bacon rind. Those who had no fat to call their own simply had to fry them in water.

More culinary options opened up when our loved ones back home were able to supply us with various kinds of ingredients such as flour, pulses, potatoes, basic ingredients for stock and other such things. Before we could set about our new recipes, some at least half-baked advice had to be brought in. It was given gladly and in lively conversation. Pleasant cooking aromas often wafted through the barracks. Fried potatoes, browning and crisping, and fragrant fritters stared out at us from the pans. Broad beans together with the occasional piece of meat grinned up at us, and soup with specks of fat eyed us from the pans. The owners of these magnificent treasures would stand around, eyes shining, hands pressed to their stomachs, attentively following every visible sign of progress in the pan. Rejoicing, they would then carry their culinary masterpieces back to their own dens. Tranquillity would descend for minutes on end, and all that could be heard was the chomping of jaws.

What a place of honour we granted you in our culinary world, dear, stomach-filling custard! There were times when this custard was almost the only

2/6?	VORBEREITUNG	KOCHEN ~	ESSEN

DER PUDDING

| Two shillings and sixpence? | Preparation | Cooking | Eating |

Custard

supplement to our meals. Custard powder was easily obtained. The custard powder used in England also contains nutrients including cornflour and sugar. Even the powder on its own was enough to prepare a so-called blancmange. Mostly, though, when combined with oats, porridge, leftover bread, and particularly with cocoa, it entered into the most harmonious of partnerships.

Lazy individuals, and those who lacked the raw ingredients they suspected others of having, clamoured for cooking cooperatives. As a result of this, small cooking groups emerged with some members taking a more active role than others. However, not everything they turned their hands to resulted in intoxicating aromas. Led by a strong survival instinct, the barracks majority often had to defend themselves against the smell emanating from the witches' brew being concocted in the various pots and pans. Cooking in the barracks reached dizzying heights in the winter of 1918/19, when, owing to the coal shortage, the kitchen was no longer able to brew afternoon coffee and had to leave the task to us. The resulting pushing and shoving at the stove was perilous. Pots of manifold shapes and sizes were deployed in long rows. We considered distributing 'cooking tokens' in order to regulate the operation. Some clever individuals would set their pots ready on the stove at midday. Our trusty stove thus not only provided us with a warmth that invigorated our bodies, it was not only the meeting point for the stove council, no, it was also the sacred hearth of the house and contributed immensely towards heightening a sense of family.

Yet, given that its moderate output only sufficed to heat one pot at a time, it was not nearly enough to meet the many demands placed upon it. The POW needed to use his ingenuity in searching for other sources of heat. In the end, the gas pipes that were suspended from the ceiling were angled upwards and a burner that had been 'found' was placed on top. A soot-blackened pot swayed above it, suspended from a strong hook.[*] Most of the time this little cooking idyll was to be found high up in the gods, between the rafters. Caution was an absolute necessity. The English had long since become aware of the tremendous amount of gas being used. They had several times already caught these 'gas cooks' in the act, in the wash-houses, and had threatened to cut off the gas supply. Therefore, when cooking one kept an eagle-eyed lookout for the sergeant roaming the barracks. The cry of alarm, 'The Yorkshire Boar's coming' was enough to see the cooking area turned into a clattering, tumbling pandemonium. Up in the rafters, one would hear heavy puffing and blowing, and the obelisk built of suitcases, on top of which two legs had just been visible,

Forbidden cooking.

would thunder to the ground like Cyclopean masonry. A human being would descend to earth from on high, amidst a shower of pots and pans, knives, forks, spoons and splashing water. In spite of his crimson face and almost asthmatic wheezing, he would turn out to be a quite harmless individual. Yet, mostly the alarm had been merely spiteful comrades playing a trick on us.

We could purchase pots of a more or less decent size, from tin-plated iron ones with protruding handles to bare metal or enamel ones, from Mr James in the canteen with his winning smile. The high price he asked for them always ripped a depressingly large hole in our meagre funds. The poorer amongst us and those who took particular pleasure in making things themselves would turn their back on Mr James with a curse and make their own cooking equipment. We fried in empty herring cans, cooked in milk tins, and drank coffee out of tin cups made from food tins. In the hands of a skilled person, an ordinary pair of scissors could be used to trim the tin and a handle could be soldered on with a soldering iron and lead. A simple, yet first-rate frying pan

---

[*] According to the detailed research of our expert (Adolf Sanio), the use of gas in the camp through the forbidden pipe was equivalent to at least 82 light bulbs.

would first see the light of day by cutting away the lid of a flat square herring tin so that it was still attached at one side, then bending it over and binding it to a wooden handle. The potato grater was made out of an empty milk tin cut into two even pieces, the upwardly curving, serrated holes being made by forcibly hammering a nail into the surface many times. Spoons were regularly whittled out of wood. We would drink coffee and tea from ordinary drinking glasses; the wealthy sipped from cups. The sink served not only for washing dishes but also frequently for food preparation e.g. kneading the dough of certain flour-rich agriculturalists.

As our provisions began to improve in the spring of 1919, cooking in the barracks gradually petered out."

Hegermann & Wannemacher.

For long weeks, life in the camp had been under the terrible shadow of the influenza epidemic. Our mourning for those comrades who had passed away and the sight of the many convalescents who were recovering only slowly in the bad weather dampened our spirits. The camp only returned to normality around Easter time. After many rainy days, the weather cleared up in mid-April and the Easter celebrations had more of a shine to them. On Good Friday and Easter Sunday religious services resumed for the first time; the sermons reverberated with the terrible suffering of the previous weeks. Our Catholic comrades walked down into Skipton to the little church of St Stephen's. The kitchen served better food again. In the evenings we watched good stage performances of Oscar Wilde's *The Importance of Being Earnest*. Other than that, the Easter period passed quietly by.

Mercifully, the English heavens then saw fit to send us the most glorious weather. Heating stopped. Summer began. Our lives developed more richly than in the previous year. Only the gardening was not on the same scale. After all, we were hoping for repatriation. Why sow for others to reap? Once again, the hills turned green and full of flowers before our eyes, and we prisoners often stood looking out deep in thought across the wide sun-drenched Skipton valley to the distant surrounding hills in the direction of home. Outside in the woods the birds were singing. And, even in here, caged behind the wire, we had …

Our Camp's Animal Kingdom

which an animal-loving comrade describes for us.

"First there were cats. Three or four of them, for example our Peter and our Minnie, walked around the camp constantly and delighted audiences with solo performances or duets. Their playful mating rituals, in particular, never failed to draw a large crowd of onlookers. They managed to get everywhere. On two occasions one of these cats proudly trod the boards during one of the camp's theatrical performances. However, during musical performances, they were never to be seen. And quite rightly, for how should these English cats ever gain an understanding of the art of music? In contrast, these creatures showed a peculiar fondness for the rooms we had dedicated to academic study. I doubt that it was understanding that led them there. But in those hallowed halls it was warm, at least sometimes. And many are indeed attracted to things they do not understand. So, these cats must have observed how we prisonörs would sit on our chairs and armchairs for hours on end, with our heads bent over books as if we were sleeping. 'This must be the height of wisdom and bliss!' the cats were certainly thinking, since no sooner had we left the area than they would climb gracefully onto the chairs and – fall asleep. Twice, a mother cat chose Room A for her confinement. On those occasions the ice around even our coarse warriors' hearts melted into tenderness. No one could work during these major events. Some built a soft den, others fetched milk, and one fellow with deep insight into feline psychology produced a charming symbolic mother-cat epic.

And dogs, what about the dogs that were so popular with the German officers and men? I tried once to imagine what it would have been like if every German prisoner here in the camp had his own dog. Seven hundred dogs of various breeds, sizes and genders together in the smallest of spaces. That would have been fun! Or maybe not. I remember a captain who did have his dog with him until Le Havre. Presumably no German dog came further than that. Here in the camp itself, there wasn't a single dog. Only the mutt belonging to the aforementioned uncle visited us now and then. This creature took little notice of us and we took little notice of him. Only when he occasionally ventured recklessly onto the sports field did he delight us with the authentic English doggedness with which he tried to catch the ball, which was much too big for him, during the dance around the martyrs' stake, otherwise known as basketball. For a few weeks in June, a small, young pinscher appeared, who showed a touching attachment to our kitchen staff. He would yelp at the doors and from time to time he would inspect the officers working in room A.

Our most profound joy came from the bird life. We would stand for a long time in front of the ash trees in the camp, often with necks craned, watching the tiny young beaks pushing out of a hole in the box up there. There were cages hanging outside many of the barracks. Their prisoners enjoyed the loving care of our prisonörs, who deprived themselves of their own jam and other food to feed their winged fellow sufferers. And we imagined pleasant scenes. On the day of our release, our prisoners too were to be returned to the sunny skies: after all, happiness shared is happiness doubled.

The most popular animal in the camp was a dove. Who knows where she came from! In any case, she was suddenly there, around the time that the end of the war was in sight. We built her a little house out of an old porridge box and cared for her throughout the winter. She was kept prisoner for a long time. But when the beautiful spring days came, the little door was opened.

Away she flew. Would she ever return? She did indeed. First, she came alone, but then she brought her lovey-dovey with her. And then every day many people, especially older family men, could be seen lingering in front of the dovecote and delighting in the charming family life taking place within.

Even when it became quite lively up there and feathers flew, some still thought, 'Yes, yes, just like at home!' And the interest became even greater when cage after cage appeared outside Barrack 33 and the fertile original couple raised a fivefold brood over the course of spring and summer. There were large-scale pilgrimages to observe the doves' daily feuding, the first flight attempts of the young and other such momentous events. An astounded dove colony received the most staggering proof of the affection of their foster father when this 'Hun' packed up his pets on our return home and smuggled them back to Germany."

Schrader.

During the period of fine weather, participation in sport flourished surprisingly. In the previous year it had been curtailed by bad weather and the reprisals. Now, almost seventy percent of the camp's inmates were taking part in enjoyable games on the grass. So let us now have a brief overview of our …

Camp Sport

"The sports ground: a grassy field, approximately a hectare in size, just about large enough for a football pitch. It does, however, slope down steeply towards the southern corner. But what does that matter? A true footballer will overcome such obstacles if necessary. So, with the goal posts erected and some balls purchased, the sports ground is ready for use! There is the main field, which is the football pitch. And further north, separated from the football pitch by a hedge consisting of young trees and an old ash, there is a second field the same length as the main field but only half the width – but without a steep slope. Entrance to the smaller field is via a wide gap in the hedge at the lower end or a narrow gap at the upper end. This field is very useful for games requiring a smaller pitch and for practising athletics. Placed at the disposal of the 500 German officers and 100 men condemned by fate to be prisoners of war, how could such a sports field fail to provide them with joyful and energetic activity!

And yet, during the summer of 1918, it was not to happen due to external circumstances. Soon after the sports ground was opened, the English reprisals came into force, which included the closure of the sports ground. When it became accessible again in the late summer, the continually poor weather meant that very little sport could take place.

In 1919 things were entirely different. The summer was exceptionally dry with week after week of good weather. We were allowed increasingly longer access to the sports ground; eventually it could be used from early in the morning until late in the evening. This was the time when our sporting activity reached its peak and when the most colourful images and the most lively activity could be seen on the sports ground.

The colourfulness of the scene, in the literal sense of the word, arose firstly from the multi-coloured sporting attire. In comparison with its otherwise renowned wide range of stock, Mr James' cheap and cheerful shop stocked a relatively small range of sports garments, meaning that his suppliers had a good distribution outlet for their left-over items. Alongside plain black or plain white shorts and white sports shirts there were red and white sweat shirts, sports jackets with red, black, brown and purple stripes, rowing suits and bathrobes, calf-length rubber boots, bast shoes and black plimsolls. The most consistent thing about all the items was the price. In the interests of increased variation the young sportsmen also added their own accessories. When the individual compartments of the barracks had fallen victim to the influenza, the material that became available found no better use than for making gym shorts: the boxes[58] became boxer shorts. The 'Tünnerhoff'[59] brand, which celebrated its greatest triumphs in the blue and green shorts of Barrack 18, received well-deserved acclaim and was soon copied by others. Two comrades from Barrack 27 even appeared on the sporting arena wearing shorts with a pink flowery pattern.

Just as the sportsmen of the camp were unable to choose their clothing on the grounds of practicality and tasteful simplicity, the sporting activities themselves were designed to fit in with the particular conditions and requirements of the camp.

The variety of activities on offer was large enough to cater for the most diverse of wishes and yet very quickly, out of necessity and for everybody's benefit, was restricted to a small but wide-ranging selection of games and exercises. With the exceptions of *Barlauf*,[60] which was only played a few times, and tennis which was taken up very late, only four games were played regularly in the camp: football, *Schlagball*,[61] fistball and basketball. Athletics events consisted of running, jumping and throwing (discus, throwing a *Schleuderball*,[62] shot put) in addition to regular gymnastic exercises (without apparatus). But this small number of exercises and games provided sporting activity that was healthy, enjoyable and kept us physically fit, as well as providing amusement for those few comrades who were only spectators. Let us visualise some moments from those summer days, evoking for one or the other of us the memory of a dear figure or an amusing event.

About one in ten comrades in the camp participated in football. The game requires skills that cannot be learnt at an advanced age or in a matter of a few weeks. We only had 3-4 teams of 11 players, who all knew each other very well personally, and were part of the same community. This number was too small to provide an incentive for real competition, and in this respect the camp football matches could be compared to those of a local football club whose spark is only fully ignited by the prospect of competition against teams from further afield. In the games between officers and men, one could definitely detect more of a will to win, but it was enacted with an acrimony arising from the depths of the non-sporting soul.

Nevertheless, the advantages of the beautiful game were apparent to everyone. It instils endurance and courage, lightning-quick assessment of the situation, rapid response, participation in methodical, shared work, and camaraderie. The physical advantages of the game are also great, as only the arms remain inactive, necessitating complementary athletic exercises or games involving hitting and throwing such as tennis or *Schlagball*.

Schlagball was also embraced by a dedicated group during the winter. Like football it requires particular skills: throwing, catching and hitting the ball. These skills cannot be acquired overnight. It is expedient to prepare by means of childish ball games. Once a certain level of competence with the ball has been reached, however, the game acquires a wonderful finesse. Physically, the versatility of the game is almost perfect: there are short sprints, the elasticity of evasion and pursuit, high leaps for the ball, sideways jumps, diving to protect the wicket, long-distance throwing, throws aimed at an opponent, wide swings of the bat and bold catches performed with a sure steely eye and a firm hand. The physical aspect of the game is accompanied by pleasant psychological processes, similar to those experienced in football. But *Schlagball* is more enjoyable – it is the most pleasurable of all the finely developed competitive games. Contact with the opponent is never direct; it is only through shots with the harmless leather ball that one attempts to get the better of him. There is a great deal of pleasure to be had in the game. Lying comfortably by the hedge and watching, I always sensed a similarity between the game of *Schlagball* and the play of young dogs, in that there seems to be an element of humour. They scrap with and bite each other but all in a good-natured way. Now the game is on, they hang their ears and crouch attentively, waiting for the other to move: this is when the shot is played and none of the runners dare to move from the crease. Now! Suddenly the group of runners is dashing towards the home base. What have our dogs been doing? One of them has jumped up, followed by the second one and then the others, back and forth, up and down, their antics accompanied by loud and excited yapping. The shouts of the *Schlagball* players are also loud and excited and then there is the roar of 'got him' when he is thrown out. What now? The ball flies out of bounds and they have to chase after it, the game is stopped, some of the players sit on the grass, the crease keeper leans lethargically against his post. One of the dogs has discovered a bone, the others sniff around him, an older dog lies down, panting with its tongue hanging out; but the bone isn't really what they want, it's not worth interrupting the enjoyable game for, and with high-pitched yelps the chase starts again.

In football we found none of this joyfulness, and there were no playful dogs – here we saw the fighting bull, heavy and powerful on its feet, but often unexpectedly lithe, continually attempting to take its opponent by the horns and with magnificent steadfastness to break through towards the target. The entire attacking team could also be likened to the image of the fighting bull. The goal keeper is the Espada, who has to fell his approaching opponent with a decisive push lest he be overrun and trampled underfoot, unless he manages at the last moment to grab the bull by the horns and thus avert the worst outcome. Encounters with the opponent are much more direct than in *Schlagball* and don't have the same humorous, often ironic guile; the clashing opponents are certainly wily, but we don't sense any humour; they are raging, and opponents are brutally pushed aside; they always have a red rag before their eyes.

Our third main game in the camp, the game of fistball, has something bear-like about it. Just as Goethe's bear Meister Petz stands up on his hind legs, the fistball player continually returns to take up his position on a particular spot like the chained dancing bear. Initially, observers will notice a certain ungainliness but soon it becomes apparent that the best results are achieved only with the most nimble movements – just as moments of great agility can be witnessed when observing bears. This combination of bear-like power and agility is apparent in the way the ball is handled, one moment hit with resounding force, the next guided lightly forward with a skip and a jump. In fistball there is also an element of the good-naturedness of the bear. The opponents are separated by a rope and only come into contact with each other as a result of ineptitude. Essentially they should have nothing to do with one another, just as polar bears and brown bears are separated by a fence in a zoo. It is only through superior ball handling skills that one can score against the opposing side. It is more a game of skill than a game of combat, akin to

View from the sports ground to the camp.

billiards and tennis. Therefore it is less crucial to have a series of different opponents to maintain motivation. In contrast to games such as football or basketball, it can be played regularly against the same opposition without a significant loss of fulfilment, as the main satisfaction comes from skilfully striking the ball. In addition, the game only permits five players on each side, so a team can easily be assembled or reassembled if broken up by the extreme irritability typical of prisonörs. The game also requires only a relatively small amount of space, meaning that four games can be played simultaneously. And so it was especially popular in the camp during the hot summer, particularly as little training was required in order to achieve a modest level. For the amateur player it was enough at first if he could thump the ball hard in its English face – what happened to the mistreated ball after that did not really concern him. The spectators would be all the more delighted; the first attempts of a certain team of more senior players were in particular a lasting source of mischievous pleasure for the spectators watching openly or surreptitiously.

Requiring even less prior experience than fistball is basketball, which we should count as the fourth of our main games in the Skipton camp. The technique required is the ability to grasp the ball naturally with both hands then throw it to another player and run – these skills are possessed sufficiently by every healthy person to allow him to pick up the game quickly. While football and *Schlagball* are played at national level, or could be, basketball and fistball are supplementary games or games played between seasons – fistball more for the warmer months and basketball for the colder months. Fistball is mainly a game for adults, very popular among older gentlemen who have started to accumulate fat around their midriffs; basketball is distinctly a younger person's game, full of action and bubbling with life. The rule that a player holding the ball with two hands cannot be attacked makes it an excellent game for girls.

As we played it in the camp, basketball was a game of panthers. The agility was cat-like, the leaping, the grabbing, the lithe power, the determination and the resolute tenacity of the best players. Cat fights were common. There was none of the awkward good-naturedness of the fistball bears, none of the humorous scuffles of the *Schlagball* stars, but also none of the stubborn force of the football buffaloes. No! What we saw there before us were fighting tigers, growing in stature, in the full sinewy strength of their lean bodies. Listen! A threatening growl is emitted from jaws which are attempting to bite. We feel we are only a hair's breadth away from the beasts drawing blood in earnest. In the days leading up to Whitsun, when the basketball competitions had reached their climax, the behaviour of the spectators and the arrangement of the seating in rows was reminiscent of a Roman amphitheatre. At the front the wide-armed basket chairs represented the boxes of the Caesars and other powerful figures, then came the chairs and the benches of the horsemen, with the shouting plebeians standing behind.

For the sake of consistency I must also include in my animal comparisons the game of tennis, which was taken up by one or two dozen comrades right at the end of the autumn playing season. However, this conflicts somewhat with the overriding significance of the instrument, the racquet, when the game is being practised; the tool is an indicator for the elevation of the human being above the level of animals. Actually, tennis was also considered to be the most refined and aristocratic of all the ball games; certainly for this reason it has more of a tendency than others to incite sports fanaticism and foppishness. Of course, I do not wish to belittle the fine and powerful game. Alongside its particular advantages, every game also has its inherent dangers.

And if we firstly take our eyes off the players and look straight at the ball itself and how it constitutes the moving focal point of performance in the game of tennis – how it flies, springs, bounces, lightening quick, dilated, elastic and yet precise – the image of playing squirrels as a comparison is probably justified. We have discovered two of them playing their delightful games on the trunk of that spruce. They chase after each other up the trunk in short little leaps, we see them appear on the left and on the right alternately, every now and again using adjoining branches to spring from. Similarly the ball sweeps swiftly back and forth over the net. But the rushing of the squirrels up the thin branch is suddenly followed by a magnificent arcing leap to the end of the branch; one of the players has saved himself from a frantic rally by hitting a high volley to the rear of the court in a steep arc with a smooth rotation of his body; the ball slams down firmly and rebounds up again, just as over there the branch bows down under the springing weight of the animal and then springs upwards again. Has the game finished? It almost seems like it has. At any rate one of the animals is sitting calmly at the top of the tree, while the other sits below in the large fork of a branch. But soon one of them makes a sudden movement, to which the other responds with a powerful counter-leap. Well, what did you expect? Likewise, in the game of tennis, after every point there is a pause during which one player prepares himself to serve and the other to return the shot, and only the completed serve initiates once again the swaying, seesawing, springing motion of the bouncing sphere. And when the animals' game is suddenly interrupted by a mistimed jump or a slip and one of the squirrels falls to the ground from the bough with a heavy thud, it is as much a discordant note as a clumsy shot in the tennis game which sends the ball over the net and beyond the white line into the safety netting – or to use 'Skipton-speak' – into the barbed wire. Even the aristocratic nature of the game of tennis is mirrored in the squirrels' game. The football bull has to wade through the quagmire which often forms in front of the goals; the *Schlagball* dogs have muck hanging from their bellies (sometimes they also slide along on their backsides across the slippery surface in front of the base line). The basketball tigers and football bears live in their cages, which are not always very clean, but the tennis court on the other hand is clean and smooth or it is empty: the squirrels also only play in the clean and airy areas of woodland trees or in majestic parks. To be truthful, it must however be noted that the over-enthusiasm of some Skipton tennis players, who were sporting novices, did not always conform to this stereotype.

Alongside the games in the camp, athletic exercises became increasingly popular following the formation of the athletics society in April 1918. A sandpit was prepared for long jump and high jump, which unfortunately had to be made slightly too narrow because of the adjacent fistball pitch. A 400m track was marked out as well as was possible given the unsuitable terrain. We also obtained some simple equipment: a 7¼kg shot put, 2 discuses and 1 *Schleuderball*. With this simple set-up, the athletes in the camp were able to do their training, which, though falling short of the full range of events in the classical Greek pentathlon, nevertheless enabled excellent physical exercise for the attainment of both strength and beauty. There were various throwing, jumping and running exercises, in other words ancient forms of meaningful human movement in which the relative attainments of all participants emerge clearly and automatically. Thus they provide all the attractions of competitive sports, just as, of course, they constitute regulated elements of other sports, the effect of which on the spectator is akin to the enjoyment of art.

Let us take another walk in our mind's eye around our sports field on one of the beautiful July mornings when many men are participating in athletics training in the foreground.

We have barely gone through the narrow entrance when we see a *Schlagball* or cricket ball coming towards us, having been thrown from the area near the top football goal. Some comrades are training for the long-throwing competition by practising with the *Schlagball*. Complacently we observe the lovely arc described by the expertly-thrown ball against the sky. Nearby we then see the flowing movement of the limbs and torso of the thrower when he swings back his arm to take aim and transfers all his momentum into the small ball.

Next to this we see another type of throwing: the launching of the large, heavy leather ball with a strap attached. In this case, again, the strength of the arms alone is not sufficient to achieve a good distance: full power must be transmitted into the ball at the very moment it is launched via the rotational force of the body and the arms, while avoiding any loss of energy.

Yet another group of officers is practising throwing the discus. This throw requires even more energetic rotation around the axis of the body and constitutes excellent training for the abdominal muscles.

Participation in the various running disciplines was particularly enthusiastic. If one wished to find out in advance of the races what the competitors were capable of, one had to be an early riser! No other discipline generates so much excitement among the spectators, as here a person pushes himself to his highest speed and power in order to fight for victory. The pinnacle of this can be observed in the sprints, where within a few seconds the heart, lungs and legs must give everything they have got, while in the middle and long distance running events intelligent economy of effort and an awareness of the actions of one's fellow competitors is necessary for success. Furthermore, running is an activity which requires extreme caution at any age, but particularly for those of more advanced years. It seemed to me that the many new sports enthusiasts in the camp did not always take their health seriously enough.*

The greatest non-sporting interest, where the focus was exclusively on the winners, was generated by the relay races, which were not just about camaraderie and personal relationships, but also the element of risk involved in the handover of the baton. The amount bet on these team races was therefore especially high and indeed the totaliser played a major role in sport because of the conditions produced by camp life. It must, however, be said that all forms of betting must be regarded as an enemy of pure physical exercise and should be discouraged.

The third main group of physical exercises becomes apparent as we reach the sandpit on the upper sports field. We only see a small number of examples of triple jump and the standing long jump of the classical pentathlon. On the other hand, the normal long jump and high jump are being practised diligently, the latter not often with a straight run-up but with an approach from the side, the so-called 'Scottish jump'. In the best examples of this the body of the jumper rolls over the string in an almost horizontal position, having pushed off the ground with the foot furthest from the take-off position so that the entire wonderful movement appears as a more purposeful and, for that reason, more beautiful run punctuated by a jump. We are struck by how short the run-up is; there should not be an excessive forward velocity; instead the momentum should be carried into the upward leap. In the long jump it is different – here, the take-off speed should be as high as possible, and so the run-up is long and the effort is apparent in the facial expressions, similar to those of the sprinters. So it is no surprise that the winner of the long jump and the sprint is often the same person.

Next to the sand pit we can see the shot put with the iron ball which, as with all the throws, demands a unity of strength and agility, and requires the maximum performance of the entire human frame.

The whole range of enjoyable yet seriously and keenly undertaken sports and games that have just been briefly paraded before our eyes came together gloriously in the camp sports festivals.

---

* Those who wish to know more about the health parameters for athletic activities should refer to two good German works: F.A. Schmidt, *Unser Körper*, written for sportsmen and quite detailed; Hüppe, *Die Hygiene der Körperübungen*, less detailed but an excellent overview of the subject.

When, with the start of the good weather, the wish for a combined sports festival was expressed more widely and began to take shape, the compiler of this report held a lecture entitled 'How shall we organise our camp sports festival?' believing that a successful demonstration of camp games and traditional competitions, enhanced by universal participation and the presentation of awards, framed by an opening speech and a small post-event celebration, would encourage physical activity in the camp and promote an understanding of sensible sporting activity. Immediately before the first sports festival he held a second lecture entitled 'Introduction to the camp sports festival from patriotic and educational perspectives.'

Certificate.

In total, three large sports festivals were held in the Skipton camp, or four if the tennis tournament is included. All of them were blessed with superb weather. The first major sports and games festival was opened by the senior German officer with an entertaining speech on the afternoon of Whit Sunday. The main events were on Whit Monday.

The second camp sports festival, on 27th July 1919, featured only athletics competitions but with a much wider range of events. Contributions from comrades enabled us to provide numerous handsome prizes with a total value of around £30.

The autumn competition on 7th September was a smaller affair, involving only the members of the athletics club who had not previously won prizes.

The tennis competitions that took place in October 1919 were similarly organised. Two tournaments were held, the second of which had handicaps. Unfortunately these provoked so much antagonism that even the spectators were affected by unease. However, a series of enjoyable matches took place, and the progress of some of the players during the tournament week was quite remarkable.

Without doubt, sport was a ray of light in the lives of the prisoners of war, both individually and collectively. It would not be exaggerating to say that it was only through sport in our prisoner-of-war camp that some men experienced for themselves the benefits of habitual daily activity in the fresh air, within healthy limits, for the maintenance of physical fitness as well as for intellectual capability and for refreshing the mind; and that habitual physical activity within the limits imposed by one's work can actually be considered a moral obligation of every citizen.

More attention will have to be paid to sport and games in post-war Germany, and they will have important functions to fulfil. What is most important, alongside the appropriate organisation of physical and patriotic development, is the German concept of sport as a schooling of the body to higher moral purposes. May I conclude by expressing the wish that every 'Skiptoner' who, as a father, educator or citizen, will one day have to concern himself with the issue of physical fitness or physical education, might be inspired by his own experience in the camp to adopt a positive attitude."

Eppensteiner.

For the Whitsun weekend we were blessed with glorious sunshine. The morning service sought to offer a religious understanding of Germany's fate and, in the light of this new article of faith, to awaken in us the courage to face the new life of the German people. The big sports festival took place on the afternoon of Whit Sunday and on Whit Monday. The orderlies, in their high-spirited humour, combined it with the bustle of a lively fair. There were stalls with a wheel of fortune and tombolas. A chamber of horrors revealed its terror. Fortune tellers and bears with their keepers wandered through the crowds. The 'dance hall' was filled with couples in charming costumes. The following Tuesday gave us the opportunity to demonstrate our grateful veneration to our beloved senior officer and head of our administration since March, Corvette Captain Sachsse, on the occasion of his birthday. At the early hour of 6.30am a piano was secretly 'smuggled' into the staff officers' barracks, and actors and singers soon followed, stepping quietly. The day got off to a festive start with two songs from the choir, performances from a section of our orchestra and an address. Despite the early hour, many comrades had gathered around the staff officers' barracks and joined in enthusiastically with the three cheers that rang out loudly and strongly over the baffled Tommies and down into the

Western side of the sports ground.

valley. In the evening we had a jolly get-together in the Old Mess, attended by representatives of every barracks.

Our administration had operated loyally and diligently over a long time period, despite the fact that it was often quite difficult to accommodate the wishes and demands of 550 officers and 120 men, while at the same time following the orders of the English. May the following reports shed some light onto this so-far unmentioned activity:

Our Administration Office

"The highest authority in our small, autonomous kingdom was represented by the senior German officer. As indicated by his name, this position was held by the highest ranking officer in the camp. His position was by no means easy. Many were of the opinion that his post suffered from its inherently vague status, given that it had neither a civilian nor a military stamp and that it was not in the least bit similar to the position of commander in the military sense. The argument went that there was no provision for it in our peacetime regulations, and that hence its status rested on no actual authority or disciplinary power. While, towards the end of the war, the German government had conveyed to us through the Swiss Legation the essential remit of the office, it was argued that this merely reiterated in general terms that in captivity the military hierarchy remained in force and therefore any offences would be dealt with once we were back home. Beyond that, it contained nothing of substance on which to base the position of a senior officer and the scope of his authority. Seeing that we were all still soldiers, his authority could not be civilian in character either.

One can therefore appreciate the difficulties to which this amorphous role gave rise. But nevertheless it worked well because we had to get on with each other. We made our own small laws; orders were given when necessary and the German officer obeyed. But in general, all of our interactions were based on comradely solidarity, and only in rare cases might it perhaps have been desirable to have a constitutionally secured and legitimated senior officer.

At the heart of the camp's system of governance was the central administration led by the director. He was based in the administration office, where all correspondence and financial matters were dealt with. Alongside this office, or under its control, came all the sub-offices required for the organisation of the camp. Firstly there was the mess administration, staffed by a number of officers, which was responsible for the operation of the kitchen, the store and the bar; then, each managed by one officer, there were the carpentry, tailors and cobblers, the barber's, the gardeners and the laundry administration; next there were the two postal officers, the shower officer, the officer responsible for firewood and coal distribution, the officer for barracks occupancy and inventories, the sports officer, the officer for pathway maintenance, and the firefighting officer; the officer responsible for tobacco distribution (during the time of rationing), the head of teaching and the lecture programme, the officer in charge of ordering books from London, the newspaper distribution officer, the officer in charge of the newspaper reading society; and not forgetting the director and the heads of the individual sections of the music, choir and theatre society, the head of the enlisted men, the enlisted men's catering officer, the officer responsible for checking the enlisted men's canteen fund, the committee for checking accounts, which once a month reviewed the ledgers and accounts of every department, the library officers, and finally the barrack captains, who were the representatives of each accommodation barracks. All these functions, and in addition others that were newly created or subsequently improved upon as practice progressed and experience was gained, always followed the aim of contributing to our general wellbeing and making our imprisonment more bearable.

The following account will allow the reader to gain an insight into the department responsible for handling all the camp correspondence.

When, at the outset, four keen officers met to divide up the writing tasks and book-keeping between them in a brotherly fashion, the question arose as to whether there would actually be any work to do. But scarcely had ink and paper been acquired when the work started to pile up. The names of all officers present in the camp were listed in alphabetical order; lists with precise personal details, dates, status and place of birth gave information about every inmate and provided a means of checking the accuracy of the information already contained in the large personnel files held by the English, who were often very good at misinterpreting our excellent German handwriting. Indispensable and most urgently needed both for ourselves and for the English was a list of the residents of each barracks, accurately naming the occupant of each bed in turn, which was vital for the formation of the daily roll calls. Election to the councils of honour necessitated reference to lists based on service seniority; a rapidly instituted chronological check-list of camp numbers made it possible to see, for instance, the daily tally of arrivals and departures and the total number of men in the camp on a daily basis. But it soon became apparent that maintaining all these hand-written records was far too time-consuming and that, in order to complete the work more quickly with so few workers available, the procurement of a typewriter was an urgent necessity.

One was promptly obtained and it did not break down during our time in Skipton, despite the fact that sometimes it was rattling away from dawn to dusk with many hands relentlessly pushing it to the limit.

In the beginning, compiling the lists meant a lot of work. Because of the constant arrival of groups of men at frequent intervals from our original camp of Colsterdale and later on from the Front, the lists were being continually revised and usually had to be compiled from scratch. They were always reproduced in seven or eight copies as they were in urgent demand by various departments. These personnel lists were abandoned as it became almost impossible to continue producing new lists as the influx of officers increased. They were replaced by a card index system, which operated until the end.

In fact, by far the greater part of the correspondence was with the camp commandant and the Swiss Legation. Since, except in the most pressing cases, direct communication between inmates and the commandant was not permitted, all suggestions, complaints, petitions and proposals were processed in the administration office, translated into English and produced in duplicate. If the commandant forwarded such petitions, then he required a third copy for himself.

Requests for powers of attorney made for considerable extra effort and a lot of vexation. Claiming that the German government was applying restrictions to power of attorney cases for British prisoners, the War Office responded with similar regulations. The dispatch by post of full power of attorney was, and always remained, prohibited. Only in specific cases was special power of attorney admissible, e.g. for court cases, in cases involving family law and inheritance, as well as for money transfers, in which there had to be absolute clarity concerning the whys and wherefores and in particular the amount of money in question. In short, no power of attorney 'whose consequences could be detrimental to the British Empire or its allies' was permitted. Prior to its dispatch every power of attorney required the permission of the Treasury, which in addition to the restriction clauses meant a further delay of up to three weeks. The regulations required six copies of every power of attorney, four versions in English, two in German – probably to fill up the wastepaper baskets as it went through the bureaucratic channels. At times there was no possible means of progressing the power of attorney through the often arbitrary procedures of the Treasury, despite strict compliance with the regulations in every respect.

Our work also involved a steady stream of inquiries about missing persons, which the Red Cross in Germany forwarded to us from their branches in Frankfurt am Main and Leipzig. Hundreds of these inquiries were lodged, but only in a relatively few instances was it possible to provide specific information.

Every morning between 11.00 and 12.00 the senior German officer, and in the early days the officer who acted as interpreter, spoke with the commandant and conveyed to him the concerns and requests of the camp's inmates. For his part the commandant then made known any new regulations or other items of information. He would also no doubt complain about any irregularities.

Notification of all orders and instructions were made to the camp via the administration office. Minor or frequently occurring routine matters were announced at the midday meal. More important and more extensive announcements were posted on the noticeboard or were conveyed at meetings of the barrack captains.

The occasional elections to positions on the councils of honour were also handled by the administration office. All orders and instructions issued by the administration office, which initially only existed in a single copy, were duplicated and made available to each group. The lists were kept up to date and from time to time were re-issued. Later, a special officer was assigned to assist the commander of the councils of honour. This officer dealt with all matters pertaining to the councils of honour and in particular took responsibility for the lists.

One position that likewise helped to take the pressure off the administration office was the position of 'duty officer'. His tasks were confined to drawing up the daily lists of those going on walks, distributing the official letter-writing forms and the sorting and dispatch of outgoing post on Mondays and Thursdays. Later on, these tasks were taken on by an orderly who was assigned to the administration office to do a variety of routine jobs.

There were plenty of other things that often completely filled up the day. In particular, the acquisition of a duplicating machine widened the scope of our activity. Copy for the camp newspaper, for concert, theatre and other performance programmes (assuming the camp's artists had not written things in their own hand), were type-written onto the waxed sheets of paper needed for the duplicating machine. All the newspaper items of interest and reports from home, talks on particular camp events, extracts from the stipulations of the peace treaty translated into German, major announcements to the camp and so forth would be reproduced in many copies. Beyond that, individual requests were considered whenever possible.

We should also mention the so-called 'pocket-handkerchief reports'. When, in 1918, the exchange took place of comrades who had been imprisoned for more than 18 months, or who were seriously wounded or sick, many officers took the opportunity to prepare detailed accounts about their captivity, their last field reports and full powers of attorney to share with those back home. They were not intended for British eyes and would certainly have had very little chance of getting past the censors. All these statements were typed on strips of handkerchiefs and then sewn into clothing, caps and boots, places where body searches and inspections of belongings by the Tommies would never uncover them, whereas paper often gave itself away by rustling. It gave us great satisfaction to learn that all these accounts reached their destination, having been missed by the lynx-eyed Tommies, most of whom thought they were very clever.

A diary enumerating the most important happenings in the camp was started only at the beginning of 1919, but it nevertheless contained much that has been useful for the present volume.

As the time for repatriation drew nearer, the administration office also got itself ready and made the final preparations. Important records to be handed over to the German authorities, and in particular documents concerning the influenza epidemic, were included; less important documents were destroyed. Some of the fixtures such as the typewriter and duplicating machine were bought by the canteen manager at half price."

Kohlenbusch.

The Military Leadership of the Camp

The administration office also worked closely with the military authorities responsible for the Skipton prisoner-of-war camp.

"The Skipton officer prisoner-of-war camp belonged to the military district of Northern Command, which was headquartered in York. Initially, General Maxwell was in charge. This gentleman had earned his reputation during the bloody fighting in the Easter Rising in Ireland in 1916. He won further laurels for himself thanks to his verbal abuse of the prisoners in his care. When he was officially opening a hospital he said in his speech, which was heard by nurses and children, 'The German prisoners are like dogs. They definitely bark, but when you hit them, they go on licking your hands.' A letter of complaint about this incident was sent from the Lofthouse Park civilian internment camp near Wakefield to the Swiss Legation. This letter would have been but one of many letters that never reached its destination. Once, the general even favoured us with a visit. In a friendly post-breakfast atmosphere he listened to our complaints, made a lot of promises, but kept none of them. That evening we then read in the *Yorkshire Evening News* that he had used the dog comparison again over breakfast: 'The German dog has now got its tail between its legs'. We experienced something mildly similar with his successor, General Maxse. On the occasion of his visit to the camp, to use camp jargon, he stuck his boot in. When we protested about this, we received a very skilfully worded reply, which we again found very hard to swallow. The following transcription of the formal correspondence regarding this incident supplies further information:[63]

'12th July 1919
To the commandant of the Skipton POW Camp
   In the name of the German officers at the Skipton Camp I must bring the following to your attention. Yesterday when General Sir I. Maxse was speaking to Lieutenant X, he said the following with reference to German air force officers: 'From all I came across they were the only men I found chivalrous.' He repeated this statement twice, and the final time, when Lieutenant X tried to respond, he said quite distinctly; 'Don't talk about. From all I came across, officers and men, they were the only ones who showed chivalry.'
   This remark is not surprising in itself, seeing that similar slanderous statements made by British statesmen and the press are to be found every

day in the newspapers. What does surprise us is the fact that the general used the occasion of a visit to a prison camp to make such comments, when these officers have in fact been entrusted to his protection by his own government, and he is well aware that these officers are in no position to defend their honour under the present circumstances, if that honour is not upheld by his own sense of chivalry.

The officers of the camp are indignant to discover that they themselves are being denied this essential protection. The only recourse open to them is to rebuff this affront to the German Officer Corps in the strongest of terms.'

To this communication we received the following reply:

'1. The general understands the point of view of the German officers, and their endeavour to attribute a specific meaning to the words he used is natural, when one takes account of the length of their captivity. But to the best of his recall, the conversation with Lieutenant X took place somewhat differently.

2. As a matter of fact it was Lieutenant X who initiated the conversation. He mentioned that he was a member of the German air force, and the general's comment about his chivalry seemed to give him pleasure. As far as he remembers, the general believes that Lieutenant X replied in excellent English that they were all decent sporting fellows. If the two or three German officers, who could possibly have overheard the general's words, were irritated by them, 'it could not be helped.'

3. This was one of several conversations in which the German officers seemed willing to engage with the general during his one-hour visit to the camp. There was no parade. The commandant only received news about the intended visit shortly beforehand. The purpose of the unofficial visit was to ascertain whether the German officers had grievances to make about their physical living conditions, and the general made a point of asking the two senior officers whether they had any such grievances to make, or any suggestions for alterations.

4. If this objection is the only serious grievance that the German officers wish to make, then the general states with satisfaction that the arrangements at the camp are good.'

In his response the general has neglected to mention that: (1) we had not invited him to visit us; (2) that Lieutenant X, together with a few other officers, had been ordered by the commandant to present themselves before the general; and (3) the senior officer had made only one request, for permission to write more letters, and in response to the general's reply that British prisoners in Germany were not permitted more letters either and that there was still a war going on (11th July 1919), answered that: 'If the general draws such comparisons, there is no point in making any request whatsoever, and I will not do so again.'

Initially, we had as our camp commandant a Colonel Hunter, a somewhat unknown quantity. In any case, the top hat which he donned following his secondment to Skipton suited him better than a khaki cap. Under him was the assistant commandant, Lieutenant Colonel Eley. His tall, stiff, gaunt figure, his finely chiselled, haughty, monocled face gave him an air of unapproachability. However, his conduct was punctilious in all respects.

Another wonderful 'little man from Wales' (Lloyd George was the first to be described in these words), Adjutant Captain Parkhurst was the third-in-command of the camp. 'His appearance was against him', and in addition he always carried around with him that curse of the vertically challenged, who fear not being noticed or not receiving due respect. This mistrust, combined with an air of self-importance and officiousness, often made him more zealous than we would have liked. He therefore had few friends among the prisoners. Goaded on by Sergeant Major Green he

The Heads of our Loved Ones: Colonel Ronaldson.

would stick his nose into everything, would always find something and often caused trouble for us. But perhaps he was misunderstood: for example, when he was creeping about under the huts he wasn't really sniffing for tunnels, no, it was the lure of the mushrooms that grew there in abundance. Hence, he was not quite as dangerous as he appeared. If he thought that he was being genuinely appreciated, he became very obliging and affable. Under the positive influence of the new commandant he became an entirely different person and did many things for us beyond the call of duty. And this is how we can show our gratitude: by the inclusion of his picture in the history of the camp, he has joined the ranks of the immortals.

The new commandant, Colonel Ronaldson, was in all respects the opposite of his predecessor. After 25 years' service in India and South Africa, he first took part in warfare at the Suez Canal and then in France. He returned to Britain wounded and now wanted to conclude his military career as commandant of our prison camp. We can only look back at him with respect and gratitude. Having had many bleak experiences particularly with the attitude of more senior British officers (one has only to think of the shameless attacks of British generals and admirals on our highest leaders), Colonel Ronaldson convinced us, despite the contrary opinion of the English themselves who feared that this class of person had become extinct, that there was still one gentleman left in England, and it was him. Even during the war, he interpreted his official orders in our favour as much as possible. He settled breaches of camp regulations in a manner that testified to his goodwill and complete understanding of our position. Some of the misdemeanours might otherwise have proved costly to the perpetrators. After the Armistice in particular he did everything in his power to alleviate our situation. The War Office showed no inclination to grant us any latitude and so his hands were tied. Under Ronaldson, Parkhurst was in the meantime promoted to major and assistant commandant. The new adjutant, Captain Cotton, followed wholly in the footsteps of the commandant.

In the barracks next to the commandant's office the two duty interpreters sat and whiled away their working hours. When their children ask 'Daddy, what did you do during the Great War?' (this question could be seen frequently under a picture on posters encouraging men to enlist in the British Army), they would have to reply: 'Supervised distribution of parcels, sorted letters, occasionally translated a few formal requests into English, read out names

Der Adjutant.

The Adjutant.

at roll call.' In so far as they were able, the interpreters passed the time by reading through the German books which were to be censored. Letters were all censored in London. The virtues and failures of the various interpreters are given ample space elsewhere in this book. Suffice it to mention here that the last two interpreters shared a pleasant characteristic with their comrades in the commandant's office: the gentlemen in question greatly enjoyed a tipple. Indeed the older members of the British officers' mess were frequently enveloped in the sweetish smell of whisky when they reported for duty in the camp with its uneven pathways – but we will say no more of that, as further remarks could be construed as an outpouring of pure envy. And if we ever wanted to slurp a glass of whisky, well – discretion is the better part of valour.

The administration of the inventory is always a thankless task, and especially so here in the camp. Quartermaster Williamson was not to be envied, because woollen blankets can be made into smart civilian suits and bed sheets into sports kit, whilst chairs and wooden bedsteads burn really well. The British Army administration, which squandered millions during the war, is at the lower levels of command even more meticulous and bureaucratic than the old German one ever was. Furthermore, it was to our financial advantage that the quartermaster did his best to keep things in order and was miserly in issuing new items. In personal dealings he was very obliging and accommodating.

Of our guards inside the barbed wire, the only ones who were with us from beginning to end, apart from Parkhurst and Williamson, were the sergeants Lloyd, Turner and Green. The first two were calm, reasonable men who did their duty according to the regulations and overlooked many minor infringements. Sergeant Green by contrast, despite his ample stature, was a dangerous Briton. He was certainly a zealous soldier, but he had an interest in occasionally trying to make trouble for us. Unfortunately Parkhurst allowed himself to be entirely influenced by him.

The guard changed very frequently. The officers only came into contact with us on walks and when doing their rounds in the evening and at night. Apart from a few minor confrontations with the younger men over disrespectful greetings, inappropriate language, petty incidents on walks and too much noise during the nightly checks of the huts, we got on well with all of them. Some of the guard officers, such as Lieutenants Williams and Gray, earned the particular thanks of our fast walkers for taking them on longer walks. Towards the end, several men who had been in German captivity were in charge, and these men seem to have experienced no maltreatment there, as they were all very amiable."

Sachsse.

Our Cashier's Office

"The task of the cashier's office was to regulate the financial transactions between the English and the German officers. The salaries received by the German officers were:

- staff officers and captains: 4 shillings and 5 pence per day
- 2nd lieutenants and lieutenants: 4 shillings per day

Salaries were paid monthly to the cashier's office after a deduction by the English of 2 shillings per officer per day for food and 1 penny per day for coal. From the remaining amount the administration, which organised the finances of the camp businesses, deducted amounts owed by comrades in the camp.

An agreement between the German and Swiss governments permitted German officers in Britain to be paid extra allowances as follows:

1. Captains and higher ranking officers: 1 shilling per day
2. Officers below the rank of captain: 6 pence per day

These extra allowances were implemented from 1st January 1918. Separate statements detailing these payments were submitted quarterly to the Swiss envoy, clearly showing how this money had been distributed. Any money received from home was credited to the private accounts of individual comrades. The statements of these accounts were held by the cashier's office. Each officer was allowed to withdraw up to £3 of his money per week. The total amount of money requested was withdrawn by the English paymaster at the beginning of each week and paid out to the account holders. The cashier's office was responsible for the bookkeeping of twenty accounts, with the books being balanced monthly.

The Canteen Fund

When it came to purchasing food, clothing, etc., we relied solely on the Army & Navy Stores canteen. The store added a specific surcharge to the purchase price. It added 20% to all items sold in the store and 12% to all rationed and other food items we purchased for the kitchen. At the end of every month we were reimbursed 10% of the surcharge on non-kitchen purchases and 5% on kitchen purchases. Of this monthly income, 25% was paid into a bond account, which was only available to the English for payments required due to damage and wear and tear of the buildings and their fittings as 'perpetrated' by us. The remaining 75% was transferred to the canteen fund, which, in agreement with the British commandant, we used for expenses relating to sport, theatre and music, as well as to supplement the pay of the orderlies.

The general expenses of the camp administration amounted to £75 in March; our total assets in that month amounted to £922. The wages of our orderlies, who received 1 pound 5 shillings per month on average, amounted to £154. For extra work the orderlies were paid 1½ pence per hour. Men not assigned to a specific role received 20% on top of their earned wages. The turnover for the canteen amounted to £2,076 in December, with £418 for the kitchen store (the February figures were £1,644 and £387 respectively). Catering expenses for March amounted to 1,798 shillings and the amount paid to the English laundry for March came to 74 shillings.

The Loan Fund

The loan fund was established with a one-off contribution of 2 shillings each from 350 men. The fund allowed newly-arrived comrades from the Front to borrow up to £1 during their first four weeks, enabling them to buy the items they urgently required from the canteen, in addition to tobacco supplied by the German administration, and food items such as honey and margarine available from the mess. These purchases could only be made by means of vouchers, which had to be countersigned by the cashier's office. The loans would be repaid as soon as money had arrived from home, or by two monthly deductions of 10 shillings each. Sixty officers were supported through the fund."

Brünger, Schmalhoff.

Tobacco Administration

"After the introduction of rationing of tobacco, cigarettes and cigars in December 1917, no officer or orderly was able to buy more than 3 ounces of tobacco per month. This put an end to what had previously been a free market. The tobacco products bought from the Army & Navy Stores were distributed amongst the individual barracks as soon as they arrived each month. On public holidays there was usually a larger amount of tobacco available to the camp. The prices for cigarettes and cigars were always high (on average 2 to 3 shillings for twenty cigarettes, 8 pence apiece for cigars and 6 pence per ounce of pipe tobacco); cheap cigarettes were provided only for the orderlies' rations, 5 to 6 pence for ten cigarettes. Twenty cigarettes equated to one ounce of tobacco.

Tabaksausgabe.

Tobacco distribution.

The tobacco was sold in the camp at the purchase price. With around 600 men in the camp, approximately 30,000 cigarettes and 60 English pounds' weight of pipe tobacco were needed for one month's rations; the demand for cigars was comparatively low due to their high price and in most cases poor quality. Obtaining a sufficient supply of matches proved very difficult; there was a constant shortage in the camp. Each man was supplied with two small boxes of matches per month. Then, in early 1919 a golden era for the camp's smokers began: rationing ended. Each man was able to purchase from the canteen as much of the precious weed as his heart desired."

Thomsen.

Our Tailors' and Cobblers' Workshop

"To start with, the equipment in our workshops was rather basic as we lacked the essential tools for tailoring and the necessary material needed to patch up jackets and trousers. Therefore, various comrades provided old pieces of clothing for us to cut up and use for patching. After four weeks, we even managed to obtain a sewing machine, a vintage Singer model, which despite its age showed no signs of weakness during its service to us. The sewing machine and other tools for the tailors and cobblers were obtained in the camp from the Army & Navy Stores, who also supplied all the thread, lining

Tempora mutantur

...et nos mutamur in illis

material, buckram, leather, nails and much more to the workshops, with a 10% surcharge rather than the 20% usually applied to all goods.

In addition to repairing uniforms, we gradually started turning jackets, trousers and overcoats inside out, a practice which proved to be extremely practical and soon became very popular. Then, however, new fabric of a similar colour to our military clothing became available from the English canteen, albeit at huge expense. Thus, the already flourishing workshops of the Skipton Camp were able to branch out into the production of jackets and trousers (breeches and long trousers).

In the second half of 1918, the business grew so rapidly that new workers repeatedly had to be found. By the end of 1918, there were seven tailors and four cobblers working in the camp. Among the tailors was a cap maker who rendered an exceptional service in providing headgear for the men.

A few statistics demonstrate the importance that the workshops had on our life in the camp. Within six months, the tailors produced 38 new pairs of trousers, 39 new jackets and 54 new caps, turned 27 pairs of trousers and jackets, as well as effecting 1543 sundry repairs. Within the same period of time, the cobblers soled 296 pairs of boots and carried out 907 repairs."

Luckey.

Our Carpentry Workshop

"The tools required for our workshop were initially bought with the funds pooled by the camp inmates. However, this created some difficulties because the English feared that escape attempts might be made with the help of the workshop tools. In order to prevent this, we had to sign an honour-bound agreement that neither tools nor materials would be used for escape attempts. Additionally, all tools had to be handed over to the guards at night.

And so the two trusty NCOs who were to run the workshop could then set to work – and work was waiting for them in abundance. The English, in their kindness, provided nothing that could make our lives any easier at all. At first there was a great demand for tables, so in the course of the first nine months approximately 200 small tables were supplied. A lot of serious intellectual work was carried out on these sometimes incredibly weak structures, many a sad letter was written but many entertaining games of *Skat* and

Die Paketliste –

The parcel list.

Doppelkopf were also played. The tables also served as chess boards, helping many of the prisoners to get through difficult times. With the conclusion of the Armistice, the demand for tables ceased as everyone was hoping to return home soon. Consequently, the demand for suitcases became much greater. By April 1919, approximately 125 suitcases of varying sizes had been produced and all older ones freshly painted and repaired. At times the demand was so great that the workshop had to be closed to new orders for weeks on end, even though three carpenters and one painter were employed there. The other main products included bookshelves, wall shelves and windowsills, of which over 300 were supplied in all manner of sizes up until April 1919. The carpenters' help was also much needed in the construction of the boxes we built around our beds and the initial construction of the theatre. Music stands, blackboards for the classrooms, lecterns, trays and many other items were also produced by the carpenters.

The procurement of materials was a difficult issue. In England, wood is a rare commodity. This was particularly apparent in wartime. It was only through much cajoling and a lot of money that we occasionally succeeded in obtaining planks and posts through our canteen manager. The workshop mainly relied on old boxes from the canteen. But these did not come cheap either (3 to 5 shillings). Necessity is the mother of invention, and so every remotely usable plank in the camp became fair game. Some struts were stealthily removed from the barracks and repurposed as stage supports or as table legs. This had to be done very carefully, because the English watched us closely and once even threatened one of our carpenters with imprisonment for theft. It did them no good: we continued to take whatever we needed.

Like the price of wood, the prices of glue, nails, suitcase fittings, etc. were also high. For example, a pound of carpenter's glue cost 5 shillings, a pound of one-inch tacks cost 3 shillings, an ordinary suitcase lock cost 3 shillings and sixpence, and so on. But we were happy to be able to obtain these items at all. In our workshop a small table cost 10 shillings, a small suitcase cost 12 shillings and a larger suitcase 20 shillings. The average monthly turnover was £20."

Möller.

Six orderlies worked in the barber's shop. Given the large number of camp inmates, the post office also had a considerable amount of work to do. Apart from our regular work with parcels from home, many Red Cross shipments arrived from Denmark, Spain and Holland. The Danish parcels were often damaged upon arrival, and sometimes items were missing. The monthly number of parcels in the last half year was 3,000 (January 2491, February 2940, April 2631), and on average 150 to 200 letters arrived daily. Of course, letters often failed to appear for days or even weeks. After our complaints to the War Office (through the Swiss Legation), suddenly 500 to 1,000 letters would often arrive daily without having undergone the English postal censorship. According to the British Government and the Swiss Legation, the delay was due to the German postal censorship.

Our Orderlies

On 12th December 1917, 49 enlisted men from the Brocton prisoner-of-war camp arrived at the newly established Skipton camp to make preparations for the arrival of the expected German officers, most of whom had been reluctant to leave their old 'home'.[64] Their vast parent camp had offered an abundance of organised diversions such as a theatre, music groups and libraries. They could not rely on finding this in a new camp. After the first officers arrived, the orderlies were reinforced by a further 80 men on 25th January 1918. Thus, their company rose to some 120 men and remained at this number from then on. In charge of the orderlies was one of the officers at the camp, whose authority was eventually recognised by the English.

The orderlies were responsible for performing a wide range of duties. In the officers' kitchen eight of them peeled, cooked and baked; in the enlisted men's kitchen there was one NCO and two men. Six nimble pairs of hands worked in the scullery. In the mess barracks, twenty-two orderlies in white jackets and waiters' aprons served at the tables. In the accommodation barracks, another forty-eight made certain that the bachelors' messiness did not get out of hand. They made the beds, swept, beat the covers and bed-side rugs, cleaned the washstands, fetched water, and from time to time gave the rooms a good scrubbing. Six barbers worked industriously at transforming noble heads into objects of beauty and elegance. In the workshops, six tailors, six cobblers, two carpenters and one painter variously hammered and nailed, snipped and sewed, sawed, glued and painted. A gardener tended the camp garden, whilst the shower officer with his irresistible call of 'b-a-a-th time!' was a popular camp figure. Two orderlies on outdoor duty swept the camp

Baracken schrubben.

Scrubbing the barracks.

pathways and kept them clean, whilst another four helped the director of path repairs with their upkeep. Another served as window-cleaner. Perched on his ladder at a dizzying height, busily wiping away, he made certain that the window-panes had a chance of fulfilling Otto Ernst's exhortation to *Let the Sun in!* Two orderlies were assigned to the hospital to attend to the sick, and one NCO and two orderlies were assigned to sundry other duties under the heading of 'outdoor work'. Apart from those working in all these designated occupations there were another thirteen non-assigned men who formed the reserve. The sergeant major served as a guiding light through this prodigious workload. The basic pay was 15 shillings per month, later 25 shillings. For extra duties the pay was 1½ pence per hour. Lance Corporal Foraita will now tell us about the ...

Daily Life of an Orderly

"There can be no uniform answer to the question of how the day passed for the prisoner who was neither an officer nor an NCO: it varied. It is probably true to say that a man whose 'home' was an enlisted men's camp and who possessed a medical certificate to say he was unfit for work had it made; that is to say, apart from having to be present at two roll calls, he could spent the entire day lying on his straw mattress or otherwise occupy his time as he pleased. However, as a rule, strenuous physical exertion was not to be recommended; that was a luxury reserved for those who received enough food parcels from home. Others would probably be found sitting with their noses in a book or lying on a mattress dreaming of life back home. But a man who was fit to work would be detailed by the English to work in road or rail construction, in a quarry or on a farm. For an eight-hour working day the rate was 8 pence, worth about 65 pfennigs in peace-time, along with supplementary labourer's rations, which consisted of 1 ounce (28g) of ground maize, 1 ounce of cheese and 4 ounces of bread.

In officer camps, conditions were rather different. This is where the camp doctor sent any man deemed fit enough for light duties when there were insufficient numbers of volunteers, which was mostly the case. Here every one of these men, or *orderlies*, was assigned to his position. There were no labourer's rations here, which partly explains why very few volunteers came forward to work in officer camps.

Up with the lark, the barrack orderly was already at work with brush and polishing cloth to make the officers' boots gleam. The orderly had to have his work finished even before the bugler had announced reveille, so that the officers found their clothes and boots clean and ready when they awoke. Our breakfast was at 7.30: every man received his two cups of tea, and anyone who had not eaten his bread from the previous evening did so now. Then everyone went about his business. The mess orderlies rushed to the dining rooms to serve the officers with their breakfast; the men on washing-up duty, known as scullery skivvies, rolled up their sleeves and got ready for the 500 breakfast plates and cups which were brought across from the messes; the barrack orderlies set about cleaning the huts allocated to them, making the beds, etc. and even the window cleaner got down to work, even if with some hesitation, and had only one wish on his mind: 'If only it would rain!' It was with the same hope that the path repairers scrutinised the weather prospects. But when the indications were that the weather was going to be fine, they finally got down to work and our German sergeant major on his rounds could rejoice at the diligent activity of his flock.

Kohlenholer.

Coal collectors.

Shortly before 10 o'clock came the call 'Fix bayonets', which in camp language meant 'coal collectors, look lively!' Immediately twenty men armed themselves with wheelbarrows and were escorted by a guard (with his bayonet fixed, of course) to the coal-yard, from where they brought the coal for the day into the camp in several small trips. We much preferred the call 'Assembly!', a notification that the post had arrived and that the lists of lucky recipients had been posted. On the other hand, little enthusiasm was generated by the call 'Charge', which summoned us to a fire drill. That was when everybody had to drop what they were doing, grab a fire bucket and hurry to the parade ground, where a so-called fire officer announced the location of the fire and issued precise orders. Although an older prisonör always had time on his side and rarely bothered to hurry on these occasions, everyone was to be seen rushing backwards and forwards and going through the motions of panting for breath. The reason for this was the presence of an English guard watching over us: anyone who appeared to be lagging behind faced unpleasant consequences. We quickly formed a human chain to the nearest water source and 'through the long chain of hands the buckets veritably flew'. Fortunately, performances like this seldom lasted longer than half an hour, and it was with genuine pleasure that we heard the trumpeter telling us to 'get back to quarters.'

When the morning had passed in this way, we all streamed into the enlisted men's dining room with our mess tins and spoons (no need for knives and forks!). This place always struck me as the most unfriendly place in the entire camp. In some places the walls were whitewashed; elsewhere they were bare. Some of the windowpanes were smashed; rain and sunshine came in from above and everywhere else – but it was mainly rain because of the many gaps in the wooden walls and roofing. The concrete floor was damaged here and there, and in the corner stood an erstwhile iron stove that did not quite know what it was doing there. This was where the food was routinely served up, which, Sundays excepted, was always the same: a soup made of rice, peas, potatoes and tiny pieces of chopped up meat all boiled to death. Even the most eager of stomachs could not in the long run stand the invariable monotony of the menu. Although the food itself might be palatable enough, it was not really surprising that most men could not finish their portion and had to throw their left-overs in the slop bucket.

As a rule things were quieter in the afternoons. When the midday roll call was over and the rations had been handed out, it was tea-time. With that, the enlisted men's kitchen had done its day's work and closed its hatches. A man would now sit in front of his ration of 8 ounces of bread and agonise over the question, 'Should I eat this now or later this evening, or save it for tomorrow morning?' And for all his bitter experience he was not always quite strong enough to put it to one side. If he did not do that, then inevitably he would be left 'twiddling his thumbs,' to use the technical term, until the following lunch time. However, that did not bother most men. One tightened one's belt and put up with it. In July 1919 there was at last an improvement, as we received supplementary rations in the form of a plate of ship's biscuits and a quarter pound of tinned beans.

When the weather was favourable, the playing field soon became lively with sports enthusiasts. The orderlies' favourite games were football, fistball and *Schlagball*. There were often matches between teams of officers and orderlies. This of course resulted in a surge of anticipation on both sides. A proper tote was set up, whereby punters betting on one team or the other could easily be parted from their money. But all these events could not disturb the imperturbable zeal of the so-called hard labourers. There were some of these even among the orderlies. During their free time these gold miners sat in the quiet room, otherwise known as the 'stink room', and sought to dig out their own little nuggets of gold from the most diverse pathways of knowledge. Some could be heard murmuring Spanish, French and English to themselves; here, a few sought to fathom out the mysteries of conic sections; there, somebody revelled in differentiation and integration; at this table somebody was bent over an atlas, because he wanted to go to Argentina eventually; at that table balance sheets were laid out, and words such as current account, transit account, endorsement and other fine bits of commercial jargon could be heard, enough to make the hair of the non-commercially minded stand on end. Men who had no interest in such endeavours would stand in the wash-house and set about their own or somebody else's washing with soap and brush and, to make the work more appealing, engage their neighbour in a bit of a chinwag. Polite conversation helped the work to go on at a cheery pace. Not that these conversations were always polite.

When the trumpet called the officers, they made haste – not to face a reprimand, but to get their evening meal in the mess. In the meantime the barrack orderlies prepared the officers' barracks for the night and fetched water for the next morning's ablutions. When all this had taken place, their duties were also completed. The kitchen lads, like the mess orderlies, 'went home' after they had done the washing-up and had laid out everything ready for the next day. And so the barracks slowly filled up. Those who arrived in good time were guaranteed a place near the hot stove. The thing was, that there were few days in England when one could do without its reviving warmth. Then it was time for spinning yarns. Generally the conversations revolved around four main topics: (1) the prospects of being exchanged; (2) the economic situation in Germany; (3) memories of life before the war; (4) our officers. In one corner an old sea-dog would gather about himself a circle of listeners and concoct an incredible story, perhaps to do with the Indian Ocean, involving an awful lot of sharks. The hair of his unfortunate listeners would stand on end. Or he would tell the tale about how his tub was sunk, all richly spiced up with strong language like 'death and damnation', or –

and this accomplishment was much appreciated by the younger generation
– he would give instruction in the fine art of spitting. I have never seen such
incredible proficiency as that of our old 'Johnny'. At five paces he could
guarantee a direct hit into the stove! Every now and then one or another of us
would recall his own musical skills and produce his mandolin, guitar, violin
or clarinet and strike up a song and the others would join in, *Von den Bergen
fliesst ein Wasser* [*From the mountain flows a stream*], *Das Leben ist ein Traum*
[*Life is a dream*], and so forth. Mainly they were songs that had a dash of
melancholy. There were no songs about soldiers and war. The chaps could
no longer get enthusiastic about the war and its consequences. Rarely did we
hear any talk about their experiences on the battlefields. If nobody was in the
mood for singing, then we would get out the playing cards. The most popular
games were *Skat*, *Schafkopf* and *Schwarzer Peter*, the latter mainly because
of the face blackening which nobody was excused from. Before we went to
bed, almost everybody would have been the Peter several times and we would
have rubbed soot from the stove onto our noses and foreheads with varying
degrees of dignity. It was just as well that we did not have white bedsheets!

So it was that the evening seldom dragged. Even so everyone was glad
when the English rang the bell and soon afterwards our trumpeter gave the
familiar 10 o'clock signal. Then we would stretch out on our straw mattresses
and wrap ourselves in our bedcovers with a sigh of relief, 'Thank God,
another day has passed!' "

Food Supplies

As already suggested, the orderlies' food allowance was wholly inadequate.
Our fine lads were ravenously hungry. The English supplied food sufficient
only for a convalescent diet. There
was a daily allowance of 1 ounce of
rice, 2 ounces of peas, 20 ounces of
potatoes, 9 ounces of bread, 4 ounces
of vegetables and ¾ ounce of butter,
plus a weekly allowance of 40 ounces of
horse meat (divided into four portions),
10 ounces of herring (in two portions),
and 1⅗ ounces of bacon. Later on, the
officers' kitchen helped with providing
an evening meal (rice and porridge), for
which each man had to pay 3 shillings
and sixpence monthly, which was later
reduced to 2 shillings and sixpence and
then 1 shilling and sixpence. April 1919
saw an increase in the ration, amounting
on a weekly basis to ½ ounce of bread,

Path repairs.

⁴/₅ ounce of horse meat and 1³/₁₀ ounces of margarine. From time to time, the canteen fund found money to improve our diet.

Lectures

Even if the scope of intellectual activities and stimulation available to the enlisted men in the Skipton Camp was nowhere near as extensive as that in the parent camp, there were still plenty of opportunities. The orderlies could attend lectures, religious worship and performances organised for the officers. In addition the following special lectures were put on for them:

1. Chile
2. Questions of law
3. Persia
4. Social legislation in the German Reich
5. China (two lectures)
6. Germany and the revolution
7. Marx and Lassalle, the founders of German socialism
8. Alcohol and public health.

Various educational courses were set up for the enlisted men: English (two courses), Spanish, French, shorthand and typing (two courses), book keeping, art history and mathematics.

During the period when, in a state of high suspense, we were awaiting the start of the great German offensive, which the British press announced with all too evident trepidation, every evening an officer would read aloud to the men from the newspapers and provide explanatory and instructive commentaries. When Hindenburg's hammer-blow struck the Western Front, our worthy lads used large maps to follow our troops as they pressed forward, with proud joy and yet with a slight feeling of sadness that we could not be there, until finally everything came to a stop again. Later, on some evenings the senior German officer would read out to us the latest reports on the work of the peace conference and on the peace treaty.

Through the voluntary contributions of the officers and some of the men it was possible at the end of May 1918 to establish a small library. We also received a number of books from the Düsseldorf Main Office of Voluntary Charitable Assistance. The Berlin Scholars' Commission also sent us a substantial collection of 216 volumes in January and February 1919.

Worship

Lutheran worship was held every three weeks and Catholic worship every two weeks in the music room.

In August 1918 the orderlies established their own theatre, for which Dr Markel's organisation in London supplied the props. *Pension Schöler* was performed, and a number of musical evenings graced our world-famous stage. A vocal octet was formed in December 1918, which delighted us with its first performance at Christmas. On several Sunday evenings dance music could be heard in the enlisted men's dining room and witty recitals amused the throng, who, some of them dressed in colourful attire, enjoyed the dancing and the extremely weak beer and dubious wine. At Whitsun 1919, the sports festival was accompanied by all the diversions of a lively summer fair.

Christmas 1918 cast its benign light into the monotonous dreariness of everyday life. Lance Corporal Foraita will now describe the celebrations.

Christmas Celebrations

"Christmas had come around again, for many of us for the fifth time whilst in captivity. But this time it had a special meaning: the old Christmas message *Peace on Earth* had at least partly come true; the Armistice had put an end to the war. What the peace would be like, nobody could yet imagine. On the contrary! Since the terms of the Armistice were so harsh, peace would surely be all the more bearable. There was hardly anything left that the opposing side had not demanded and been granted. So hope for the peace dawned in our hearts like the promise of spring. The possibility that we might soon go home shone as brightly before our trusting eyes as any shimmering mirage ever appeared to a man wandering in the desert. So this last Christmastime of our captivity was the first we planned to celebrate with unadulterated joy – and we did celebrate! It was the best Christmas I experienced in England.

A few days before, a small tree was brought to each of the barracks. Of course, we only had modest means available to decorate them: paper and cotton wool, but nevertheless in the skilled hands of some especially talented men these were crafted into little works of art, and when the green denizens of the forest appeared in all their glory, with a stretch of the imagination, we could almost recognise our dear old German Christmas tree whose magic first enchanted us in childhood and had still not yet quite faded away.

It is said that it is hard to study properly on a full stomach, but the reverse can also be argued: it is hard to celebrate on an empty stomach. In view of this important fact the enlisted men's kitchen had taken steps in good time to address this serious issue – the constant emptiness of the prisoners' stomachs. With some earlier thriftiness and a few under-the-counter purchases (we called it *Schiebung*), on Christmas Eve it was possible to provide every man with a bowl of fried potatoes, and this unusual event of actually having an evening meal did wonders for our mood. When the lights were lit, our faces also shone with contentment. Then the sound of our dear old Christmas carols opened up our hearts. It is an old truth that '... out of the abundance of the heart the mouth speaketh'.[65] Our conversation turned again and again to thoughts of home, parents, wives and children. What else would we have talked about on Christmas Eve! Some of us who had been together in the Brocton camp must have remembered the Christmas Eve of 1917, when our Christmas treat consisted of four pickled herrings to be shared between the forty men in each barracks, and when we sat together huddled in overcoats and blankets, freezing because the camp commandant had refused to give us coal. Even this memory made us feel all the more content because the difference between that day and this was so obvious and palpable.

Then came Christmas Day, bringing us a number of pleasant surprises. The kitchen administration and the camp sergeant major seemed determined to amaze us - and they certainly succeeded. Only someone who has actually been a prisonör in England can really appreciate what a blessing a mouthful of good coffee is after all that tea. And this blessing was given to us – and with milk too! There was even cake to go with it, proper cake with proper raisins, properly baked, with proper sugar on top! However much we doubted it, we had to accept the incredible fact that such things actually did still exist. For some however, especially the family men, with every bite came the sad realisation that their loved ones at home would certainly not have such a festive breakfast. I am convinced that many of us would rather have packed up the whole glorious thing and sent it home. I might just mention in passing that the festive mood at the midday meal was enhanced by the goulash and custard instead of our usual 'Bolshevik soup'.

The actual celebration took place in the afternoon and evening of Christmas Day. For this purpose the enlisted men were allowed to use the Old Mess, a large hall-like room, at one end of which rose a mighty fir tree. On long rows of tables, arranged in a horseshoe and covered by white tablecloths, 135 cups of festive cocoa steamed invitingly. We were delighted that the senior German officer came to join the enlisted men's celebration. The first part was a typical Christmas celebration. The venerable words of the Christmas gospels spoke more poignantly to our hearts than they might have done in better times; for some of us it may even have been only through war and captivity that they became meaningful at all. So our lovely German carols about the 'silent, holy night' and the 'joyful blessed time'[66] of Christmas rang out strongly throughout the hall. And in his speech, the sergeant major put into words what we were feeling: as he spoke we could see in our mind's eye the Christmas celebrations of the last few years, feel once more the burning longing for home that becomes particularly acute at this season, feel also the deep despair that always overcame us with the realisation that our wishes could not be fulfilled, and pull ourselves together once more, determined to face the cold, hard fact that we would simply have to bear it. But then the image changed and he painted a picture of home for us brush-stroke by brush-stroke until we could see it before our eyes, with hill and vale, stream and meadow and the little cottage that we call home, in which live two dear old people with white hair and work-worn hands, gazing with silent joy at their strapping lad who has finally returned from England. And after this enticing picture he added the words: 'Soon comrades, this will be reality.' Oh how eagerly one listens to someone talking about home!

Eight comrades who were proficient singers had got together to form an octet and entertained us with the traditional hymn *Es ist ein Ros entsprungen* [*Lo, how a rose e'er blooming*] and Beethoven's *Hymn to the Night*. And then came Father Christmas' companion, Ruprecht, in costume, with a big sack and a big beard! The beard was false but the sack was real and contained the presents that the officers in the camp had provided for the men. There was something for everybody: some were given pocket knives, tobacco pipes, cigar and cigarette holders, others board games, soap, shaving soap, braces and many other things that brought great joy. But Father Christmas' companion Ruprecht also knew quite well that 'It is the spirit who gives life'[67] and had inserted a little verse into each parcel, good-humouredly but aptly mocking the greater and lesser weaknesses of the recipient in language that admittedly was not always suitable for 'polite society' and did not always conform to the norms of poetry, but was always comical. Gales of laughter accompanied the reading out of these pearls of German poetry and Ruprecht was quite right to stroke his beard in contentment.

After a break of about two hours, the second, more general, part of the celebrations began, dedicated to merriment. Introduced by a prologue spoken by the poet himself (we counted quite a number of artistic types in our midst), the evening began with a vocal quartet performing Zöllner's[68] humorous *Der Speisezettel* [*The Menu*].[69] Under normal circumstances the tempting abundance of this menu would have made our mouths water, but that day's never-ending stream of pleasures for both body and soul had dulled our senses a little so that most of us limited ourselves to the observation, sometimes spoken out loud, that there must have been some *Schiebung* going on. An 'original Viennese *Schrammelband*', consisting of two violins and a guitar, excelled in a colourful series of 'classical' pieces, alternating with a variety of solo performances, both serious and light-hearted. Even a woman appeared on stage! Fake, of course like Ruprecht's beard, but still a welcome sight for eyes accustomed to seeing only men. Now and then, the hall resonated with the heavy stamping of a *Schuhplattler* folk dance group performing their 'national' dance with all the rustic energy of Upper Bavaria. But it was most probably Töpfer who was the greatest success, with his comic turns, including some phrases that later became proverbial, and secondly our little *Liebknecht*[70] with his gripping performance: *I am down and out* (in a Berlin accent) – as if we needed to be told. We would have known this just by looking at him.

So the evening passed in the most cheerful of atmospheres. The bell for lights out rang all too soon. 'Let's hope it was for the last time!' With this hope we went our separate ways to seek our usual solace in dreamland from the harsh realities of days past and future."

About twenty of our orderlies had already borne the heavy burden of captivity for more than five years. We do not need to emphasise how much the privations of that period had undermined their physical strength and their nerves. And in everyone, even the newest prisoners, there burned a great longing for home. Germany's defeat weighed on their spirits like a heavy, exhausting burden. The orderlies, too, succumbed to the influenza epidemic, robbing us of ten dear comrades, who found their last resting place in the cemetery in Keighley beside the thirty-seven officers, cheated of their homecoming. The shockwaves of Germany's internal turmoil were even felt by us in the camp. There were brief disputes. No soldiers' council was formed, because the different sides were too diametrically opposed. However, with the cooperation of the orderly officer, a committee of elected enlisted men was set up to try to deal with all future internal issues within our circle. This body proved its worth and a number of improvements in the lives of the orderlies were made, such as the allocation of a 'quiet room' and their own barber's shop.

Deputy Sergeant Major Schonek.

E. From the Signing of the Peace Treaty to our Return Home

(28th June to 28th October 1919)

The Prisoners' Despair

When the English newspapers published the news on the 29th June that, after vigorous debate, the Weimar National Assembly had ratified the Treaty of Versailles, we hoped that our release was imminent. We knew of course that we had, strictly speaking, no legal grounds for this hope, since the treaty stipulated that we would not be discharged until three great powers had signed the peace treaty. But our German idealism led us to believe that the enemy would follow that rule of humanity on which they had always prided themselves: that general nobility of sentiment common to mankind, that when a war is over an enemy is no longer an enemy upon whom to wreak vengeance, that it is inhumane then to withhold home, family and work from hundreds of thousands of men who had honourably done their duty for their nation and then spent years behind barbed wire. Germany had signed, thereby declaring its willingness to abide by the conditions of the treaty. It had been disarmed and the country was in disarray. It was no longer dangerous. And apart from that, the German prisoners were costing the English millions every day and 100,000 British soldiers were required to guard them. Yet the attempts of the German government at Spa and Versailles to expedite our release were unsuccessful. They no longer had any leverage. The Entente powers were in no hurry to ratify the peace treaty. On the contrary, France very deliberately aimed at keeping the prisoners as slave labour for as long as possible. In America, opposition to the peace treaty was growing so that there was no prospect of them signing it in the near future. 'Noble' General Maxse explained to us during his notorious visit that as far as the English were concerned, a state of war still existed and they would hold on to us as long as they needed to. So we felt that we were being seen as bargaining chips against our homeland and that, in spite of their rhetoric about humanitarianism, our enemies had no sympathy for our suffering or for that of our fellow countrymen. Accordingly, the mood of the prisoners became more and more explosive every day. We read in the newspapers about the continuing demobilisation of English soldiers and their return to ordinary peacetime occupations, but our people, who were in need of vast numbers of workers for reconstruction, did not see us return. We had for years been deprived of every influence of family life, both great and small, of productive work and all intellectual and artistic stimulation, and now we were to continue to experience the cruelty of captivity; the English newspapers had in fact criticised the destructive effects of this on their own prisoners on a daily basis in many column inches the previous year. On the evening of 2nd August we stood on the steps of our barracks and stared in impotent rage into the valley below. Celebratory bonfires lit up the evening sky, and all around rockets whizzed and the sounds of joyful gunfire and music reached us from below. England was noisily celebrating its victory. Bitterness spread through the camp. It was just as well the English no longer considered it worth censoring our letters, as here our German wrath was expressed in the strongest terms. Many changed the wording 'Prisoner of War' on the letter writing forms to 'Prisoner of Peace'. One night, somebody cut through the wire fence of our cage. Our accumulated rage had to find some release. For some, the hopelessness was so damaging that it led to outbreaks of insanity. One day, an older officer went to the commandant and begged to be shot, saying he was an idiot and did not wish to become a burden on his wife and children. Neither the English staff nor the man's friends, who hurried to his aid, could pacify him. He had to be taken to the camp hospital. Another comrade absented himself during a walk, passed unhindered through the busy streets under the astonished gaze of Skipton's residents and asked for a ticket at the railway station, saying Mr Balfour had ordered him to leave. It took a long time for the English officer to persuade him to return to the camp, under the pretext that he would have to go back to pick up his luggage. One evening one of our number ran amok across the camp threatening to kill the commandant. He said that his family and his business at home were going to rack and ruin and he wanted at least to take revenge on the 'dogs'. It took some effort to overpower him. One of our officers, who accompanied this poor man on his journey to the hospital, was himself pronounced insane and was locked up there as well. The night he spent there with screaming, raving German soldiers had a harrowing effect on him.

We applied repeatedly to the Swiss Legation, pleading for information about when we would be sent home. We always got the same bland reply: nothing was known about our return, but we would be given more information when

View from the steps of a barracks.

possible. It never came. In August we sent a new protest to the War Office. We repeated all the reasons in support of our release. Our letter closed as follows:

> "The inhumanity implicit in keeping the prisoners incarcerated will continue until the formal ratification of the treaty, after the German Army is demobilised and the peace treaty is signed. This raises the question of whether it may be the intention to continue to hold the prisoners solely as security in order to enforce new demands or to implement unacceptable conditions, should any emerge from the treaty in the course of time. This would amount to a trade-off of human beings for material interests, and every decent human being baulks at the very idea that the fate of millions should be sacrificed to such interests. Human history records terrible acts of cruelty perpetrated by victors on the vanquished, but they pale into insignificance in the face of the shame that the Allied statesmen incur by depriving millions of German women and children, suffering through no fault of their own, of their protectors and providers, and by abandoning the prisoners to physical and mental decline. What is the beautiful humane idea of a League of Nations worth in the face of the hatred engendered by the present handling of the prisoner-of-war question!"[71]

The War Office confined itself to formal legalities: the treaty would come into force after ratification. Nothing could be done until the main commission convened in Paris and the sub-commission in London. The repatriation of prisoners of war found guilty of disciplinary offences after 1st May 1919 would be delayed. In addition, Germany would be required to provide the necessary means of transport. Since transport was in very short supply, delays were to be expected. 'This is caused solely by Germany's unrestricted U-boat war, which has sunk ships of all nations, both enemy and neutral.' Of course the strong desire of German prisoners of war to return to their homes and families was understandable and deserved sympathy. 'Everything would be done to fulfil it.' Empty rhetoric!

Self-Help

So we decided to take matters into our own hands to some extent. We knew from the newspapers that there were certain groups even in England who, for religious or humanitarian reasons, deplored the unjustified detainment of prisoners. We wanted to make the most of this mood. We found out that other camps had had similar intentions and acted upon them. In one camp they had hung large placards in the streets demanding (in English) 'We want to go home!' In the next few weeks, our camp guards were astounded to see kites flying here and there in the camp and on the sports ground. Traditional diamond-shaped paper kites and box-kites floated high in the sun-drenched air or sailed across the blue sky. One of our pilots spent weeks secretly building a 2-metre-long aeroplane, which unfortunately crashed during take-off and smashed to pieces due to poor weather conditions. But that was just the beginning. On 5th August at 3pm, a communal 'Ah!' was heard throughout the camp. The prisonörs rushed out of their barracks, craning their necks to gaze in wonder at the sky. A bell-shaped red balloon, 2 metres tall, rose from inside the camp amid the smoke of the burning gas that fuelled it, and floated merrily towards Skipton. The guards watched in astonishment, uncertain whether to shoot at this German messenger as it rose ever higher towards the hills to the south west. We learned its fate from the *Daily News*. The paper reported on 20th August 1919:[72]

"Paper Balloon Propaganda

The German call to be sent home

A large, coloured-paper balloon, attached to which was a sack full of leaflets typed and signed 'The German Prisoners of War', landed in recent days in the suburban garden of a Sheffield businessman, John Biggin of Clarendon Street.

The leaflets contained a series of appeals, skilfully drafted to win our sympathy. If they are really, as seems likely, documents of genuine human sentiment, entrusted to the air by German prisoners of war, they represent the first attempt to gain freedom through propaganda. The red and yellow pieces of paper are certainly composed in an effective propaganda style, e.g. 'Housing is bad in England. Hundreds of families could live in our camp. Therefore send us home!'

There is no shortage of emotional appeals. The writer, whoever he might be, has sought to use expressions that shock, and at the end we are never without the refrain 'Send us home!' 'The German mothers are lamenting,' says one leaflet, 'Wives and children are crying. Peace has come, but our unfortunate imprisoned soldier-boys do not come yet. Send the poor prisoners home!' 'What would an English mother say had her son been in Germany after signing of peace? Send the prisoners home!'

'What pains German mothers, wives and children must suffer, who have not seen their sons, husbands and fathers, their indispensable bread-winners, for five years. Send the prisoners home!'

A Nod to Politics

The meticulous German has not forgotten to include political appeals and cunningly touches on the question of unemployment. He emphasises that '30,000 German prisoners of war are working in England depressing the wages on your labour market.' Another leaflet states: 'According to Mr Churchill, the prisoners of war are unproducing people who want a body of 100,000 soldiers to guard them.'

Whoever the author is, he not only knows the English language, but also English ways. He puts forward many and varied arguments for repatriation.

One more leaflet should be mentioned, in which a sarcastic touch is conveyed in a well-executed sketch. A bird – is it the emblem of peace? – is shown in the air, and on the ground, behind barbed wire sits a man in chains. At the bottom is the word: 'Peace?' "

The Propaganda Committee: 'Homework'

In order to exert a constant influence on English public opinion and to have sufficient resources to do so, a secret 'conspiracy' was formed in the camp. An executive committee unknown to the other prisonörs covertly recruited a large-scale propaganda department. Almost all the prisonörs joined the clandestine group and supported it with money. Behind locked doors secret discussions took place, from which the uninitiated were excluded. This undertaking required great caution, and at first there were many difficulties to overcome. English middlemen had to be won over – English money was needed. Soon the committee, which concealed its activity under the harmless code-word 'Homework', succeeded in bribing Englishmen to procure English money, to smuggle letters out of the camp, and to have them sent through the post. Numerous appeals were drawn up and sent to English pacifists, religious groups (Quakers), trade unions, members of Parliament and the press. One of our appeals appeared in the *Yorkshire Evening News*. The *Manchester Guardian* ran a leader on the ideas behind our appeal and supported it. We therefore tried to persuade that paper to share with us all the news it had about repatriation. During the rail strike we made an effort to build a rapport with the strikers.

The British War Office did almost nothing to alleviate our situation in what was for us such a difficult time. What we wanted, amongst other things, was freedom of movement, an end to rationing, subscriptions to German newspapers and the right to manage our financial affairs. Instead we were given permission to receive visits from English relatives. But who had any? And how difficult it seemed to be for the oh-so-humane English to concede to the often repeated request to be allowed to write three letters a week. Fortunately the man in charge of the camp at that time was at least a gentleman who attempted, by dint of his own personality, to compensate for the uncaring behaviour of the powers that be. Colonel Ronaldson endeavoured to contain the rising unrest in the camp by all the peaceful means at his disposal. He often assured us that he had genuine sympathy for us: 'I sympathise with you.'[73] He replied with words of comfort to a German mother who had written to him full of anxiety about her son. As far as he was able, he willingly endorsed applications for repatriation from those who were ill. He settled disciplinary cases in a calm, objective manner. Only the midday parade took place now each day. The walks were often lengthened to 3½ hours, and the number of participants on fine days rose to as many as 150 officers. He also obtained permission for us to walk or lie around in a big meadow beyond the sports field on fine days. Unfortunately the less friendly Skipton Town Council soon revoked this permission. Even *Icankillyou* now and again suppressed his often unpleasant military zeal. One day he even went round Skipton's joinery shops himself to get the sawdust that we needed for a sports day.

However, the tide of agitation in the camp rarely ebbed. There were always new reasons. The Americans had released their prisoners. From our camp, those from Alsace-Lorraine and those from occupied Prussian Poland had been released long ago. The 'Danes' went to Feltham, several Schleswigers were moved to Holyport and swiftly conveyed home in order to take part in the plebiscite.[74] Soon we received letters from the lucky ones who had reached home – but we were still stuck behind barbed wire without any hope. It was therefore understandable that the officers who had a potentially valid reason endeavoured to push through their repatriation. So then those from Saarland, Upper Silesia and many others submitted similar applications. The list of those reporting sick increased daily at an astonishing rate.

29th August and its Consequences

Then, on 29th August, the depressed mood erupted into jubilation. That evening the commandant appeared in the camp in great excitement and without his cap, waving the evening paper from afar. Soon a dense circle of prisonörs gathered around him. There, on a page he held high could be read in big bold letters: 'German prisoners to be sent home'. Underneath followed the detailed report:

> "At this morning's meeting of the Supreme Council the following resolution regarding the repatriation of German prisoners of war was agreed upon:
>
> In order to diminish as rapidly as possible the sufferings caused by war, the Allied and Associated Powers have determined to anticipate the date of the ratification of the Treaty of Peace with Germany so far as the repatriation of German prisoners is concerned.
>
> The process of repatriation will begin immediately and will be conducted under the auspices of an Inter-Allied Commission, to which will be added German representatives as soon as the Treaty comes into force.
>
> The Allied and Associated Powers desire to make it quite clear that the continuance of this benevolent policy, from which the German soldiers will so greatly benefit, must depend on the fulfilment by the German Government and people of all their obligations."[75]

The newspaper added frankly: 'It is just as much a matter of economics as an act of humanity. The prisoners are costing us £90,000 every day.'[76]

'At Once'[77]

'At once!' A magic word seemed to have been spoken. The joyful news spread like wildfire through the camp. Blown away was the mood of gloom, and happy faces could be seen everywhere. Laughter and thunderous cheers resounded from the barracks. Home already seemed almost within reach. The port of departure, the itinerary, the arrival home – everything was the subject of animated discussions. Many couldn't wait to celebrate. The store handed out all the drinks it had in stock. The commandant granted leave until 12 o'clock. The singing of the men, now released from a heavy burden, could be heard until late into the night. The next day, the barrack captains held lengthy discussions. There was so much to arrange. Like the English commandant, we were anxious to have everything as ready as possible, in order to leave our hated exile as soon as we were given the nod. A thousand questions emerged. How are we going to get everything home? Should we start on it now? Are we allowed to send home all the enormous piles of books and papers, etc., we have accumulated? Will post from home be forwarded to us? Five departure squadrons were formed with company commanders, adjutants and baggage officers. From early until late, teams of men and officers worked in the carpenter's shop making trunks and packing cases, fabricating locks and giving the pieces of luggage the obligatory blue coat of paint. The 'trial packing' began. At last the War Office had settled the baggage question. In September 1918 a harsh order had been issued to us, forbidding prisoners to take with them leather goods, raincoats or mackintoshes if they had been bought in England, and even English boots, if they possessed German footwear. As far as other necessities were concerned we were allowed 2 shirts, 2 pairs of underpants, 3 pairs of socks, 2 pairs of shoes, 1 travel blanket, 1 knitted cardigan, 1 bar of toilet soap, 1 stick of shaving soap, 1 box of matches and 1 ounce of tobacco. The total amount of luggage was not to exceed 50kg. In May 1919 we were additionally informed that on our return home, we would only be allowed to take with us £2 (enlisted men 10 shillings) as retaliation for the same measures imposed by the German government on British prisoners of war. We would be given a receipt for any additional money, and we could then claim compensation from the German government. In June 1919 these regulations were changed. Prisoners were allowed to take all that they had with them, as long as – with the exception of hand luggage – it did not weigh more than 100 English pounds (sergeant majors 80, corporals 50, enlisted men 30). 'The commandants of the prisoner-of-war camps will, however, take precautionary measures so that the prisoners do not buy any more than required for their personal use.'[78] The rule about money was also lifted. We were permitted to take all our money with us (exchange rate: 2 shillings and 1 penny = 10 marks).

With these instructions in mind, we prisonörs stowed away our valuables. We were ready to march. Once again, on four consecutive days, 100 of us at a time, we travelled to Keighley to visit the graves of our dead comrades and to say goodbye to them. In the camp, the workshops were cleared out, credit was no longer granted. The barber's shop only gave out cards for half subscriptions. Most of the courses were cancelled, the lectures stopped. The theatre, orchestra and male-voice choir gave their 'final' performances and concerts. Farewell celebrations of small groups took place earlier than intended. 'Confirmed' reports were whispered into ears: 'Hey you, next Friday for sure!' The store had a large clearance sale and everyone packed once more – Friday passed by uneventfully. 'Wednesday! Word of honour! Bribed an Englishman! Read it myself in the commandant's office!' Wednesday also went by. Then came the set-back, the fall from the heights of hope into the depths of depression. Repatriation fever gripped even the strongest. Then that peculiar time period, no doubt characteristic of all prisoner-of-war camps, set in, a time of ...

Troubled Mood

As long as the war lasted we had borne imprisonment without complaining. It was simply a part of our war service. Now, however, almost a year had gone by since the Armistice. There was no longer any valid reason for our detention; common human decency called for our repatriation. We heard that our fellow prisoners kept in British-occupied France were arriving home every day, whereas we had to remain. News in letters from home and in German newspapers reported that German ships had set off from home. We heard nothing about their arrival. Some groups of prisoners were even supposed to have arrived back in Germany, but that was an English lie; they could only have been talking about a few of the sick. Precious time was racing by. Many of the young comrades, whose training had been set back many years by the war, felt that their intellectual powers were weakening and that they had less and less hope of secure jobs. Others, who were already established in their professions, learned that their jobs had been taken by others. Those officers, who after repatriation would have to take up other professions, saw valuable time go by needlessly. The sick felt their suffering more keenly than before, as did the wounded whose injuries were not yet fully healed. Work, which had previously occupied and calmed the mind, was not possible in the state of nervous collapse that now affected so many. Our long-weakened nerves could no longer withstand this tension, this sudden switching between hope and despair. The mood oscillated between unbridled pessimism, both angry and defiant at the idea of even more years of imprisonment, and groundless optimism, which always believed in 'next week'. One day, some cynical wags pinned a mood thermometer on the blackboard: it graphically described the mood swings of our ever-changing emotions from 'rejoicing to heaven' to 'grieving to death'.[79] The staff in the administration offices were confronted from morning till night with the question: 'No news?' We applied to the War Office for permission to be allowed to charter a ship ourselves – naturally without success. And we were constantly on edge, aware of suffering unjustly, of being powerless, at the mercy of others' whims, cheated of the best years of our lives and of a man's duty to work for his family and our ruined Fatherland. Yes, the British seemed to be making fun of us. They 'sympathised' with us, which is why they kept us so long. They fed us with comforting news: we should be the first for evacuation. Instead of treating our patriotic feelings with consideration, the War Office dared one day to allow the Danish agitator, Hansen, into our camp so that he could peddle his propaganda before the very eyes of us Germans. The British War Office appeared to believe that its concern for our welfare had broken our German sense of honour. How little they were justified in this assumption should have been shown by our protests, in which we declared ourselves, as German soldiers and regardless of any party-political standpoint, to be against the judicial condemnation of the Kaiser and our army leaders. We thank the British Government and Herr Hansen publicly for giving us the opportunity, in response to the provocation of an agitator, to reawaken our collective German patriotic feelings even in the bleakness of a prison camp. One camp comrade wrote the following in an open letter to his relatives, which was also published in the *Täglichen Rundschau*:[80]

"Today we have experienced something that will certainly remain for me the only good memory of Skipton. A certain Pastor Hansen, a Dane (probably from North Schleswig), came into the camp and attempted to use promises to persuade some comrades from Schleswig-Holstein to vote Danish! Each of these comrades gave him a sharply worded reply and rejected his suggestion in no uncertain terms. Meanwhile the camp flocked together and there was an uproar. A stone was thrown at the commandant's barracks, which Pastor Hansen had entered, and like a hurricane they roared: *Deutschland, Deutschland über alles!* As the Dane emerged, surrounded by English officers, such a rage and storm of indignation was raised that the senior German officer only just saved the fellow's life. Suddenly, from a tall barracks near the camp gate, the German flag was unfurled, black-white-red, and it fluttered giant-sized and high over the English guards as they were rushing out, and once more *Deutschland über alles* rang out, and then again *Schleswig-Holstein meerumschlungen* [*Schleswig-Holstein, embraced by the sea*].[81] Once the Dane was outside the camp and far enough away from the wire fence of our cage, he turned around, mocking and threatening us and made a circle with his hand in front of his forehead. Probably he wanted to indicate that he had a screw loose. As shameless as the man was, his knees were still shaking with bravery. We had a little Jewish salesman in the canteen, who knew only three German words: 'Hau bloss ab' [just clear off], and these he shouted at Herr Hansen. That was the humorous aspect of the affair. The camp was once again agitated; something had happened and we had taken action. And that is what is lacking in imprisonment – happenings and action."

The behaviour of the British government convinced many that it was deliberately leading us astray and deceiving us with spurious news. The bitterness of many was also directed at the commandant, who repeatedly gave us definite statements that did not materialise. We felt this behaviour all the more painfully, as we had cancelled letters and parcels in expectation of our imminent return and many had now had no news from home for months. The Red Cross had also advised our relatives at home against sending us things. Our growing bitterness was also directed against the German government, which was accused of a lack of concern and of inaction – an accusation which, according to all the letters and news reports, was without foundation. The more thoughtful prisonörs were aware that Germany was facing considerable difficulties in organising transport.

The news that the German seamen's strike was delaying our transport home was also unwelcome. Then, one day when we at last felt more cheerful, the English railwaymen's strike set in and destroyed all our hopes.

The explosive mood in the camp became increasingly inclined towards 'trouble', i.e. action against the English. This had at first found expression in vigorous debates, as we discussed how we would counter General Maxse's insults. These debates revealed that even in our very midst there were fundamental differences of opinion about how to behave towards the English. A number of our comrades took the position that we should make as many difficulties as possible for them and, that in cases such as the Maxse affair, we should be at our most awkward. They argued that the English were our national enemy and deserved no consideration, for they had insulted and betrayed our people and were threatening to annihilate us by means of the peace treaty. Furthermore, our national honour required that we should only undertake the most necessary dealings with them and that we should reject every kindness from the commandant. The overall administration and kitchen, which we ran saving the British a lot of work, should be handed over to the enemy so that they would have to use as much effort as possible on our behalf. Also, by continually stirring up unrest (refusing parades, etc.) it was hoped to induce the commandant to present a report to his superiors and thereby exert pressure on the War Office to expedite our repatriation. In contrast, those with the opposite view emphasised that because of our powerlessness, petty acts of insubordination would merely aggravate our miserable situation. Significant gains would never be achieved by these means and we would then just be shamefaced in front of the English. If the English were to take over the administration, in particular the kitchen, it would affect the catering, financial payments and also create other serious difficulties, and our dependence on the English would be doubly felt. Apart from that, only our kind-hearted commandant would be affected by these troubles and not, however, the higher echelons, whose orders were the cause of our misery. Minor actions would lead to nothing. More serious action, for example attacking and capturing the English guards – in fact a few prisoners were working on real storm trooper tactics – could have only temporary success and would then make our position even worse. In the Maxse affair, a simple protest had been sufficient for us, in the knowledge that we were above being offended by such a tactless individual.

Trouble flared up again when our rations were reduced and coal was withdrawn as a consequence of the great rail strike. There were no more showers, and on the first cold October days we had to sit in unheated rooms, while outside smoke was rising merrily from the Tommies' barracks. In great agitation, the occupants of the camp tore up the paths and pulled out the wooden planks for burning. *Icankillyou*, indignantly rushing out shouting 'stop that', was welcomed with whistles and rude gestures, and fled from our fury. The senior German officer made representations in the strongest terms to the commandant and explained to him that the officers were at the end of their tether and that from now on he himself would have to relinquish all responsibility for the German Officer Corps. The commandant now made a serious effort to obtain coal so we could at least once again continue our dreary existence in heated rooms.

However, after a few days a new wave of anger surged through the camp. The commandant announced to us that, according to information from the War Office, we would only be in the camp for 'a few more days'. The mood thermometer abruptly reached its optimistic peak again. Yet again however, day after day went by with the assurances coming to nothing. One morning gigantic white letters appeared on the commandant's office written in English:

> 14th September: in a very few days
> 17th October: in a very few days, now?

Laughing, the prisonörs gathered around the scene of the crime enjoying the sarcasm, which, white on black, beamed so audaciously into the camp. *Icankillyou* foamed with rage and immediately telephoned the commandant, who lived in the town. He immediately cancelled the trips to Bolton Abbey planned for the next few days, and ordered the staff officers and the captains to attend a meeting the next day. An impassioned meeting of the barrack captains was held. Sharply contrasting opinions came to light about the judgement of the commandant, about the justification of what had been written, about its removal ('since the commandant doesn't get the joke') and above all about our behaviour towards the English. One well-meaning comrade erased the text with the good intention of defusing the situation, but it was written up again during the night and then erased again. The bitterness intensified, leading to personal disputes and resignations. The following day, the commandant addressed the staff officers and captains. He justified his announcement, which he had given in all good faith, explained that he too had regarded the graffiti as a joke and said that from now on he would only share with us strictly official news. The situation calmed down. Explanations were given, reconciliations took place. So our agitation rose and fell. The mood once again became calm and weary, and we waited – waited – how much longer now?

Problems in the Kitchen

In this difficult time, when almost all the artistic groups in the camp gradually ceased their performances, teaching and lectures stopped, and the capacity to work diminished through mental lethargy, the kitchen administration quite unexpectedly provided outstanding service to the camp. The prospects for our rations in July were looking far from rosy. The price of food had risen considerably. The daily rate for our rations rose from 2 shillings to 2 shillings and 3 pence. Mr James had had to give up his profitable activities, as the commandant, after many warnings, caught him engaging in *Schiebung* yet again. The new manager, Mr Strickland, in the light of the shocking fate of his predecessor, rejected any willingness to indulge in *Schiebung*. What was to become of us? The high expenses during the influenza epidemic, the increased price of food and many other factors led one day to the surprising discovery that we had overspent by some £350. We had to dig deep into the camp's finances, and we resolved, in the light of this painful haemorrhage, to budget more carefully in future. A new, improved kitchen administration, which included competent businessmen, ran the whole of our catering establishment on strictly commercial lines. They worked thriftily and carefully and yet we had good ample meals. Those who were permitted to enter the hallowed halls of the kitchen and saw at first hand the hard work of the orderlies and the demands on the chef, busy from dawn to dusk, knew how much we had to thank our mess administration for our wellbeing. They had to struggle with inadequate boiler systems and a shortage of coal. The English often delivered the raw ingredients so late that the menu could only be drawn up at the last minute. On many occasions, in order to prepare lunch, the chef had to buy essential ingredients (e.g. flour) from comrades who were lucky enough to receive parcels. In spite of the scant resources, an effort was always made to create variety in the weekly menu, to limit less appealing dishes (such as boiled fish, herring, rice) and to continue efforts to improve the cooking (pea soup, cabbage). The canteen manager, responsible for purchasing, saw to it that his store was stocked up regularly (fruit, fat, jam, sausage, extra bread, sardines, kippers, chocolate, etc.) and he took pains to ensure that good quality provisions were delivered. Pressure was put on Mr Strickland and he was forced to go down the route of his predecessor and engage in *Schiebung*. Were he to sell us inferior products, the mess administration would give the signal, and he would be boycotted by the whole camp. However, it was the mess administration, in particular their tireless finance officer, who earned the most credit for its action against the Army & Navy Stores. We had heard from officers and men in the camps at Redmires and Catterick that bread there was only half the price. This was confirmed by our observations in English newspapers. Thereupon the finance officer spent days checking the accounts and established that the English had, over a period of time, defrauded us of 30,000 shillings. The commandant passed our figures and our application for repayment to the War Office, which could not deny

View to the Old Mess and the kitchen.

the facts (Mr James had cheated us!) and ordered the Army & Navy Stores to pay back the money immediately. This favourable outcome, which we were able to announce to the camp before a theatre performance, naturally gave rise to riotous joy and satisfaction. The senior manager of the stores, Mr Bourne, appeared the next day to settle the account as ordered. But he was already in the clutches of the kitchen administration and the Price Watch Committee that we had just set up. It was made clear to the unfortunate 'Mister' that he had profiteered through our purchases in a completely outrageous way. In the end, confronted by the facts, he saw no other way out but to declare that he was prepared to compensate us. He promised to supply goods (mainly obtained by *Schiebung*) to the value of £500 free of charge. In addition, all future prices were of course to be held at the national rate. Mr Bourne was said to have gone away remarking that he would not forget our finance officer in a hurry.

So not only did considerable amounts of cash pour into the pockets of the prisonörs (and £300 was paid into the camp kitty) but also vast quantities of fat and jam were now provided for our physical wellbeing. The commendable mess administration arranged musical evenings to satisfy the desire for entertainment that this gave rise to, enabling these unbearably large sums of money to come back into circulation.

Saturday 25th October

A bright October morning dawns over the camp. The prisoners have shovelled down their porridge and drunk their coffee. Now individuals are strolling slowly to the sportsground. Others are sitting in the quiet rooms reading the newspaper that has just arrived. Then someone shouts: 'Monday – departure!' They hear this very significant word with indifference at first – it is bound to be another 'latrine'. But someone who suspects it might be true decides to run out and he comes back beaming: 'It's true! Monday – departure!' In the blink of an eye, the quiet room is empty. A joyful throng fills the camp's pathways. It really is true! The senior German officer comes out of the commandant's office with his cap on the wrong way round – this is the long-agreed sign. Then our captain himself appears as well and confirms everything – everything. This writer finds himself quite unable to describe these hours. He could speak of the happy faces of the prisoners, of their irrepressible flow of words, of their wild gesticulations, he could write about the jubilation in the barracks, the cheerful chatter accompanying the packing, but the inner jubilation, the rising and falling waves of joy, the images surging through our minds – he cannot and will not describe all that.

At midday there is a big gathering of the barrack captains. The administration is well prepared. The final arrangements are made. In the afternoon any large pieces of luggage must be handed in. Breathing heavily, the prisonörs drag these into the Old Mess. There they are weighed, but the Tommies make no protests about the weight, which is often over the limit. *Icankillyou* experiences yet another attack of zeal and in the evening orders a check of the luggage that has already been handed in. The interpreters join us in performing a cheery comedy. They make spot-checks: touching the lock with the key is enough to satisfy them.

Sunday passes in a blur of relentless activity. Here, there are prisoners – today even the laziest – dragging equipment to the collection point in room C. There, others are collecting food for the journey. The reinforced finance committee works hard all day. There is so much to be done: payment of wages, the winding up of accounts, conversion of camp money into German notes. In the afternoon the prisonörs receive their bags of riches. Once again the senior German officer gathers all officers and men in front of the Old Mess. He thanks us all for our support in spite of many difficulties, enabling him to fulfil his duties, and in particular he thanks those who have made an effort to serve the common good. To everybody he gives his most heartfelt good wishes for the future. To the comrades who must return to occupied areas,[82] he calls: 'It is with shame that we have lost you; we will bring you back again with honour!' Far over the barbed wire down into Skipton's valley the German anthem *Deutschland über alles!* rings out.

The prisonörs disperse. One of them takes one last glance into what was the quiet room, others wander through the camp, and many take a last walk around the sports field. It is not a painful farewell, but this patch of earth still holds many memories – and not just bitter ones. That is why one comrade stands high up on the sports field and gazes at the quiet valley, hazy in the evening mist.

The sun has gone down behind the hill,
But above the peaks a light glows still,
Reaching to me through the frosty night,
As I stand here speechless, up on the height.

The dale draws into the dusk's tight embrace,
A blue veil of mist hides its beautiful face.
Drifting up through the branches, a song's last refrain,
A violin sings, full of longing and pain.

Not foreign fields, but of God himself a measure,
Faithful land, will you now take back this treasure
That you gave us so freely, a vision of eternity?
In you I have seen my own immortality.

Let me stand here and gaze one last time at this view.
They say that we're leaving, can it really be true?
Tomorrow, yes tomorrow, we shall be free.
Salas-y-Gomez,[83] silent valley, – what that means to me!

                                                        Stoltenberg.

In the evening in room A, from which all the tables have disappeared, the last religious service takes place. The sermon looks back again on our days of captivity and explains that we have endured much suffering, but that the righteous prevail in all situations in life. Thus our captivity may be a blessing, as it has forced us into self-contemplation and stimulated in us a strong and clear desire to work for the future. In the evening many prisonörs sit together, still celebrating. Thoughts rush back and forth. In the camp garden a big fire is burning; it is fed with English tar barrels and tables which have served their purpose. Soon most of the prisoners go to bed. But our last sleep in Skipton is not at all restful. Around midnight someone dashes through the barracks: 'Every prisonör can collect another 40 Marks – the rest of the camp's money!' – a pleasant, but untimely invitation.

Our Last Day

Early the next day, still in complete darkness, we get up again. Coffee is brewed for the last time. At 7.30am the companies are standing at the gate ready to march off. Our bugler plays once more – not a call to coffee: an emotive German melody rings out over the deserted barracks. *Icankillyou* runs busily to and fro, full of charming kindness. The gates open, and once again the Yorkshire Boar tries to count us, in vain as usual, then we stride off into freedom. At a quick march we proceed through the town and board the train hurriedly. Soon it is carrying us through the Aire valley, into the morning heavy with rain. Via Keighley, where once again we quietly remember our dead comrades, we pass through Leeds, dark and overcast, and arrive in Hull at 11.30am. The Humber rumbles to our right. Slowly the train pulls alongside the quay. For a long time we stand at the window looking out for the ship from our homeland. Then comes a joyful cry: 'The Lisboa!' We hastily leave the train, a short pause, a last rueful glance at *Icankillyou*. Then we are on board our ship, which was once laden with ore, but today is to carry its sons to the Fatherland. We are greeted joyfully by comrades from Redmires camp, who have already embarked.

At 1.30pm the ship casts off. The departure is without ceremony; no yearning holds us back. We stow ourselves and our luggage in the hold, and in the twilight we search for our bunks which are in tiers three and more high. We strike up conversations with the sailors to hear from German mouths what is going on at home. Many visit the little canteen, others send telegrams to relatives. We get a good helping of beans from a German galley. Most of our comrades linger on deck. In the rainy misty greyness the inhospitable English coastline slips by. By late afternoon we are sailing on the open sea. A heavy swell makes the ship pitch and toss. Gradually, the spectre of seasickness grips the former prisonörs. Quietly, one after another, we creep into the bowels of the ship and hit the hay.

Vadding's Return Home[84]

Vadding E from Schleswig Holstein clambers up into his fourth tier bunk. Soon he is under the covers, the twilight is seeping into the room. Monotonously the engines throb, the ship pitches violently. Then Vadding's thoughts become hazy. The recent past drifts by, as if it were much longer ago, and it merges with the near future. In Vadding's imagination fantastic pictures are conjured up in this prisonör's epic poem:

> Vadding was a prisonör, so we hear,
> Over in England for year after year,
> In a little place full of mud and mire
> Up in the north-west, in Yorkshire.
> In wooden huts they sat and wove
> Their plans around the smoking stove.
> Many worked hard, by night and day,
> Studying their wits away.
> Here there's bacon and porridge cooking,
> And every day the stove keeps smoking.
> Bit by bit our Vadding grew
> Into such a prisonör through and through
> That the prison way of life is easy to trace,
> It's clear to read upon his face.
>
> At last, after many long years of captivity
> The promised freedom becomes a reality.

Vadding packs up his case, with no hesitation,
And soon steps out onto Hamburg Main Station.

Out in the entrance hall, teeming with life,
Stood, waiting for hours, his own wee wife.
Is waiting to take her Vadding home,
She makes her way through the crowded room.
He can't stand still, there is no doubt,
And little by little he makes his way out.
Crash! Without warning there's almost a wreck
As his wee Mother flings her arms round his neck,
And gives him such a hearty kiss
That Vadding feels his heartbeat miss.
Then she inspects her beloved one
From front to back to see how he's done,
And says with joy, 'May God be praised!
I feared you'd be suffering from some malaise
From living with hunger in God knows where,
But that's quite a pot belly that you've got there!'
'That's no pot belly', his laugh is merry,
'That there is just my porridge belly!'

Not best pleased, she seeks the knowledge
What sort of food is this here porridge?
But before he's able to answer as he oughtta
Up leaps his very own young daughter.
With arms flung round his neck, this young miss
Plants on his face a loving kiss.
Then she looks up and rubs his chin,
'Nay, what do you look like, our Vadding?
Vadding, looks like you've been in trouble,
Our Vadding's got a full beard and not just stubble!'
But Vadding says with his voice full of pride,
'That's my Bolshevik beard that you have spied!'

And so at last, they homeward dash,
And our wee Mother, quick as a flash,
Flies into the kitchen like a bolt of lightning,
In case something in there might be igniting.
For bubbling away in pans on the stove
Are all the good things from her treasure trove,
She's been hoarding away for Vadding's return,
And it would be a shame to let it all burn.
But now what's up? What's all this palaver?

Vadding dashes off into the parlour,
And starts to tip everything out of his case,
In one big muddle all over the place.
And then he strips off from head to toe,
All his mucky old clothes must go.
He's just pulling his shirt up over his head
When in comes Mother, and then she said,
'Now what are you up to? I'm astounded!'
And stares at him, like she's dumbfounded:
'Surely you're not going to bed straight away?'
'That would be nice; but not yet, nay.
You see, I'm not quite sure – can you explain?
I thought we'd have to be searched again!'
But, finally, he began to see
That here that is not necessary.
And so he pulls his clothes back on,
But here comes Mother back again.
'Now come on Vadding, shift your feet!
Can't you see that we're all ready to eat!'
So he sits at the table and stares at his dish.
First comes the soup, and then the fish.
But all the while Vadding keeps looking round
As if at the door he can hear a sound,
And all of a sudden it seems to him
That someone outside has knocked to come in.
And Oopla! He jumps up with all his might,
So that Mother turns quite pale with fright.
And from within his beard he shouts,
'Here comes the Yorkshire Boar! Watch out!'
But then, as if nothing has happened at all
He sits back down, and lets his head fall,
Gives a wry little smile, then he's laughing away,
'Of course, there is no parade today!'

So they fetch in the ham quite hastily –
He'll surely want something tasty for tea.
He's barely finished with his fish,
When a lump of bread lands on his dish.
A bit of jam and it's looking fine.
They've even got a bottle of wine.
Vadding stares at this spread and he's amazed,
Looks up at his dear wee Mother and says,
'Listen here Mother, I may be wrong ...
But it looks like there's been a bit of *Schiebung*!'

'What's that?' she asks, looking at her man,
And so his story then began;
He starts to explain, to make it all clear,
How over there, every day, every year,
They scraped together every penny they had
To obtain cigarettes and eggs and lard.
And once he'd started to let it all out
He just couldn't stop, he continued to spout,
Whilst snacking on this and tasting the rest,
All the good things that he liked best.
Then all of a sudden his stories were spent,
And our Vadding's tale came to an end.
He's about to storm off, in a mad rush,
Until Mother calms him, 'Hush, now, hush!'
'Oh yes', says he, 'I'm sorry to shout!
I just wanted to see if the post list was out!'

The following morning, in dawn's early light,
Once more he gave one and all a great fright!
He still had Skipton so fixed in his head,
That at eight o'clock sharp he leapt out of bed.
He thought they'd all slept in and were late,
The bugle has blown, the porridge won't wait.
He ran downstairs, headed straight for the door,
But Mother was waiting there, just to be sure.
She pulled him close, 'Oh Vadding my love,
Where are you off to, heavens above!
In your nightshirt and slippers, at this early hour?'
'Oh, I'm just heading over the road for a shower!'

The ship pitches violently. Vadding half opens his eyes. With a smile, a comrade peeps up to his bed! 'Hey lad, you're talking in your sleep and saying such funny things!'

But Vadding murmurs, drunk with sleep:

'You're laughing? You think that when you get home,
It will all run smooth as a metronome?
Take care, my friend, this prisoner madness
Will send you out of your mind with gladness.
But it's sure to wear off, bit by bit,
If you just wait a while, and quietly sit!'

Eggers.

Track through the camp.

Home Again

On Tuesday night we sail into the mouth of the Elbe, and at about 7 o'clock in the morning into the Kaiser-Wilhelm-Canal. Around 8 o'clock the ship anchors in Brunsbüttelkoog. We set foot on the longed-for soil of our homeland, welcomed by our dear compatriots. Soon we are sitting in a large hall, at tables spread with white cloths, and we gratefully accept the refreshments our homeland offers. A strange feeling creeps over us as, led by their choir-master, little children sing beautiful German songs to us with their high pitched voices. Yes, we rejoice from the heart to be able to spend time with our own people once again after our long absence. And yet this joy is subdued by something invisible, which stares us in the face everywhere and weighs heavily on our hearts, and by the words of the welcoming speaker: 'You went to war from a proud, strong Fatherland, you are returning to a Reich which is crushed and completely broken!' But we pick ourselves up and pledge ourselves to the words that our senior officer had addressed to everybody in his speech of thanks: 'The Reich is shattered, we are returning to rebuild it!'

The train takes us into Lockstedt Camp. After a few days, we ex-prisonörs, who have spent months and years together in joy and sorrow in an enemy country, go our many separate ways to our families and friends, to a new life and new work. However, the words of our former senior officer light our homeward paths as a pledge made by all of us:

'We will build the Fatherland anew!'

Appendix I

Map Showing Homes of
Skipton Prisoners of War

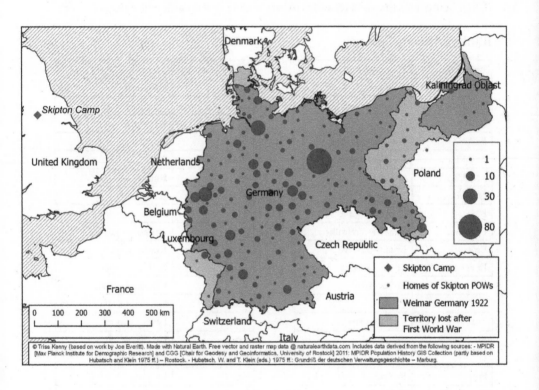

© Triss Kenny (based on work by Joe Everitt). Made with Natural Earth. Free vector and raster map data @ naturalearthdata.com. Includes data derived from the following sources: - MPIDR [Max Planck Institute for Demographic Research] and CGG [Chair for Geodesy and Geoinformatics, University of Rostock] 2011: MPIDR Population History GIS Collection (partly based on Hubatsch and Klein 1975 ff.) – Rostock. - Hubatsch, W. and T. Klein (eds.) 1975 ff.: Grundriß der deutschen Verwaltungsgeschichte – Marburg.

Appendix II

List of Skipton Prisoners of War

The details in the table of POWs have been transcribed directly from the records of the ICRC. Sometimes the same term was abbreviated in several different ways.

Rank Abbreviations

Abbreviation	Meaning	Abbreviation	Meaning
Adj.	Adjutant	Hpt.	Hauptmann
Bmt.	Bootmannsmaat	I.	Infanterie
Bt.-Kmdr.	Bataillon-Kommandeur	Inf.	Infanterie
Bt.Adj.	Bataillon Adjutant	J.	Jäger
[...] d.Lw.	[...] der Landwehr	Jäger	Jäger
[...] d.R.	[...] der Reserve	K.	Kürassier
[...] d.Res.	[...] der Reserve	Kan.	Kanonier
E.	Ersatz – Reserve	Kfw.	Krankenwärter
Einjfreiw.	Einjährig-Freiwilliger	Kfw.	Kriegsfreiwilliger
Eres.	Ersatz – Reserve	Kktr.	Krankenträger
Ersatz-res.	Ersatz – Reserve	Korvk.	Korvettenkapitän
Ert.	Ersatzrekrut	Kpl.	Kapitän-Leutnant
F.	Füselier	Landwm.	Landwehrmann
Fha.	Feldhilfsarzt	Lcorp.	Lance-Corporal
Flr.	Flieger	Lrt.	Landsturmrekrut
Fr.	Fähnrich	Lstm.	Landsturmmann
Frw.	Freiwilliger	Lt.	Leutnant
Fü.	Führer	Lwm.	Landwehrmann
Fua.	Feldunterarzt	Min.	Marine-Ingenieur
Füs.	Füsilier	Msk.	Musketier
Fw.	Feldwebel	Musk.	Musketier
Fwl.	Feldwebel-Leutnant	Oasp	Offizier-Aspirant
G.F.	Geschützführer	Oaz.	Offizier auf Zeit
Gef.	Gefreiter	Obermatr.	Obermatrose
Gefr.	Gefreiter	Ogef.	Obergefreiter
Gem.	Gemeiner	Olt.	Oberleutnant
Gfr.	Gefreiter	Om.	Obermatrose
Gmnr.	Gemeiner	Otlt.	Oberstleutnant
Gr.	Grenadier	Pi.	Pionier

Abbreviation	Meaning
R.	Reserve
Res.	Reserve
Rkt.	Rekrut
Rtm.	Rittmeister
Sa.	Sappeur
Sch.	Schütze
Serg.major	Sergeant Major
Sgf.	Sanitätsgefreiter

Abbreviation	Meaning
So.	Soldat
u.	und
Uo.	Unteroffizier
Vfw.	Vizefeldwebel
Wehrm.	Wehrmann
Wm.	Wehrmann
[...] z.S.	[...] zur See
[...] z.See.	[...] zur See

List of Skipton Prisoners of War

Serial No.	Surname	Christian Names	Rank	Military Particulars	DoB/Approx. Year of Birth
58908	Achnig	Adolf	Msk.	R.I.122/12/54.	09/06/1896
169212	Albrecht	Hermann	Lt.d.Lw.	I.470/2/-; Lw.	09/03/1889
126880	Allert	Otto Karl	Fwl.	I.454/7/-; Lw.II.	27/08/1877
59294	Allmendinger	Hermann Theo Emile	Gem.(Kfw.)	R.I.109/2/364	22/09/1894
141894	Almstedt	Erich	Lt.d.R.	I.77/3/-; R.	26/06/1892
190669	Altmeyer	Adolf Josef	Lt.d.R.	I.345/MGK.1/19; R.	27/08/1895
205650	Altmeyerhenzien	Paul Theobald	Lt.	R.I.49/-/-; R.	23/12/1891
141895	Ammenn	Ernst Fredinand Karl	Lt.d.R.	I.79/5/-; R.	04/10/1889
152291	Andresen	Heinrich Johannes	Lt.d.R.	I.84/4/-; R.	07/06/1891
167336	Andrich	Johannes	Lt.	Gebirge Mga.221/-/-; R.	24/02/1887
213119	Arendt	Erich	Lt.d.Lw.	G.2/9/-; Lw.	08/05/1896
170936	Arndt	Siegfried Otto	Lt.d.R.	R.I.207/3/-; R.	08/11/1889
133034	Arnecke	Arthur Waldemar Friedrich	Lt.	I.26/1/-; R.	23/08/1892
156751	Arnold	Franz Thomas Otto	Lt.d.R.	Bay.R.I.11/12/-; R.	30/09/1892
12696	Artelt	Robert	Füs.	Füs.-Rgt.35. Kp.5. Nr.258/220 Res.	1885
96937	Auernhammer	Xaver	Uo.	Bay.R.I.1/7/5404	20/05/1893
213120	Ausfeld	Rolf	Lt.d.R.	G.Gr.2/Stab./-; R.	15/02/1897
152292	Baade	Konrad	Lt.	Lw.I.387 (Stab) /-/-; R.	20/12/1894
98054	Baars	Walther Bernhard	Lt.d.R.	R.I.76/4/-	30/08/1896
126338	Bach	Georg	Lt.d.R.	Bay.R.I.20/8/1121; R.	06/07/1892
75956	Bach	Valentin	Inf.	R.I.111/12/866	18/11/1896
117565	Bachor	Gustav	Gem.	I.44/10/812	18/09/1895
58260	Bangerter	Karl Friedrich	Msk.	R.I.122/2/29; R.	03/10/1894

Serial No.	Surname	Christian Names	Rank	Military Particulars	DoB/Approx. Year of Birth
154562	Banke	Wilhelm Hermann Hugo Paul	Olt.	Gr.10/3/-; R.	27/08/1884
31490	Barrenpohl	Paul	Msk.	I.R.13, Kp.12, Nr.520, Eres.	1894
141852	Bartel	Paul Karl	F.	F.34/10/988; Lst.	19/03/1896
136931	Bartels	Erwin Johannes Wilhelm	Lt.	R.J.24/2/-; R.	16/01/1897
166870	Bartoszewicz	Stanislaus	Lt.d.R.	I.53/12/-; R.	15/09/1890
166021	Basten	Hermann Josef	Lt.d.R.	G.z.F.5/4/-; R.	18/01/1893
143430	Baumeister	Alois	Lt.(Kpf.)	Bay.I.3/5/-; R.	17/03/1892
104498	Baumgarten	Friedrich	Lstm.	R.I.231/1/1508; Lst	05/10/1886
143429	Bäuml	Karl	Lt.d.Lw.	Bay.I.22/10/-; Lw.	25/02/1883
132943	Becker	Hermann Wilhelm	Gef.	I.26/1/584; Eres.	07/03/1885
22333	Beckmann	Heinrich Paul Louis	Wehrm.	Res.Inf.Rgt 213, Kp. 10.Landw.	1885
106076	Bednarek	Paul	Gem.	I.51/6/570	18/01/1894
157458	Behn	Wilhelm Johann August	Wm.	Lw.I.387/11/556; Lw.	18/04/1876
168800	Behnecke	Ernst	Lt.	F.A.2/-/-; R.	02/08/1890
60237	Behrendt	Paul	Msk.	I.72/10/298	26/05/1896
152293	Behrmann	Carl	Lt.d.R.	Fdrt.108/8/-; R.	13/10/1889
210002	Berckenhagen	Kurt	Lt.	R.Fdrt.3/3/-; R.	02/12/1891
281120	Berke	Hermann Walter	Sch. (Lrt.)	R.I.262/MGK.2/5408.	16/04/1898
98057	Berleuing	Heinrich Karl	Lt.d.R.	Bay.I.4/4/-; R.	30/09/1889
309694	Bernsdorf	Erich Walter	Msk.(Lrt.)	I.27/9/1245.	03/02/1899
133043	Bertrab, von	Joachim	Lt.	Jsta.30/-/-	18/02/1894
34417	Betsch	Eugen	Gem.	I.R.57. Kp.8. Nr.471. Lst	1896
152295	Bibeljé	Willy Karl Theodor Rudolf August	Lt.d.R.	R.I.90(Stab) /-/-; R.	11/06/1887
170937	Biehlig	Erich Wilhelm	Lt.d.R.	R.I.48/7/-; R.	03/06/1880
168774	Bientz	Erich	Hpt.	I.360/-/-; R.	25/09/1874
249747	Bischoff	Ernst	Lt.d.R.	I.79/6/-; R.	22/09/1885
167918	Bittorf	Wilhelm	Lt.d.R.	I.466/MGK.1/-; Lw.	23/09/1885
145651	Biwer	Michel	Gem.(Ert.)	I.477/4/344	13/03/1891
9255	Blanke	Ernst Richard Max	Gmnr.	Fü. Rgt. 35. Nr. 159, Res.	1891
136011	Blechschmidt	Arno	Vfw.d.R.	I.94/7/587; R.	11/05/1895
67773	Bloch	Robert	Lt.d.R.	Bay.I.14/9; R.	03/03/1894
152296	Blume	Gerhard Heinrich	Lt.d.R.	R.I.90/-/-; R.	15/07/1894
96437	Bock	Franz	Inf.	Bay.I.25/1/164	15/08/1896

Serial No.	Surname	Christian Names	Rank	Military Particulars	DoB/Approx. Year of Birth
99066	Böhme	Oskar Karl Otto	Lt.	R.I.263/MGK.3/-; R.	17/01/1892
152299	Böker	Hans Friedrich Wilhelm	Lt.d.R.	R.I.90/12/41; Lw.	09/08/1887
189811	Bold	Paul	Lt.	R.I.88/12/-; Lw.	14/10/1878
284235	Bollerey	Gustav	Pi.	Pi./187/409; Lst.	11/03/1895
114766	Bolte	Friedrich	F.	F.73/10/905	01/05/1897
115595	Borgwardt	August	Gr.	Gr.9/6/1379	09/11/1893
189812	Borkenhagen	Paul Julius Johannes	Hpt.	I.330/-/-; R.	27/03/1875
189813	Bornhard	Otto Ernst	Hpt.d.R.	R.I.232/-/-; R.	06/05/1878
96597	Borowietz	Georg	Inf.	R.I.10/1/-; Eres.	26/07/1897
141900	Borsikowski	Kurt	Lt.d.R.	G.z.F.5/2-; R.	29/11/1894
13806	Bösche	Wilhelm Friedrich	Gefr.	H-Rgt 3. Kp.I. Nr.19.	1893
167676	Bostelmann	Arthur	Lt.(Kpf.)	I.466/1/-	08/11/1892
166693	Böttcher	Bruno Gerhard Waldemar	Lt.	F.A./-/-; R.	01/09/1896
158186	Brandt	Wilhelm	Lt.d.Lw.	I.84/11/-; Lw.	26/05/1887
155838	Bredow, von	Hermann Paul Max Werner	Lt.z.See	Vorpostenboot "Kehdingen", Nr.1	04/11/1893
197470	Breitenfeld	Fritz	Lt.d.R.	G.Gr.2/MGK.3/-; R.	12/08/1890
152300	Bremer	Walther Erich Emanuel Friedrich	Lt.d.R.	R.I.90/-/-; R.	08/06/1887
166871	Brendel	Joseph	Lt.d.R.	R.I.227/12/-; R.	11/08/1879
169472	Brendel	Fritz	Lt.d.R.	I.471/5/-; R.	04/05/1888
46222	Brettmann	Otto	Eres.	Res.I.R.22. Kp.4. Nr.679	1880
94683	Breyer	Herbert Friedrich Wilhelm	Olt.z.S.	U.C.32	30/11/1887
98060	Bröcker	Heinrich	Lt.	Bay.I.8/7/-	05/11/1894
20455	Broda	August	Gem.	Inf-Rgt 172, Kp.11	1891
60724	Brosi	Wilhelm Karl	Gem.	R.I.122/3/288	23/03/1895
99067	Brucker	Georg	Lt.d.R.(Kfw.)	Bay.R.I.1/MGK.1/-	02/11/1896
117928	Bruhn	Hans Eggert	Lt.z.S.	U.C.29; R.	20/12/1892
170098	Brüll	Friedrich Franz	Lt.	I.118/12/-	26/06/1897
122212	Brünger	Heimar	Vfw.	I.61/1/-	06/10/1893
169213	Buchholz	Walter Franz Albert	Lt.d.R.	I.156/5/-; R.	03/08/1894
178401	Büchler	Franz	Lt.	Pi.7/Mw.13/-; R.	10/09/1892
170938	Buchs	Joseph	Lt.	Bay.I.9/3/759; R.	13/09/1893
168775	Bühring	Heinrich	Lt.	I.360/Stab./-; Lw.I.	06/07/1884
149995	Bültzingslöwen, von	Max Heinrich	Major	Gr.10/-/-. Karl v	03/04/1874

Serial No.	Surname	Christian Names	Rank	Military Particulars	DoB/Approx. Year of Birth
142985	Burchardt	Anton	Msk.	R.I.49/12/638; Lst.	17/01/1898
189814	Bürger	Otto Gustav	Lt.d.R.	I.116/MGK.1/-; R.	06/11/1895
86081	Burghagen	Walter Ernst Adolf	Lt.z.S.	S.M.S. Unterseeboot	21/09/1891
141901	Burgmann	Adolf	Lt.	I.470/MGK.1/-/; R.	02/03/1888
189815	Burmann	Georg	Hpt.	I.450/-/-.	04/09/1882
156753	Busch	Hermann	Fwl.	R.I.65/8/-; Lw.	27/08/1875
110088	Busch	Adolf	Msk.	I.459/8/244	05/01/1895
70271	Büsch	Heinrich	Inf.	Bau.I.18/4/1020; Lst.	03/07/1880
189816	Buschendorff	Otto Max Albert	Hpt.	R.I.232/-/-.	16/02/1883
117422	Buscher	Adam	Gem.	Bay.I.18/11/385; Lst.	18/05/1886
190670	Busse	Erich	Lt.d.R.	I.132/1/-; R.	12/01/1893
170939	Cartsburg	Hans Fritz Carl	Lt.d.R.	R.I.207/1/-; R.	30/10/1894
189817	Caspary	Rudolf Nikolaus	Lt.	Gr.5.Stab/-/-.	22/12/1897
154935	Chlappik	Karl	Sa.	M.1.2/2/713	18/10/1898
190671	Christoph	Emanuel	Lt.d.R.	I.373/2/-; R.	02/02/1896
186374	Cleve	August Ernst Hermann	Oaz.d.R.	R.I.91/-/-; R.	05/08/1890
170099	Clodt	Fritz	Lt.d.R.	I.455/6/-; R.	17/05/1886
152301	Cossmann	Willy Max Georg	Olt.	R.I.52/4/45; R.	12/01/1883
189818	Courtus	Eberhard Friedrich Karl	Lt.	I.116/4/-.	18/02/1896
167919	Croonen	Max	Lt.d.R.	R.I.213/-/-; R.	16/09/1896
83444	Czaja	Raphael	Rkt.	I.62/8/85.	25/10/1897
166213	Czechura	Carl Paul Heinrich	Lt.	I.76/3/-; R.	13/07/1894
186375	Czerwinski (Dr.)	Bruno Carl Hermann	Aa.u.Bt. Arzt.d.R.	R.I.232/-/-; R.	21/08/1891
134566	Daniels	Johannes	Fwl.	I.358/10/-; Lw.II.	28/03/1877
59774	Danielsen	Emil	Gem.	I.186/MGK/170	1894
114586	Danne	Joseph	Gef.	Nkb.220/1008	22/05/1894
141903	Danz	Wilhelm	Lt.d.R.	I.77/4/-	12/06/1892
156754	Danz	August	Fwl.	R.E.I.1/1/-; Lst.	05/05/1872
263019	Dauscher	Jacob	Lt.d.R.	R.J.20/3/-; R.	06/06/1895
14857	Deise	Kurt Karl Paul	Husar.	Hu-Rgt 17. Kp.I. Nr.51.	1895
140322	Dellian	Rudolf	Lt.	Bay.I.13/MGK.1/-; R.	06/01/1895
152302	Demant	Hinrich	Lt.d.R.	I.84/6/-; R.	18/11/1879
167920	Demeter	Karl	Lt.d.R.	Bay.R.I.5/1/-; R.	26/07/1892
189819	Denner	Albert	Lt.	I.124.Stab/-/-.	01/08/1895
60698	Dettmann	Walter Wilhelm	Gem.	I.183/8/484	31/01/1895

Serial No.	Surname	Christian Names	Rank	Military Particulars	DoB/Approx. Year of Birth
189820	Dick	Georg	Lt.d.R.	I.120/MGK.2/-; R.	15/09/1890
348543	Diederich	Eno	Msk.	Esb.1/1/-. Frl	08/03/1882
171973	Dietrich	Fritz Friedrich Albert Otto	Min.	"U.55"	24/03/1890.
190672	Dietz	Christian Ferdinand	Lt.d.R.	Fdrt.25/1/-; R.	18/04/1895
166872	Dinnemann	Wilhelm	Lt.d.R.	F.36/6/-; R.	03/01/1891
135700	Dobbek	Wilhelm	Lt.	I.141/4/-; R.	29/05/1888
137792	Doege	Karl Paul Friedrich	Fwl.	I.363/8/; Lw.II.	25/01/1879
170940	Doerk	Waldemar Ludwig	Lt.d.R.	R.I.237/Mw./-; R.	11/12/1893
46080	Donizka	Josef Karl	Gem.	Eres.I.R.22. Kp.8. Nr.595	1893
157407	Döring	Friedrich	Gem.	I.143/9/234	16/12/1887
268033	Döring	Willy August	Kktr.	I.347/6/731; Lst.	14/04/1899
98062	Dorn	Hans	Lt.d.R.	Bay.I.8/-/158; R.	05/02/1890
145079	Dreger	Paul	Gem.	R.I.42/7/973	31/08/1895
148940	Duhm	Wilhelm	Msk.	I.471/12/74; Lst.	26/01/1895
166873	Düker	Oswald Karl August	Lt.d.R.	R.I.91/Stab/-/5; R.	25/11/1881
152304	Düne	August	Lt.d.R.	Lw.I.387/4/-; R.	11/12/1896
152305	Dunkelgod	Erich	Lt.d.R.	I.84/3/-; R.	08/03/1897
152306	Dunkhase	Otto Kurt Arthur	Lt.d.R.	Lw.I.387/1/-; R.	06/03/1891
119499	Dünow	Friedrich	Msk.(Ert.)	I.61/10/1120	12/02/1897
144451	Ebel	Ernst Julius Wilhelm	Lt.d.R.	G.z.F.5/11/-; R.	14/09/1892
167921	Ebert	Wilhelm Friedrich Theodor	Lt.d.Lw.	I.466/-/-; Lw.	12/02/1886
217842	Eckenberger	Max	Lt.	Bay.I.7/10/-; R.	29/07/1898
190673	Eggebrecht	Gottfried	Lt.	R.I.217/MGK./-; R.	03/07/1893
152307	Eggers	Nikolaus Leopold	Lt.	I.84/MGK.1/-; Lw.	19/10/1891
58892	Ehlers	Heinrich	Gem.	R.I.91/4/373; Eres.	08/02/1894
60283	Ehrlich	Josef	Gem.	Bay.I.16/1/480; Lst.	17/03/1887
169473	Eichelseder	Franz Seraph August	Lt.d.R.	Bay.R.I.2/8/-; R.	11/06/1893
139614	Eider	Friedrich Adolf	Lt.d.R.	I.417/1/-; R.	08/03/1897
195459	Eisenlohr	August	Hpt.d.Lw.	I.362/-/-; Lw.	29/12/1880
128716	Ekel	Heinrich	Sch. (Lrt.)	I.455/13/241	13/04/1896
169474	Elias	Wilhelm Ernst	Lt.d.R.	R.I.28/10/-; R.	09/10/1897
73806	Ellmers	Klaus	Lcorp.	R.I.72/10/438	01/10/1891

Serial No.	Surname	Christian Names	Rank	Military Particulars	DoB/Approx. Year of Birth
189821	Elsner	Bruno Otto Emil	Lt.d.R.	I.116/-/-.	23/12/1886
152308	Encke	Alwil Wilhelm Heinrich	Olt.	R.I.90/1/-; R.	21/11/1887
181535	Endler	Walter	Lt.	Flr.Trp./-/-;.	06/08/1896
345329	Engel	Konrad	Msk.	I.76/Mw.2/701	31/08/1898
190674	Engelhardt	Karl Paul Ernst Richard Bernhard	Lt.d.R.	R.I.18/-/-; R.	18/10/1885
68789	Engster	Valentin	Gem.	R.I.211/6/525;Eres.	05/09/1891
189822	Eppensteiner (Dr.)	Friedrich Johann	Hpt.	F.122/-/-; Lw.	29/11/1880
152309	Ernst	Albert	Hpt.	Lw.I.387/2/-; R.	04/10/1869
133033	Ernst	Wilhelm Karl Heinrich Friedrich	Lt.	I.26/3/-	17/02/1898
189823	Ernst	Hermann	Lt.	I.124/12/-; Lw.	24/10/1885
22514	Espig	Willy Guido	Ersatz-res.	Res-Inf-Rgt 241, Kp. 12, Nr. 88.	1886
143433	Essenwanger	Franz Anton	Lt.	Bay.I.3/5/-; R.	08/01/1888
96251	Eule	Walter Helmuth Alfred	Lt.	Gr.10/12/462; R.	21/04/1897
45759	Exner	Alfred	Gef.	Res.I.R.11. Kp.3 Nr.269. Res	1886
170112	Exner	Hanz Robert Alfons Adolf	Lt.d.R.	F.A.A.219/-/-; R.	15/02/1895
189824	Faber	Friedrich	Fwl.	I.124/Nk./-.	12/01/1879
104507	Fähndrich	Heinrich Bernhard	Msk.	R.I.229/11/2097	15/06/1896
152310	Falk	Erick Johannes Hermann	Lt.	R.I.90/3/-; R.	03/02/1885
179816	Fasen	Johannes	Lt.d.R.	I.13/MGK.1/-.R.	07/04/1890
249746	Fehrs	Hermann	Rtm.d.R.	U.15/1/-; R.	01/10/1880
189825	Feiling	Karl	Lt.d.R.	R.I.87/5/18; R.	08/08/1888
117270	Feser	Michael	Inf.	Bay.I.9/1/1271	16/04/1894
144452	Fiedler	Wilhelm Georg Heinrich Conrad	Lt.d.R.(Kpf.)	R.I.233/5/-	01/08/1888
132986	Figel	Otto Julius	Lt.(Kpf.)	I.414/1/4; R.	07/03/1893
152312	Filter	Heinrich Friedrich	Fwl.	R.I.90/6/-; Lw.	02/02/1883
308382	Fischer	Hugo Ernst	F.	F.33/Nrz./-; Lst.	15/01/1882
168776	Fitzau	Paul Max Heinrich	Lt.	Pi./304/-	14/05/1895
171977	Fleck	Otto Heinrich	Min.(Lt.)	Unterseeboots-Abt.; R.	03/03/1887
143435	Fleischmann	Hans	Lt.d.R.	Bay.R.I.13/9/-; R.	19/12/1887

Serial No.	Surname	Christian Names	Rank	Military Particulars	DoB/Approx. Year of Birth
182300	Flinker	Friedrich	Lt.	R.I.265/5/-; Lw.	01/03/1882
117182	Florczak	Andreas	Gr.	Gr.4/8/798	16/11/1895
152313	Flügge	Heinrich	Lt.d.R.(Adj.)	I.84 Stab; R.	17/04/1888
190675	Folschweiller	Nikolaus	Lt.d.R.	Lb.I.117/11/-; R.	09/01/1887
121673	Fölz	Johann	Gr.	R.G.2/3/989; Lst.	11/07/1898
114798	Foraita	Bruno	Gef.	R.I.98/4/768; Lst.	20/06/1887
159377	Forell	Paul	Gef.	I.50/12/910	24/04/1892
169475	Forster	Josef	Lt.d.R.	Bay.R.I.2/6/-; R.	24/09/1898
168777	Förster	Johannes Herbert	Lt.d.R.(Kpf.)	R.I.133/6/125; R.	07/09/1891
96253	Frank	Josef	Lt.(Bt.Adj.)	Bay.R.I.2 Stah/-/-; R.	17/01/1892
170100	Freundlich	Leo	Fwl.	I.456/9/-; Lw.	14/11/1886
117950	Freyberg	Heinrich	Otlt.	I.44/-/-	21/10/1865
148477	Freytag	Johannes Alfred Paul	Msk.	I.128/2/868; Lst.	29/11/1880
141906	Fricke	Arnold	Lt.d.R.	I.92/8/-; R.	28/03/1894
186376	Friedländer	Johannes Carl Otto	Oaz.	R.I.232/-/-.	27/12/1890
307425	Fritz	Paul Herbert Willi	J.	R.G.J.11/4/1032; Lst.	16/11/1899
6158	Frosch	Karl	Musk.	Inf.Rgt.27. Kp.9. Nr.144. Res.	1890
167337	Fuchs	Reinhold Karl Hermann	Lt.	R.I.212/4/-; R.	17/03/1897
117575	Füchsel	Max	Hpt.(Bt.-Kmdr.)	Bay.I.9/-/-; R.	02/11/1872
5456	Fuder	Bernhard	Jäger	G-J. Bat. Nr.245.Res.	1890
304181	Gans	Karl Richard	Gef.(Kktr.)	M.I.2/12/-; R.	07/03/1891
75465	Ganser	Ludwig	Inf.(Lstm.)	Bay.I.14/5/1720	07/04/1892
189826	Ganter	Marcel	Lt.d.R.	I.450/9/-; R.	17/06/1898
189827	Garben	Erich	Olt.d.R.	Gr.5/-/-; R.	05/10/1885
126985	Garms	Hermann	Lt.	I.455/12/-; R.	08/09/1893
96255	Gärtner	Erich Ludwig Johannes	Lt.d.R.	Bay.I.25/MGK.1/-; R.	13/08/1885
13503	Gauger	Paul Karl	Gefr.	Füs.-Rgt.35. Kp.8. Nr.20	1890
12217	Geercken	Heinrich Johannes Hans	J.	J-Batt 9. Nr.84	1893
138541	Geitel	Max	Lt.d.R.	MGSSA.9/-/-; R.	29/01/1889
190676	Gentz	Wilhelm	Olt.	Lb.I.117/-/-.	16/07/1893
189878	Gerken	Hinrich	Lt.d.R.	I.345/4/-; R.	12/05/1896
189828	Gerlach	Curt Heinrich	Lt.Kpf.	R.I.88/6/-.	10/03/1895
149365	Gerlich	Ewald	Vfw.	I.477/1/936; Lst.	20/06/1892
167338	Gewecke	Ferdinand	Lt.d.R.	R.I.64/6/-; R.	30/07/1889

Serial No.	Surname	Christian Names	Rank	Military Particulars	DoB/Approx. Year of Birth
22739	Gierlinski	Ludwig	Landwm.	Res-Inf-Rgt 211, Kp. 3, Nr. 75.	1880
168921	Glas	Adalbert	Lt.	Bay.R.I.2/-/-.	23/04/1880
167339	Gleich	Hermann Viktor	Lt.	I.140/1/-	29/07/1898
74970	Göbel	Fritz	Inf.	Bay.I.5/12/643; Lst.	23/12/1889
216119	Göbel	Gustav	Lt.	R.I.206/8/-; R.	08/12/1889
193542	Gockel	Franz	Lt.d.R.	MGSSA.19/2/238; R.	18/03/1895
152314	Goerg	Otto	Lt.	Lw.I.387/MGK.1/-; R.	08/01/1891
37013	Göhring	Ernst	Gem.	Res.I.R.246. Kp.12. Nr.65. Eres	1889
264544	Göldner	Walter	Msk.	I.46/3/1259; Lst.	02/07/1898
152315	Goltz	Eduard	Fwl.	R.I.52/-/-; Lw.II.	13/09/1878
45505	Goraus	Rudolf	Msk.	I.R.157.Kp.8.Nr.615.Lst	1893
175788	Gorol	Leo	Lt.	R.I.84/3/-; R.	30/03/1897
157912	Gorran	Wilhelm	Lwm.	I.143/-/1323; Lw.	31/01/1880
161503	Görtz	Wilhelm Heinrich	Lstm.	I.84/10/620; Lst.	29/09/1884
292751	Gossler	Franz	Msk.	R.I.226/10/1087; Lst.	04/10/1899
170941	Gottwaldt	Alfred Ernst Emil Franz	Lt.	I.48/5/-	06/08/1897
149996	Götz	Albert Christian Georg	Lt.	I.172/Sturm/-; R.	08/04/1889
185232	Greiner	Eberhard Maximilian Otto	Lt.	I.18/MGK.3/-.	20/02/1893
126896	Grelle	Friedrich Johann Hermann Nicholaus	Lt.d.R.	I.94/7/-; R.	27/10/1893
132268	Griesch	Fritz	Msk.	I.455/8/44; Lst.	21/06/1898
18877	Griessbach	Heinrich Johann	Gem	Inf-Rgt 134, Kp 5, Nr. 204	1891
55408	Grimm	Robert	Gem.	R.I.99/9/597; Lst.	25/09/1883
111895	Grosch	Peter	Uo.	Bay.I.4/6/142; R.	16/05/1889
142191	Grueber, Ritter und Edler von	Curt Johannes Moritz Ernst	Oasp	G.z.F.5/1/-; R.	21/09/1874
170942	Grussdorf	Walter Max Ludwig	Lt.	R.I.207/12/-; R.	26/03/1891
154561	Gummich	Otto Ernst	Lt.	Gr.10/1/-; R.	14/10/1886
53938	Günth	Fritz	Msk.	R.I.111/11/467	14/05/1893
139389	Gunther	Karl Philipp Alfons	Fha.	Bay.R.I.4/-/-; R.	25/03/1891
111955	Günther	Gustav Max Hermann	Uo.	R.I.263/2/78	29/07/1892

Serial No.	Surname	Christian Names	Rank	Military Particulars	DoB/Approx. Year of Birth
170101	Günther	Erich	Lt.d.R.	I.469/MGK.3/–; R.	28/11/1891
190298	Günther	Franz	Lt.	I.452/–/–; R.	08/06/1893
60971	Guther	Marcus	Gef.	Bay.I.16/MGSST.87/–	22/10/1895
189931	Haack	Wilhelm Max	Hpt.	Lb.I.117/–/–.	28/09/1876
34542	Haase	Heinrich	Gem.	I.R.57. Kp.4. Nr.497	1892
102258	Haberla	Paul	F.	F.38/MGK/436	18/01/1897
235363	Häberle	Georg	Lt.	Bay.R.Fdrt.1/3/–; R.	21/08/1891
169476	Haberreiter	Adalbert	Lt.d.R.	Bay.R.I.2/2/–; R.	19/12/1889
264557	Hackl	Hans Johann	I.	Bay.Lb.I./3/3497;E.	03/05/1895
170113	Haehner	Paul Ernst Karl	Lt.d.R.	Flr.Trp./–/–; R.	05/03/1891
7516	Hahn	Thomas	Jäger	J-Bat.9. Nr.192. Res	1888
75289	Hahn	Adolf	Kktr.	Bay.San.2/363; Lst.	26/11/1890
182943	Hahn	Johannes	Lt.	R.I.217/Mw.2/–; R.	11/08/1892
139696	Halfmann	Wilhelm Hermann Heinrich Leonhard	Lt.d.R.	I.85/10/404; R.	12/05/1896
168778	Halm	Max	Lt.d.Lw.	I.362/5/–; Lw.I.	04/02/1883
142192	Hameyer	Richard Friedrich	Lt.d.R.	R.J.16/3/–; R.	10/01/1893
169214	Hammer	Rudolf Karl Friedrich	Lt.d.R.	I.393/11/–; R.	30/05/1894
169405	Hammerschmidt	Herbert	Lt.d.R.	I.23/9/–; R.	25/10/1895
169215	Hannemann	Fritz Theodor	Lt.d.R.	I.470/4/–; R.	14/05/1889
234291	Hannemann	Theodor	Lt.	R.G.1/4/–; R.	26/11/1890
220256	Hansen	Friedrich	Lt.d.R.	I.84/11/382.	18/12/1890
169216	Harig	Ludwig Johann	Fwl.	I.363/7/–; Lst.	23/10/1875
138389	Harter	Emil	Lt.d.R.	E.I.28/7/–	27/02/1894
307912	Haupt	Walter Heinrich Willy	Sch.	I.24/MGK.1/–/	24/10/1897
239368	Hauschildt	Nicolaus Heinrich	Lt.d.R.	R.I.31/7/–.R.	25/07/1892
185260	Hausmann	Heinz	Fha.	I.157/–/–; R.	16/02/1890
195460	Haverkamp	Alfred	Lt.	I.360/MGK.1/–; R.	03/12/1892
167342	Haymann	Claus	Lt.d.R.	R.I.15.5.–; R.	17/08/1881
152317	Hegermann	Bernhard Franz Emil	Lt.d.R.	I.84/8/–; R.	11/11/1886
166874	Heider	Carl	Lt.	I.53/12/–; R.	09/08/1888
140069	Heidke	Otto Bernhard Hermann	Fwl.	I.369/10/–; Lw.	04/03/1880
217841	Heilmann	Hans	Lt.d.R.	I.402/MGK.2/–; R.	06/05/1885
188446	Hein	Max	Lt.d.R.	Bay.I.9/3/–; R.	03/02/1891
152464	Heinrich	Arthur	Fwl.	I.50/9/1049; Lw.II.	12/11/1878

Serial No.	Surname	Christian Names	Rank	Military Particulars	DoB/Approx. Year of Birth
57864	Heissel	Karl	G.F.	G.F.-/-/-.452	28/01/1883
249812	Held	Rudolf Joseph	Lt.d.R.	MGSSA.70/1/-; R.	19/08/1893
139607	Hell	Fritz	Lt.d.R.	I.29/9/-; R.	23/06/1884
55925	Hellmuth	Joseph	Msk.	R.I.109/10/374	24/04/1896
166887	Helm	Paul	Fha.	F.73/-/-; R.	24/08/1888
59767	Helms	Friedrich	Inf.	Bay.I.16/2/438; Lst.	03/07/1888
168780	Henkel	Heinrich	Lt.d.R.	I.360/3/	24/09/1888
93106	Henkel	Josef	Gem.	G.2/2/949	30/05/1897
62834	Henneberg	Richard	Msk.	I.26/10/65; Lst.	1890
179819	Henning	Johann Heinrich	Lt.	R.I.202/6/-; R.	19/10/1896
166022	Hensellek	Herbert	Lt.	I.452/2/-; R.	20/11/1896
168360	Hentschel	Kurt	Lt.	R.I.104/Mw.4/-; E.	26/09/1890
196545	Herbig	Karl	Fwl.	I.453/4/-; R.	11/11/1896
189829	Herbst	Heinrich Friedrich Carl	Hpt.d.R.	I.363/-/-; R.	21/10/1876
306626	Herbst	Heinrich Wilhelm	Msk.	I.44/10/1367; Lst.	16/09/1896
168806	Hering	Max	Lt.d.R.	R.I.107/12/-; R.	26/02/1883
306867	Hermani	Johann	Gef.	F.33/3/659.	29/03/1893
152318	Hermsdorff	Carl	Major	R.I.90/-/-	27/12/1869
189830	Herwegen	August	Hpt.d.R.	I.172/-/-; R.	17/10/1879
167922	Hesse	Artur Friedrich	Lt.d.R.	I.79/5/-; R.	07/03/1894
170943	Hesske	Kurt Hermann Botho	Lt.	R.I.237/12/-	30/01/1894
114386	Hesterberg	Wilhelm	Msk.	I.84/-/636; R.	15/09/1896
157239	Heth	Hugo Julius	Gef.(Ert.)	R.I.90/11/1011	20/02/1896
103175	Heyde, von der	Gustav	Lt.	G.z.F.5/10/-; R.	06/04/1891
168779	Heydenreich	Ernst Theodor	Lt.d.R.	Fdrt.90/7/-; R.	02/08/1895
126902	Heyer-Patzschke	Kurt	Lt.	I.94/2/-; R.	19/09/1893
283776	Heyne	Franz	Kan.	Fdrt.63/7/214; Lst.	22/09/1899
64074	Hickethier	Otto	Gem.	I.179/7/653	1895
126903	Hildebrand	Paul	Lt.	I.94/9/- R	04/07/1890
128226	Hilger	Friedrich	Lt.	I.455/11/-; R.	23/07/1892
189831	Hilger	Bruno Ulrich Ludwig Karl	Olt.	I.450/10/-.	11/02/1894
159317	Hillig	Alwin Friedrich	R.	Pi./107/219; R.	05/04/1889
152319	Hinrichsen	Hans Nikolaus	Lt.	I.84/2/-; R.	18/08/1891
270139	Hintze	Georg Paul Robert	Fwl.	I.50/3/-; Lw.II.	21/10/1878
187188	Hoeppe	Ernst	Gef.	R.I.201/8/1160.	18/12/1883

Serial No.	Surname	Christian Names	Rank	Military Particulars	DoB/Approx. Year of Birth
156755	Hoffmann	Georg Friedrich Ernst	Hpt.d.R.	I.58/-/-	23/02/1874
189937	Hoffmann	Hans	Lt.d.R.	I.345/MGK.1/-; R.	01/06/1894
152320	Hofmann	Richard	Lt.d.R.	R.I.19/3/-; R.	08/09/1891
52674	Hofmeier	August	Eres.	R.I.111/7/542;Eres.	1883
168801	Hofmeister	Ludwig	Lt.d.R.	Bay.F.A."A"294/-/-; R.	05/12/1887
169406	Högemann	Heinrich Franz	Lt.d.R.	Flr.Korps/-/-; R.	15/10/1892
147316	Höhn	Karl	Vfw.	R.J.24/2/888; E.	11/09/1893
168802	Höhne	Karl Arthur Georg	Lt.d.R.	F.A."A"248/-/-; R.	29/01/1895
155578	Höhne	Heinrich Wilhelm Ludwig	Lt.	I.84/12/-; R.	30/08/1892
307057	Holland	Joseph	Sch.	R.I.28/MGK.2/336.	01/03/1895
65842	Hölscher	Friedrich	F.	F.73/1/697	23/02/1898
156756	Holtz	Hans Jürgen	Lt.	I.140/5/-	22/09/1893
152321	Holz	Karl Gustav Louis	Lt.d.R.	R.I.90/8/-; R.	26/04/1889
5384	Hönow	Paul	Jäger	Garde-Jäger Bat.1 Comp. Nr76 Aktiv.	1892
142193	Hörchner	Walter	Lt.d.R.	R.I.233/5/-; R.	27/06/1892
138254	Hörich	Karl	Lt.	R.I.6/12/-; R.	14/02/1894
58317	Hoyer	Willy	Inf.	I.26/10/515.	16/11/1896
252931	Hübbe	Friedrich Wilhelm Adolf	Lt.	I.363/1/-	31/05/1898
135711	Hückelheim	Heinrich	Gem.	I.67/6/1093	28/03/1898
52732	Hügle	Ernst	Msk.	R.I.111/11/598	11/03/1895
189832	Hühn	Curt	Lt.d.R.	I.159/12/-; R.	07/01/1892
182731	Hülsemann	Julius	Lt.	Fdrt.79/Stab.Abt.II./-.	04/09/1894
189833	Hunczek	Franz	Lt.d.R.	R.I.440/3/-.	22/12/1895
132988	Ibscher	Friedrich	Fwl.	Bay.Eres.I.3/10/-; Lw.I.	06/12/1882
170102	Ilchmann	Karl	Fwl.	I.455/6/-; Lw.II.	15/11/1878
185233	Imhof	Alfred August	Lt.d.R.	I.169/2/-.; R.	28/07/1891
189834	Immel	Heinrich	Lt.d.R.	R.I.88/10/-; R.	24/01/1887
189897	Intra	Hans Heinrich	Lt.d.R.	I.116/3/-; R.	29/11/1897
189835	Jaeck	Karl Peter	Lt.u.Adj.	R.I.87/-/-.	02/12/1894
95521	Jaenchen	Otto Friedrich Walter	Lt.	R.I.93/11/-; R.	15/05/1890
154567	Jander	Wilhelm Wolfgang	Lt.	I.79/12/-	02/07/1898
156382	Jänsch	Richard	Msk.	I.72/5/1167; E.	19/06/1897
46890	Jarzab	Valentin	Lstm.	Res.I.R.22. Kp.8. Nr.642	1890
155418	Jenichen	Otto	Uo.	Lw.I.387/7/7; Lw.	11/12/1876
114797	Jensen	Thomas	Msk.	R.I.263/5/477; Lst.	22/01/1886

Serial No.	Surname	Christian Names	Rank	Military Particulars	DoB/Approx. Year of Birth
172655	Jentzer	Kurt	Lt.	Flying Corps (U.8/-/-).	30/10/1889
186377	Jeran	Friedrich Wilhelm Erich	Lstm.	I.453/-/-; Lst.(Arzt).	18/10/1885
147947	John	Hermann	Msk.(R.)	R.I.212/1/1332	17/02/1890
155749	Johnson	John Leopold	Serg.major	I.84/8/1001	08/10/1898
189836	Joost	Alexander Emil Willy	Lt.d.R.	R.Pi.23/2/-; R.	07/02/1885
139694	Jordan	Albert August	Lt.d.R.	R.I.212/10/-; R.	27/07/1896
140812	Jucknischke	Max	Gem.	I.79/MGK.1/273; Lst.	02/05/1898
168781	Juhre	Hermann	Lt.	I.360/3/-; R.	01/03/1894
262090	Juhre	Paul Richard Robert	Msk.	I.46/9/-; Lst.	16/07/1898
174538	Jung	Joseph	Lt.d.R.	Lw.I.31/4/817; R.	20/10/1893
95837	Junggebauer	Max	Lt.d.R.	Gr.10/12/N.A.85; R.	11/10/1889
182735	Kaczke	Theophil	Lt.d.R.(Kpf.)	I.152/12/-; R.	11/04/1892
126906	Kaebsch	Erwin Kurt	Lt.d.R.	I.94/10/-; R.	29/10/1895
53398	Kahl	August	Msk.	I.99/9/-; R.	1896
172277	Kahles	Ludwig Friedrich	Lt.d.R.	I.180/11/4161	23/07/1894
190283	Kalinowski	Methodius	Lt.d.Lw.I.	I.176/8/-,Lw.I.	03/09/1889
168803	Kalkofen	Gustav	Lt.	Flr.Korps/-/-	26/11/1895
249739	Kalmbach	Georg	Lt.d.R.	R.I.120/5/6066; R.	11/05/1896
186378	Kammerer	Wilhelm Ludwig	Oaz.	R.I.77/-/-; R.	28/07/1887
47168	Kampka	Carl	Wm.	Res.I.R.22. Kp.8. Nr.651. Lw.	1884
29388	Kampmann	Fritz	Gem.	I.R.13. Nr. 356	1895
167993	Kamutzky	Fritz	Lt.	I.152/-/-; R.	20/12/1895
135859	Kasperek	Paul August	G.F.	L.I./5/1740; Lst.	03/09/1891
306743	Kater	Adolf	Gef.	R.I.90/1/1777.	15/08/1895
170103	Kaufhold	Ludwig Karl Heinrich	Lt.d.R.	R.I.93/6/-; R.	15/10/1892
332957	Kaune	Richard Robert Heinrich	Msk.	I.371/5/935; Lst.	28/08/1899
182670	Kayser	Ernst	Fwl.	R.I.52/4/-; Lst.	30/09/1883
105060	Kecht	Joseph	Inf.	Bay.I.1/12/248; Lw.	10/03/1883
167343	Keesenberg	John	Lt.d.R.	R.I.85/4/-; R.	17/12/1891
167992	Keil	Edmund	Lt.	Flr.Trp./-/-; R.	21/08/1892
306741	Keller	Julius	Gef.	R.I.249/2/1276.	30/09/1898
189837	Kempter	Johann Baptist	Lt.d.R.	I.120/8/-; R.	11/08/1895
189838	Kessler	Rudolf Valentin	Hpt.	I.81/-/-.	25/04/1884
170104	Kesting	Wilhelm Bernard	Lt.d.R.	I.450/2/-; R.	12/03/1891
142195	Ketelsen	Christian	Lt.	R.J.24/3/-	07/02/1898

Serial No.	Surname	Christian Names	Rank	Military Particulars	DoB/Approx. Year of Birth
234331	Ketelsen	Lorenz Georg Otto	Lt.	I.89/5/-,	03/05/1894
4784	Kiefer	Bernhard Jacob Peter	Ob.Sign Gast.	S.M.S. "Mainz".	1893
182293	Kieser	Felix	Lt.d.R.	R.I.201/5/-; R.	22/07/1887
59388	Kirchdörfer	Heinrich	Inf.	Bay.R.I.21/8/-	1894
58538	Kirsch	Otto	Lstm.	I.190/1/422; Lst.	18/06/1879
182946	Kirschke	Erich Fritz	Lt.d.R.	I.376/MGK.3/-; R.	28/07/1892
308816	Kishner	Franz	Msk.	R.I.118/Nrz./1085.	07/10/1895
152322	Kisker	Hans Alexander Wilhelm	Lt.d.R.	I.84/1/1259	13/04/1891
154551	Klein	Karl	Lt.	Bay.I.22/11/-; R.	10/10/1893
64762	Klein	Heinrich	Msk.	I.29/3/886	25/05/1894
182732	Klein	Heinrich	Lt.	Fdrt.27/5-; R.	08/07/1884
138152	Klein	Ernst	Gem.	Bay.R.I.4/2/2022; Lst.	25/08/1897
64663	Kleinloff	Kurt Friedrich Albert Viktor	Lt.d.R.	I.170/12	18/05/1894
216248	Kleist, von	Rülekin	Major.	G.U.3/-/-.	03/11/1874
126908	Klement	Karl Paul Ernst	Lt.	I.95/7/-; R.	04/07/1891
192943	Klemtke	Willy Wilhelm	Lt.	Gr.2/-/-.(st).	05/04/1894
72878	Klenke	August	Msk.	R.I.77/4/591; Lst.	15/01/1881
156757	Klenske	Bruno Ernst	Lt.d.R.	Gr.9/5/-; R.	26/03/1894
96357	Klimas	Josef	Gem.	F.36/MGK.1/441; Lst	13/02/1897
152323	Kmet	Gustav Matthias Johannes	Lt.d.R.	R.I.19/MGK.1/-; R.	08/09/1884
189839	Knapp	Viktor Wilhelm	Lt.d.R.	I.124/MGK.2/251; R.	10/01/1897
139707	Knauer	Emil	Lt.d.R.	R.I.93/5/-; R.	02/09/1887
188318	Knauer	Wilhelm Adolf	Lt.	I.453 Stab./-/-; R.	26/03/1897
167344	Knecht	Theodor	Lt.	Gr.9/2/-	17/09/1898
170105	Knichel	Friedrich	Lt.d.R.	R.Frt.3/5/-; R.	28/05/1895
143052	Knieps	Joseph	Msk.	I.73/10/1341; Lst.	25/10/1896
168782	Kniesberg	Andreas Christian	Lt.Adj.	I.362/-/-; R.	31/01/1890
50670	Knittermeier	Wilhelm Carl Heinrich	Om.	S.M.S."Greif", Nr.64	1892
138256	Knocke	Hermann	Lt.	I.395/2/-; R.	08/11/1893
85900	Kobarg	August Ernst Fritz	Msk.	R.I.111/10/742	15/11/1879
150001	Kober	Rudolf Julius Ludwig	Lt.d.R.	Gr.10/10/A.290; R.	06/01/1894
102184	Koch	Willy	Msk.	I.51/11/1086; Lst.	09/08/1887
174784	Koch	Josef	Lt.	R.I.13/7/-; R.	13/09/1892

Serial No.	Surname	Christian Names	Rank	Military Particulars	DoB/Approx. Year of Birth
156758	Kohlenbusch	Hans	Lt.	I.143/9/-	08/05/1894
137764	Köhler	Heinrich	Lt.	R.I.77/5/—	28/07/1884
232889	Köhncke	Ernst	Lt.d.R.	F.A./-/-; R.	22/06/1889
150000	Köhr	Hermann Heinrich Wilhelm	Lt.d.R.	I.132/12/-; R.	01/03/1891
69183	Koltermann	Johann	Kktr.	Lw.San.Kp.38/54; Lw.	06/07/1877
168783	Koltzer	Hans Karl August	Lt.	I.360/6/-; R.	02/11/1892
221501	Konczikowski	Josef	Gef.	I.50/MGK.1/244; Lst.	07/09/1897
111869	Köpke	Adolf Emil August	Uo.	I.163/11/757; R.	27/08/1894
170944	Koppe	Paul Max	Lt.	R.I.207/4/-; Lw.	25/05/1897
168784	Korthals	Erich Friedrich	Lt.d.R.	I.362/6/-; R.	17/09/1892
169477	Köstlin	Helmut	Lt.	I.471/8/-	26/10/1895
170106	Kötter	Hermann Karl	Lt.d.R.	I.456/11/-; R.	27/07/1887
97826	Kraft	August	Inf.	Bay.I.8/11/632; Lst.	22/04/1889
229333	Kraft	Otto Arthur	Lt.	R.I.19/9/-; R.	30/10/1895
36720	Krampe	Wilhelm	E.	I.R.132.Kp.11.Nr.650. Eres	1885
81042	Kraus	Hans	Lt.	I.95/MGK.1	03/02/1896
138646	Kraus	Peter	Fwl.	Bay.I.11/8/-; Lst.	29/06/1875
52234	Krause	Gustav Hermann	Lstm.	R.I.109/7/687; Lst.	27/12/1876
147187	Krause	Hermann	Vfw.(Kfw.)	R.J.24/4/638	11/08/1891
188447	Krause	Friedrich Karl Kurt Rudolf	Lt.d.R.	R.I.15/11/- R.	09/01/1893
232930	Krauss	Karl Wilhelm	Lt.	I.413/MGK.3/-; R.	26/10/1892
171975	Krech	Günther	Kpl.	"U.85"	29/01/1886
54664	Kremer	Benedikt	Msk.	I.186/10/384; Lst.	18/12/1893
154572	Kress	Rudolf Martin Friedrich Balthasar	Lt.u.Kpf.	Bay.I.22/MGK.3/-; R.	18/03/1890
150002	Kretzschmer	Hans Theo	Lt.	Gr.10/-/-.	23/11/1895
168785	Kreuss	Otto Walter	Lt.d.R.	R.I.133/5/-; R.	25/12/1891
139700	Kries	Arthur	Lt.d.R.	R.I.441/3/-; E.	02/06/1894
67712	Kruck	Franz	F.(Rkt.)	F.73/MGK/352	03/06/1896
188448	Krueger	Erwin Franz Leopold	Lt.d.R.	Fdrt.183/2/-; Lw.I.	21/12/1891
74585	Krügel	Hans	Msk.	Bay.I.7/-/4031. Joh	10/08/1894
152324	Krüger	Ewald Franz Bernhard	Lt.	R.I.19/3/-; R.	14/09/1892
235357	Krüger	Georg Karl Martin	Lt.d.R.	Fdrt.507/2/-; R.	04/02/1897
263119	Krüger	Richard	Lt.	I.359/2/232; Lst.	10/11/1885

Serial No.	Surname	Christian Names	Rank	Military Particulars	DoB/Approx. Year of Birth
168918	Kühlewein, von	Otto Gustav Friedrich	Hpt.	I.363/8/-	17/07/1889
198490	Kümmel	Franz Andreas	Lt.d.Lw.	MGSSA.67/3/-; Lw.	19/12/1882
139830	Kunz	Ehrhard Constantin Ferdinand	Lt.	I.79/-/-; R.	06/07/1888
150754	Küppers	Josef	M.Fua.	S.M.H."Kronprinz Wilhelm"	1896
89226	Kürbs	Harry	Lt.d.R.	M.Feld.F.A.1; R.	25/07/1890
156759	Kurre	Theodor	Lt.d.R.	I.94/3/-; R.	04/06/1890
169217	Kurzeje	Othmar Gregor Franz	Lt.d.R.	I.156/7/-; R.	15/11/1884
170945	Kusel	Peter Wilhelm Christian August	Lt.d.R.	I.455/6/-; R.	31/07/1891
169486	Küspert	Theodor	Olt.	Bay.R.I.2/2/-	05/09/1891
169487	Kuttig	Konrad Paul Adolf	Lt.d.R.	I.361/1/570; R.	17/07/1893
127228	Küttner	Hugo	Gem.	I.392/4/1365	02/09/1896
142196	Laak, von	Dietrich	Lt.d.R.	I.471/MGK.2/-; R.	09/10/1889
147118	Lafrenz	Claus Peter	Kpl.	S.M. "U.C.65"	09/01/1887
15245	Lambertz	Michael	J.	J-Bat 7, Esk 1, Nr. 161	1893
183571	Lampertz	Heinrich	Lt.	Flr.Corps./-/-.	26/12/1896
117589	Langer	Ernst Karl Wilhelm	Gef.	G.Gr.5/2/943; Lst.	26/08/1891
126909	Langer	Robert Gregor Franz	Lt.	I.94/-/-; R.	25/05/1891
178818	Langner	Karl	Lt.	I.15/MGK.2/-; Lw.	19/10/1894
174384	Lanz	Fritz	Lt.d.R.	R.I.31/3/5692; R.	21/07/1889
96960	Laskus	Hans	Lt.	I.51/MGK.3/-; R.	24/12/1896
189840	Lassen	Georg	Lt.d.R.	I.450/10/-; R.	10/12/1895
155147	Laue	Arno	Lt.	I.84/5/1559	10/07/1894
139608	Lauff	Wilhelm	Lt.d.R.	I.29/10/-; R.	18/02/1891
171079	Launer	Hans	Hpt.	Flr.Trp.	22/11/1886
219344	Lauterfeld	August	Gef.	R.I.226/MGK.2/35.	23/08/1892
156709	Ledebur, Freiherr von	Karl	Hpt.d.R.	Schutz-Trp	1870
168786	Lehmann	Fritz Karl Adolf	Lt.d.R.	I.360/MGK.2/-; R.	18/02/1891
7486	Lehmann	Emil	Gefr.	Res-Inf-Rgt 16, Kp 5,Nr. 30.	1888
25824	Lehngut	Karl	Gr.	G-Rgt-z-F. 1, Kp. 4, Nr. 338	
75319	Lehrmann	Heinrich	Msk.	I.66/1/122; R.	02/04/1888
167345	Leiner	Simon	Lt.d.R.	I.479/4/-; R.	25/12/1894
168787	Lemcke	Johannes	Lt.d.R.	I.362/1/-; R.	20/07/1887

Serial No.	Surname	Christian Names	Rank	Military Particulars	DoB/Approx. Year of Birth
189841	Lemcke	Walter Friedrich Christian Hartwig	Hpt.	I.448/-/-.	20/12/1884
69090	Lemke	Otto	Eres.	R.I.210/5/393; Eres.	08/12/1895
189842	Lemke	Hans	Lt.d.R.	Gr.5/-/-; R.	05/04/1898
185238	Lemmens	Franz Peter	Fha.	San./29/-; R.	25/01/1891
189843	Lendle	Friedrich	Lt.d.R.	R.I.88/12/587; R.	05/04/1898
220229	Leonhardt	Karl	Msk.	I.81/3/265.	11/05/1896
124117	Liebchen	Paul	Gr.	G.Gr.5/2/1350; Lst.	22/05/1897
189844	Liebendörfer	Gerhard	Lt.d.R.	I.124/-/-; R.	22/07/1894
99288	Liebler	Nikolaus	Gem.	Bay.I.8/9/856; Lst.	13/04/1882
166875	Lieske	Carl Friedrich	Lt.	R.I.46/7/-; Lw.	27/12/1883
150166	Lilienhoff Zwowitzki, von	Werner Hugo Ernst Karl	Lt.	Gr.10/MGK.3/-	02/07/1895
168807	Linnepe	Max	Lt.d.R.	Fdrt.61/1/-; R.	29/08/1894
135701	Linse	Eugen	Lt.	I.414/MGK.1/894; R.	31/12/1894
170946	Lipp	Joseph Ludwig Wolfgang	Lt.d.R.	R.I.207/8/-; R.	30/10/1882
83650	Lissek	Albert	Inf.	R.I.55/2/828; Eres.	09/06/1889
189845	Locher	Josef	Lt.	Fdrt.13/7/-; R.	16/04/1890
31331	Löffler	Georg	Gem.	Bay.Res.I.R.5, Kp.10, Nr.536.	1895
156760	Loll	Ernst Johann	Lt.d.R.	I.58/9/-; R.	09/02/1893
88745	Loos	Hermann	Pi.	Pi.16/-/955	04/10/1896
55073	Loose	Paul	Gef.	R.I.99/11/183; R.	24/02/1889
130846	Lorenz	Karl Johann Bernhard	Res.	I.94/8/1025; R.	10/09/1888
266524	Lottes	Theodor Franz	Kktr.	R.I.208/3/1660; Lst.	02/06/1887
169488	Lotz	Paul Heinrich	Lt.	R.I.225/12/-; Lw.I.	14/07/1883
132990	Luckey	Alfred	Lt.	I.145/1/-; Lw.	02/04/1883
168788	Lüders	Waldemar Friedrich	Lt.d.R.	I.362/-/-; R.	29/07/1884
182611	Ludszuweit	Fritz	Lt.d.R.u.Adj.	I.373/-/-; R.	25/09/1888
180476	Luedtke	Johann Friedrich	Lt.	R.I.269/12/-; Lw.	09/03/1891
142198	Luft	Fritz Theodor August	Lt.d.R.	R.J.8/3/-; R.	18/09/1892
173233	Lühe, von der	Vicco	Olt.z.See.	UB16/-/-.	09/06/1890
166869	Lurmann	Johannes Bernhard Anton	Lt.	I.78/Mw./-; R.	04/10/1895
292414	Maass	Kurt	Gem.	I.27/3/-; Lst.	08/02/1899
170947	Mahr	Hans Adam Johannes	Lt.d.R.	R.I.207/4/-; R.	13/08/1893

Serial No.	Surname	Christian Names	Rank	Military Particulars	DoB/Approx. Year of Birth
139752	Malo (gen Ahlfeld)	Fritz Wilhelm Hermann	Lt.d.R.	R.I.212/Mw.2/-; R.	27/07/1886
63146	Maneke	Friedrich	Msk.	I.165/5/656	27/01/1895
339169	Mangold	Max	I.(Rkt.)	I.153/10/-	06/06/1899
167923	Manthey	Johann	Lt.d.R.	I.58/-/-; R.	12/10/1889
159981	März	Karl Heinrich	Msk.(Lrt.)	Bay.I.22/9/677	17/10/1898
169489	Massmann	Joseph	Lt.d.R.	Fdrt.31/8/-; R.	15/11/1894
133041	Matt	Stephan	Lt.u.(Kpf.)	I.26/12/-	26/01/1886
143439	Matthei	Ernst Fedor Fritz Bodo Alfred	Lt.	I.160/-/-	07/10/1894
150167	Matthiass	Gerhard	Lt.	Gr.10/-/-.	16/06/1894
139613	Matthies	Julius Christian Georg Gustav	Lt.d.R.	I.417/1/60; R.	21/09/1892
167924	Matthies	Walter Julius	Lt.d.R.	I.58/11/-; R.	25/11/1883
67783	Matthiesen	Axel Peter Louis Von Wowern	Lt.d.R.	R.I.209/11; R.	24/02/1896
121062	Mau	Adolf	Msk.	I.162/2/607	28/05/1896
9296	Meier	Willi Edmund Paul	Fü.	Fü.-Rgt. 35, Kp.8, Nr.120	14/05/1892
104509	Meier	Carl	Gef.	R.I.230/MGK.2/157	10/09/1895
93581	Meier	Franz Anton	Inf.	Bay.I.25/4/936	21/07/1896
160440	Meister	Philipp	Gem.	I.84/1/1563; Lst.	05/07/1881
2411	Mertens	Casper Gottfried	Obermatr.	S.M.S. "Mainz". Nr. 386	1890
150168	Meske	Hans	Lt.u.Kpf.	R.I.205/5/-; R.	02/08/1887
159128	Metzroth	Josef Emil Robert	Lt.d.R.	I.153/5/-; R.	06/11/1889
143440	Meyer	Oskar Hermann Waldemar	Lt.d.R.	I.160/4/-	26/03/1893
132928	Meyer	Wilhelm	Msk.	I.26/9/985.	08/04/1894
175787	Meyer	Karl	Lt.d.R.(Kpf.)	R.I.265/8/-; R.	13/04/1890
189846	Meyer	Heinrich	Lt.d.R.	I.124/9/-R.	01/10/1891
29967	Meyer	August	Msk.	I.R.16, Kp. 5, Nr. 613.	1895
166876	Meyerhoff	Ernst	Lt.d.R.	G.F./Mw./-; R.	12/08/1890
150170	Michaelis	Otto Karl August	Lt.d.R.	R.Fdrt.36/5/-; R.	07/02/1893
169218	Miethner	Georg Anton Hans	Hpt.	I.50/-/-; Lw.I.	30/08/1872
185234	Minnich	Aloys	Lt.d.R.	I.58/3/-; R.	15/07/1885
152400	Möllenberg	Paul	Lt.d.R.	Mw.240/440; R.	08/12/1891
168789	Möller	Emil	Lt.	I.362/2/-; Lw.	06/10/1882

Serial No.	Surname	Christian Names	Rank	Military Particulars	DoB/Approx. Year of Birth
228736	Möller	Erich Ernst Friedrich August	Lt.d.R.	I.84/1/-; R.	19/04/1893
170107	Moritz	Max Karl	Lt.d.R.	I.184/2/-; R.	11/03/1897
64412	Mörk	Christian	Gem.	Gr.119/12/834; Lst.	16/03/1886
152466	Mory	Herbert Walter	Lt.	I.84/7/277	23/11/1895
126917	Most	Martin Louis Karl Ferdinand	Lt.d.R.	I.28/3/-; R.	15/05/1892
48408	Mucha	Stephan	Msk.	I.R.157. Kp.4. Nr.616	1894
140412	Müller	Karl	Msk.	R.I.229/2/1391; R.	02/08/1898
46913	Müller	Johann	Wm.	Res.I.R.22. Kp.6. Nr.709	07/06/1879
152401	Müller	Wilhelm Josef Hubert	Lt.d.R.	Lw.I.384/3/-; R.	02/07/1891
91597	Müller	Josef	Fw.	R.I.10/MGK.2/3	26/01/1894
153532	Müller	Friedrich Wilhelm Heinrich	Lt.z.S.	U-Boot; R.	04/10/1888
59874	Müller	Rudolf Fr. Heinrich	Msk.	I.184/6/375; Lst.	05/12/1879
170108	Müller	Heinrich Friedrich August	Lt.d.R.	I.94/11/-; R.	11/04/1891
118190	Müller	Anton Josef	Lt.	Bay.I.17/9/-; R.	10/11/1892
151225	Müller	Adolf	E.	I.76/8/-; E.	09/02/1887
263121	Müller	Moritz	Lt.	I.105/11/-; R.	24/06/1887
56376	Müller	Wilhelm	Lstm.	R.I.111/2/574; Lst.	11/08/1879
152402	Münnich	Theodor	Lt.d.R.	I.50/12/-; R.	24/09/1885
152403	Nagel	Friedrich Wilhelm	Lt.d.R.	Lw.l.387/MGK.3/-; R.	06/02/1894
82441	Nagel	Friedrich	Inf.	R.I.55/12/2; Eres.	02/11/1888
120635	Narz	Hermann	Vfw.	R.I.261/9/498; R.	18/02/1893
167589	Nathan	Paul Albert	Lt.	R.I.247/12/959; R.	30/12/1880
186921	Nehring	Adolf	Gem.	I.46/3/1436.	10/01/1895
189847	Nettelbeck	Hermann Englebert	Lt.d.Lw.	I.159/3/-; Lw.	27/04/1881
271980	Neuendorf	Otto	Kktr.	R.I.270/6/837; E.	15/03/1890
168790	Neumann	Kurt Ernst	Lt.	I.148/1/-; R.	25/09/1890
170948	Neumann	Claus Edmund Bernhard	Lt.d.R.	R.I.207/12/-; R.	05/11/1895
126920	Nickel	Alfred Louis Hermann	Lt.d.R.	R.I.31/10/-; R.	11/04/1887
168791	Niebuhr	Heinrich	Lt.d.R.	I.362/3/534; R.	17/05/1895
92770	Niedermöller	Fritz	Inf.	I.22/MGK.2/194; Lst.	11/06/1884
139697	Nöhricke	Karl Franz	Lt.d.R.	R.I.441/1/579; R.	06/12/1886

Serial No.	Surname	Christian Names	Rank	Military Particulars	DoB/Approx. Year of Birth
142202	Nölke	Theodor Karl Robert Friedrich	Lt.d.R.	R.J.24/2/-; R.	03/04/1893
137784	Nothdurft	Friedrich	Gem.	Ers.I.28/5/832; Lst.	23/04/1885
189848	Nowoczyn	Leo Emil	Lt.d.R.	I.450/MGK.3/-; R.	12/01/1889
166877	Nürnberger	Heinz	Hpt.	R.I.440/-/-	28/06/1878
142203	Nützel	Hans Heinrich	Lt.	I.470/8/-; R.	27/11/1895
179818	Obertrifter	Willi	Lt.	I.55/9/-; Lw.	30/11/1896
152465	Offenheimer	Ernst	Lt.	Lw.I.387/-/-; R.	19/05/1892
59915	Ogorek	Karl	Sch.	R.I.51/MGK./559; Lst.	09/12/1893
168792	Ohl	Carl	Lt.	I.362/MGK.3/-; Lw.	28/12/1886
189849	Ohling	Albert Heinrich	Lt.d.R.	R.I.440/1/-; Lw.	22/01/1893
57091	Okon	Paul	Msk.	I.62/5/411	15/01/1893
73012	Oleff	Werner	Gem.	R.I.238/8/515; Lw.	03/03/1886
105114	Opitz	Hans	Gem.(Lrt.)	I.451/3/-	25/09/1898
55870	Oster	Josef Franz	Gem.	R.I.111/8/-; R.	03/03/1886
150171	Ostoyke	Waldemar	Lt.d.R.	Gr.10/MGK.1/-; R.	19/03/1887
61414	Otto	Adolf	Gem.	Mw.3.664; Lst.	24/09/1896
142204	Otto	Willy Emil Hermann	Fwl.	R.I.233/1/-	31/10/1884
189850	Pape	Richard Hermann Rudolf	Lt.d.R.	Gr.5/11/-; R.	25/03/1897
62821	Paps	Richard Friedrich Otto	Lstm.	R.I.133/10/643; Lst.	18/05/1878
170818	Parlasca	Curt	Fr.	I.48/5/1230	23/07/1898
167346	Partenschy	Johannes	Lt.d.R.	R.I.229/6/-; E.	10/07/1884
72632	Paschenda	Hugo	Msk.	I.157/4/959	03/12/1892
118193	Paschkewitz	Hans Leo Karl	Lt.	I.44/7/-; R.	07/08/1898
249801	Penseler	Ernst Friedrich Wilhelm	Lt.d.R.	R.I.87/1/-; Lw.I.	27/07/1880
126922	Peper	Ludwig	Lt.d.R.	R.I.240/6/-; R.	10/07/1889
126923	Peter	Christoph	Fwl.	Fdrt.19/1/-; Lw.	13/11/1878
152404	Peters	Rudolf	Lt.d.Lw.Kpf.	Lw.I.384/MGK.3/-; Lw.I.	22/11/1878
181170	Petri	Erich	Msk.	R.I.266/11/1120; Lw.	05/03/1879
195454	Petry	Alfred	Lt.d.R.	R.I.121 Stab./-/-; R.	15/09/1894
152405	Petz	Michael	Lt.	Frt.37/4/-; R.	25/02/1889
34839	Petzke	Bruno	Gem.	I.R.57. Kp.2	1892
356356	Petzold	Willy	So.	I.106/1/-; Lst.	15/09/1887
168793	Pfeiffer	Peter Hermann Joseph	Lt.d.R.	Bay.E.I.3/5/498; R.	03/02/1896
201816	Pitz	Hubert	Gem.	Fdrt.58/1/476; Lst.	26/09/1898
156761	Plagge	Karl	Lt.	I.116/4/971.	10/07/1897

Serial No.	Surname	Christian Names	Rank	Military Particulars	DoB/Approx. Year of Birth
82444	Pliefke	Hermann	Inf.	R.I.55/11/586	08/08/1893
150172	Plischke	Walter Max Paul	Lt.	Gr.10/-/-.	09/08/1898
154571	Ploss	Karl Wilhelm Hermann	Lt.	G.Gr.5/9/-; R.	14/09/1895
252932	Podlaszewski	Edmund	Fha.	I.61/-/-; Lst.	20/01/1892
108643	Pohl	Heinrich	Msk.	R.I.76/5/468	26/11/1893
213118	Pohl	Richard	Lt.d.R.	I.403/7/-; R.	14/09/1882
189851	Pohlmann	Hartwig Wilhelm	Lt.	Gr.5 Stab/-/-	
70605	Popp	Georg	Gef.	R.I.211/10/378; Eres.	10/02/1892
142217	Pousette	Joseph Emanuel	Hpt.	I.92/-/-.	28/04/1888
139711	Preisser	Wolfgang Albrecht Hermann	Lt.	I.92/MGK.2/-	15/07/1894
167347	Priebe	Ernst Otto Ferdinand	Lt.d.R.	I.140/9/-; R.	12/05/1894
65829	Pries	Hermann Johannes Max	Gem.	I.76/7/629; Eres.	09/02/1884
135708	Przybilla	August	Gem.	R.I.261/2/653; Eres.	21/12/1895
96951	Punde	Wilhelm	Gr.	R.I.261/1/261; R.	22/08/1893
112275	Pundsack	Johann	Uo.	I.162/6/46	30/11/1890
355359	Purrmann	Kurt	Msk.	I.164/7/1245	19/11/1898
300486	Püschmann	Max	Gef.	I.104/2/1547; Lst.	31/12/1896
166343	Puttkamer, Freiherr von	Georg Dietrich	Lt.d.R.	Flr.Trp; R.	30/12/1888
158004	Quantmeyer	Carl Christian Wilhelm Ferdinand	Lt.	R.I.90/6/-; E.	13/08/1889
152658	Rachse	Kurt	Gef.	R.I.52/9/1033	21/11/1897
302536	Rahm	Michael	I.	Bay.I.26/10/695; R.	04/02/1888
75685	Rambatt	Karl	Gef.	Lw.I.74/9/588	19/11/1872
203125	Ramien	Kurt Klemmens Wilhelm Oskar	Kpl.	U.B.109.	03/10/1889
189852	Rampf	Heinrich	Lt.d.R.	I.124/MGK.3/1017; R.	10/02/1897
36171	Rasche	Hugo	Gem.	I.R.56. Kp.3. Nr.881	1889
314091	Rasche	Martin Heinrich	So.	I.106/5/1438; Lst.	04/09/1899
178943	Rathjen	Heinrich	Lt.	Flr.Corps/-/-; R.	12/05/1887
152406	Rattay	Gotthard	Lt.	Lw.I.387/MGK.2/-; R.	25/04/1892
8744	Rau	Oskar	J.	J-Bat.4. Nr.95.	1894
166882	Raue	Richard	Lt.	R.I.218/12/-; R.	08/12/1887
168159	Rausche	Walter	Lt.	I.360/2/-; R.	08/12/1886

Serial No.	Surname	Christian Names	Rank	Military Particulars	DoB/Approx. Year of Birth
57144	Ravoth	Normann	Lt.	I.186/12/-;.	1897
179820	Reck	Paul	Lt.	R.I.202/11/-; R.	21/06/1880
176934	Recum, Freiherr von	Otto Heinrich Georg Andreas	Lt.z.See.	U.C.75	28/06/1895
164568	Regber	Robert Karl Friedrich	Wm.	I.387/3/448; Lw.	10/05/1877
139703	Reichardt	Rudolf Theodor	Lt.d.R.	I.371/1/359; R.	31/05/1884
167348	Reichardt	Ernst	Lt.d.R.	Fdrt.267/7/-; E.	28/08/1887
170109	Reichel	Oskar Wilhelm	Lt.d.R.	I.62/7/-; R.	03/03/1896
167448	Reinicke	Emil Max Reinhold	Lt.	I.54/12/-; Lw.I.	12/01/1874
139615	Reins	Meinhard Johann	Lt.d.R.	I.188/5/631; R.	24/12/1892
282507	Rellensmann	Werner Friedrich	Sch.	I.24/MGK.3/417.	02/09/1899
198480	Reuss	Heinrich	Lt.	R.I.51/8/-.R.	03/01/1889
152407	Reuter	Fritz Gustav	Lt.d.R.	R.I.27/1/-; R.	26/04/1885
282431	Rieck	Otto	K.	K.5/3/447.	11/09/1894
128193	Riemann	Heinrich	Lt.	R.I.82/8/-; R.	20/02/1893
189853	Riese	Ludwig	Olt.	Pi./341/-.	22/02/1893
308514	Rinke	Friedrich Karl	Kan.	Fdrt./907/3330; Lst.	17/09/1897
126434	Ritter	Heinrich	Inf.	Bay.R.I.8/1/843	07/04/1897
126926	Rocholl	Martin	Hpt.	F.73/-/-	30/08/1883
152340	Roesch	Eugen	Lt.d.R.	R.I.52/12/-; R.	04/12/1887
126929	Roestel	Werner	Lt.d.R.	I.95/9/-; R.	22/04/1892
167439	Rohr	Wilhelm Paul	Lt.	I.396/10/-	29/10/1898
189854	Rolefs	Karl Hermann	Lt.d.R.	I.450/9/-; R.	25/02/1890
96524	Romberg	Erich	Lt.d.R.	Pi.9/4/-; R.	12/03/1891
169219	Roschlau	Fritz Otto	Lt.d.R.	I.50/-/-; R.	26/11/1891
186379	Rosenbaum (Dr.)	Otto Gottschalk Karl	Oaz.	R.I.77/-/-; R.	04/03/1890
314348	Rossel	Georg	So.	I.105/7/1444; Lst.	11/07/1899
126928	Rost	Hermann	Lt.d.R.	I.94/MGK.2/-; R.	17/06/1897
55447	Roth	Ernst	Msk.(Frw.)	I.186/10/70	03/05/1894
166878	Rother	Werner Erich Fritz	Lt.d.R.	R.J.2/2/458C; R.	05/06/1894
159807	Rücker	Adolf	Lt.d.R.	F.A.7/-/-; R.	28/02/1884
152341	Rühle	Theodor	Lt.d.R.	I.84/MGK.1/-; R.	30/06/1887
103249	Rühlicke	Franz Albert Friedrich	Lt.d.R.	R.I.263/3/-; R.	27/03/1894
152408	Rühlmann	Kurt Alfred	Lt.d.R.	R.I.27/10/-; R.	16/09/1893

Serial No.	Surname	Christian Names	Rank	Military Particulars	DoB/Approx. Year of Birth
126931	Rumpf	Theodor Richard	Lt.d.R.	R.Eres.I.1/-/-; R.	10/01/1889
182318	Rust	Heinrich	Fwl.	R.I.266/6/-; Lst.	29/07/1875
114481	Rütten	Quirin	Sch.	R.I.25/MGK.1/480; Eres.	10/08/1888
181300	Sachsse	Fritz Walther	Korvk.		10/06/1875
189855	Saebens	Peter Ludwig	Lt.d.R.	I.116/3/-; R.	23/03/1886
185235	Sander	Adolf Gustav Hermann	Lt.d.R.	R.I.440/3/-; R.	05/03/1890
189856	Sanders	Kurt Gustav Josef	Lt.	I.450/5/-.	19/09/1896
295552	Sandrock	Friedrich	Msk.(Lrt.)	I.94/3/286.	21/05/1899
168804	Sanio	Adolf	Lt.d.R.	H.13/-/-; R. (Flr.Korps)	21/05/1891
152343	Saucke	Adolf	Lt.d.R.	I.84/6/-; R.	18/12/1891
189859	Schaaf	Karl Hermann	Lt.d.R.	I.450/12/-; R.	25/03/1891
168794	Schacht	Erich Hermann Louis Wilhelm	Lt.d.Lw.	I.362/MGK.3/188; Lw.I.	04/11/1893
158797	Schaerf	Willy	Msk.	I.84/3/1372; Lst.	14/08/1898
68322	Schäfer	Martin	Inf.	Bay.I.17/6/586; Lst.	26/06/1889
239371	Schäfer	Alfred Oskar	Lt.	R.I.6/9/-; R.	22/07/1890
140323	Schäfke	Rudolf Theodor	Lt.	I.79/3/-; R.	17/02/1895
42792	Schatz	Jacob	Msk.	I.R.126. Kp.2. Nr.724. Lst	1887
171976	Scheer	Werner Emil Hermann	Olt.z.See	"U.85"	06/06/1893
139702	Schenke	Paul Otto Albin	Lt.d.R.	R.371/1/-; R.	14/12/1888
166879	Schiller	Richard	Major.	R.I.32/-/-	12/12/1874
167350	Schirach, von	Max	Lt.	Lb.G.109/-/-.	14/06/1895
166880	Schimmrigk	Max	Fwl.	I.92/6/-; Lw.	10/07/1882
143442	Schloesser	Erich Alfred Wilhelm	Lt.	I.160/MGK.1/-	04/07/1896
6789	Schlünzen	Hermann	Jäger	J. Bat. 9. No 106	1892
152347	Schluter	Heinrich	Lt.d.Lw.	I.84/12/-; Lw.	13/10/1880
152409	Schmalhoff	Hans	Lt.d.R.	R.I.27/MGK.1/-; R.	02/09/1897
96325	Schmenger	Gustav	Gef.	Bay.I.17/1/1008	15/11/1896
142206	Schmidt	Willi	Lt.d.R.	R.J.8/2/-; R.	31/08/1894
152349	Schmidt	Wilhelm Karl	Lt.d.R.	I.84/11/-; R.	28/04/1889
152410	Schmidt	Fritz	Lt.d.Lw.I.	Lw.I.386/-/-; Lw.	19/04/1889
152411	Schmidt	Ernst Wilhelm Gustav	Lt.d.Lw.II	L.I.384/-/-; Lw.II.	15/01/1878
170951	Schmidt	Walter Albert Georg	Lt.	I.48/8/-	17/05/1897
28816	Schmidt	Hermann Wilhelm	Msk.	I.R.13. Kp.10.	

Serial No.	Surname	Christian Names	Rank	Military Particulars	DoB/Approx. Year of Birth
169491	Schmitt	Armin	Hpt.	Bay.I.22/-/-; R.	12/04/1880
176933	Schmitz	Walter Edward Alexander	Olt.z.See.	U.C.75	01/02/1891
301861	Schmoy	Max	Msk.	R.I.86/11/1221; Lst.	04/03/1898
52595	Schnappauf	Peter	Gef.	Bay.R.I.6/5/226; R.	1887
170950	Schneider	Heluo Carl Wilhelm Elias	Lt.d.R.	R.I.207/8/-; R.	11/10/1891
139610	Schnelting	Friedrich Wilhelm	Lt.	I.417/4/-; Lw.II.	13/08/1884
73044	Schnitzler	Heinrich	Msk.	R.I.239/9/666	19/01/1895
167351	Scholl	Robert Traugott	Lt.d.R.	Gr.123/5/-; R.	24/02/1893
126934	Scholz	Hans	Lt.	I.456/6/-	01/03/1876
179815	Scholz	Johann August	Lt.d.R.	I.13/3/-. R.	05/01/1893
167925	Schomberg	Heinrich	Lt.d.R.	I.58/8/-; R.	13/11/1895
170220	Schömberg	Friedrich	Lt.	I.48/6/-; R.	26/05/1883
47147	Schöneberg	Wilhelm	Msk.	I.R.93. Kp.5. Nr.808	1895
112215	Schonek	Adolf Gustav	Vfw.	Pi.18/3/707; R	11/12/1892
91023	Schorling	Ludwig Georg	Lt.d.R.	R.G.2/10/-; R.	17/04/1896
152412	Schrader	Ernst	Lt.d.R.	I.77/1/1004; R.	30/01/1878
142208	Schreiner	Helmuth	Lt.d.R.	R.J.24/-/-; R.	02/03/1893
126936	Schreiter	Fritz	Lt.d.R.	I.96/5/-; R.	12/07/1894
152350	Schriefer	Henry Georg	Lt.d.R.	I.84/10/-; R.	04/09/1895
82708	Schröder	Bernhard	Inf.	I.62/5/982; Eres.	23/08/1889
126307	Schröder	Alfred	Lt.	R.I.226/11/703; R.	21/12/1896
152413	Schroeter	Botho Albert	Lt.	Lw.I.386/11/-; R.	11/09/1893
99204	Schröter	Max Otto	Lstm.	I.51/11/1125; Lst.	15/04/1881
152351	Schubert	Joachim Carl	Olt.	R.I.90/10/-	28/01/1890
7268	Schubert	Franz	Wehrm.	Landw. Inf-Rgt 13, Nr. 200.	1881
152414	Schüler	Max	Lt.d.R.	I.50/10/343	26/01/1892
170952	Schüler	Georg Wilhelm Konrad	Lt.d.R.	I.48/1/-; R.	21/08/1887
156763	Schulte	Heinz Heinrich	Lt.d.R.	Fdrt.237/6/-; R.	02/12/1891
157179	Schulte	Franz Robert	Lt.	G.z.F./-/-; R.	12/08/1893
179817	Schulte	Franz Kaspar	Lt.	I.13/4/157; R.	30/04/1892
241415	Schultes	Paul	Sgf.	Bay.R.I.20/8/1365.	05/05/1895
126940	Schultz	Albert Ludwig Bernhard Friedrich	Fwl.	R.I.86/5/-	15/11/1880
75519	Schulz	Paul Friedrich Karl	Gem.	R.I.240/MGK/272; R.	19/08/1887
106102	Schulze	Friedrich	Msk.(Lrt.)	R.I.263/11/884	28/05/1896
124674	Schumacher	Hans Carl	Olt.	F.A.277/-/-	02/04/1891
78067	Schüssleder	Albert	Gem.	R.I.66/10/871; Lst.	08/11/1876

Serial No.	Surname	Christian Names	Rank	Military Particulars	DoB/Approx. Year of Birth
135430	Schütte	Wilhelm August Hermann	Lt.d.R.	I.165/11/226; R.	25/03/1889
152352	Schütz	Ernst August Theodor	Lt.	I.84/9/-; Lw.	12/07/1895
118955	Schwab	Vinzenz	Gef.	Bay.I.17/9/447	31/12/1892
235508	Schwalbe	Gerhard Sylvester	Lt.d.R.	I.63/3/-; R.	31/12/1894
82183	Schwarz	Hans Theodor	Lt.	Fdrt.21/6.	30/08/1896
152353	Schwarz	Franz Wilhelm Heinrich Johann	Lt.d.R.	I.84/3/-; Lw.	13/01/1888
152415	Schwarz	Karl Hermann Berthold	Lt.	I.470/7/-.	10/07/1895
168795	Schweitzer	Alfred	Lt.d.R.	R.I.133/6/215; R.	21/07/1887
192944	Schwencker	Albrecht	Lt.d.R.	Fdrt.71/3/-; R.	21/09/1896
152063	Schwill	Ewald	Lt.	R.I.52/12/-; R.	13/04/1884
189857	Scriba	Eduard Hermann	Lt.d.R.	R.I.222/2/-; R.	13/04/1892
72860	Seeberger	Karl Friedrich	Lt.d.R.	R.I.72/7; R.	04/07/1891
169490	Seeger	Fritz Paul	Lt.d.R.	I.363/11/-; R.	30/08/1893
189858	Seeger	Johannes	Lt.d.R.	I.124/MGK.3/-; R.	31/12/1892
186380	Segall	Ivan	Fha.	I.451/-/3693; R.	08/07/1894
139706	Seifert	Hans Paul Freedrich Johannes	Lt.d.R.	I.92/11/-; R.	27/06/1896
182944	Seifert	Walter	Lt.d.R.	I.152/2/-; R.	18/06/1891
170949	Seippel	Wilhelm	Fwl.	Fdrt.69/9/-	22/05/1894
137702	Sellner	Max	Gef.	G.F./12/-; Lst.	10/02/1890
219912	Sharnack	Emil Karl	So.	I.181/12/1003; E.	24/04/1886
5574	Shrader	Artur	Schütze	G,Schüt.Bat. No 91	1894
156762	Sichler	Helmuth Friedrich Richard Peter Paul	Lt.d.R.	I.94/11/855; R.	18/11/1895
152344	Siemon	Ernst Peter	Lt.d.R.	I.84/8/-; R.	17/06/1892
180180	Siems	Friedrich Hermann	Lt.	I.71/12/-; R.	08/11/1896
132991	Sierk	Johannes	Lt.d.R.	Fdrt.108/4/83; R.	07/05/1893
47261	Sievert	Fritz	Res.	I.R.13. Kp.6. Nr.237. Res	1890
167349	Simon	Arthur	Lt.	I.140/9/-; R.	23/01/1893
249748	Solbrig	Hugo Otto	Lt.d.R.	I.64/8/-; R.	24/06/1884
117285	Sommer	Julius Theodor	Lt.	R.I.120/3/-; R.	15/03/1887
152416	Sourell	Martin	Lt.d.R.	I.363/-/-; R.	07/12/1892
170110	Spaetgens	Hubert	Lt.d.R.	R.I.257/11/-; R.	06/04/1889

Serial No.	Surname	Christian Names	Rank	Military Particulars	DoB/Approx. Year of Birth
169492	Spangenberg	Alfred Friedrich Bertram	Lt.d.R.	I.471/4/–; R.	21/07/1897
126941	Spies	Carl	Lt.	I.94/10/–; R.	05/09/1888
170953	Spillner	Fritz	Lt.	I.188/11/–; R.	12/05/1888
121220	Stabolepszy	Richard	Uo.	I.181/MGK.2/91	03/12/1892
54051	Stärker	Richard Julius	Gef.d.Res.	R.I.110/12/213; R.	22/01/1890
132220	Stasch	Albert	Gem.(Lrt)	I.50/12/1341	17/02/1898
102536	Staschitzek	Johann	Gem.	Gr.10/3/–; Lst.	01/04/1891
98093	Steghöfer	Fritz	Lt.	Bay.I.8/12/1454; R.	28/03/1884
143444	Stehenmüller	Helmut Hans	Lt.	Bay.I.22/9/–	14/08/1896
139612	Stein	Georg Emil Julius	Lt.d.R.	I.417/2/17; R.	20/08/1896
152417	Steinmann	Franz	Lt.d.R.	Lw.I.387/6/–; R.	27/05/1895
174383	Stelzner	Otto	Lt.Kpf.	I.179/3/–; Lw.I.	23/04/1886
82492	Stender	Karl	Inf.	R.I.55/7/357 Eres	11/04/1885
96948	Stetzkamp	Heinrich	Msk.	R.I.99/10/–; R.	18/05/1897
126944	Steuding	Walter Rudolf Hermann	Lt.d.R.	I.94/–/–; R.	05/08/1892
155629	Stieding	Ernst	Sch.	I.370/MGK.1/175	16/02/1898
152418	Stoltenberg	Joachim Ernst Wilhelm	Lt.d.R.	R.I.27/1/–; R.	27/12/1887
167352	Stoof	Reinhold Karl Bruno	Lt.	I.52/11/–; Lw.	12/01/1887
143445	Storck	Clemens Friedrich Ewald	Lt.d.R.	I.160/4/–; R.	11/09/1886
182234	Straehler	Herbert Ludwig Karl Alexander	Olt z.See,	Marine Wilhelmshaven.	06/01/1887
117102	Strang	Paul	Flr.Lt.	Sfa.II; R.	08/09/1884
152419	Strauss	Richard	Lt.d.R.	Lw.I.384/10/–; R.	09/10/1892
201943	Streckmann	Hugo	Lt.	I.82/7/–.	25/05/1899
136344	Stresow	Gustav	Vfw.	I.26/8/1029; R.	22/08/1889
60014	Strobelt	Max Richard	Gem.	I.183/12/345	12/05/1895
192945	Stüdemann	Werner	Lt.d.R.	I.55/11/–; Lw.I.	28/11/1884
66562	Studerus	Otto Julius	Lt.d.R.	Bay.I.14/12; R.	04/09/1888
68114	Stühmer	Wilhelm	Dem.	R.I.211/2/424	08/09/1891
169510	Südhoff	Gottfried	Lt.d.R.	I.470/4/–; R.	19/06/1883
114120	Sujata	Johannes Heinrich Otto Martin Theodor	Bmt.	S.M.T."S.20",II.Z.Flottille	25/01/1899
142205	Sumpf	Adolf Heinrich Konrad	Lt.	R.J.24/–/–; Lw.	21/01/1884

Serial No.	Surname	Christian Names	Rank	Military Particulars	DoB/Approx. Year of Birth
152044	Sünderhaus	Alfred H.	Lt.	Lw.I.387/5/-; Lw.	27/11/1876
6778	Szezganski	Felix	Jäger	J.Bat.9. No.111	1893
168796	Tannebring	Fritz	Lt.d.R.	Fdrt.90/9/-; R.	28/08/1893
152420	Tautz	Franz	Lt.d.R.	I.471/12/-; R.	27/05/1893
98095	Telthörster	Bernhard Heinrich	Lt.	Bay.I.8/8/-; R.	05/09/1891
360480	Tetzlaff	Martin	Msk.	I.27/9/-	13/09/1899
152354	Teuber	Wilhelm Erwin Heinz Maximilian August	Lt.	I.84/2/-	15/01/1893
167353	Thalheim	Georg Karl	Lt.d.R.	R.I.91/6/-; R.	25/02/1895
175789	Thee	Peter	Lt.d.R.	R.I.90/2/-; R.	17/08/1887
61997	Thiede	Siegfried Erich Wilhelm	Lstm.	I.12/1/1054; Lst.	27/01/1891
152355	Thiele	Rudolf Franz Christian	Lt.d.R.	Lw.Frt.40/5/-; R.	14/07/1893
53962	Thoma	Philipp	Msk.	R.I.111/11/435	20/04/1894
82413	Thomasi	Dominick	Msk.(Lrt)	Ers.I.29/2/239	10/09/1877
123191	Thomsen	Joachim	Lt.z.S.	Seeflugstation Zeebrügge Oblt	08/04/1896
98099	Thomsen	Carlo Zino	Lt.	R.I.76/5/-; R.	29/08/1890
126947	Thon	Paul	Lt.d.R.	I.94/11/-; R.	23/03/1885
9043	Thörmer	Carl Otto Eduard	Einjfreiw.	G-Schütz-Bat, Nr. 116	1892
308548	Tichauer	Artur	Gef.	I.51/Na./-.	29/05/1896
152421	Tielcke	Leopold Johannes Paul	Lt.	Lw.I.386/6/-; Lw.II.	22/08/1881
112291	Tietjen	Heinrich	Uo.	Pi.9/-/142	18/09/1892
98097	Tilch	Alfred	Lt.d.Lw.I.	I.51/12/-; Lw.I.	26/10/1884
152356	Tilger	Wilhelm	Lt.d.R.	R.I.90/10/-; Lst.	02/03/1888
302959	Töpfer	Oskar August Albert	Kktr.	I.175/2/1366; Lst.	15/05/1882
176551	Trautmann	Eduard	Lt.	R.I.31/4/49; R.	19/12/1896
167926	Treppe	Werner Fritz	Lt.	I.58/7/-	28/11/1896
235360	Tröster	Ludwig	Lt.d.R.	I.128/1/-; R.	12/03/1893
77662	Trübe	Otto	Gem.	R.I.109/3/437	07/01/1893
170954	Tünnerhoff	Wilhelm	Lt.d.R.	Flr.Trp./-/-; R.	19/11/1890
142211	Tuphorn	Curt	Lt.d.R.	R.I.233/4/-; R.	20/11/1895
252929	Uecker	Richard Wilhelm Ernst	Lt.d.R.	I.141/11/-; R.	31/01/1888
139708	Ueckert	Paul Otto Karl	Lt.d.R.	R.I.93/2/-; R.	04/03/1897
152422	Ueter	Hermann	Lt.d.R.	I.470/12/-; R.	26/06/1890

Serial No.	Surname	Christian Names	Rank	Military Particulars	DoB/Approx. Year of Birth
58335	Ulrich	Arthur Friedrich Wilhelm	Lstm.	I.184/6/524; Lst.	11/01/1877
134562	Unruh	Fritz	Lt.	I.358/MGK.3/–; R.	13/05/1893
56744	Urnstein	Max	Msk.	I.186/12/485; Lst.	09/06/1896
139609	van Spankeren	Karl August Ludwig	Lt.	I.28/6/–	04/05/1896
169675	Verschner, Freiherr von	Theodor Hans Georg Christoph	Lt.	I.469/11/–	28/07/1893
12603	Vester	Johannes Ferdinand Fritz	Gfr.d.Res.	Füs-Regt. 35. Kp.5. Nr.125	1891
166937	Viol	Rudolf	Lt.	I.140/5/–.	18/04/1899
70129	Vogt	Karl	Inf.	Bay.I.23/5/976; Eres.	20/10/1893
217453	Voss	Richard	Lt.	R.I.261 Stab/–/–; R.	10/06/1892
152357	Vulmahn	Walter	Lt.d.R.	Lw.I.387/4/–; R.	04/09/1887
139695	Wagner	Rudolf	Lt.	R.I.212/11/–; R.	10/02/1882
97149	Wagner	Johann	Vfw.	Bay.R.I.1/12/726; R.	29/03/1890
168797	Wagner	Hans	Lt.d.R.	I.362/1/–; R.	24/06/1895
138393	Wallbaum	Hans Johann Friedrich	Lt.d.R.	R.I.229/MGK.2/–; R.	01/07/1893
68263	Wallhausen	Hermann	Inf.	R.I.229/5/906; Lst.	02/12/1885
46324	Walta	Wilhelm	Msk.	I.R.22. Kp.5. Nr.780. Lst	1888
156764	Wannenmacher	Johann	Lt.d.Lw.	I.30/–/1114; Lw.	01/05/1879
186381	Warnecke	Fritz Bernard Joachim	Fha.	I.451/–/–; R.	26/05/1886
114525	Wasel	Reiner	Gem.	I.25/7/955; Lst.	02/03/1887
6750	Weckmann	Otto Gottfried	Schütze	G-Schütz-Bat.3 Kp. Nr. 39	1892
167446	Wedel	Carl Wilhelm	Lt.d.R.	R.J.16/–/–; R.	10/08/1892
152423	Wegener	Johannes	Fwl.	Lw.I.384/10/–; Lst.	28/08/1872
256502	Wehe	Friedrich Wilhelm August	Msk.	I.68/3/1134.	09/06/1897
139723	Wehrmann	Heinrich Friedrich August	Lt.d.R.	I.79/7/–; R.	15/01/1893
308557	Weidner	Fritz	Gr.	Gr.10/1/1177; Lst.	06/05/1896
142214	Weiger	Hubert Joseph Anton	Lt.d.R.	I.124/5/–; R.	27/07/1896
126952	Weimes	Jack Johann	Lt.	R.I.240/5/–; Lw.I.	26/10/1883
63546	Weingärtner	Heinrich	Msk.	R.I.122/1/460	04/07/1894
29262	Weinrauth	Arno	J.	J-Bat. 11, Nr. 414.	
167927	Weiser	Paul	Lt.d.R.	I.466/3/–; R.	20/04/1884
139616	Weiss	Johann	Lt.d.R.	I.188/8/–; R.	23/09/1891

Serial No.	Surname	Christian Names	Rank	Military Particulars	DoB/Approx. Year of Birth
306559	Weissleder	Eduard	Gef.	R.I.251/9/1467; R.	14/04/1883
134564	Wendel	Eugen	Lt.	Gr.119/4/-; R.	25/04/1893
126951	Wendt	Rudolf Heinrich William August	Lt.d.R.	R.I.31/11/-; R.	11/08/1887
171974	Wenninger	Ralph	Kpl.	"U.55".	22/04/1890
29726	Werner	Josef	Msk.	I-R-16. Kp.11. Nr.567	1895
138387	Werner	Karl Erich	Lt.	R.I.229/5/-; R.	02/01/1894
266927	Werno	Josef	Msk.	R.I.3/2/1583; Lst.	09/03/1898
185236	Werth	Gustav Adolf Robert	Lt.d.R.	R.I.263/MGK.3/-; R.	08/07/1896
156765	Wessel	Karl	Lt.d.R.	I.30/5/-; R.	19/12/1888
7267	Westerhoff	Georg	Wehrm.	Landw.Inf-Rgt 13, Nr. 224	1882
235358	Westphal	Fritz Friedrich Gerhard Günther	Lt.	I.46/7/1085.	23/08/1897
170111	Weygandt	Gustav	Lt.d.R.	I.88/Mw.Abt./-; R.	08/09/1891
142221	Wichmann	Paul Friedrich Wilhelm	Lt.d.R.	I.79/10/-; R.	26/07/1892
167438	Wiedmann	Gustav Heinrich Walter	Lt.d.R.	F.122/4/-; R.	23/09/1888
167928	Wiegand	Karl Otto Friedebald	Lt.d.R.	I.466/2/-; R.	21/03/1891
96603	Wielpütz	Julius	Ogef.	Lw.Frt.47/4/38; R.	08/01/1891
207193	Wilhelm	Willy Ernst	Lt.	I.94/3/; R.	08/09/1891
168798	Wilke	Albin Joseph	Lt.d.R.	I.371/6/-; R.	15/09/1897
183235	Will	Georg	I.	Bay.I.7/2/1195; E.	09/11/1899
156766	Wilmanns	Erich	Lt.d.R.	I.67/6/-; R.	01/08/1895
132183	Windolf	Hans	Gef.(Kfw.)	I.26/9/420	20/10/1895
126953	Windscheid	Friedrich Karl Otto	Lt.	Pi.235/Mkw.435/-; R.	15/12/1893
168799	Winklemann	Johann Heinrich Friedrich Louis	Lt.	I.362/6/-; R.	13/02/1898
263118	Wintermeyer	Karl	Lt.d.R.	I.82/1/-; R.	10/01/1892
30621	Wittkämper	Friedrich Fritz	Gem.	I.R.16, Kp.10, Nr.516.	1892
297209	Wittmann	Karl	Msk.	Bay.I.27/8/650; Lst.	25/02/1882
12537	Wodetzki	Hugo	Füs.	Füs.-Rgt.35. Kp.11. Nr.46	1890
77168	Wolf	Friedrich	Gem.(Res)	R.I.240/6/27	12/12/1890
185237	Wolff	Karl Friedrich	Fwl.	I.14/11/-.	28/12/1890
66397	Wolfsen	Jes Ingwert Heinrich	J.	R.J.9/2/247; Lw.I.	27/10/1884
152424	Wommer	Emil	Lt.d.R. (Frw.)	Lw.I.387/MGK	23/12/1893

Serial No.	Surname	Christian Names	Rank	Military Particulars	DoB/Approx. Year of Birth
143447	Wörthmüller	Hans	Lt.	Bay.I.22/9/–	27/10/1893
113636	Wortmann	Heinz	Lt.	R.I.25/MGK1/–; R.	29/05/1895
169220	Wülfing	Otto	Lt.d.R.	I.370/10/–; Lw.	18/02/1877
166881	Würffel	Conrad Albert Heinrich	Lt.d.R.	R.I.46/7/–; R.	03/11/1892
182737	Wüstefeld	Hans	Lt.(Kpf.)	I.18/12/–; Lw.I.	06/07/1881
22709	Zanhow	August Karl Friedrich	Landwm.	Res-Inf-Rgt 211, Kp. 5, Nr. 228	1877
168805	Zech	Franz Josef	Lt.	Bay.F.A.48/–/–; R.	05/08/1892
149846	Zenker	Wilhelm Heinrich August	Lt.d.R.	Gr.10/2/–; R.	16/09/1893
127831	Zimmermann	August Friedrich Wilhelm	So.(Rkt.)	I.392/4/409	09/02/1896
114428	Zinnen	Hübert	Res.	R.I.69/12/–; R.	13/01/1891
152425	Zscheyge	Ernst	Lt.d.R.	I.470/6/–; R.	24/05/1881
169221	Zühl	Helmuth Martin	Lt.d.R.	I.26/11/–; R.	06/09/1895
328519	Zylla	Johann	Msk.	I.63/4/836.	22/08/1897

Notes and Sources

Introduction

1. It is difficult to establish an exact figure. According to War Office file WO 394/20 (The National Archives), the greatest number of military prisoners and civilian internees held by the British at home and abroad at any one time was 507,215 in January 1919. Of this figure 122,121 were Germans held in Britain, which included just over 18,000 civilians leaving approximately 104,000 military personnel. The total number held in Britain over the course of the war will be higher, as by January 1919 some prisoners previously held in Britain had been repatriated.
2. The project was funded by the National Lottery Heritage Fund. The project website is at https://skiptonww1camp.co.uk/.
3. The film entitled *The Story of Fritz Sachsse and how he ended up in Skipton* can be accessed via the project website: https://skiptonww1camp.co.uk/project/refugee-project/.
4. Heather Jones gives an estimate of 7 to 9 million in *Violence Against Prisoners of War in the First World War: Britain, France and Germany, 1914–1920*, 2011, p. 2. Reinhard Nachtigal believes the figure to be nearer 9 million ('Zur Anzahl der Kriegsgefangenen im Ersten Weltkrieg', *Militärgeschichtliche Zeitschrift* 67, 2008, pp. 345–84.)
5. Heather Jones, 2008, 'A Missing Paradigm? Military Captivity and the Prisoner of War, 1914–18', *Immigrants & Minorities*, vol. 26, nos 1–2, pp. 19–48.
6. Uta Hinz, 2006, *Gefangen im Grossen Krieg: Kriegsgefangenschaft in Deutschland, 1914–1921*, p. 9. The German expression 'eine vergessene Geschichte' is used.
7. Graham Mark, 2007, *Prisoners of War in British Hands during WWI. A study of their history, their camps and their mails.*
8. Brian Feltman, 2015, *The Stigma of Surrender. German Prisoners, British Captors, and Manhood in the Great War and Beyond*, p. 4.
9. See note 1.
10. Panikos Panayi, 2012, *Prisoners of Britain. German Civilian and Combatant Internees during the First World War.*
11. Oliver Wilkinson, 2017, *British Prisoners of War in First World War Germany.*
12. Clare Makepeace, 2017, *Captives of War. British Prisoners of War in Europe in the Second World War.*
13. Matthew Stibbe, 2008, *British Civilian Internees in Germany, The Ruhleben Camp 1914–18.*
14. Heather Jones, 2011, *Violence Against Prisoners of War in the First World War: Britain, France and Germany, 1914–1920.*
15. Ibid., p. 71.
16. This book, p. 127.
17. This book, p. 127.
18. Peter Simkins, 'Pals Battalions', *1914–1918-online. International Encyclopedia of the First World War*, 2018. Online at https://encyclopedia.1914-1918-online.net/article/pals_battalions (accessed 26 January 2020).
19. David Raw, 2005, *Bradford Pals. A Comprehensive History of the 16th, 18th & 20th (Service) Battalions of the Prince of Wales' Own West Yorkshire Regiment 1914–1918*, p. 29.
20. Ibid., pp. 57–70.
21. Kathryn Hughes, n.d., 'Bradford Pals', *Bradford WW1 Social, Local and Family History Research*. Online at http://www.bradfordww1.co.uk/bradford-pals.html (accessed 19 January 2020).
22. *Bradford Weekly Telegraph*, 6 November 1914.

23. David Raw, 2005, *Bradford Pals. A Comprehensive History of the 16th, 18th & 20th (Service) Battalions of the Prince of Wales' Own West Yorkshire Regiment 1914–1918*, p. 80. The full list of forty-four hut names is given.
24. This book, p. 42.
25. 'Raikeswood Camp to be dismantled', *Craven Herald and Wensleydale Standard*, 11 June 1920.
26. The Wartime Memories Project, *21st (Wool Textile Pioneers) Battalion West Yorkshire Regiment during the Great War*. Online at https://www.wartimememoriesproject.com/greatwar/allied/battalion.php?pid=5045 (accessed 19 January 2020).
27. Information obtained from the records of the International Committee of the Red Cross, *Prisoners of the First World War, the ICRC archives*. Online at https://grandeguerre.icrc.org/ (accessed 25 January 2020). See also note 17 to the translation.
28. 'A German Invasion', *Craven Herald and Wensleydale Standard*, 18 January 1918.
29. International Committee of the Red Cross. *Prisoners of the First World War, the ICRC archives*. Online at https://grandeguerre.icrc.org/ (accessed 25 January 2020).
30. Ibid.
31. Ibid.
32. This book, pp. 126 and 259.
33. Report dated 21 March 1919 of inspection to Skipton Camp by the Swiss Legation on 24 February 1919 (The National Archives, FO 383/506).
34. International Committee of the Red Cross, *Prisoners of the First World War, the ICRC archives*. Online at https://grandeguerre.icrc.org/ (accessed 25 January 2020).
35. Wenninger was captured on 22 April 1918 when in command of the *U-55*, which hit a mine in the English Channel. Further details about his career and capture can be seen in Innes McCartney, 2002, *Lost Patrols: Submarine Wrecks of the English Channel*.
36. Airmen identified using the ICRC records. For more on Joachim von Bertrab see, for example, Greg VanWyngarden, 2013, *Aces of Jagdstaffel 17* (Aircraft of the Aces), p. 10.
37. International Committee of the Red Cross, *Prisoners of the First World War, the ICRC archives*. Online at https://grandeguerre.icrc.org/ (accessed 25 January 2020).
38. Home addresses obtained using ICRC records. In most cases the place of birth of the prisoner was also the place of residence.
39. This book, p. 212.
40. See, for example, John E. Moser, 2015, *Global Great Depression and the Coming of World War II*, p. 35.
41. For more detail see, for example, Derek Howard Aldcroft, 1977, *From Versailles to Wall Street, 1919–1929 (History of the world economy in the twentieth century)*.
42. Hans H. Hildebrand and Ernest Henriot, 1990, *Deutschlands Admirale 1849–1945. Die militärischen Werdegänge der See-, Ingenier-, Sanitäts-, Waffen- und Verwaltungsoffiziere in Admiralsrang. Band 3: P–Z*, pp. 174–5.
43. 'Meine Flucht durch China', *Stralsunder Tageblatt, Unterhaltungs-Beilage*, Nr. 54, 5 March 1938.
44. Charles Burdick and Ursula Moessner, 1984, *The German Prisoners of War in Japan, 1914–1920*, pp. x–xi.
45. 'Meine Flucht durch China', *Stralsunder Tageblatt, Unterhaltungs-Beilage*, Nr. 54, 5 March 1938.
46. Charles Burdick and Ursula Moessner, 1984, *The German Prisoners of War in Japan, 1914–1920*, pp. 25–37.
47. 'Meine Flucht durch China', *Stralsunder Tageblatt, Unterhaltungs-Beilage*, Nr. 65–Nr. 66, 18–19 March 1938.
48. Ibid.
49. Ibid.
50. Ibid.
51. Charles Burdick and Ursula Moessner, 1984, *The German Prisoners of War in Japan, 1914–1920*, p. 47.
52. 'Meine Flucht durch China', *Stralsunder Tageblatt, Unterhaltungs-Beilage*, Nr. 54–Nr. 66, 5–19 March 1938. The ICRC records show that Fritz Sachsse was travelling under the

name of Hans Edeler (see Plate 4) and Herbert Straehler was using the name Herbert Ungerer.

53. This book, p. 127–8.
54. This book, p. 245.
55. Hans H. Hildebrand and Ernest Henriot, 1990, *Deutschlands Admirale 1849–1945. Die militärischen Werdegänge der See-, Ingenier-, Sanitäts-, Waffen- und Verwaltungsoffiziere in Admiralsrang. Band 3: P–Z*, pp. 174–5.
56. 'Abschied vom Alt-Landesgrßmeister Br. Willy Coßmann', *Zirkelkorrespondenz* (monthly magazine of the Freemasons in Germany), 1970, pp. 303–5.
57. Willy Cossmann, 1915, *Die Entwicklung des Gerichtsgedankens bei den alttestamentlichen Propheten* (Beihefte zur Zeitschrift für die alttestamentliche Wissenschaft).
58. 'Abschied vom Alt-Landesgroßmeister Br. Willy Coßmann', *Zirkelkorrespondenz* (monthly magazine of the Freemasons in Germany), 1970, pp. 303–5.
59. International Committee of the Red Cross, *Prisoners of the First World War, the ICRC archives*. Online at https://grandeguerre.icrc.org/ (accessed 25 January 2020).
60. 'Abschied vom Alt-Landesgroßmeister Br. Willy Coßmann', *Zirkelkorrespondenz* (monthly magazine of the Freemasons in Germany), 1970, pp. 303–5. See also this book, pp. 166–72.
61. Archiv der Bibliothek für Bildungsgeschichtliche Forschung des Deutschen Instituts für Internationale Pädagogische Forschung, DIPF/BBF/Archiv: GUT PERS 372, p. 18.
62. 'Abschied vom Alt-Landesgroßmeister Br. Willy Coßmann', *Zirkelkorrespondenz* (monthly magazine of the Freemasons in Germany), 1970, pp. 303–5.
63. Alan Bernheim, 2014, 'United Grand Lodge and United Grand Lodges of Germany 1946–1961', *Ars Quatuor Coronatorum*, vol. 127, pp. 61–104. Also mentioned in *Zirkelkorrespondenz* (ibid.).
64. Hague Convention, 1907: Hague Convention (IV) respecting the Laws and Customs of War on Land and its annex: Regulations concerning the Laws and Customs of War on Land. The Hague, 18 October 1907, ANNEX TO THE CONVENTION: REGULATIONS RESPECTING THE LAWS AND CUSTOMS OF WAR ON LAND – SECTION I: ON BELLIGERENTS – CHAPTER II: PRISONERS OF WAR – REGULATIONS: ART. 5. Online at https://ihl-databases.icrc.org/applic/ihl/ihl.nsf/ART/195-200015?OpenDocument (accessed 7 January 2020).
65. Hague Convention, 1907: Hague Convention (IV) respecting the Laws and Customs of War on Land and its annex: Regulations concerning the Laws and Customs of War on Land. The Hague, 18 October 1907, ANNEX TO THE CONVENTION: REGULATIONS RESPECTING THE LAWS AND CUSTOMS OF WAR ON LAND – SECTION I: ON BELLIGERENTS – CHAPTER II: PRISONERS OF WAR – REGULATIONS: ART. 6. Online at https://ihl-databases.icrc.org/applic/ihl/ihl.nsf/ART/195-200016?OpenDocument (accessed 7 January 2020).
66. See, for example, British Parliamentary Papers: Cd. 8590, *An Agreement between the British and German Governments concerning Combatant and Civilian Prisoners of War* (London, 1917); Cd. 9147, *An Agreement between the British and German Governments concerning Combatant Prisoners of War and Civilians* (London, 1918).
67. Ibid., Cd. 9147.
68. 'Report on the Directorate of Prisoners of War', September 1920 (The National Archives, WO 106/1451).
69. Bradley P. Tolppanen, 2005, 'Maxwell, Sir John Grenfell (1869–1929)', in Spencer Tucker and Priscilla Mary Roberts (eds), *World War I: Encyclopedia*, vol. 1, pp. 763–4. See also this book, p. 250.
70. John A. Hutcheson Jr, 2005, 'Maxse, Sir Ivor (1862–1958)', in Spencer Tucker and Priscilla Mary Roberts (eds), World War I: Encyclopedia, vol. 1, p. 763. See also this book, p. 250.
71. This book, p. 250.
72. This book, p. 250.
73. This book, p. 252. See also Skipton Camp inspection reports February 1918 (The National Archives, FO 383/432), and June 1918 (Bundesarchiv Berlin-Lichterfelde, R901/83146).
74. This book, p. 128.
75. This book, p. 129. See also Skipton Camp inspection report February 1918 (The National Archives, FO 383/432).

76. This book, pp. 128 and 252–3. See also Skipton Camp inspection report March 1919 (The National Archives, FO 383/506).
77. This book, pp. 246–54.
78. This book, p. 245.
79. Skipton Camp inspection report March 1919 (The National Archives, FO 383/506).
80. This book, p. 246.
81. Oliver Wilkinson, 2017, *British Prisoners of War in First World War Germany* (Studies in the Social and Cultural History of Modern Warfare), pp. 187–9. Wilkinson's observations refer to the British POW camps in Germany, which functioned in a similar way to the camps in Britain, in that senior-ranking prisoners maintained order among their own men.
82. This book, p. 248.
83. Oliver Wilkinson, 2017, *British Prisoners of War in First World War Germany* (Studies in the Social and Cultural History of Modern Warfare), p. 167.
84. Ibid., p. 76.
85. Joan Beaumont, 1983, 'Rank, Privilege and Prisoners of War', *War and Society*, vol. 1, no. 1, pp. 67–94.
86. Ibid.
87. This book, p. 198. A War Office report gives details of an agreement between the British and German governments for officers to be 'permitted to give a temporary parole for the purpose of taking exercise outside camp limits' ('Report on the Directorate of Prisoners of War', September 1920, p. 41, The National Archives, WO 106/1451).
88. Panikos Panayi, 2012, *Prisoners of Britain. German Civilian and Combatant Internees during the First World War*, p. 80.
89. Inspection report Skipton Camp February 1918 (The National Archives, FO 383/432); Inspection report Skipton Camp June 1918 (Bundesarchiv R 901/83146); Inspection report Skipton Camp March 1919 (The National Archives, FO 383/506).
90. This book, pp. 36, 96, 117, 248, 250 and 259.
91. Oliver Wilkinson, 2017, *British Prisoners of War in First World War Germany* (Studies in the Social and Cultural History of Modern Warfare), pp. 161–2.
92. 'Report on the Directorate of Prisoners of War', September 1920, pp. 47–8 (The National Archives, WO 106/1451). One of those who reached Germany was the famous aviator Gunther Plüschow. Graham Mark has used newspaper reports to compile a list of nearly 500 escapes from British camps (*Prisoners of War in British Hands during WWI. A study of their history, their camps and their mails*, 2007).
93. This book, pp. 118–23.
94. *Clitheroe Advertiser*, 5 July 1918.
95. *Clitheroe Times*, 5 July 1918.
96. *Craven Herald and Wensleydale Standard*, 5 July 1918.
97. John Beckett, 2018, 'The Great Escape … from Sutton Bonington!'. Online at https://www.nottingham.ac.uk/alumni/newseventsandfeatures/news/news-items/2018-news/the-great-escape...from-sutton-bonington.aspx (accessed 12 January 2020). Brian Feltman also discusses the escape from Sutton Bonington (*The Stigma of Surrender. German Prisoners, British Captors, and Manhood in the Great War and Beyond*, 2015, pp. 99–100).
98. Information obtained from the records of the International Committee of the Red Cross, *Prisoners of the First World War, the ICRC archives*. Online at https://grandeguerre.icrc.org/ (accessed 25 January 2020).
99. This book, p. 118.
100. This book, p. 123.
101. 'Report on the Directorate of Prisoners of War', September 1920, pp. 18 and 38 (The National Archives, WO 106/1451). See also Oliver Wilkinson, 2017, *British Prisoners of War in First World War Germany* (Studies in the Social and Cultural History of Modern Warfare), p. 138.
102. Oliver Wilkinson, 2017, *British Prisoners of War in First World War Germany* (Studies in the Social and Cultural History of Modern Warfare), p. 139; Brian Feltman, 2015, *The Stigma of Surrender. German Prisoners, British Captors, and Manhood in the Great War and Beyond*, pp. 90–1 and 105.

103. International Committee of the Red Cross, *Prisoners of the First World War, the ICRC archives*. Online at https://grandeguerre.icrc.org/ (accessed 25 January 2020).

104. Unpublished analysis by Triss Kenny and Alice Craft, 2019. Alice Craft was a student intern, whose research was funded by the Leeds Q-Step Centre.

105. Niall P.A.S. Johnson and Juergen Mueller, 'Updating the Accounts: Global Mortality of the 1918–1920 "Spanish" Influenza Pandemic', *Bulletin of the History of Medicine* 76, no. 1, 2002, pp. 105–15.

106. This book, p. 129.

107. This book, pp. 212–26.

108. International Committee of the Red Cross, *Prisoners of the First World War, the ICRC archives*. Online at https://grandeguerre.icrc.org/.

109. A.L. Vischer, 1918, *Die Stacheldraht-Krankheit*. Translated in 1919 as: *Barbed Wire Disease. A Psychological Study of the Prisoner of War*.

110. Ibid., pp. 53 and 59.

111. Unpublished analysis of ICRC data by Triss Kenny, 2019. It is believed that the data is at least 99 per cent complete.

112. See, for example, Matthew Stibbe, 2008, *British Civilian Internees in Germany. The Ruhleben Camp, 1914–18*, p. 101 (Stibbe also refers to the work of Alon Rachamimov and Rainer Pöppinghege); Brian Feltman, 2015, *The Stigma of Surrender. German Prisoners, British Captors, and Manhood in the Great War and Beyond*.

113. *Instructions and Rules of Guidance for the Conduct of Every German Soldier Who is Taken Prisoner* (translation), July 1918 (The National Archives, ADM 137/3868).

114. Brian Feltman, 2015, *The Stigma of Surrender. German Prisoners, British Captors, and Manhood in the Great War and Beyond*, pp. 138, 142, 146.

115. Ibid., pp. 149–61.

116. This book, pp. 132–5.

117. 'German Prisoner's Escapade', *Craven Herald and Wensleydale Standard*, 17 October 1919; this book, p. 270.

118. 'German Prison Camp at Skipton', BK424 Herbert A. France archive, scrapbook no. 7, p. 9, Keighley Local Studies Library. Subtitle 'Pioneeer Special' indicates likely source to be *West Yorkshire Pioneer and East Lancashire News*, October 1919.

119. *The Times*, 3 April, 23 April, 1 May, 8 May, 14 May 2020.

120. *Craven Herald and Wensleydale Standard*, 11 June 1920.

121. 'End of Raikeswood Camp', *Craven Herald and Wensleydale Standard*, 25 June 1920.

122. Ibid.

123. Imperial War Museums. *Rylstone and District War Memorial Hall*. Online at https://www.iwm.org.uk/memorials/item/memorial/29542 (accessed 12 January 2020).

124. Helen Wallbank (Tosside Community Link and Slaidburn Archive), 2016, email to Robert Freeman, 27 February.

125. Geoffrey Rowley, 1983, *The Book of Skipton*, p. 117.

126. Ken Ellwood, 2003, *Images of England, Skipton and the Dales*, p. 116.

127. Geoffrey Rowley, 1983, *The Book of Skipton*, p. 117.

128. Geoffrey Rowley, 1983, *The Book of Skipton*, p. 117.

129. 'Zum 80. Todestag würdiges Gedenken an Claus Lafrenz', *Fehmarn 24*, Online at https://www.fehmarn24.de/fehmarn/todestag-wuerdiges-gedenken-claus-lafrenz-8099216.html (accessed 16 January 2020).

130. Karl-Friedrich Hildebrand, 1992, *Die Generale der deutschen Luftwaffe 1935–1945. Band 3: Odebrecht bis Zoch*, pp. 567–9.

131. International Committee of the Red Cross, *Prisoners of the First World War, the ICRC archives*. Online at https://grandeguerre.icrc.org/ (accessed 25 January 2020).

132. 'Hofmeister Ludwig', *Kickersarchiv*. Online at http://www.kickersarchiv.de/index.php/Main/HofmeisterLudwig (accessed 16 January 2020).

133. 'Hofmeister & Seitz – Legenden unserer Bayern', 2018, *Kurt Laundauer Stiftung eV*, Online at https://www.facebook.com/kurt.landauer.stiftung/posts/872663929586071/ (accessed 16 January 2020).

134. 'Hofmeister Ludwig', *Kickersarchiv*. Online at http://www.kickersarchiv.de/index.php/Main/HofmeisterLudwig (accessed 16 January 2020).

135. Carl Schuchhardt, Paul Jacobsthal, R.A. Stewart Macalister, 1926, 'Nekrolog: Walther Bremer', *Prähistorische Zeitschrift*, vol. 17, pp. 281–7.
136. Ibid.
137. This book, p. 158.
138. Royal Society of Antiquaries of Ireland. 'Proceedings', *The Journal of the Royal Society of Antiquaries of Ireland, Sixth Series*, vol. 17, no. 1, Jun. 30, 1927, pp. 69–78.
139. Carl Schuchhardt, Paul Jacobsthal, R.A. Stewart Macalister, 1926, 'Nekrolog: Walther Bremer', *Prähistorische Zeitschrift*, vol. 17, pp. 281–7.
140. Royal Society of Antiquaries of Ireland, 1927, 'Proceedings', *The Journal of the Royal Society of Antiquaries of Ireland, Sixth Series*, vol. 17, no. 1, Jun. 30, pp. 69–78.
141. See notes 139 and 140 and also Gustav Behrens, 'Walther Bremer †', *Gnomon*, Band 3, 1927, pp. 502–4.
142. Karl-Heinz Fix, 2007, 'Schreiner, Helmuth', *Neue Deutsche Biographie* 23, pp. 538–9. Online at https://www.deutsche-biographie.de/pnd118761706.html#ndbcontent (accessed 16 January 2020).
143. This book, pp. 89–94. Schreiner's handwritten copies of the sermons he gave in the camp are in the archive of the Universitäts- und Landesbibliothek Münster, along with a number of letters he wrote home from Skipton and other camps.
144. Karl-Heinz Fix, 2007, 'Schreiner, Helmuth', *Neue Deutsche Biographie* 23, pp. 538–9. Online at https://www.deutsche-biographie.de/pnd118761706.html#ndbcontent (accessed 16 January 2020).
145. International Committee of the Red Cross, *Prisoners of the First World War, the ICRC archives*. Online at https://grandeguerre.icrc.org/ (accessed 25 January 2020).
146. Information from Michael Good's book, *The Search for Major Plagge, The Nazi who Saved Jews*, 2006, and Good's website. Online at https://searchformajorplagge.com/ (accessed 16 January 2020).
147. Documentary: 2018, *The Good Nazi* (dir. Bienstock and Niski). Online at: https://www.imdb.com/title/tt8574722/?ref_=ttpl_pl_tt and https://uktvplay.uktv.co.uk/shows/the-good-nazi/watch-online/ (accessed 16 January 2020).
148. This book, pp. 212–26.
149. 'German Graves in an Airedale Cemetery', *Keighley News*, 1 March 1919.
150. 'Die deutschen Gräber in Keighley', *Kriegsgräberfürsorge*, vol. 10, no. 8, August 1930, p. 7.
151. 'German Widow Visits War Grave at Morton', *Keighley News*, 10 July 1937.
152. 'Homage to the Fallen', *Keighley News*, 19 March 1938.
153. 'Hindenburg Drops Flowers', *Yorkshire Observer*, 23 May 1936.
154. British Movietone News, *Hindenburg' Drops a Letter at Keighley*. Online at https://www.youtube.com/watch?v=NbayO6fhb4U (accessed 17 January 2020).
155. Oliver Denton, 2003, *The Rose and the Swastika*.
156. Film: Our Lady of Victories Media, 2015, *Our Hindenburg*. Online at https://vimeo.com/132979086 (accessed 19 January 2020); 'Pupils get the red carpet treatment at Keighley children's film festival', *Keighley News*, 17 July 2015. Online at https://www.keighleynews.co.uk/news/13439797.pupils-get-the-red-carpet-treatment-at-keighley-childrens-film-festival/ (accessed 19 January 2020).
157. 'Riddlesden man made famous by crucifix-find dies aged 89', *Keighley News*, 18 July 2014. Online at https://www.keighleynews.co.uk/news/11351372.riddlesden-man-made-famous-by-crucifix-find-dies-aged-89/ (accessed 19 January 2020).
158. Commonwealth War Graves Commission, *Cannock Chase German Military Cemetery*. Online at https://www.cwgc.org/find-a-cemetery/cemetery/4007266/cannock-chase-german-military-cemetery/ (accessed 19 January 2020).
159. Letter from German War Graves Commission (*Volksbund Deutsche Kriegsgräberfürsorge*) to Town Hall Clerk, Keighley, 30 January 1961.
160. 'Morton to lose graves of prisoners of war', *Keighley News*, 20 August 1960.
161. *Keighley News*, 8 December 1994 and 26 December 1997.
162. Tim Grady, 'Burying the "Enemy": German First World War Graves in Britain, 1914–1967', *International Society for First World War Studies Conference Leeds, 10–13 September 2019.*

163. Archiv der Bibliothek für Bildungsgeschichtliche Forschung des Deutschen Instituts für Internationale Pädagogische Forschung, DIPF/BBF/Archiv: GUT PERS 372 p. 18.
164. Hans H. Hildebrand and Ernest Henriot, 1990, *Deutschlands Admirale 1849–1945. Die militärischen Werdegänge der See-, Ingenier-, Sanitäts-, Waffen- und Verwaltungsoffiziere in Admiralsrang. Band 3: P–Z*, pp. 174–5.
165. 'A Yorkshire prisoner-of-war camp from within', *Times Literary Supplement*, 21 April 1921.
166. The records of the ICRC show the first group of non-officers arriving on 11 January 1918 and the first officers on 17 January 1918.
167. This book, p. 107.
168. For example, Michael Foley, 2015, *Prisoners of the British. Internees and Prisoners of War during the First World War*, p. 71, and Paul Cohen-Portheim, 1932, *Time Stood Still: My Internment in England 1914–1918*, pp. 44–5.
169. 'Die Weihnachts-Revue', *Stobsiade* (Stobs camp newspaper), no. 9, 30 January 1916 (translation Anne Buckley). There is a poem entitled '*Schiebung*' in the previous issue of *Stobsiade*, no. 8, 14 January 1916. Online at http://www.stobsiade.org/ (accessed 19 January 2020).
170. Michael Foley, 2015, *Prisoners of the British. Internees and Prisoners of War during the First World War*, p. 71.

Translation of *Kriegsgefangen in Skipton*

1. In the play *Faust* by Johann Wolfgang von Goethe, Wagner is Faust's assistant.
2. This is likely to be an error and should probably read north-east.
3. The prisoners erected partitions in an attempt to create some private space (see pp. 139–45).
4. There was no newspaper called the *Bradford Evening News* in 1919. The story was reported in the *Yorkshire Observer* on 16 September 1919 and the *Craven Herald and Wensleydale Standard* on 19 September 1919. The German wording in *Kriegsgefangen in Skipton* would appear to have been translated from the *Craven Herald and Wensleydale Standard* article so it is this wording that has been reproduced here.
5. Maria Stuart (Mary Stuart, Queen of Scots) is also the title of a play by Friedrich Schiller (1759–1805), a work which would have been known to the prisoners.
6. Halliwell Sutcliffe (1870–1932).
7. Likely to be referring to Aireville Hall.
8. Likely to be referring to Thorlby House.
9. The 'Green Palace' is the prisoners' nickname for Scale House, a property on Grassington Road north of Skipton.
10. Wordsworth's poem 'Brave Schill' written in 1809 was a tribute to Ferdinand von Schill (1776–1809).
11. Latin: 'Times are changed'.
12. A reference to *Faust* by Johann Wolfgang von Goethe.
13. A reference to Friedrich Schiller's *Der Handschuh* (The Glove).
14. Latin: 'All that is mine I carry with me'.
15. *Dreischichteneinsatz* in the original German text. This was also the name of a type of gas mask – see, for example, Wilhelm Waldmann and Wilhelm Hoffmann, 1936, *Lehrbuch der Militärhygiene*, p. 27.
16. A native African hut village in southern Africa. The term 'Kaffir' was used in the colonial period to refer to native southern African people but its use would now be viewed as highly offensive. The term 'kraal' refers to a group of native African huts. The German officers use of 'Kaffir kraal' to describe the camp as they first arrived suggests that they were disappointed at what they saw.
17. According to *Kriegsgefangen in Skipton*, a group of enlisted men arrived in Skipton on 12 December 1917 to prepare the camp for the officers – see section entitled 'Our Orderlies' on p. 259. However, the records of the ICRC show the first group of non-officers arriving on 11 January 1918.
18. *Doppelkopf* and *Skat* are traditional German card games.
19. The concept of *Schiebung* is discussed in the Introduction on pp. 18–19.
20. A War Office report states: '*Measures to prevent escapes from camps* [...] In officers' camps precautions were never relaxed, and measures were taken in addition to those mentioned

above as being applicable to all camps. Metal tokens of the value of 10s., 2s. 6d., 1s., and 6d. took the place of all except copper coins. Those issued to a particular camp were punched with a special mark to avoid their use elsewhere and, in order to prevent forgery, each die bore a secret mark which was communicated confidentially to the commandant.' See 'Report on the Directorate of Prisoners of War', September 1920, pp. 47–8 and Appendix 20 'Regulations for the use of tokens in officers' camps', p. 138 (The National Archives, WO 106/1451).

21. *Leberecht Hühnchen* is a character who knows the art of happiness in a book of the same name by Heinrich Seidel.

22. The author is quoting the erroneous German of the British guards – it should be 'Gute Nacht'.

23. A joke: the soldier has made a Latin-sounding name from the word Kommiss (army).

24. From 1914 to 1916 soldiers wore leather helmets with a spike called *Pickelhauben*. From 1916 onwards these were replaced by steel helmets. See, for example, David Stone, 2015, *The Kaiser's Army: The German Army in World War One*, pp. 218–22.

25. Winston Churchill used this term to refer to the Germans following the bombing of Scarborough on 16 December 1914. See, for example, the *Daily Telegraph*, 21 December 1914, p. 9.

26. See section on the reprisals on pp. 116–17.

27. See note 4.

28. A note dated 23 November 1917 from the War Office states 'The Director of Military Intelligence presents his compliments to the Director of the Intelligence Division Admiralty and begs to inform him that arrangements have been made whereby all enemy Prisoners of War captured on the Western Front who are in possession of information of naval interest will be sent if unwounded to Cromwell Gardens, London, if wounded to Prisoners of War Hospital, Belmont, Sutton, Surrey.' (The National Archives ADM 137/3868. p. 33).

29. Charles Algernon Fryatt was a British merchant seaman who was executed by the Germans in 1916 for attempting to ram a U-boat in 1915. See, for example, James Brown Scott, 1916, 'The Execution of Captain Fryatt', *The American Journal of International Law*, vol. 10, no. 4, pp. 865–77.

30. The transit camp in Southampton consisted of a large private house and a skating rink that could accommodate 80 officers and 800 men ('Report on the Directorate of Prisoners of War', September 1920, p. 45, The National Archives, WO 106/1451).

31. Likely to be referring to Friedrich Müller, a reservist lieutenant on the *U-58* submarine, which was attacked and sunk by two American destroyers off the coast of Ireland on 17 November 1917. The story was reported in the *New York Times*, 30 December 1917. Müller was imprisoned in Taunton before being transferred to Skipton on 7 March 1918. He was transferred to the American authorities on 9 April 1918 and moved to the Fort McPherson camp in the state of Georgia – see Plates 5, 6 and 7.

32. The War of the Sixth Coalition (March 1813–May 1814), part of the Napoleonic Wars.

33. Eugen Sandow (1867–1925) was a famous Prussian strongman, bodybuilder and showman. He sold magazines and exercise equipment, such as the 'Sandow Apparatus', which he designed to train the upper limbs and shoulders. See, for example, Caroline Daley, 2002, 'The strongman of eugenics, Eugen Sandow', *Australian Historical Studies*, vol. 33, no. 120, pp. 233–48.

34. *Skat* terms: calling 'Contra!' doubles the stakes in the game, while 'Re!' quadruples them.

35. See note 9 above.

36. The wording that follows is the translation of the German from *Kriegsgefangen in Skipton*. The original correspondence has not been found.

37. Royal Warrant: 'Maintenance of Discipline among Prisoners of War', 4 August 1914 (The National Archives, WO 32/5367). Later amendments to the 1914 document are referred to in 'Report on the Directorate of Prisoners of War', September 1920, Chapter VI (The National Archives, WO 106/1451).

38. Likely to be a reference to Heinrich von Winkelried, a medieval knight who, according to legend, slayed a dragon.

39. Likely to be a reference to Menelaus, a king of Mycenaean Sparta in Greek mythology.

40. Part of *Schäfers Sonntagslied* by Ludwig Uhland.

41. Accounts of instances of this type of behaviour by British soldiers on the Western Front can be found in The National Archives, e.g. in files FO 383/505 and FO 383/432.
42. See p. 255.
43. See Introduction, p. 7.
44. The wording that follows has been translated from the German in *Kriegsgefangen in Skipton*. The original letter has not been found. However, similar letters written from other British camps can be found in The National Archives, e.g. FO 383/502 (Letter from Redmires Camp), FO 383/506 (Letter from Brocton Camp), FO 383/516 (Letter from Oswestry Camp).
45. This wording has been taken from *The Times*, 16 November 1907.
46. See pp. 166–72.
47. L. Rothschild, 1911, *Taschenbuch für Kaufleute – Ein Lehr- und Nachschlagebuch der gesamten Handelswissenschaften in allgemein verständlicher Darstellung*.
48. In *Zollvereinsblatt*, no. 2, 8 January 1843. Georg Friedrich List (1789–1846) was a German-American economist.
49. Likely to be referring to the aria from Bizet's Carmen, *Die Liebe vom Zigeuner stammt*, also known as Habañera, which was very popular in Germany.
50. Jeremiah 29:11.
51. In the German this is a play on words using the adjective *lauschig* (secluded) and the verb *lauschen* (to eavesdrop).
52. This wording is taken from a bilingual German and English parole form from the Ripon camp (Bundesarchiv-Militärarchiv, Freiburg im Breisgau MSG200/1599). The same wording also appears in 'Report on the Directorate of Prisoners of War', September 1920, p. 41, where details are given of an agreement between the British and German governments for officers to be 'permitted to give a temporary parole for the purpose of taking exercise outside camp limits.' (The National Archives, WO 106/1451).
53. See note 38.
54. Likely to be Major Pounden who was named as one of the medical officers in the 1919 camp inspection report (The National Archives, FO 383/506).
55. Likely to be Captain Wellburn who was named as one of the medical officers in the 1919 camp inspection report (The National Archives, FO 383/506).
56. *Ich hatt' einen Kameraden* or *Der gute Kamerad* – a traditional lament of the German Armed Forces.
57. Added by the German authors to the original *Keighley News* report.
58. See section on 'box building', pp. 139–45.
59. Wilhelm Tünnerhoff was one of the prisoners.
60. A game played between two teams of five players each that was popular during the first half of the twentieth century.
61. A game played between two teams of twelve players each, similar to rounders or baseball.
62. A leather ball with an attached strap.
63. The wording that follows is the translation of the German from *Kriegsgefangen in Skipton*, apart from the quotes, which were in English within the German text. The original correspondence has not been found.
64. See note 17.
65. Matthew 12:34.
66. *Stille Nacht, heilige Nacht* and *O du fröhliche*.
67. John 6.63.
68. Carl Friedrich Zöllner (1800–60).
69. There are a number of recordings of performances of *Der Speisezettel* available online, for example, by Ensemble Amarcord, 2003, online at https://www.youtube.com/watch?v=9ki0nn7o5n0 (accessed 19 January 2020).
70. Karl Liebknecht (1871–1919) was a German socialist politician and a co-founder of the Spartacus League. He was a revolutionary who was opposed to the First World War and was executed in the Spartacus Revolt of January 1919. (See, for example, Tim Grady, 2017, *A Deadly Legacy. German Jews and the Great War*, pp. 100, 158 and 195–8).
71. This letter has not been found. This wording is a translation of the German wording in *Kriegsgefangen in Skipton*.

72. The original article from the *Daily News* has not been found. However, a report on the incident has been found in the *Sheffield Independent* of 19 August 1919. The wording of the leaflets and most of the final paragraph has been taken from this report while the remaining wording has been translated from the German in *Kriegsgefangen in Skipton*.
73. This quotation was in English in *Kriegsgefangen in Skipton*.
74. Two plebiscites took place in early 1920 to determine the future border between Germany and Denmark. The people of northern Schleswig voted to become part of Denmark, while the people in southern Schleswig voted to remain in Germany. See, for example, Norman Berdichevsky, 1997, 'The Chameleon Territory of South Schleswig (Slesvig): Fluctuations in the Perception of National Identity', *Boundary & Security Bulletin*, vol. 5, no. 1, pp. 65–70.
75. Wording from *The Times*, 30 August 1919.
76. Wording translated from the German in *Kriegsgefangen in Skipton*.
77. This phrase was in English in *Kriegsgefangen in Skipton*.
78. The original document has not been found. This wording is translated from the German in *Kriegsgefangen in Skipton*. The baggage weight allowances are detailed in the War Office 'Report on the Directorate of Prisoners of War', September 1920 (The National Archives, WO 104/1451, pp. 138–9).
79. The original German formulations are quotations from Klara's song in Goethe's drama *Egmont* (Act 3, Scene 2) that have become proverbial.
80. A daily newspaper published in Berlin.
81. The unofficial anthem of Schleswig-Holstein, also known as *Wanke nicht mein Vaterland*. It expresses the desire for a united, independent and German Schleswig-Holstein.
82. See Introduction, p. 5.
83. An uninhabited Chilean island in the Pacific Ocean. It was mentioned in a poem by Adelbert von Chamisso.
84. The nickname *Vadding* is likely to have been inspired by the satirical cartoon drawings of 'soldier Vadding' by the German caricaturist and illustrator Heinrich Zille, published in 1915 and 1916.

Bibliography

Archival Sources
Archiv der Bibliothek für Bildungsgeschichtliche Forschung des Deutschen Instituts für Internationale Pädagogische Forschung
DIPF/BBF/Archiv: GUT PERS 372

Bundesarchiv, Berlin-Lichterfelde
Abteilung R: Deutsches Reich 1495–1945
R 901, Auswärtiges Amt

Bundesarchiv-Militärarchiv, Freiburg im Breisgau
Militärgeschichtliche Sammlungen
MSG 200: Elsa Brändström Gedächtnisarchiv-Sammlung Kriegsgefangenenwesen seit 1867

International Committee of the Red Cross
Prisoners of the First World War, the ICRC archives. Online at https://grandeguerre.icrc.org/

Keighley Local Studies Library
BK424 Herbert A. France archive

National Archives, USA
Record Group 165: Records of the War Department General and Special Staffs, 1860–1952

Naval History and Heritage Command, USA
NH Series

Skipton Library
Rowley Ellwood Collection

The National Archives, Kew, London
Records of the Admiralty Office
ADM 137: Historical Section: Records used for Official History, First World War
Records of the Foreign Office
FO 383: Prisoners of War and Aliens Department: General Correspondence from 1906 and 1915–19
Records of the War Office
WO 32: War Office and Successors, Registered Files (General Series)
WO 106: Directorate of Military Operations and Military Intelligence, and predecessors: Correspondence and Papers
WO 394: Department of the Secretary, C5 Statistics Branch: Statistical Abstracts

Universitäts- und Landesbibliothek Münster
Nachlass Helmuth Schreiner

Official Publications
British Parliamentary Papers
Cd. 8590. An Agreement between the British and German Governments concerning Combatant and Civilian Prisoners of War. London: His Majesty's Stationary Office, Harrison & Sons, 1917.

Cd. 9147. An Agreement between the British and German Governments concerning Combatant Prisoners of War and Civilians. London: His Majesty's Stationary Office, Harrison & Sons, 1918.

Hague Convention, 1907: Hague Convention (IV) respecting the Laws and Customs of War on Land and its annex: Regulations concerning the Laws and Customs of War on Land. The Hague, 18 October 1907, ANNEX TO THE CONVENTION: REGULATIONS RESPECTING THE LAWS AND CUSTOMS OF WAR ON LAND – SECTION I: ON BELLIGERENTS – CHAPTER II: PRISONERS OF WAR – REGULATIONS: ART. 5. Online at https://ihl-databases.icrc.org/applic/ihl/ihl.nsf/ART/195-200015?OpenDocument (accessed 7 January 2020).

Hague Convention, 1907: Hague Convention (IV) respecting the Laws and Customs of War on Land and its annex: Regulations concerning the Laws and Customs of War on Land. The Hague, 18 October 1907, ANNEX TO THE CONVENTION: REGULATIONS RESPECTING THE LAWS AND CUSTOMS OF WAR ON LAND – SECTION I: ON BELLIGERENTS – CHAPTER II: PRISONERS OF WAR – REGULATIONS: ART. 6. Online at https://ihl-databases.icrc.org/applic/ihl/ihl.nsf/ART/195-200016?OpenDocument (accessed 7 January 2020).

Newspapers and Periodicals (Including Camp Newspapers)
Clitheroe Advertiser
Clitheroe Times
Craven Herald and Wensleydale Standard
Daily Telegraph
Fehmarn 24 (online)
Keighley News
Kriegsgräberfürsorge (newsletter of the German War Graves Commission)
New York Times
Sheffield Independent
Stobsiade (newspaper of Stobs camp)
Stralsunder Tageblatt
The Times
Times Literary Supplement
West Yorkshire Pioneer and East Lancashire News
Yorkshire Observer
Zirkelkorrespondenz (monthly magazine of the Freemasons in Germany)

Primary Sources
Cossmann, Willy. *Die Entwicklung des Gerichtsgedankens bei den alttestamentlichen Propheten* (Beihefte zur Zeitschrift für die alttestamentliche Wissenschaft). Giessen: Verlag von Alfred Töpelmann (Vormals J. Ricker), 1915.

German War Graves Commission (Volksbund Deutsche Kriegsgräberfürsorge), 1961, Letter to Town Hall Clerk, Keighley, 30 January.

List, Georg Friedrich, 'Die deutsche Flagge', *Das Zollvereinsblatt*, no. 2, 8 January 1843.

Secondary Sources
Aldcroft, Derek Howard. *From Versailles to Wall Street, 1919–1929 (History of the world economy in the twentieth century)*. Berkeley: University of California Press, 1977.

Beaumont, Joan. 'Rank, Privilege and Prisoners of War', *War and Society*, vol. 1, no. 1, 1983.

Beckett, John. 'The Great Escape ... from Sutton Bonington!', *University of Nottingham Alumni News*, 2018. Online at https://www.nottingham.ac.uk/alumni/newseventsandfeatures/news/news-items/2018-news/the-great-escape...from-sutton-bonington.aspx (accessed 12 January 2020).

Behrens, Gustav. 'Walther Bremer †', *Gnomon*. Band 3, 1927, pp. 502–4.

Berdichevsky, Norman. 'The Chameleon Territory of South Schleswig (Slesvig): Fluctuations in the Perception of National Identity', *Boundary & Security Bulletin*, vol. 5, no. 1, 1997, pp. 65–70.

Bernheim, Alan. 'United Grand Lodge and United Grand Lodges of Germany 1946–1961', *Ars Quatuor Coronatorum*, vol. 127, 2014, pp. 61–104.

Bienstock, Ric Esther and Yaron Niski (directors). *The Good Nazi*, 2018. Online at: https://www.imdb.com/title/tt8574722/?ref_=ttpl_pl_tt and https://uktvplay.uktv.co.uk/shows/the-good-nazi/watch-online/ (accessed 16 January 2020).

British Movietone News. *Hindenburg Drops A Letter at Keighley*. Online at https://www.youtube.com/watch?v=NbayO6fhb4U (accessed 19 January 2020).

Burdick, Charles and Ursula Moessner. *The German Prisoners of War in Japan, 1914–1920*. Lanham and London: University Press of America, 1984.

Cohen-Portheim, Paul. *Time Stood Still: My Internment in England 1914–1918*. New York, E.P. Dutton & Co., 1932.

Commonwealth War Graves Commission. *Cannock Chase German Military Cemetery*. Online at https://www.cwgc.org/find-a-cemetery/cemetery/4007266/cannock-chase-german-military-cemetery/ (accessed 19 January 2020).

Daley, Caroline. 'The Strongman of Eugenics, Eugen Sandow', *Australian Historical Studies*, vol. 33, no. 120, 2002, pp. 233–48.

Denton, Oliver. *The Rose and the Swastika*. Settle: Hudson History, 2003.

Ellwood, Ken. *Images of England, Skipton and the Dales*. Stroud: Tempus Publishing Limited, 2003.

Ensemble Amarcord. *Der Speisezettel 2003*. Online at https://www.youtube.com/watch?v=9ki0nn7o5n0 (accessed 19 January 2020).

Feltman, Brian. *The Stigma of Surrender. German Prisoners, British Captors, and Manhood in the Great War and Beyond*. Chapel Hill: The University of North Carolina Press, 2015.

Fix, Karl-Heinz. 'Schreiner, Helmuth', *Neue Deutsche Biographie* 23, 2007, pp. 538–9. Online at https://www.deutsche-biographie.de/pnd118761706.html#ndbcontent (accessed 16 January 2020).

Foley, Michael. *Prisoners of the British. Internees and Prisoners of War during the First World War*. Stroud: Fonthill Media Limited, 2015.

Good Michael. *The Search for Major Plagge, The Nazi who Saved Jews*. New York: Fordham University Press, 2006.

——. *The Search for Major Plagge* (website). Online at https://searchformajorplagge.com/ (accessed 16 January 2020).

Grady, Tim. *A Deadly Legacy. German Jews and the Great War*. New Haven & London: Yale University Press, 2017.

——. 'Burying the "Enemy": German First World War Graves in Britain, 1914–1967', *International Society for First World War Studies Conference Leeds, 10–13 September 2019*.

Hildebrand, Hans H. and Ernest Henriot. *Deutschlands Admirale 1849–1945. Die militärischen Werdegänge der See-, Ingenier-, Sanitäts-, Waffen- und Verwaltungsoffiziere in Admiralsrang. Band 3: P–Z*. Osnabrück: Biblio Verlag, 1990.

Hildebrand, Karl-Friedrich. *Die Generale der deutschen Luftwaffe 1935–1945. Band 3: Odebrecht bis Zoch*. Osnabrück: Biblio Verlag, 1992.

Hinz, Uta. *Gefangen im Grossen Krieg: Kriegsgefangenschaft in Deutschland, 1914–1921*. Essen: Klartext Verlag, 2006.

Hughes, Kathryn. 'Bradford Pals', *Bradford WW1 Social, Local and Family History Research*. Online at http://www.bradfordww1.co.uk/bradford-pals.html (accessed 5 January 2020).

Imperial War Museums. *Rylstone and District War Memorial Hall*. Online at https://www.iwm.org.uk/memorials/item/memorial/29542 (accessed 12 January 2020).

Johnson, Niall P.A.S. and Juergen Mueller. 'Updating the Accounts: Global Mortality of the 1918–1920 "Spanish" Influenza Pandemic', *Bulletin of the History of Medicine* 76, no. 1, 2002, pp. 105–15.

Jones, Heather. *Violence Against Prisoners of War in the First World War: Britain, France and Germany, 1914–1920*. Cambridge: Cambridge University Press, 2011.

——. 'A Missing Paradigm? Military Captivity and the Prisoner of War, 1914–18', *Immigrants & Minorities*, vol. 26, nos 1–2, 2008, pp. 19–48.

Kickersarchiv. *Hofmeister, Ludwig*, Online at http://www.kickersarchiv.de/index.php/Main/HofmeisterLudwig (accessed 16 January 2020).

Kurt Laundauer Stiftung eV. *Hofmeister & Seitz – Legenden unserer Bayern*. Online at https://www.facebook.com/kurt.landauer.stiftung/posts/872663929586071/ (accessed 16 January 2020).

McCartney, Innes. *Lost Patrols: Submarine Wrecks of the English Channel*. Penzance: Periscope Publishing Ltd, 2002.

Makepeace, Clare. *Captives of War. British Prisoners of War in Europe in the Second World War* (Studies in the Social and Cultural History of Modern Warfare). Cambridge: Cambridge University Press, 2017.

Mark, Graham. *Prisoners of War in British Hands during WWI. A study of their history, their camps and their mails*. Exeter: The Postal History Society, 2007.

Moser, John E. *Global Great Depression and the Coming of World War II*. Abingdon and New York: Routledge, 2015.

Nachtigal, Reinhard. 'Zur Anzahl der Kriegsgefangenen im Ersten Weltkrieg', *Militärgeschichtliche Zeitschrift* 67, 2008, pp. 345–84.

Our Lady of Victories Media, 2015, *Our Hindenburg*. Online at https://vimeo.com/132979086 (accessed 19 January 2020).

Panayi, Panikos. *Prisoners of Britain. German Civilian and Combatant Internees during the First World War*. Manchester: Manchester University Press, 2012.

Pöppinghege, Rainer. *Im Lager unbesiegt. Deutsche, englische und französische Kriegsgefangenen-Zeitungen im Ersten Weltkrieg*. Essen: Klartext, 2006.

Rachamimov, Alon. 'The Disruptive Comforts of Drag: (Trans)Gender Performances among Prisoners of War in Russia, 1914–1920', *American Historical Review*, vol. 111, no. 2, 2006, pp. 362–82.

Raw, David. *Bradford Pals. A Comprehensive History of the 16th, 18th & 20th (Service) Battalions of the Prince of Wales' Own West Yorkshire Regiment 1914–1918*. Barnsley: Pen & Sword Books Ltd, 2005.

Rowley, Geoffrey. *The Book of Skipton*. Buckingham: Barracuda Books Ltd, 1983.

Royal Society of Antiquaries of Ireland. 'Proceedings', *The Journal of the Royal Society of Antiquaries of Ireland, Sixth Series*, vol. 17, no. 1, Jun. 30, 1927, pp. 69–78.

Schuchhardt, Carl, Paul Jacobsthal, R.A. Stewart Macalister, 'Nekrolog: Walther Bremer', *Prähistorische Zeitschrift*, vol. 17, 1926, pp. 281–7.

Scott, James Brown. 'The Execution of Captain Fryatt', *The American Journal of International Law*, vol. 10, no. 4, 1916, pp. 865–77.

Simkins, Peter. 'Pals Battalions', *1914–1918-online. International Encyclopedia of the First World War*, ed. by Ute Daniel, Peter Gatrell, Oliver Janz, Heather Jones, Jennifer Keene, Alan Kramer, and Bill Nasson, issued by Freie Universität Berlin, Berlin 2018-03-29. Online at https://encyclopedia.1914-1918-online.net/article/pals_battalions (accessed 26 January 2020).

Stibbe, Matthew. *British Civilian Internees in Germany. The Ruhleben Camp 1914–18*. Manchester: Manchester University Press, 2008.

Stone, David. *The Kaiser's Army: The German Army in World War One*. London and New York: Conway Bloomsbury, 2015.

Tucker, Spencer and Priscilla Mary Roberts (eds), *World War I: Encyclopedia*, vol. 1, Santa Barbara: ABC-CLIO, 2005.

VanWyngarden, Greg. *Aces of Jagdstaffel 17* (Aircraft of the Aces). Oxford: Bloomsbury Publishing (UK), 2013.

Vischer, A.L. *Die Stacheldraht-Krankheit*. Translated as: *Barbed Wire Disease. A Psychological Study of the Prisoner of War*. London: John Bale, Sons & Danielsson, Ltd, 1919.

Waldmann, Wilhelm and Wilhelm Hoffmann. *Lehrbuch der Militärhygiene*. Berlin: Springer Verlag, 1936.

Wallbank, Helen (Tosside Community Link and Slaidburn Archive), email to Robert Freeman, 27 February 2016.

Wartime Memories Project. *21st (Wool Textile Pioneers) Battalion West Yorkshire Regiment during the Great War*. Online at https://www.wartimememoriesproject.com/greatwar/allied/battalion.php?pid=5045 (accessed 5 January 2020).

Wilkinson, Oliver. *British Prisoners of War in First World War Germany* (Studies in the Social and Cultural History of Modern Warfare). Cambridge: Cambridge University Press, 2017.

Index